Managing Successful Projects with PRINCE2

Office of Government Commerce

London: TSO

Published for the Office of Government Commerce under licence from the Controller of Her Majesty's Stationery Office

First edition Crown copyright 1996

Second edition Crown copyright 1998

Third edition Crown copyright 2002

Ninth impression 2004

The OGC is now the authority for best practice in commercial activities in UK Government, combining a number of separate functions with related aims.

OGC will build on the popular guidance developed by the former CCTA and others, working with organisations internationally to develop and share business and practitioner guidance within a world-class best practice framework..

ACKNOWLEDGEMENTS

The consortium of Duhig Berry, WS Atkins and Penzer Allen, under contract to the former CCTA, is acknowledged for the original design and development of PRINCE2. Parity Consulting is acknowledged for assisting the consortium in the design and development of the PRINCE2 model.

OGC would also like to thank the following individuals and organisations for their contributions and support throughout the original design and development of PRINCE2.

Mike Allen	Department of Education and Employment
Rob Herson	Parity Consulting
Jeremy Cox	Parity Consulting
Patrick Mayfield	Pearce Mayfield Associates
Colin Bentley	Hampshire Training Consultants
Dick Bennett	Duhig Berry
Alan Berry	Duhig Berry

In particular, OGC would like to express special thanks to all members, over 150 individuals and organisations, of the PRINCE2 User Review Panel, and the large number of other contributors, who gave their time freely to input ideas and comments during the Quality Reviews.

OGC has continued to develop and improve the definition and presentation of PRINCE2 within this reference manual. OGC would like to thank the following individuals and organisations for their contributions and ongoing support to PRINCE2:

Colin Bentley	Hampshire Training Consultants
Dick Bennett	Abbas Associates
Alison Thurlbeck	Methodica
Alan Ferguson	AFA
Tony Levene	Quality Projects
Mike Kirk	Promit
Barry Wall	Vega Consultancy Division
Graham Connellan	Independent Consultant
Ken Bradley	SPOCE
Peter Weaver	PWA

Brian Coombes	The Projects Group
Tim Lulham	DHL Systems
Ian Santry	Civil Service College
Nick Morgan	Xansa (formerly Duhig Berry)
Mark van Onna	Pink
Bem van der Wijngaart	Tanner James Management Consultants

FOREWORD

Nowadays, most organisations are experiencing unprecedented levels of change. Change has become a way of life for organisations that need to remain effective and competitive in order to thrive. It is essential to manage the inherent risk associated with change and innovation.

Projects bring together resources, skills, technology and ideas to deliver business benefits or to achieve business objectives. Good project management helps to ensure that these benefits or objectives are achieved within budget, within time and to the required quality.

PRINCE2 is a project management method designed to provide a framework covering the wide variety of disciplines and activities required within a project. The focus throughout PRINCE2 is on the business case, which describes the rationale and business justification for the project. The business case drives all the project management processes, from initial project set-up through to the finish of the project.

Many organisations are employing the skills and services of external suppliers, working alongside in-house resources, to enhance their ability to deliver successful projects. PRINCE2 provides a mechanism to harness these resources and enable the project team to work together effectively.

PRINCE2 embodies many years of good practice in project management and provides a flexible and adaptable approach to suit all projects.

I commend the PRINCE2 approach to you. May PRINCE2 help you to achieve successful outcomes to your projects!

Bob Assirati
Executive Director,
IT Directorate,
Office of Government Commerce

CONTENTS

1 INTRODUCTION

PRINCE (**PR**ojects **IN** Controlled **E**nvironments) is a structured method for effective project management. The method was first established in 1989 by CCTA (the Central Computer and Telecommunications Agency). PRINCE was developed from PROMPTII, a project management method created by Simpact Systems Ltd in 1975. PROMPTII was adopted by CCTA in 1979 as the standard to be used for all government information system projects. PRINCE superseded PROMPTII in 1989 within government projects.

CCTA (now the Office of Government Commerce) continued to develop the method, and PRINCE2 was launched in 1996 in response to user requirements for improved guidance on project management on all projects, not just information systems. PRINCE2 is based on the experiences of scores of projects, project managers and project teams, who have contributed, some from their mistakes or omissions, others from their successes.

PRINCE2 is a *de facto* standard used extensively by the UK government and is widely recognised and used in the private sector, both in the UK and internationally. PRINCE2 remains in the public domain and the contents of this manual are Crown copyright.

1.1 Why use a project management method?

Project failures are all too common – some make the headlines, but the vast majority are quickly forgotten. The reasons for failure are many and varied. Some common causes are:

- Insufficient attention to checking that a valid business case exists for the project
- Insufficient attention to quality at the outset and during development
- Insufficient definition of the required outcomes, leading to confusion over what the project is expected to achieve
- Lack of communication with stakeholders and interested parties, leading to products being delivered that are not what the customer wanted
- Inadequate definition and lack of acceptance of project management roles and responsibilities, leading to lack of direction and poor decision making
- Poor estimation of duration and costs, leading to projects taking more time and costing more money than expected
- Inadequate planning and co-ordination of resources, leading to poor scheduling
- Insufficient measurables and lack of control over progress, so that projects do not reveal their exact status until too late
- Lack of quality control, resulting in the delivery of products that are unacceptable or unusable.

Without a project management method, those who commission a project, those who manage it and those who work on it will have different ideas about how things should be organised and when the different aspects of the project will be completed. Those involved will not be clear about how much responsibility, authority and accountability they have and, as a result, there will often be confusion surrounding the project. Without a project management method, projects are rarely completed on time and within acceptable cost – and this is especially true of large projects.

A good project management method will guide the project through a controlled, well-managed, visible set of activities to achieve the desired results. PRINCE2 adopts the principles of good project management to avoid the problems just identified and so helps to achieve successful projects. These principles are:

- A project is a finite process with a definite start and end
- Projects always need to be managed in order to be successful
- For genuine commitment to the project, all parties must be clear about why the project is needed, what it is intended to achieve, how the outcome is to be achieved and what their responsibilities are in that achievement.

1.2 Benefits of using PRINCE2

Organisations are becoming increasingly aware of the opportunities for adopting a project approach to the way that they address business change. They are aware of the benefits that a single, common, structured method for project management can bring:

- A method that is repeatable
- A method that is teachable
- Building on experience
- Ensuring that everyone knows what to expect, where, how and when
- Early warning of problems
- Being proactive, not reactive, but able to accommodate sudden, unexpected events.

Projects may exist in their own right, may have relationships with other projects or may be part of a larger programme of work. PRINCE2 is applicable in all these situations. PRINCE2 provides the organisation with:

- Controlled management of change, in terms of investment and return on investment
- Active involvement of users and stakeholders throughout the project to ensure that the product(s) will meet the business, functional, environmental, service and management requirements
- An approach which distinguishes the management of the project from the development of the product(s), so that the management approach is the same whether the project is to build a ship or implement new working practices.

PRINCE2 provides benefits to the managers and directors of a project and to an organisation, through the controllable use of resources and the ability to manage risk more effectively.

PRINCE2 embodies established and proven best practice in project management. It is widely recognised and understood, providing a common language for all participants in a project.

PRINCE2 encourages formal recognition of responsibilities within a project and focuses on what a project is to deliver, why, when and for whom.

PRINCE2 provides projects with:

- A controlled and organised start, middle and end
- Regular reviews of progress against plan and against the Business Case
- Flexible decision points
- Automatic management control of any deviations from the plan
- The involvement of management and stakeholders at the right time during the project
- Good communication channels between the project management team and the rest of the organisation
- Agreement on the required quality at the outset and continuous monitoring against those requirements.

Project Managers using PRINCE2 are able to:

- Establish terms of reference as a prerequisite to the start of a project
- Use a defined structure for delegation, authority and communication
- Divide the project into manageable stages for more accurate planning
- Ensure that resource commitment from management is part of any approval to proceed
- Provide regular, but brief, management reports
- Keep meetings with management and stakeholders to a minimum but at the vital points in the project.

Those who will be directly involved with using the products or outcomes of a project are able to:

- Participate in all the decision making on a project
- If desired, be fully involved in day-to-day progress
- Participate in quality checks throughout the project
- Ensure that their requirements are being adequately satisfied.

For senior management of the project, PRINCE2 uses the 'management by exception' concept, i.e. management agree a plan, and then let the Project Manager get on with it unless something is forecast to go wrong. Senior managers are kept fully informed of the project status without having to attend frequent, time-consuming meetings.

1.3 Support for PRINCE2

There are many service providers offering training, consultancy, tools and services for PRINCE2, thus ensuring a competitive supply of services available to support organisations in their implementation and use of the method.

There is an international accreditation programme for trainers and consultants, ensuring a high quality and consistent level of service to organisations. There are professional qualifications in PRINCE2 that assess an individual's knowledge of the method and ability to apply it to project scenarios. In addition, there is an active user group dedicated to the support, promotion and strengthening of the method.

1.4 Structure of the manual

There are five major parts to this manual, as shown in Figure 1.1.

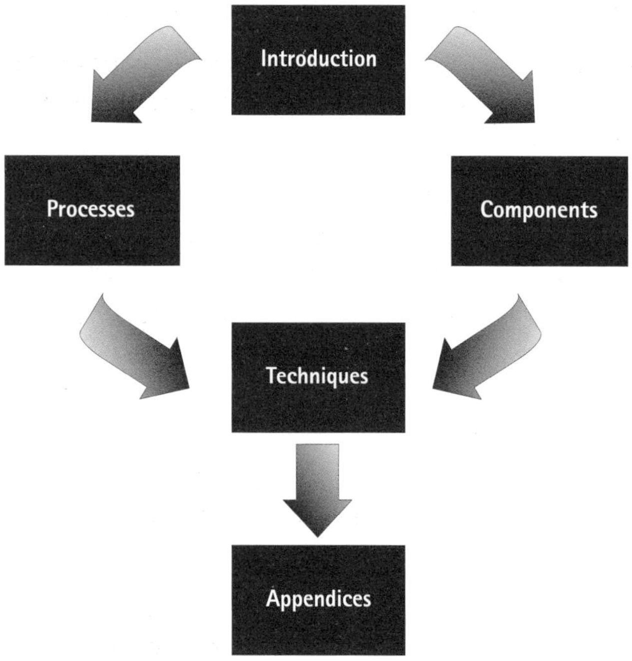

Figure 1.1 Structure of the manual

Introduction presents the basic principles governing project management and how PRINCE2 addresses them; it also shows how PRINCE2 fits with the related topic of programme management.

Processes describes the PRINCE2 process model, explaining what has to be done to manage the project by bringing together and applying the principles in a successful manner.

Components explains and describes the major elements of project management, such as organisation and control, and how PRINCE2 incorporates them. These components represent the 'raw materials' of good project management, including quality management and the management of risk.

Techniques explains some techniques of project management that are specific to PRINCE2.

Appendices offer Product Description outlines for PRINCE2 management products, role descriptions and a series of 'healthcheck' questions for organisations to ask themselves when using PRINCE2, risk categories and a suggested filing scheme for management documents.

In addition, there is a full glossary of terms.

1.5 Using the manual

This manual is aimed at people who will be playing a part in a PRINCE2 project or those who wish to understand how PRINCE2 contributes to the project management process; this would include senior managers responsible for the overall direction of a project, Project Managers, project auditors, quality assurance personnel and members of the project team. In addition, line managers of project personnel may find it useful to gain an appreciation of their staff's involvement in a project by reviewing Chapter 2, *An introduction to PRINCE2*.

This manual has been designed to provide a complete reference to the PRINCE2 method. As such, the entire manual provides essential reading for all Project Managers. However, the following is offered as a focus for specific groups:

- For Project Managers coming to PRINCE2 for the first time:
  - read and understand Chapter 2, *An introduction to PRINCE2*, to appreciate the overall approach that PRINCE2 takes to creating and managing the project
  - use the process descriptions in the Processes section as the basis for planning a project and deciding on resource requirements
  - read and understand the Components section in order to familiarise themselves with the interaction between the Components and the Processes
- For Project Managers already familiar with PRINCE2: read and understand the process model described in the Processes section to appreciate the changes of emphasis and process-driven approach
- Senior managers who will be involved in the project at Project Board level should gain an appreciation of PRINCE2 and their roles within a project by studying the Introduction (Chapters 1 and 2), *Business Case* (Chapter 13), *Organisation* (Chapter 14) and the description of the process, *Directing a Project* (Chapter 6)
- Programme managers with PRINCE2 projects in their programme should gain a clear understanding of the approach that PRINCE2 takes to creating and managing a project.

1.6 PRINCE2 terminology

The following terms are the most important to understand with regard to PRINCE2 and are all included in the Glossary. Readers should familiarise themselves with them to prevent any possible confusion when using PRINCE2.

Business Case is used to define the information that justifies the setting up, continuation or termination of the project. It answers the question 'Why should this project be done?' It is updated at key points throughout the project.

Customer is used to represent the person or group who has commissioned the work and will be benefiting from the end results.

Product is used to describe everything that the project has to create or change, however physical or otherwise this may be. Results of projects can vary enormously from physical items, such as buildings and machinery, to intangible things such as culture change and public perception.

Programme is a collection of projects that together achieve a beneficial change for an organisation.

Supplier is used to mean the group that is providing specialist resources and skills to the project or is providing goods and services, to create the project outcome required by the customer and user(s).

User is defined as the person or group who will use or operate the final product. In some situations, the customer and user may be the same group of people.

2
AN INTRODUCTION TO PRINCE2

2.1 What is a project?

PRINCE2 defines a project as:

a management environment that is created for the purpose of delivering one or more business products according to a specified Business Case

Another definition of a project might be:

a temporary organisation that is needed to produce a unique and predefined outcome or result at a prespecified time using predetermined resources

PRINCE2 additionally supposes that those responsible for the project will not have experience of working together to produce a similar set of outcomes or results for the same customer in the past; that co-ordination between those working on the project will need to be well organised; and that the responsibilities shared among those undertaking the work, those managing it and those sponsoring it will need to be clearly defined.

A PRINCE2 project, therefore, has the following characteristics:

- A finite and defined life cycle
- Defined and measurable business products
- A corresponding set of activities to achieve the business products
- A defined amount of resources
- An organisation structure, with defined responsibilities, to manage the project.

Each project falls within a specific business context. A project may be stand-alone, it may be one in a sequence of related projects or it may form part of a programme or corporate strategy.

A project, by its nature, is a temporary structure, created to achieve a specified business benefit or objective. When the work has been completed, the project is disbanded.

A project has a life cycle, which is the path and sequence through the various activities to produce the final product. The term 'life span' is used to describe the life of a product. The two should not be confused. Figure 2.1 shows how a *product life span* might start from the initial idea or conception, through to the operation of the product, finishing with the eventual scrapping of the product when it comes to the end of its usefulness. The *project life cycle* covers the tasks of specifying and designing a product, through to its testing and hand-over into operational use. PRINCE2 covers the project life cycle plus some pre-project preparation.

Within any project there are stakeholders with an interest in the project and its product, including:

- Customers, who have commissioned the work and will be benefiting from the end results
- User(s), who will use or operate the final product. The customer and user may be the same group of people
- Suppliers, who are providing specialist resources and/or skills to the project or are providing goods and services
- Sub-contractors, who provide products or services to the supplier.

The customer/supplier environment assumes that there will be a customer who will specify the desired product, make use of the final products and (in most cases) pay for the project and a (prime) supplier who will provide resources and skills to create that product. PRINCE2 is written from the standpoint that these two parties come from separately managed areas and typically from commercially separate organisations. Where, as may often be the case, both customer and supplier have a common management, this will influence the composition of the project management team.

Whatever the team composition, the customer should always participate (throughout the project) in the creation and verification of products.

A project, by its nature, is set up to deal with change and the future is always less predictable than with routine work. During the project, the specification of products will inevitably need to change. These changes need to be controlled because they can easily destroy the project's chance of success. Controlling changes is linked to version control, a topic that is covered within PRINCE2 under configuration management. Configuration management is an essential part of project control as it is focused on controlling the products being delivered, knowing where they are at any point in time, what their status is, who is working on them and which is the latest version.

In addition, projects can be large and complex, dealing with novel or unusual factors. Risk is therefore a major factor to consider during project management and PRINCE2 incorporates the management of risk into its processes.

Whatever the nature or size of the project, PRINCE2 defines an initiation stage that covers the planning and definition of the project. The initiation stage enables a management review before making any commitment to later stages and their associated resources and costs.

There will be many higher level issues surrounding the project. These will need to be dealt with by other methods and approaches, such as programme management. PRINCE2 is aimed at the middle ground between these higher level, more strategic, issues and the specialist techniques required to create the technical products.

Few projects can be completed entirely in isolation from other work. PRINCE2 projects may exist as part of a programme, contributing to the realisation of benefits of a larger organisational change. In a programme context, the outputs from one project may be used as input by another project. There may be other dependencies between projects, such as shared resources. PRINCE2 places strong emphasis on the products that the project is required to deliver and so provides a firm basis for defining the boundaries.

Feasibility studies

In some situations, a feasibility study might be required to investigate the situation and determine options for the way ahead. Using PRINCE2, the optimum approach would be to handle the study as a separate and distinct project and then operate a second project to implement the results of the study.

Figure 2.3 shows the (relatively) simple life cycle for a feasibility study project. It has one Project Plan, Business Case and set of risks. The possible options may each vary enormously in their cost and timescales. Each option would have a different Project Plan, Business Case and set of risks. Having chosen the appropriate option, the second project would proceed with a straightforward set of project information.

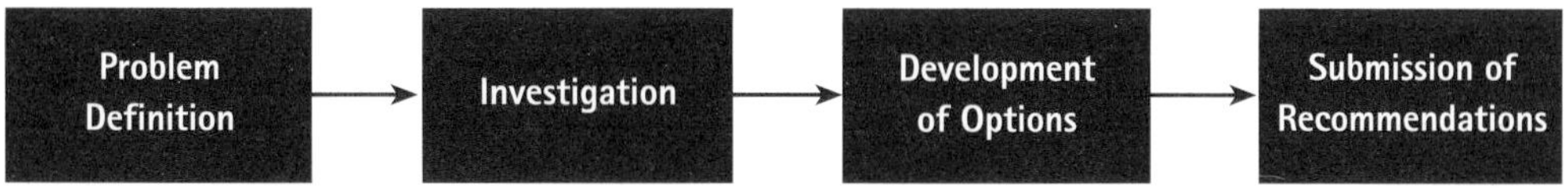

Figure 2.3 Life cycle of a feasibility study project

2.4 Overview of PRINCE2

PRINCE2 is a structured project management method based on the experience of scores of project managers, who have contributed, some from their mistakes or omissions, others from their success.

PRINCE2 has a process-based approach to project management. The processes define the management activities to be carried out during the project. In addition, PRINCE2 describes a number of components that are applied within the appropriate activities. Figure 2.4 shows the components positioned around the central process model.

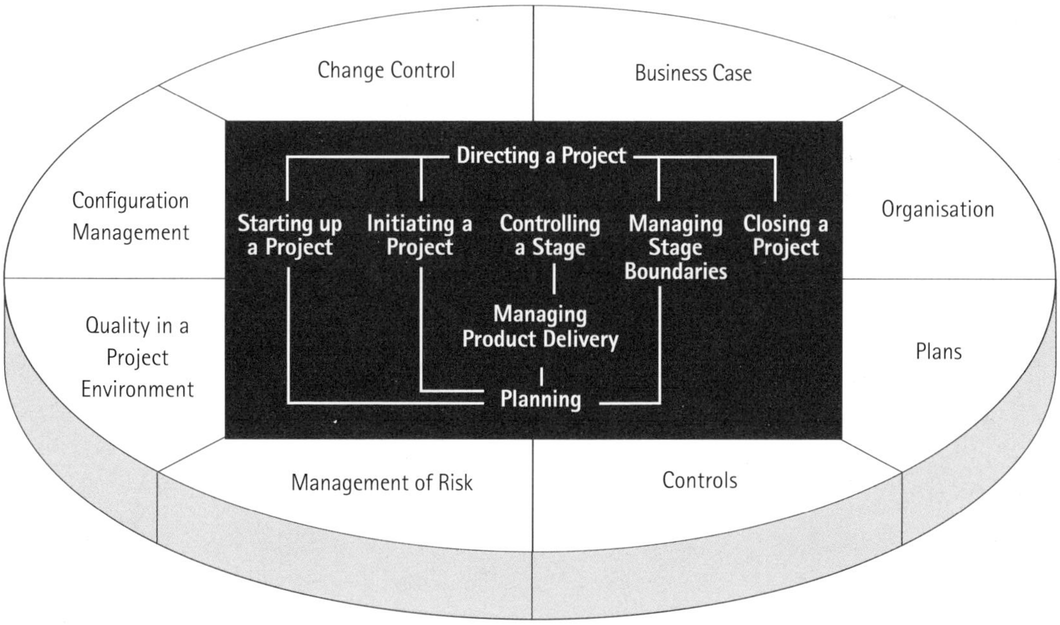

Figure 2.4 PRINCE2 processes and components

2.5 The processes

The PRINCE2 process model, shown in Figure 2.5, consists of eight distinctive management processes, covering the activities from setting the project off on the right track, through controlling and managing the project's progress, to the completion of the project. The common Planning process is used by many of the other processes.

Any project run under PRINCE2 will need to address each of these processes *in some form*. However, the key to successful use of the process model is in tailoring it to the needs of the individual project. Each process should be approached with the question: How extensively should this process be applied on this project?

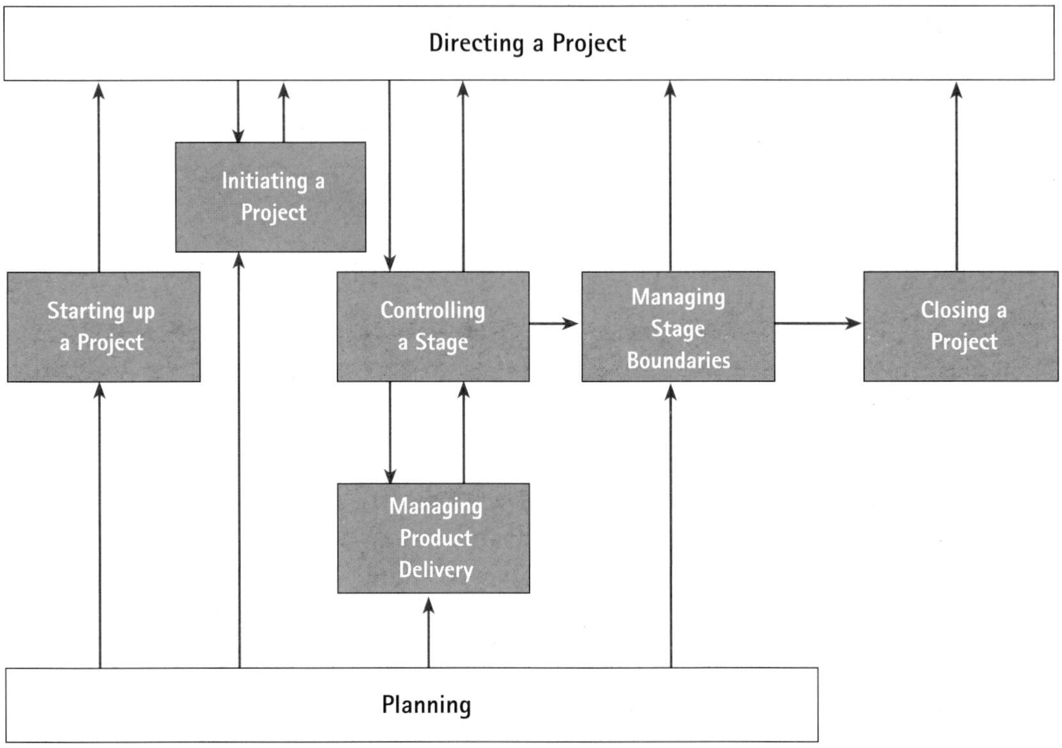

Figure 2.5 The PRINCE2 process model

2.5.1 Starting up a Project (SU)

This is the first process in PRINCE2. It is a pre-project process, designed to ensure that the prerequisites for initiating the project are in place. The process expects the existence of a Project Mandate that defines in high-level terms the reason for the project and what product is required. The process should be very short.

The work of the process is built around the establishment of six things:

- The design and, as far as possible, appointment of the project management team
- The Project Brief
- The Project Approach (in general terms how a solution will be provided)
- The customer's quality expectations

- A Risk Log
- The initiation Stage Plan.

2.5.2 Directing a Project (DP)

Directing a Project runs from the end of *Starting up a Project* (SU) until the project's closure.

This process is aimed at the Project Board, a group of managerial decision makers representing business, users and suppliers. (The Project Board is fully explained in Chapter 14, *Organisation.*) The Project Board manages by exception, monitors via reports, and controls through a number of decision points.

The key processes for the Project Board break into four main areas:

- Initiation (starting the project off on the right foot)
- Stage boundaries (commitment of more resources after checking results so far)
- Ad hoc direction (monitoring progress, providing advice and guidance, reacting to major threats to plans or benefits)
- Project closure (confirming the project outcome and bringing the project to a controlled close).

2.5.3 Initiating a Project (IP)

The objectives of *Initiating a Project* are to:

- Define how the required product quality will be achieved
- Plan and cost the project
- Document and confirm that an acceptable Business Case exists for the project
- Ensure that the investment of time and effort required by the project is justified, taking account of the risks to the project
- Enable and encourage the Project Board to take ownership of the project
- Provide the baseline for the decision-making processes required during the project's life
- Agree to the commitment of resources for the next stage of the project.

The key product of the process is the Project Initiation Document, which defines the what, why, who, when and how of the project.

Three other blank products are created in readiness for use during the project. These are:

- The Quality Log
- The Issue Log
- The Lessons Learned Log.

Another required product is the next Stage Plan. This, however, comes from the process *Managing Stage Boundaries* (SB), which will occur at the end of the initiation stage.

2.5.4 Managing Stage Boundaries (SB)

This process produces the information on which the Project Board will take key decisions on whether to continue with the project or not.

The objectives of the process are to:

- Assure the Project Board that all products planned in the current Stage Plan have been completed as defined
- Provide the information needed for the Project Board to assess the continuing viability of the project
- Provide the Project Board with any other information needed to approve the current stage's completion and authorise the start of the next stage, together with its delegated tolerance level
- Record any measurements or lessons that can help later stages of this project and/or other projects.

The products of this process are:

- An End Stage Report, given by the Project Manager to the Project Board, containing information on the stage achievements
- Current Stage Plan actuals, showing performance against the original Stage Plan
- The next Stage Plan or Exception Plan, for which approval is sought
- A revised Project Plan
- The updated Risk Log, which, together with the next two products, is used by the Project Board to review the continuing viability of the project
- A revised Business Case
- The Lessons Learned Log, updated with any lessons learned from the current stage
- Any changes to the structure or staffing of the project management team.

2.5.5 Controlling a Stage (CS)

This process describes the monitoring and control activities of the Project Manager involved in allocating work, ensuring that a stage stays on course and reacts to unexpected events. The process forms the core of the Project Manager's effort on the project, being the process that handles day-to-day management of the project.

Throughout a stage there will be a cycle of:

- Authorising work to be done
- Gathering progress information about that work
- Watching for changes
- Reviewing the situation

- Reporting
- Taking any necessary corrective action.

This process covers these activities, together with the ongoing work of risk and issue management. Products produced during the stage on a cyclic basis are:

- Work Packages
- Highlight Reports
- Project Issues (and updated Issue Log)
- An updated Risk Log
- A regularly updated Stage Plan.

There may also be the need for an Exception Report.

2.5.6 Managing Product Delivery (MP)

The objective of this process is to ensure that planned products are created and delivered by the project by:

- The Team Manager negotiating details of Work Packages with the Project Manager
- Making certain that work on products allocated to the team is effectively authorised and agreed
- Ensuring that work conforms to the requirements of interfaces identified in the Work Package
- Ensuring that the work is done
- Assessing work progress and forecasts regularly
- Ensuring that completed products meet quality criteria
- Obtaining approval for the completed products.

Products created or updated during this process are:

- Team plans
- Quality Log updates, giving the Project Manager a view of quality work being done
- Project Issues (updating the Business Case)
- Risk Log updates
- Checkpoint Reports, regular progress reports from the Team Manager to the Project Manager.

2.5.7 Closing a Project (CP)

The purpose of this process is to execute a controlled close to the project.

The process covers the Project Manager's work to wrap up the project either at its end or at a premature close. Most of the work is to prepare input to the Project Board to obtain its confirmation that the project may close.

The objectives of *Closing a Project* are, therefore, to:

- Check the extent to which the objectives or aims set out in the Project Initiation Document have been met
- Confirm the customer's acceptance of the products
- Assess to what extent all expected products have been handed over and accepted by the customer
- Confirm that maintenance and operation arrangements are in place (where appropriate) including any relevant training
- Make any recommendations for future work (Follow-on Action Recommendations)
- Capture lessons resulting from the project and complete the Lessons Learned Report
- Prepare an End Project Report
- Archive the project files
- Produce a Post Project Review Plan
- Notify the host organisation of the intention to disband the project organisation and release the resources (end project notification).

2.5.8 Planning (PL)

Planning is a repeatable process and plays an important role in other processes, the main ones being:

- *Planning an Initiation Stage* (SU6)
- *Planning a Project* (IP2)
- *Planning a Stage* (SB1)
- *Updating a Project Plan* (SB2)
- *Accepting a Work Package* (MP1)
- *Producing an Exception Plan* (SB6).

Apart from a plan, the process produces:

- A Product Checklist, which is a table of the products to be produced by the work planned, with space for planned and actual dates for delivery of draft, quality-checked and approved products

- The Risk Log, updated with any risk situation changes made as a result of the planning activity.

2.6 The components

Each component is described in further detail in the Components section of this manual, showing how the particular subject affects project management and providing guidance on when and how to address the issues.

Business Case	The existence of a viable Business Case is the main control condition of a PRINCE2 project. The Business Case is verified by the Project Board before a project begins and at every major decision point throughout the project. The project should be stopped if the viability of the Business Case disappears for any reason
Organisation	PRINCE2 provides a structure of a project management team and a definition of the responsibilities and relationships of all roles involved in the project. According to the size and complexity of a project, these roles can be combined or shared
Plans	PRINCE2 offers a series of plan levels that can be tailored to the size and needs of a project and an approach to planning based on products rather than activities
Controls	PRINCE2 provides a set of controls which facilitate the provision of key decision-making information, allowing an organisation to pre-empt problems and make decisions on problem resolution. For senior management PRINCE2 controls are based on the concept of management by exception, i.e. we agree a plan, then let the manager get on with it unless something is forecast to go wrong
	In order to promote sound management control, a project is split into stages as an approach to defining the review and commitment points of a project. (Using stages also helps to reduce the amount of work that the Project Manager needs to plan in detail at any one time)
Management of Risk	Risk is a major factor to be considered during the life of a project. PRINCE2 defines the key moments when risks should be reviewed, outlines an approach to the analysis and management of risk and tracks these through all the processes
Quality in a Project Environment	PRINCE2 recognises the importance of quality and incorporates a quality approach to the management and technical processes. It begins by establishing the customer's quality expectations and follows these up by laying down standards and quality inspection methods to be used and by checking that these are being used
Configuration Management	Tracking the components of a final product and their versions for release is called configuration management. There are many methods of configuration management available. PRINCE2 defines the essential facilities and information requirements for a configuration management method and how it should link with other PRINCE2 components and techniques
Change Control	PRINCE2 emphasises the need for change control, and this is enforced with a change control technique plus identification of the processes that apply the change control.

2.7 PRINCE2 techniques

PRINCE2 offers very few techniques, preferring to leave the choice of technique to the users of the method, and according to the circumstances of the project. But in support of the method the manual does contain details of three techniques, product-based planning, change control and quality review.

PRINCE2 provides a product-based start to the planning activity. It also provides a planning framework that can be applied to any type of project. This involves:

- Establishing what products are needed
- Determining the sequence in which each product should be produced
- Defining the form and content of each product.

Part of the product-based planning technique enables the project to define the standard of quality to which each product must conform. Every project needs a technique for the control of changes. For organisations that do not already have a suitable technique, PRINCE2 describes a change control technique. PRINCE2 also describes a specific technique: quality review, which is particularly suitable for the quality testing of document-based products.

2.8 Process and component links

It is often difficult for newcomers to PRINCE2 to understand the main relationships and links between the processes, components and techniques. In which processes are the components used? Where is this technique used? Figure 2.6 gives a picture of these links.

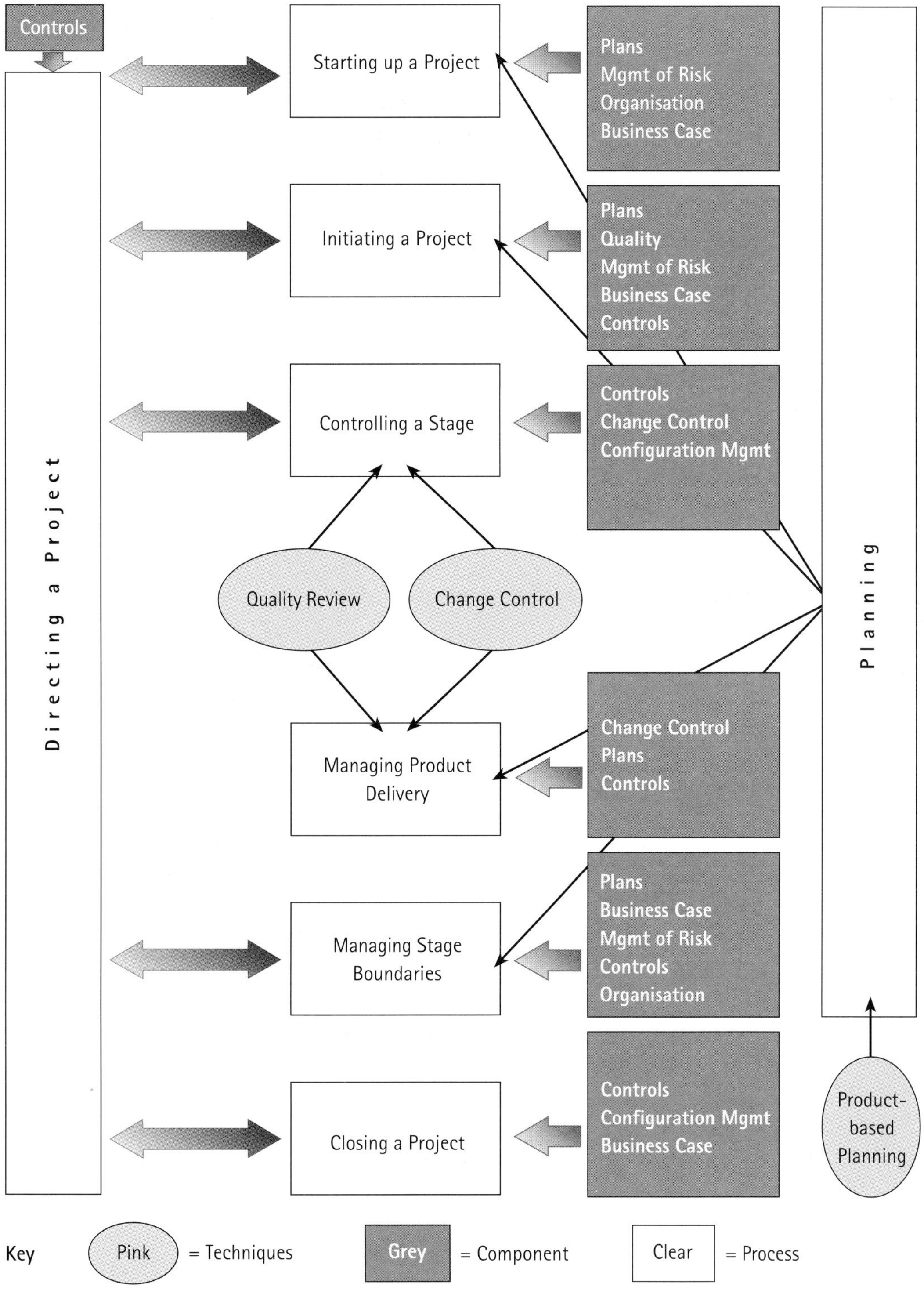

Figure 2.6 Use of PRINCE2 components and techniques in the processes

3

INTRODUCTION TO PROCESSES

3.1 Management levels

Project management is seldom straightforward enough to be a simple, linear process. In a PRINCE2 context, there are four parallel management levels to take into account (see Figure 3.1).

Figure 3.1 The four management levels

These management levels are reflected in the PRINCE2 Process model.

- At the highest level is corporate or programme management. While not part of project management as such, this higher management level is important, as it will often set the business context for one or more projects.
- Within the project itself the highest level is *Directing a Project* (the Project Board work). This level is for key decision making and direction setting.
- At the next level of managing a project a great deal of management effort is expended in day-to-day planning and control, and would largely be handled by the Project Manager.
- The lowest management level, *Managing Product Delivery*, would be handled by Team Managers.

There are two major ways in which these levels interact:

- The higher level processes exercise control over the lower levels. For example, managing a project provides the Work Packages that define the work for *Managing Product Delivery*
- The output of the lower level processes provides the inputs that allow the higher-level processes to function effectively. For example, managing a project provides essential planning and control information to enable the effective conduct of activities in *Directing a Project.*

3.2 Structure of each process description

Each process within PRINCE2 is described using the following structure and format.

3.2.1 Fundamental principles

Under this heading the following questions are addressed:

- Why have this process?
- What is it aiming to achieve in project management terms?
- Why is this process fundamental to good project management and hence a minimum requirement of PRINCE2?

3.2.2 Context

This section puts each process in context with the other processes and with activities going on outside the scope of PRINCE2. A context diagram supports each context description. The context diagram shows the major information flows into and out of the process.

3.2.3 Process description

This section describes the process by explaining the objectives and how the process fulfils the fundamental principles. The steps involved in carrying out the process are described.

No attempt has been made to lay out the steps in a strict sequence, since such a hard-and-fast sequence seldom exists. However, they have been listed in as logical a sequence as possible.

3.2.4 Scalability

Any project run under PRINCE2 will need to address each of the processes in some form. However, the key to successful use of PRINCE2 is its tailoring. Each process must be approached with the question 'How extensively should this process be applied on this project?' For each of the main PRINCE2 processes, there is a section describing the factors to consider when tailoring the process to fit the needs of the project.

3.2.5 Responsibilities

This section specifies who should be accountable for the successful conduct of the process and be responsible for its management. These are only stated for the detailed processes, as it is at that level that responsibilities can be decided.

3.2.6 Information needs

This section contains a table of the important information required for the process to function and achieve its objectives. Some entries will be products, such as plans and reports; others are in the nature of decisions.

3.2.7 Key criteria

This section highlights the main issues that will dictate the ultimate success or failure of the process.

3.2.8 Hints and tips

Projects by their nature are very varied. The environments within which they operate also vary tremendously. The PRINCE2 processes lay out the anticipated requirements for the vast majority of projects in most environments. The *Hints and tips* sections provide some guidance on the application of PRINCE2 in certain circumstances and indicate how PRINCE2 might be applied in practice. They are not expected to be a definitive guide. It is strongly advised that this section be fleshed out using best practice and normal approaches for each project environment that adopts PRINCE2.

3.3 Diagram notation

The following symbols are used in the various types of diagram used in the process chapters.

This is a repository for all management products that are created and may be used in many other processes

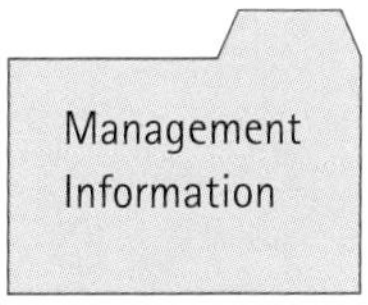

This symbol indicates the archiving of project documentation

This represents people or bodies outside the PRINCE2 identified roles, such as corporate or programme management

4

STARTING UP A PROJECT (SU)

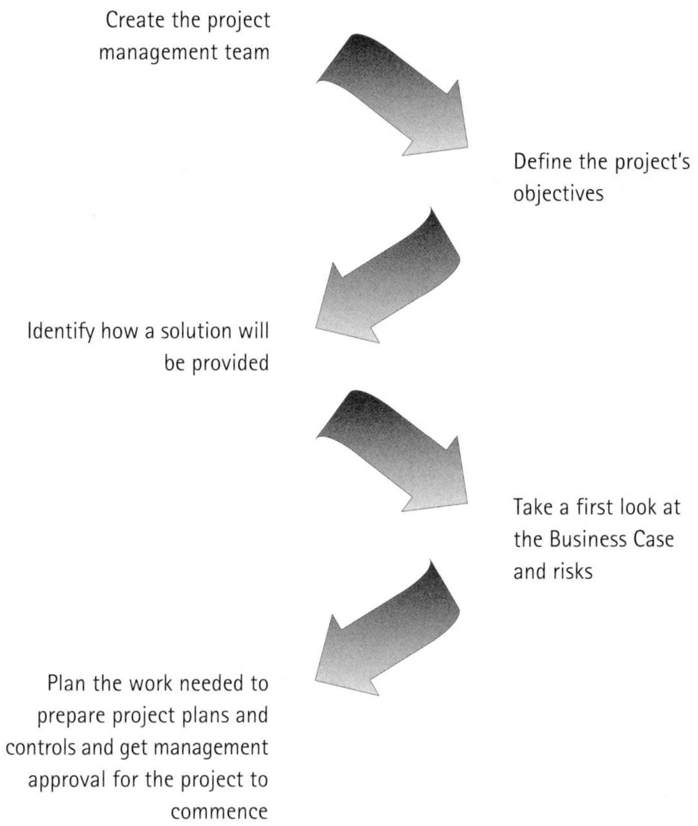
Create the project management team
Define the project's objectives
Identify how a solution will be provided
Take a first look at the Business Case and risks
Plan the work needed to prepare project plans and controls and get management approval for the project to commence

Figure 4.1 Overview of Starting up a Project

4.1 Fundamental principles

- There must be a basic business requirement that triggers the project. Indeed, before any work is commenced or resources are committed, there is a requirement to be able to answer the basic question: 'Do we have a viable and worthwhile project?'. This question must be answered honestly to ensure that resources are not committed and wasted
- Nothing can be done in the project until responsibilities are defined and key roles have been filled. Someone has to 'kick-start' the project into being and make the first decisions
- Certain base information is needed to make rational decisions about the commissioning of the project
- An initiation Stage Plan must be submitted for approval before the initiation stage can be entered.

4.2 Context

This is the first process within PRINCE2. The project begins once this process has been conducted and the Project Board has approved commencement of Project Initiation. In terms of processes, it leads to *Authorising Initiation* (DP1).

Projects can be identified in a variety of ways and thus have a wide variation in the information available to the project management team at the time of start-up. The trigger for the project is the Project Mandate. This is normally provided by corporate or programme management. It is accepted that the Project Mandate may be anything from a verbal request to a complete Project Brief.

The process expects the existence of information explaining the reason for the project and the outcome expected. This set of information has been given the title Project Mandate to avoid confusion with more rigorously defined sets of information created within PRINCE2. The process *Starting up a Project* (SU) should be of short duration relative to the size of the remainder of the project.

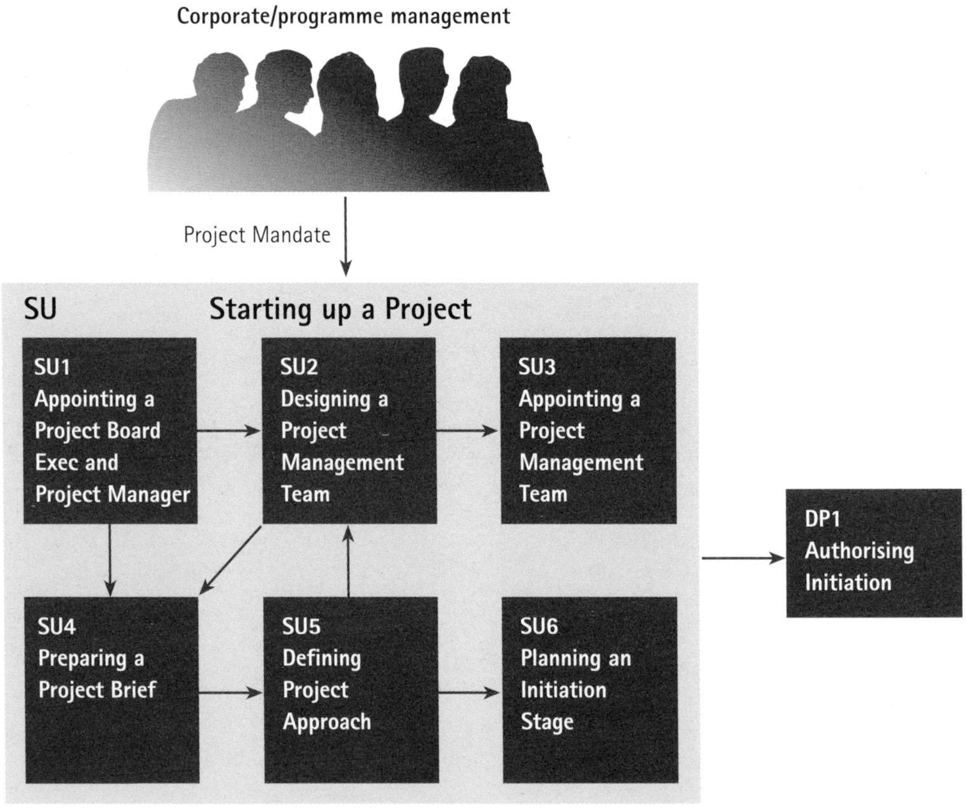

Figure 4.2 Starting up a Project

4.3 Process description

The work of the process is built around the production of six elements:

- Designing and appointing the project management team
- Ensuring that the information required for the Project Brief is available

- Establishing the Project Approach
- Establishing the customer's quality expectations
- Setting up a Risk Log
- Creating the Initiation Stage Plan.

The objective of the process is to enable a controlled start to the project by ensuring that:

- All the necessary project management authorities exist for undertaking the project
- Sufficient information is available to formalise the terms of reference for the project
- Individuals are appointed who will undertake the work required in project initiation and/or will take significant project management roles in the project
- The work required for project initiation is planned
- The organisation that will host the project team is informed of the existence and implications of the new project.

The process begins by receiving from some external source the definition of a problem or opportunity that the project has to satisfy. 'Project Mandate' is a term used for whatever information comes in to trigger the project, be it a feasibility study or details on the back of an envelope. The closer the quality of information in the Project Mandate can get to the ideal described in the Product Description outline for the Project Mandate, the easier the start-up process will be.

An additional input that will help with the creation of both the Initiation Stage Plan and Project Plan is the Project Approach, explaining the way in which it is intended that the end products of the project be produced.

If the project is part of a programme, the programme should provide the Project Brief and Project Approach and appoint some, if not all, members of the Project Board, thus eliminating much of the work required in this process.

Whilst the process model shows two parallel sets of processes to do with assembling a project management team (SU2 and SU3), and agreeing terms of reference and project approach (SU4 and SU5), in practice there will be considerable interplay between these two elements of work. This will depend on how much is known about the nature of the project, and how much has already been agreed about the structure and content of the project management team.

The target work location is informed of the impending project and requests are made for any appropriate logistical support required to carry out project initiation.

4.3.1 Scalability

There are a variety of approaches to this process, which fall into three categories:

- It is a stand-alone project and all the steps of this process will apply. If this is the case, there is little problem in deciding which steps to carry out

- This project is part of a programme. The programme has passed down documentation that is either a complete Project Brief or even a Project Initiation Document. The Project Board may already be defined; the Project Approach and the Risk Log are controlled at programme level. In other words, all the work of *Starting up a Project* (SU) and most of the initiation work has been done. In such a case, the work of this process is simply to check whether any more work needs to be done on the start-up products and that all the information provided is still correct and current
- The third possibility is that the project is very small. In such cases the process can usually be handled in an informal manner, possibly only taking a matter of minutes. A Project Manager should avoid the temptation to bypass it altogether.

Hints and tips

It will not always be appropriate, or indeed possible, to appoint the entire project management team prior to the start of initiation. But at least the Executive and the Project Manager should be appointed, so that the input to initiation can be prepared and decisions can be made.

Lessons Learned Reports from similar previous projects should be referenced to inform the set-up and conduct of this project.

4.4 Appointing a Project Board Executive and a Project Manager (SU1)

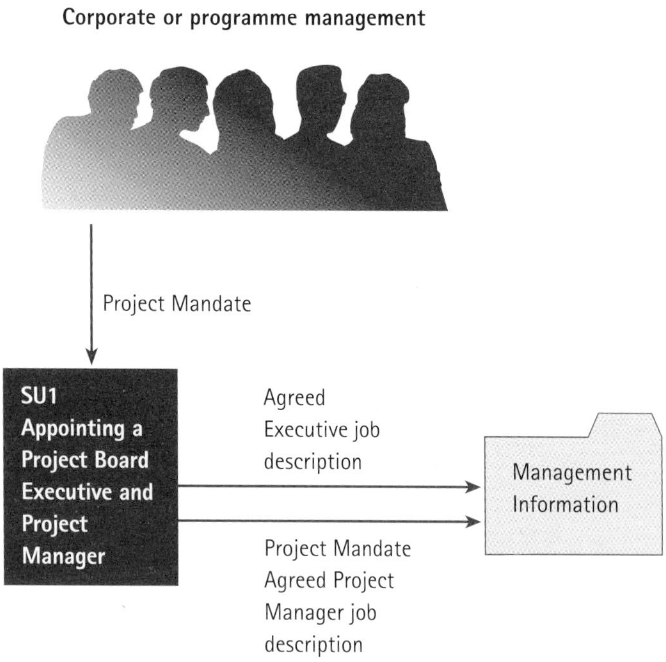

Figure 4.3 Appointing a Project Board Executive and a Project Manager

4.4.1 Fundamental principles

To get anything done in the project, you need a decision maker and someone to undertake the planning.

4.4.2 Context

Before initiation of the project can begin, there must be a plan for that initiation work. The appointment of the Executive and Project Manager is a prerequisite for this work.

4.4.3 Process description

The objectives of this process are to:

- Identify the Executive from the project's stakeholders
- Identify the Project Manager most appropriate for the project
- Confirm the selected people's availability, their acceptance of these roles and their commitment to carry them out
- Appoint them to their respective roles.

A prerequisite of this first process is the existence and availability of a Project Mandate. Because this is the process that precedes the whole of the project, it will be very variable in application, depending particularly on the quality of the Project Mandate information. The following steps will be involved:

- Ratify the key elements of the Project Mandate
- Establish any missing information
- Identify candidates for Executive and Project Manager
- Establish the responsibilities for each role
- Appoint Executive
- Appoint Project Manager
- Confirm appointments via agreement to job descriptions by corporate or programme management and appointees.

The Project Mandate should indicate the general type of project, its size and complexity and its political and business sensitivity. This information will help to identify appropriate candidates for the Project Manager role.

There may be a draft Project Plan included in the Project Mandate from earlier work. This would give an idea of the timeframe of the project – useful when confirming the availability of people to fill the roles.

The outline of the roles of Executive and Project Manager, given in Appendix B, *Project Management Team Roles*, should be used as the basis for discussion between the Executive and the Project Manager on tailoring and agreement of their roles.

4.4.4 Responsibilities

Corporate or programme management.

4.4.5 Information needs

Table 4.1 SU1 information needs

Management information	Usage	Explanation
Project Mandate	Input/Update	The trigger for the project
Agreed job descriptions for the Executive and Project Manager	Output	Basis for sign-up by the Executive and Project Manager
Appoint Executive and Project Manager	Output	

4.4.6 Key criteria

- If the project is part of a programme, will the programme management team fulfil any roles on the Project Board?
- Does the proposed Executive have the financial and functional authority necessary to support the project adequately?
- Has the availability of candidates been measured against any forecast duration of the project to ensure that individuals are available for as much of the project as possible?
- Are any candidates likely to change jobs in the near future in a direction that would remove them from the project? If so, has this information been taken into consideration when making the appointments?
- Do the appointees have the skills and knowledge required to undertake their tasks?

Hints and tips

Where the size or importance of the project warrants it, agreed job descriptions should be signed by the person or persons undertaking the role, plus, where appropriate, their line management; copies should be held by that person or persons and a signed copy also held in the project files.

For small or low-risk projects it may not be appropriate to have formal job descriptions, but the people should have read and understood the responsibilities contained in the role descriptions.

If the project is part of a programme, programme management will appoint the Executive and may influence the appointment of the Project Manager as well. The programme may leave the appointment of the remainder of the Project Board to the Executive.

4.5 Designing a Project Management Team (SU2)

4.5.1 Fundamental principles

- The project needs the right people in place, with the authority, responsibility and knowledge to make decisions in a timely manner.
- The project management team needs to reflect the interests of all parties who will be involved, including business, user and supplier interests.
- Project management requires resources and calls for a range of skills, which must be available within the project management team.
- It is important that consideration is given to all the activities that are involved in managing the project, so that no important aspects are overlooked. It is also important that all the skills needed by the project are made available. All the roles identified in the *Organisation* component must be filled in some way in each project.

4.5.2 Context

Having identified an Executive and the Project Manager, the next job is to review the project size, complexity and areas impacted by the final outcome, then design the project management team with appropriate representation of user, supplier and Project Support.

In practice it is normal that this process and the next, *Appointing a Project Management Team* (SU3), will have considerable overlap.

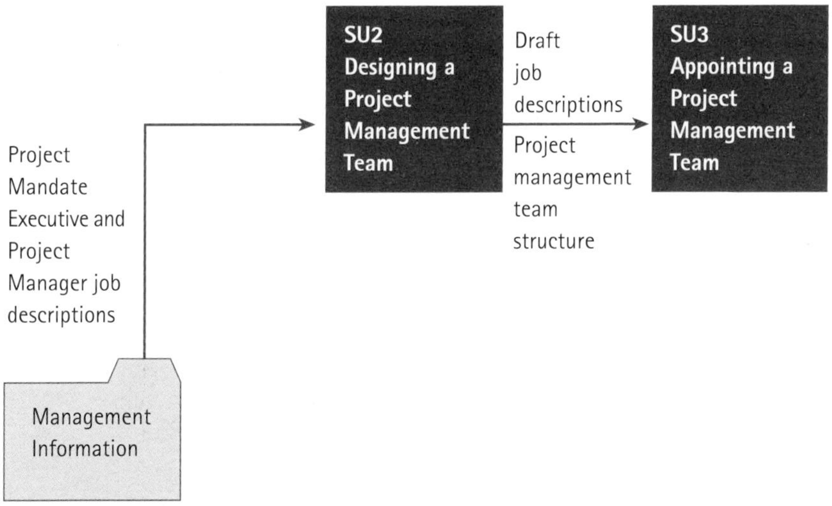

Figure 4.4 Designing a Project Management Team

4.5.3 Process description

The objectives of the process are:

- Design the project management team structure appropriate to the size and nature of the project and the groups involved

- Identify candidates for each role in order to produce a recommended project management team
- Determine the responsibilities and requisite skills required for each position
- Where the project is part of a programme, programme management has responsibility for ensuring the establishment of an appropriate Project Board. If this is done, most of this process will not be required. The programme may, however, leave the appointment of the remainder of the Project Board to the Executive.

The PRINCE2 project management team structure described in the *Organisation* component (Chapter 14) and Appendix B, *Project Management Team Roles*, should be used as a basis for the process. There are certain steps that must be undertaken:

- Identify candidates for the Project Board roles and create their job descriptions
- Assess whether any members of the Project Board are likely to delegate any of their assurance responsibilities; this will assist the Project Manager to advise on the design of any assurance roles and the selection of candidates to fill them; this aspect may need to be revisited after the other Project Board roles are actually appointed
- Consider whether separate individuals are likely to be needed as Team Manager(s) or whether the Project Manager will be filling this role personally; the final decision on this may not be taken until the planning of each stage
- Examine the Project Manager role definition and propose any Project Support roles required; a checklist of potential project support responsibilities is shown in Appendix B, *Project Management Team Roles*
- Assign candidate names to all roles identified; the design should state whether each role will be allocated to one individual, shared or combined with another role, also assess the time and effort required to fill the role
- Identify who will need to approve these appointments in the next process, SU3.

It may be necessary to obtain information from the Project Brief and Project Approach in order to complete this process.

4.5.4 Responsibilities

The Executive and Project Manager are jointly responsible for the design. The Executive will take specific responsibility for the Project Board design.

4.5.5 Information needs

Table 4.2 SU2 information needs

Management information	Usage	Explanation
Agreed Executive and Project Manager job descriptions	Input	Specifies the existing agreed responsibilities to avoid gaps/overlaps
Project Mandate	Input	Indicates the likely user and customer interests

Project management team structure	Output	This forms the basis of discussion with the appointees and with the senior management
Draft job descriptions for the remaining members of the project management team	Output	Ready for discussion and approval in process SU3

4.5.6 Key criteria

- Have the customer and supplier resident quality assurance and internal audit functions been catered for?
- Does the organisation design balance with the overall projected cost, criticality and importance of the project?
- Can the proposed Project Board members make the commitments required of them?
- Have all the roles and responsibilities been allocated? If not, are the exclusions justified?
- Does the design allocate roles and responsibilities to individuals with the requisite knowledge, time and authority to carry them out?
- Are all relevant stakeholders represented in the project management team?
- How should the PRINCE2 model be adapted where the customer or supplier uses methods or technology that call for specific organisation-and-control models?
- Does the project management team structure fit in with, and support, any programme management structure?
- If the project is part of a programme, is there to be programme representation on the Project Board or as some part of the project management team?
- Do any assurance and support roles fit into any overall programme or strategy assurance and support functions?

Hints and tips

If the project is part of a programme, programme management may choose to appoint all members of the Project Board or leave this to the project Executive. In the latter case, the Executive should confirm the acceptability of the design with programme management.

The user and operational interests that will be impacted by the project's product(s) should be considered for Project Board representation.

The Project Board is a decision-making body, not a discussion group. For this reason it is not a good idea to allow the Project Board to grow too large. Ideally, it should not grow beyond, say, 3–6 people for even a large project. It may not always be possible to restrict it to this size, but, for example, often a separate user group can be set up, which will appoint one of its members to act as the Senior User on the Project Board.

While it is important to give consideration to all the items discussed, it will often not be possible to provide all the information needed to make all appointments during start-up and thus there will often be a need to finish some appointments during initiation, or at the beginning of a stage.

Ensuring that quality testing has appropriate user and/or customer representation is the responsibility of the Senior User. This should be taken into consideration when discussing any delegation of the Senior User's assurance responsibilities.

It is essential to ensure that the project is not adversely affected by delays in customer or supplier management chains. This should be considered when thinking of individuals, particularly when filling the various Project Board roles.

A Project Board member should not delegate his/her role. This usually leads to a deputy who does not have the authority necessary to make the required decisions.

Where a third party is funding the project, it may be necessary for the financier to be extensively involved in the management of the project. Project Board roles should reflect this, but also emphasise the user's role in specifying what is needed and monitoring the project to ensure that the solution is going to satisfy these needs.

Where the project is part of a programme, this process can be used to design the lines of communication between project and programme. This may mean programme representation explicitly within the project management team.

4.6 Appointing a Project Management Team (SU3)

4.6.1 Fundamental principles

- An essential for a well-run project is that every individual involved in the management of the project understands and agrees:
  - who is accountable to whom for what
  - who is responsible for what
  - what the reporting and communication lines are
- There must be agreement and acceptance by everyone of their roles and responsibilities
- There should be no gaps in responsibilities once the roles have been tailored; someone should be clearly responsible for each given management aspect.

4.6.2 Context

Having created a design for the project management team in process SU2, this now needs discussion and agreement with the individuals identified.

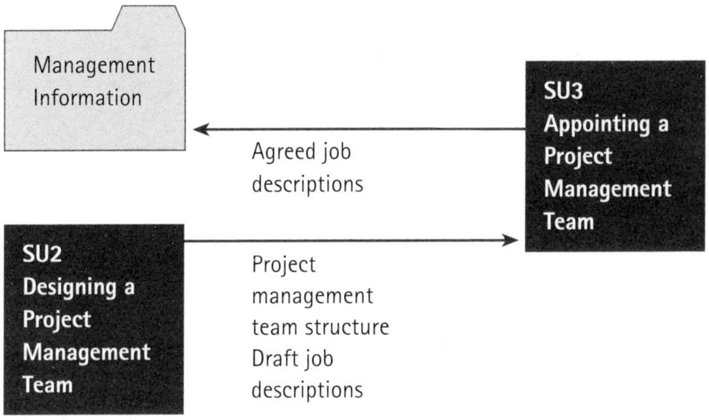

Figure 4.5 Appointing a Project Management Team

4.6.3 Process description

The objectives of the process are to:

- Appoint people to:
  - the Project Board
  - Project Assurance (where appropriate)
  - Project Support (where appropriate)
  - team management
- Ensure that these individuals understand their roles and responsibilities in the management and support of the project
- Ensure that the individuals are actively committed to carrying out their roles and responsibilities
- Confirm the reporting and communication lines, and include in management information as this will impact on the Communications Plan.

These objectives are met by a process of consultation and discussion with all the people involved and, if necessary, their line management.

As agreement is reached with Project Board members on their roles, thoughts on the delegation of any of their assurance responsibilities may change from the project management team design. This may lead to a redesign and a further round of appointments or role modifications.

Each PRINCE2 role definition will need to be tailored to the particular environment and individual. The individual concerned should sign the resulting agreed job descriptions. Copies should be held by that individual and the Project Manager.

For any Project Assurance or support personnel appointed, the Project Manager needs to confirm what their availability to the project will be.

4.6.4 Responsibilities

The Executive is responsible for the appointments, assisted and advised by the Project Manager. The Executive will have to liaise with corporate or programme management to identify the appropriate personnel and negotiate for their availability.

4.6.5 Information needs

Table 4.3 SU3 information needs

Management information	Usage	Explanation
Project management team structure	Input	Identification of the planned allocation of roles
Draft job descriptions	Input	Appointed and confirmed project management team
Agreed job descriptions	Output	Roles tailored to the project and the individual

4.6.6 Key criteria

- Did final agreement on job descriptions cause any transfer or change of responsibilities that has an impact on another job?
- Have all appointees understood and accepted the responsibilities of their role as described in the job description?
- Have the appointees the appropriate skills for the job? Have they received appropriate training to fulfil their roles? Have they sufficient time to fulfil their roles?

Hints and tips

Thought needs to be given to how the various support processes such as issue management will be handled.

The customer or supplier may have a Project Support Office in existence, from which some or all of the Project Support identified may be obtained.

If the project is part of a programme that itself has programme support, thought will have to be given as to how the project will interface with the programme.

4.7 Preparing a Project Brief (SU4)

4.7.1 Fundamental principles

Before proceeding any further, the Project Board needs to satisfy itself that the project is worth doing.

The project needs to start with a reliable statement of requirements and expectation, to ensure it is based on consistent and adequate information.

Even if the project is part of a programme and the programme has provided a Project Brief, documentation can become out of date quickly, hence it will need checking before we proceed.

4.7.2 Context

The external trigger for the project is the Project Mandate. This process checks the content of the mandate to ensure that it is still correct and enhances it, where necessary, into the Project Brief.

Where the project is part of a programme, the programme may create the Project Brief, thus reducing the work of this process. The project team should validate any provided Project Brief and may need to expand on some of the statements in it. If the Project Brief is provided by a programme, the programme management must agree any changes (for example, impacts on constraints, such as delivery dates). Such changes would need impact analysis at programme level and may cause entries in the programme and project Risk Logs.

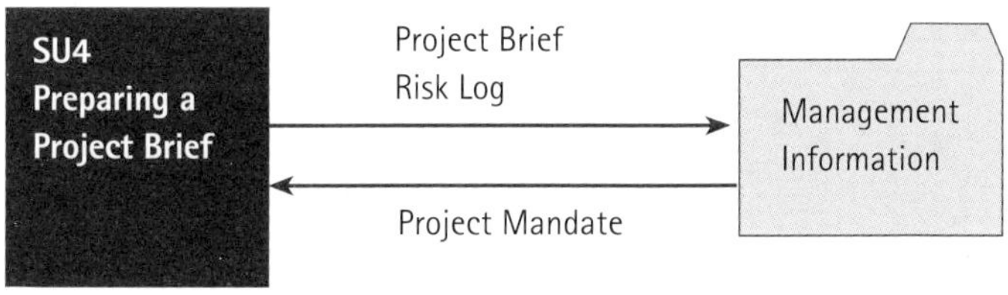

Figure 4.6 Preparing a Project Brief

4.7.3 Process description

The objectives of the process are to:

- Prepare the formal terms of reference for the project
- Establish the customer's quality expectations
- Establish the Acceptance Criteria for the project
- Begin a record of any risks facing the project
- Ensure there is an outline Business Case based on the information provided in the Project Mandate.

The Project Mandate information may not be complete or accurate. This process achieves a stable statement of project requirement in the form of the Project Brief.

The Project Brief needs to include high-level information on **what** needs to be done, **why**, the benefits to be achieved, **who** will need to be involved in the process and **how** and **when** it will be done. The aim of the Project Brief is to allow the Project Board to decide whether there is sufficient justification to warrant the expenditure proposed by the Initiation Stage Plan. The outline for the Project Brief, given in Appendix A, *Product Description outlines*, lists the information needed for this purpose.

The customer's quality expectations need to be agreed at this early stage. They will impact every part of the product development, thus affecting time and cost.

The user requirements should be prioritised. Later, if problems cause reconsideration of the project's scope, funds can then be targeted at those items promising the highest return. Part of the terms of reference should be the Acceptance Criteria, given in Appendix A, *Product Description outlines*.

The contents of the Project Brief should be discussed with all stakeholders.

The level of detail needed for each element of the Project Brief will vary with different project circumstances. However, each element needs to be considered, even if the result of that consideration is that the element is not needed.

The Business Case will be refined as part of the Project Initiation Document and throughout the project. However, the basic justification for the project needs to be understood, either defined in the Project Mandate or developed in this process and added to the Project Brief.

The customer's quality expectations will also be used in the initiation stage to create the Project Quality Plan.

Risks may come to light during this process; therefore a Risk Log should be created as early as practical within this process.

4.7.4 Responsibilities

The Executive is ultimately responsible for the production of the Project Brief. In practice, the Project Manager and any appointed Project Support staff may do much of the actual work.

4.7.5 Information needs

Table 4.4 SU4 information needs

Management information	Usage	Explanation
Project Mandate	Input	Basis of the Project Brief
Risk Log	Output	Ready to record risks, including any noted in the Project Brief
Project Brief	Output	Submission to the Project Board as part of the justification for initiation

4.7.6 Key criteria

- Does the Project Brief contain all the required information?
- Is the information in the various sections of the Project Brief consistent?
- Is the 'ownership' of the project properly defined?
- Is there any potential disagreement on the Project Brief contents from Project Board members?
- Is the Project Brief suitable for a decision to be made on whether to authorise initiation or not?

- If this project is one of a chain of related projects, does the content of the Project Brief conform to any prior projects?

Hints and tips

Check the Project Brief for the project informally with each member of the Project Board before presenting it for formal approval.

Try to determine whether there are any conflicts of interest within the parties to the project.

In small projects the Project Brief may not be produced as a separate document. It may be more appropriate to go straight to producing an outline Project Initiation Document, which would then be refined. In such a case, *Starting up a Project* (SU) and *Initiating a Project* (IP) could combine into one process.

Keep the Project Brief as small and high level as is consistent with the decisions that need to be taken in *Authorising Initiation* (DP1).

4.8 Defining Project Approach (SU5)

4.8.1 Fundamental principles

Before any planning of the project can be done, decisions must be made regarding how the work of the project is going to be approached. For example, will the solution be:

- Bought 'off the shelf'
- 'Made to measure'
- Developed in-house
- Contracted to third parties
- Based on an existing product
- Built from scratch
- Based on specific technologies?

It is also necessary to make sure that the way in which the work is to be conducted is in line with practices and guidelines currently understood between customer and supplier and does not jeopardise the project in any way.

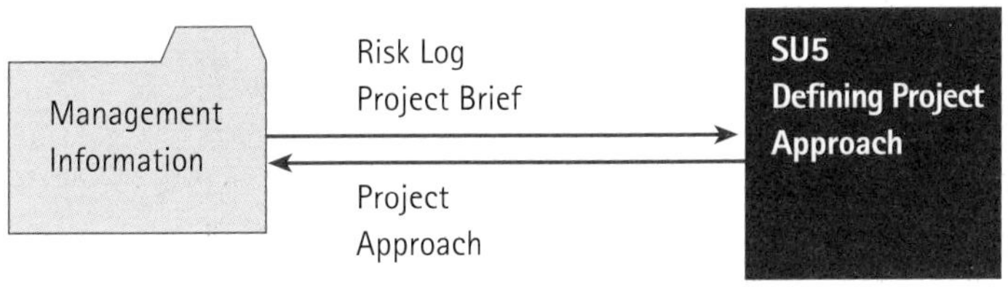

Figure 4.7 Defining Project Approach

4.8.2 Context

The process takes information from the Project Brief, together with information from a range of corporate and industry sources, to produce the defined Project Approach.

The Project Approach will be used when developing the Project Quality Plan and Project Plan in the next process, *Initiating a Project* (IP).

4.8.3 Process description

The objectives of this process are to:

- Decide how the work of the project should be approached
- Identify any constraints on the way that the work of the project must be carried out or the timing of certain product deliveries
- Identify the skills required to conduct the work of the project.

In order to achieve these objectives, various steps have to be undertaken:

- Examine, and if necessary refine, how the work is to be approached based on the overall direction given in the Project Mandate and/or Project Brief, particularly within the Project Definition and the Business Case
- Identify any constraints on time, money, quality and resource use or availability
- Identify any corporate or industry standards that should apply to this project's products or activities
- Identify any corporate or industry statements of best practice that could apply to this project's products or activities
- Identify any security constraints that apply to the creation and long-term operation of the project products
- Identify the range of options open for conducting the work of delivering the project's products
- Identify any maintenance and operational implications that might have an effect on the choice of option
- Identify any corporate strategies or statements of direction that could have a bearing on this project's products and activities
- Put the project in context with any other related work or corporate initiatives by establishing any external dependencies and prerequisites
- Identify the current thinking about the provision of solutions within the industry sectors and specialist skill areas involved
- Identify the overall business criticality of the project's outcome and the current assessment of business risk
- Consider how the finished product can be brought into use
- Identify any training needs for user personnel

- Evaluate the possible options against the identified criteria and parameters
- Select the most appropriate option.

4.8.4 Responsibilities

The Project Manager is responsible for carrying out this process. However, the work will need to be done by people skilled in the specialist areas involved, with input from Project Support and Project Assurance roles, under the overall direction of the Senior Supplier.

4.8.5 Information needs

Table 4.5 SU5 information needs

Management information	Usage	Explanation
Project Brief	Input	This product contains the information upon which decisions on this process need to be made
Risk Log	Input	Identified risks may affect the approach
Project Approach	Output	This forms part of the Project Plan description within the Project Initiation Document and is an input to *Planning Quality* (IP1) and the *Planning* (PL) process

4.8.6 Key criteria

- Has an approach been selected which maximises the chance of achieving overall success for the project?
- Have the operational and support issues been addressed when selecting the approach, to ensure that the benefits have the best chance of being realised?
- Given the approach selected, are risks being taken on a project that is critical to corporate success or that is very high profile?
- Alternatively, are opportunities being missed to experiment and potentially learn some lessons for the future, on a low-risk and/or non-critical project?
- Have risks to the various approaches been identified and evaluated so that the most appropriate options have been selected?
- Is there a need to bring in external resources? If so, does this have any impact on the mode of working?

Hints and tips

This process will be applied very differently in different environments and, as such, it must be actioned thoughtfully. The range of issues will vary tremendously, depending on the nature of the project and the corporate environment. Examples could include:

- What is the range of construction techniques available?

- Should the components or specialist skills required be bought in, or provided in-house?
- Should existing, tried-and-tested methods be used or should the project experiment with new leading-edge techniques?
- To what extent should decisions be left to a third-party *supplier*?
- To what extent should there be insistence on adherence to *customer* standards?

If the project creates a product that replaces an existing product, check whether the changeover to using the new product has implications for the Project Approach.

It may be that not everything can be decided at this stage and there will be further extension and refinement throughout the project.

The Project Manager's agreement with the Project Board on the technical and quality strategy for the project may need to take account of any planned change of suppliers during the project.

4.9 Planning an Initiation Stage (SU6)

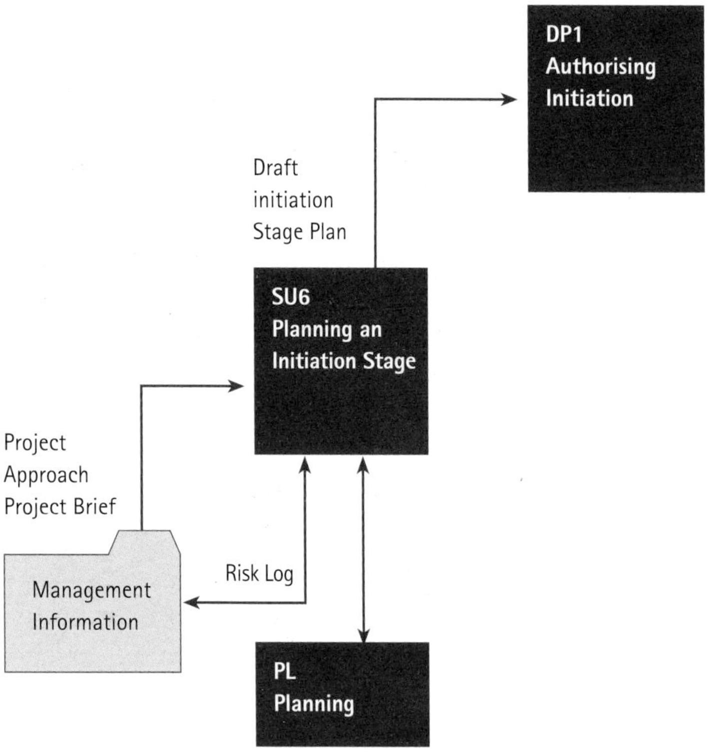

Figure 4.8 Planning an Initiation Stage

4.9.1 Fundamental principles

Initiating the project and preparing the Project Plan take time and consume resources. The work should be planned and approved like any other project work. Make sure that initiation is not aimless and unstructured.

project, and get it signe
of a verbal agreement c

In formal terms, the ob

- Document and cc

- Ensure a firm and
 the work, via the c

- Enable and encou:

- Enable and encour
 - make a decision
 - agree to the com

- Provide the benchn
 project's life

- Ensure that by carry
 time and effort requi
 the project.

5.3.1 Scalability

As stated at the beginning o
process may be reduced wh
versions of the appropriate lc
has the responsibility to ensi
complete and satisfactory.

For small projects, documen
Preparing a Project Brief, might
Stage Plan). It might have be
Starting up a Project (SU) an
Authorising Initiation (DP1) ma
Manager and Project Board.

Hints and tips

Because of the increasing
emerge during the process, i
reference to Project Board n

Where the project is well def
rapid exercise to confirm thi:

Where the project is part o
reporting structure between
Communication Plan (part of

4.9.2 Context

Having already checked in SU4, *Preparing a Project Brief*, that there is a definition of what the project is to do, plus some justification for doing it, the Project Board needs to know what effort is required to create the Project Initiation Document.

4.9.3 Process description

The objectives of the process are:

- Produce a plan (the initiation Stage Plan) that covers the production of two management products:
  - the Project Initiation Document (which includes the Project Plan)
  - the Stage Plan for the stage immediately following initiation
- Define the reporting and control arrangements for the initiation stage.

The Project Initiation Document is an extension and refinement of the Project Brief with the addition of the project management team details, the Project Plan and the Risk Log. The initiation Stage Plan needs to show the investigation and development of the extra information required, plus the development of the Project Brief into the format required for the Project Initiation Document. The initiation stage should be a short and inexpensive one, compared to the likely total cost of the project.

A stage structure for the project will be developed during initiation. At the end of initiation the Project Board will expect to see not only the Project Initiation Document but also a detailed plan for the next stage, because the extent of their actual commitment will only be for the next stage.

If the project is part of a programme, the end date for the initiation stage should be checked against that held in the programme plan. The initiation Stage Plan will also give programme management warning of any requirements from the programme and of the need to prepare to review the Project Initiation Document.

The common *Planning* (PL) process will be used to create the initiation Stage Plan.

4.9.4 Responsibilities

The Project Manager is responsible for planning the initiation stage. The appointed Project Assurance and Project Support roles will assist. In particular, whoever is responsible for business assurance needs to identify in the initiation Stage Plan how the Business Case and risk assessment will be checked.

triggered by *Authorisi*
the *Planning* (PL) pro

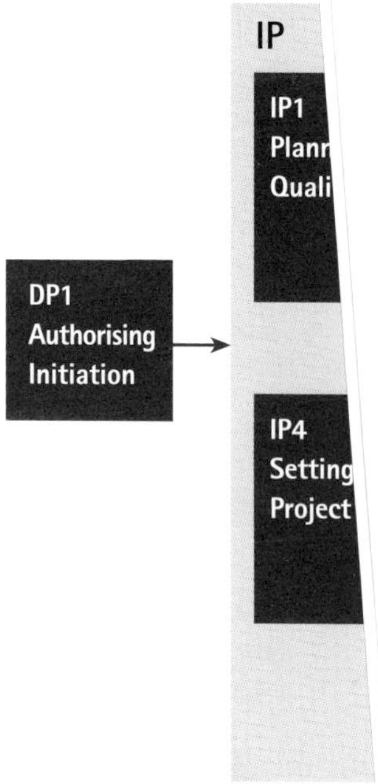

Figure 5.2 Initiating a Projec

5.3 Process descripti

The purpose of *Initiating a P*
Document between the Pr
understanding of:

- The reasons for doing
- What key products the
- How and when these w
- The scope of what is to
- Any constraints which
- Any constraints which
- Who is to be involved in
- How the quality require
- What risks are faced
- How the project is to be
- Who needs project progr
- The next commitment th

This information can be agreed a
The Project Manager should

5.4.4 Responsibilities

The Project Manager is responsible for the process, assisted by those with Project Assurance responsibilities, particularly those connected to business assurance. Where a separate quality assurance function exists within a corporate body, the work of this process must be done in close co-ordination with that function.

5.4.5 Information needs

Table 5.1 IP1 information needs

Management information	Usage	Explanation
Project Brief	Input	This document should contain the customer's quality expectations and the top-level project quality criteria. These are refined and expanded during this process
Quality standards	Input	Standards with which projects must comply
Project Approach	Input	To establish the most appropriate approach to quality, there is a need to know how the project's work is to be approached as this could have a fundamental effect on the methods and resources used
Project Quality Plan	Output	This will contain the results of *Planning Quality* (IP1) and will be an element of the Project Initiation Document output from *Assembling a PID* (IP6)
Quality Log	Output	Created in readiness to record all details of quality checks

5.4.6 Key criteria

- Have all quality standards associated with the project's area of impact been identified and considered?
- Has the customer imposed any Acceptance Criteria on the final product that will require quality-related work beyond normal expectations?
- Have all those, and only those, standards relevant to the successful final product of the project been included?
- Are the approaches to assuring quality for the project appropriate in the light of the standards selected?
- Are the quality criteria measurable or assessable by the quality control mechanisms identified?
- Are the change control and quality assurance methods appropriate for the scale, complexity and risk exposure of the project?
- How will quality assurance be provided on projects where the Project Manager is not technically qualified?

Hints and tips

Much of the information discussed earlier in this chapter, such as standards and quality assurance functions, may already be established and documented. It will usually be sufficient for the Project Quality Plan to refer to this documentation, plus clear identification and justification of any variation from the standards.

The Project Quality Plan may have to take into account any planned change of suppliers during the project, as they may have different quality standards.

5.5 Planning a Project (IP2)

5.5.1 Fundamental principles

Before committing to major expenditure on the project, the timescale and resource requirements must be established. This information is held in the Project Plan and is needed so that the Business Case can be evaluated and the Project Board can control the project.

5.5.2 Context

The process uses the common *Planning* (PL) process to produce the Project Plan. It includes the implications of the Project Quality Plan from *Planning Quality* (IP1).

The Project Plan becomes a major element of the Project Initiation Document.

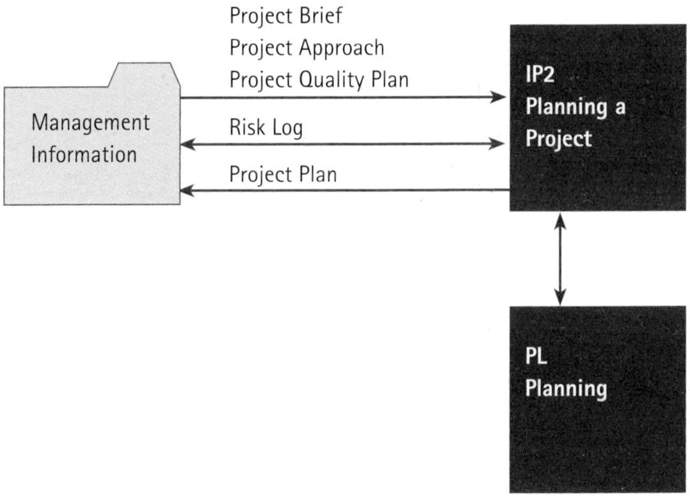

Figure 5.4 Planning a Project

5.5.3 Process description

The objectives of the process are to:

- Understand at a high level the totality of the work that is about to be undertaken by:
  - identifying and, where possible, defining the major products of the project
  - identifying the major activities to be performed to deliver the products

  - assessing the major risks of the project and putting in place countermeasures, as highlighted in *Management of Risk* (Chapter 17)
  - estimating the effort needed
  - identifying what timescales are achievable, given the project constraints and any key milestones
  - identifying the overall resource requirements and costs
- Identify the key decision and review points for the project and from these decide where the management stage divisions should be (as discussed in *Controls*, Chapter 16)
- Use the *Planning* (PL) process to produce the Project Plan.

At this time it is useful to consider the volume of change requests to the objectives or specification that are likely to be submitted during the project. If it is forecast that a number of changes are likely, the Project Manager should suggest to the Project Board that a change budget be set aside to cover the cost of these. This would avoid situations where the Executive is asked to go back to corporate or programme management for an increase in the budget to cover the cost of such changes.

It is also necessary to decide on the planning standards to be used for this project, including:

- tools and techniques
- contents and presentation of plans
- adoption or otherwise of corporate or departmental standards.

As this process is basically a planning process, the detailed steps needed to carry it out are those explained in *Planning* (PL).

5.5.4 Responsibilities

The Project Manager is responsible for this process, assisted where appropriate by Project Support roles and guided by those with Project Assurance responsibilities, who also check the results.

5.5.5 Information needs

Table 5.2 IP2 information needs

Management information	Usage	Explanation
Project Approach	Input	This product will explain what methods will be used to carry out the work of the project and provides a key input into the planning process
Project Brief	Input	This document contains the base information about the project. It is the information that this process uses as the primary start point for the planning process

Project Quality Plan	Input	This product is needed because the work carried out and the time and resources needed to conduct the work will be influenced by the quality required and the quality standards and methods to be adopted
Risk Log	Update	Risks identified in the log may affect the Project Plan. Conversely the Project Plan may create new risks or modify existing ones
Project Plan	Output	This is the ultimate product from the process and its production is the prime reason for carrying out the process

5.5.6 Key criteria

- Does the Project Plan show the appropriate balance between being comprehensive and complete and being sufficiently concise to be understandable?
- Are all the relevant parts of the Project Brief reflected in the Project Plan?
- Is the level of detail in the Project Plan appropriate for the project, bearing in mind:
  - the duration of the project
  - the levels of certainty or otherwise concerning the project's final product(s)
  - the complexity of the project, for example, the number of dependencies compared with the number of products, the number of departments or groups involved
  - the corporate and business risks involved?
- Is it supported by the other elements of the Project Initiation Document? Also is it in sufficient detail to support development of the Project Initiation Document?
- Is the Project Plan in a state suitable to support the decisions to be made in *Authorising a Project* (DP2)?
- Is the Project Plan concise enough to be of practical use for the members of the Project Board?
- Is the Project Plan consistent with corporate and/or programme plans?

Hints and tips

Make sure the Project Brief is understood, as this should provide the base from which the planning is done.

Understanding the way in which benefits are to be realised may have implications for how the project should be run.

To arrive at a final Project Plan it will often be necessary to produce a draft plan, then build the detailed next Stage Plan (triggered by process IP6, *Assembling a Project Initiation Document*), before refining the Project Plan in the light of the information gained.

There will be a need to assess the risk scenario of the Project Plan itself.

Where the project is part of a programme, it may be necessary to include provision for interaction between programme and project, for example:

- periodic audit to ensure reconciliation
- programme briefings
- project involvement in programme-level risk and change control.

5.6 Refining the Business Case and Risks (IP3)

5.6.1 Fundamental principles

When setting up, and particularly while running, the project, it is all too easy to concentrate on *what* is being done and *how* it is to be done, while ignoring *why* it needs to be done. The Business Case states *why* the work is being done and as such is a crucial element of the project.

It is also important to anticipate any problems or threats to which the project could be subject, so that appropriate actions can be taken to deal with them.

5.6.2 Context

The process takes the outline Business Case from the Project Brief and the resource requirements from the Project Plan. From these the activities of the process produce a refined Business Case that is later incorporated into the Project Initiation Document. It also updates the Risk Log with any useful expansion on risks discovered when writing the Project Brief, plus the addition of any extra risks found since.

5.6.3 Process description

This process involves creating and refining the Business Case.

The objectives of this process are to:

- Refine the Business Case in the light of what is now known about the project
- Identify how the achievement of each benefit is to be measured (benefit realisation)
- Add to the Risk Log any extra problem or threats identified during this process
- Modify the Project Plan in the light of any risk management activities.

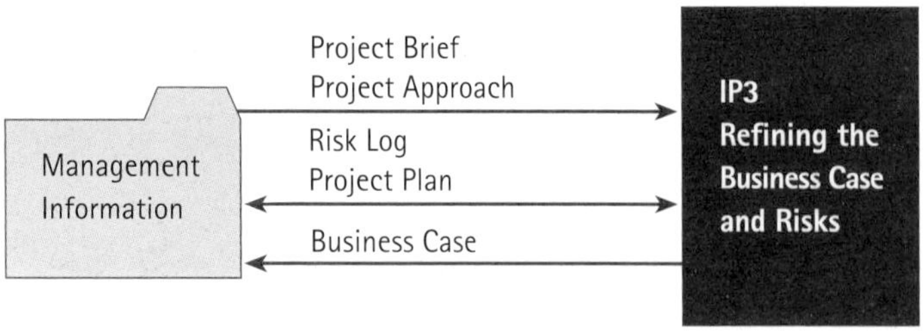

Figure 5.5 Refining the Business Case and Risks

In order to achieve these objectives, various steps have to be undertaken.

For the Business Case:

- Check whether the programme, corporate or strategic objectives that this project is expected to address are still likely to be achievable in light of the information gained so far during *Initiating a Project* (IP)
- Check whether recent external events have affected any of the benefits quoted in the Business Case held within the Project Brief
- Establish whether any additional business benefits have become apparent
- Requantify the benefits where appropriate, and identify any disadvantages that might arise from the project's completion
- Establish how the achievement of each claimed benefit would be measured and record this for the Post-Project Review Plan
- Ensure that measurements of the claimed benefits against the current situation are recorded, so that effective comparison can be made at the post-project review
- Calculate and/or refine the cost elements based on the Project Plan and the latest information regarding the likely operational and maintenance characteristics of the project's products
- Refine or calculate the financial case and recast the investment appraisal where appropriate
- Summarise any different options considered as part of *Defining Project Approach* (SU5).

For the Risk Log:

- Identify any risks that may impact the project
- Assess the likelihood of each risk occurring within this project
- Assess the impact on the project if a risk does occur
- Identify possible courses of action to reduce the risk to an acceptable level
- Prepare any appropriate contingency plans for inclusion in the Project Plan
- Where the project is part of a programme, programme management may need to be informed of any additional risks identified
- Check whether the summary of key risks included in the Business Case needs refining.

For the Project Plan:

- Evaluate the cost of the resolution actions and contingency plans against their value in reducing the risk
- Add these to the Project Plan and/or the next Stage Plan. (NB This will involve an iteration of *Planning a Project* (IP2) and possibly a revisit to the Business Case elements.)

Where a serious risk exists, the Project Board may require the Project Manager to create a contingency plan and add the budget for it – only to be used if the risk occurs. There will be a step of balancing the agreed benefits with the identified costs and risks in order to make a final decision on project viability. If the steps listed here identify any changes that have a fundamental effect on the Business Case, the Project Board will need to be informed as early as possible, since it may need to escalate the issue to corporate or programme management.

5.6.4 Responsibilities

The Project Manager is responsible for this process, assisted, where appropriate, by the Project Support roles and advised by those with Project Assurance responsibilities. The Project Manager should discuss the Business Case and risks with the Project Board informally before presentation in the Project Initiation Document.

5.6.5 Information needs

Table 5.3 IP3 information needs

Management information	Usage	Explanation
Project Brief	Input	Contains high-level views of the anticipated business benefits and risks as identified in *Starting up a Project* (SU)
Project Approach	Input	Will contain information about the way the work is to be conducted and could provide input to both Business Case and risk analysis
Risk Log	Update	Add any identified new risks. Modify with details of any changed risk
Project Plan	Update	Updated with any significant extra activities and resource requirements to counter risk exposure
Business Case	Output	Extract from the Project Brief and update with the latest (more detailed) information

5.6.6 Key criteria

- Are the risk avoidance costs less than the costs implicit in the threats?
- Is it reasonable that the benefits claimed can be achieved by the anticipated final outcome of the project?
- Has sensitivity analysis been conducted on the Business Case?
- Is the information in a form that is understandable by the Project Board?
- Are plans in place by which the user(s) of the products will realise the benefits?
- Has the Business Case been produced in line with corporate standards?

Hints and tips

Each risk effect is itself a potential cause of another effect in a cause–effect chain. The Project Manager has to decide where the chain should be cut to prevent or reduce risks.

It may be appropriate to use the risk profile model to present a summary of the risks documented in the Risk Log to the Project Board.

Where the project is part of a programme, the programme's risk monitoring mechanism must be used unless there are valid reasons not to do so. It may be sensible to combine the maintenance of all the Risk Logs at programme level.

Funding normally comes from the customer, but there are situations where the supplier fully or partially funds the project (Private Finance Initiative, for example). This may give the customer fewer rights to intervene or control the project and could affect the customer's ability to insist on the inclusion of risk avoidance or reduction activities.

The customer and supplier are likely to have different Business Cases.

The method of payment to suppliers needs to be considered. Payment may be provided on a regular basis throughout the life of the project, staged according to the delivery of particular products or in a lump sum at the end.

Benefit realisation often requires measurements of the 'before' situation to be done as part of the project. Once the new product is in place, the old situation has disappeared, making a true comparison impossible. It is sensible to take such measurements close to the time the benefit is claimed.

5.7 Setting up Project Controls (IP4)

5.7.1 Fundamental principles

Each decision on the project has to be made in a timely manner by the person or group most appropriate to make that decision, and must be based on accurate information. This process ensures that an appropriate communication, control and monitoring framework is put in place.

5.7.2 Context

The process builds on the information established in the earlier IP processes to produce a statement of project controls.

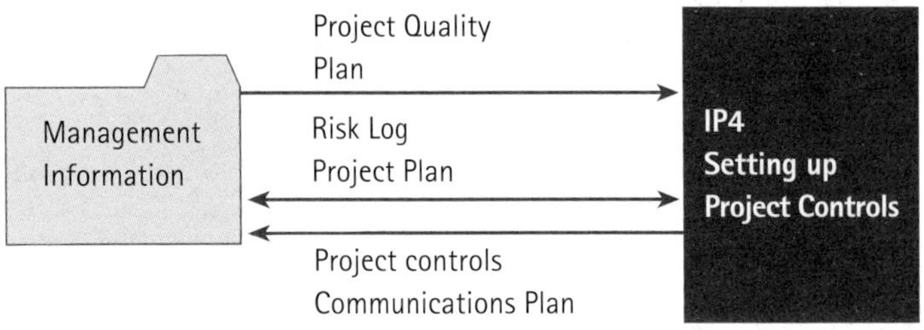

Figure 5.6 Setting up Project Controls

5.7.3 Process description

The objectives of this process are to:

- Establish the level of control and reporting required by the Project Board for the project after initiation
- Develop controls that are consistent with the risks and complexity of the project
- Establish the day-to-day monitoring required to ensure that the project will be controlled in an effective and efficient manner
- Identify all interested parties and agree their communication needs.

In order to achieve these objectives, various steps need to be undertaken:

- Allocate the various levels of decision making required within the project to the most appropriate project management level
- Establish any decision-making procedures that may be appropriate, possibly by tailoring procedures within existing quality management systems or other standard procedures
- Incorporate the control requirements specified in the Project Brief into the overall control environment as created by these two steps
- Incorporate decision-making authorities and responsibilities into job descriptions where appropriate
- Establish the information needs associated with each of the decision-making processes
- Establish monitoring mechanisms to satisfy these information needs
- Establish the resource requirements to provide the monitoring information
- Incorporate monitoring mechanisms into plans and job descriptions where appropriate
- Identify all stakeholders outside the project management team and agree with them their information needs, plus any information needed from them by the project. Define the communication content, recipient(s) and sender, method and frequency for all these external communications in the Communication Plan
- Create a Communication Plan as described in the Product Description outline

- Establish the procedures required to produce and distribute the reporting information.

Where the project is part of a programme, the Communication Plan must define how information is to be fed to the programme.

5.7.4 Responsibilities

The Project Manager is responsible, assisted by Project Support and advised by those with Project Assurance responsibilities.

5.7.5 Information needs

Table 5.4 IP4 information needs

Management information	Usage	Explanation
Project Plan	Update	This will need to be updated with activities and resource requirements for monitoring and control
Risk Log	Update	Risk levels will have an impact on the scale and rigour of control activities. New or changed risks may be noted as a result of defining control and monitoring activities. Also there is a need to put in place monitoring devices for risks as they develop
Project Quality Plan	Input	The achievement of quality is one area that must be monitored and controlled. There is, therefore, a need to co-ordinate project controls with the Project Quality Plan
Communication Plan	Output	Identify all communication paths, frequency, methods and reasons
Project controls	Output	This will form part of the Project Initiation Document

5.7.6 Key criteria

- Are the decisions being allocated to people equipped and authorised to make those decisions?

The next points are there to reinforce the motto 'Not too little, not too much':

- Are the controls appropriate to the risk, scale and complexity of the project?
- Is the level of formality established appropriate to the risk, scale and complexity of the project? This covers such things as reporting, monitoring, procedures and job descriptions
- Are all the participants committed to providing the information and acting on it?
- Have the information needs of all people with an interest in the project been considered when creating the Communication Plan?

Hints and tips

When creating the controls for the project, consider the communications requirements of the project as well as the decisions being made.

Make sure that the level of control is appropriate to the project. Don't over-control for the sake of it.

If the project is part of a programme, make sure that any programme reporting requirements will be satisfied by the defined control structure.

Where information has to be fed back to a programme, this may be done by reports from the project being examined by programme staff or by programme representation within the project.

Programme representation is recommended in estimating the impact of change.

When creating the project schedule, appropriate milestones should be identified to allow any required programme monitoring of project progress, such as the ends of stages and the production of reports required for use by either the programme or other projects.

Try to restrict external communication requests to copies of existing project reports.

In a programme context, each project may operate change management within delegated authority levels.

5.8 Setting up Project Files (IP5)

5.8.1 Fundamental principles

Once the project is under way, it is important to keep track of all the information being produced about the project and the management and specialist products. There is a need to be able to manage different versions of products and to be able to retrieve information quickly and reliably. Establishing a sensible and pragmatic project filing system at the start of the project can ease these problems.

5.8.2 Context

This process takes information from the Project Plan and adds the project filing structure to the Configuration Management Plan. A suggested project filing structure is given in detail in Appendix E.

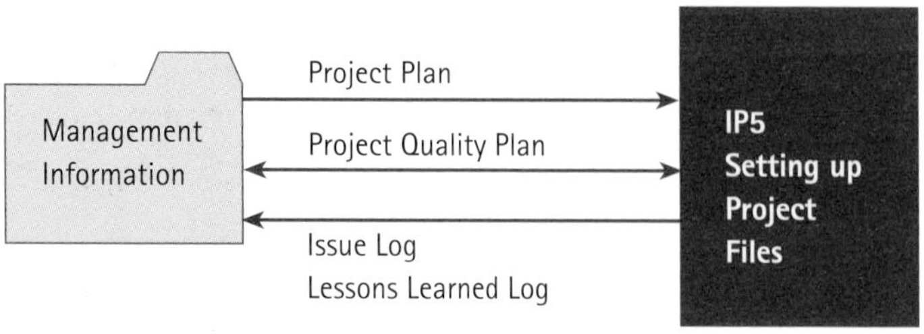

Figure 5.7 Setting up Project Files

5.8.3 Process description

The objectives of the process are to:

- Institute a system of storing and retrieving all information relevant to the management of the project, the quality checking work done and the products themselves, which will provide appropriate support to the project team and to the implementation of change management
- Assign responsibility for managing this filing system.

It may be that a configuration management system is to be used that will provide these facilities for some or all of the project's products.

In order to achieve these objectives, various steps have to be undertaken:

- Establish what information will be produced throughout the project and will need filing
- Establish what products will be produced throughout the project and the need for associated storage
- Establish what retrieval requirements the people in the Communication Plan have
- Establish filing systems that are appropriate for the identified filing and retrieval needs.

The Issue Log and the Lessons Learned Log are also created during this process.

5.8.4 Responsibilities

The Project Manager is responsible for this process, assisted by any Project Support roles and advised by those with Project Assurance responsibilities.

Where the project is part of a programme, the project-level filing structure must be consistent with that at programme level.

5.8.5 Information needs

Table 5.5 IP5 information needs

Management information	Usage	Explanation
Project Plan	Input	Contains all the information about the products that the project is expected to produce
Project Quality Plan	Update	Updated with the project filing structure as part of the Configuration Management Plan
Issue Log	Output	Created in readiness to record all Project Issues
Lessons Learned Log	Output	A blank log ready to record aspects of project management that go well or badly

5.8.6 Key criteria

- Is the formality and rigour of the project filing system appropriate for the scale, risk and complexity of the project? Does it fit with corporate culture?
- Will the retrieval system produce all required information in an accurate, timely and usable manner?
- Will the project files provide the information necessary for any audit requirements?
- Will the project files provide the historical records required to support any lessons learned?

Hints and tips

With sensible design, computerised support can avoid the need for multiple copies and ensure that staff have access to only the latest version of information.

The key to success is complete and rigorous naming conventions and version numbering, so that it is at least clear what information is being looked at and for the Project Manager to have confidence that there is firm control over all master versions of information and products.

Whether paper based or automated, create a formal configuration management system and appoint a Configuration Librarian as discussed in the *Configuration Management* chapter of this manual (Chapter 19).

Remember that 'files' do not necessarily mean paper. The project files will cover a wide range of media, all of which need to be considered.

Has due consideration been given to the implications of the geographic spread of project personnel?

5.9 Assembling a Project Initiation Document (IP6)

5.9.1 Fundamental principles

There needs to be a focal point at which all information relating to the 'what, why, who, how and when' of the project is gathered for agreement by the key stakeholders and then for guidance and information for those involved in the project.

5.9.2 Context

The process takes all the information from the other IP processes and produces the Project Initiation Document in preparation for the Project Board's decision on whether to authorise the project, covered in *Authorising a Project* (DP2). It also invokes *Managing Stage Boundaries* (SB), to summarise the performance of the initiation stage and produce a detailed plan for the next stage of the project.

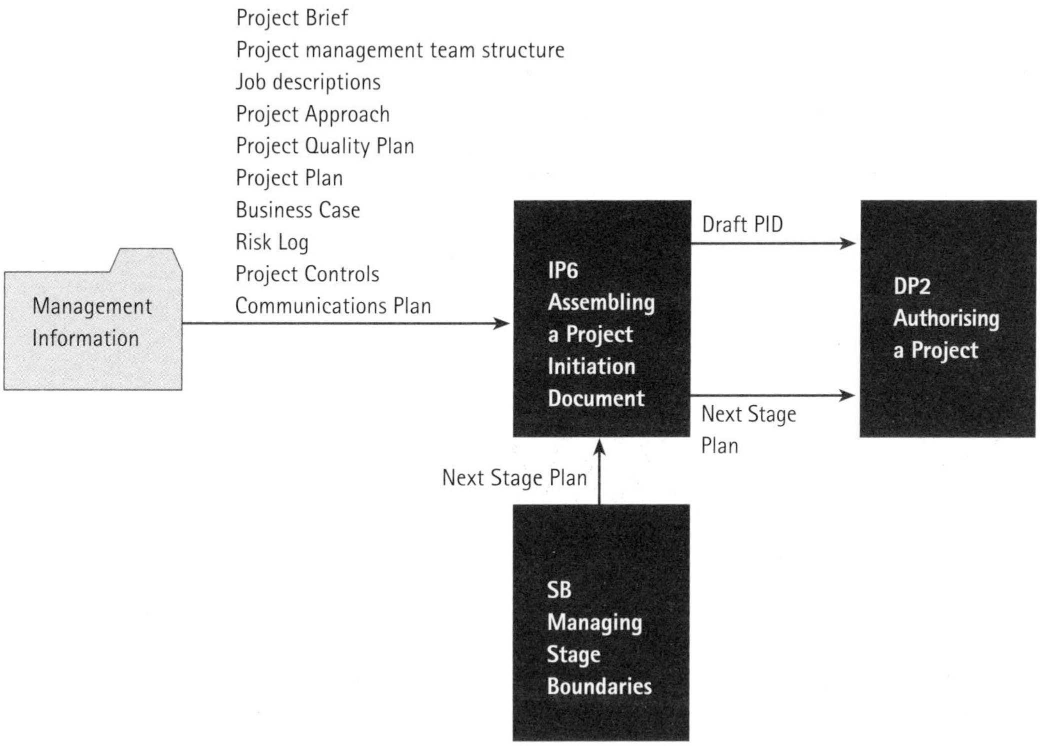

Figure 5.8 Assembling a Project Initiation Document

5.9.3 Process description

The objectives of this process are to:

- Provide a basis for the decisions to be made in *Authorising a Project* (DP2)
- Provide a benchmark for all the other management decisions that need to be made during the life of the project
- Provide an information base for everyone who needs to know about the project
- Prepare a plan for the next stage for Project Board approval.

In order to achieve these objectives, it is important to understand that the information will need to be held and presented in various ways and the Project Initiation Document may not be one physical document.

The steps required to achieve these objectives will include the following:

- Invoke the *Managing Stage Boundaries* (SB) process to prepare the next Stage Plan and draw the initiation stage to a close
- Decide how the information can best be packaged and held so that these objectives can be met for this particular project
- Assemble the information from the previous processes
- Assemble the Project organisation structure from the project management team structure and job descriptions

- Construct the project definition from the contents of the Project Brief and Project Approach, modified by the Project Plan contents
- Carry out a final cross-check of the information in the various elements to ensure that they are compatible
- Add any narrative, explanatory, or navigational information required, including the background
- Create the Project Initiation Document
- Forward the information required for *Authorising a Project* (DP2).

Where the project is part of a programme, programme management must examine the Project Initiation Document for any changes affecting the programme's portfolio. Where there are changes that have been agreed, these need to be reflected in the portfolio. If the changes are likely to have an impact on other projects (for example, a product required by another project will be produced later than previously scheduled), then all projects in the programme should be informed.

5.9.4 Responsibilities

The Project Manager is responsible for the production of the document, assisted by Project Support and advised by those with Project Assurance responsibilities as required. There should be close consultation with the Project Board on the content as it is developed.

5.9.5 Information needs

Table 5.6 IP6 information needs

Management information	Usage	Explanation
Project Brief	Input	Provides information that will be extracted/developed into part of the Project Initiation Document (PID)
Project management team structure and job descriptions	Input	To be developed into part of the PID
Project Approach	Input	To be incorporated into the PID
Project Quality Plan	Input	To be incorporated into the PID
Project Plan	Input	To be incorporated into the PID
Business Case	Input	To be incorporated into the PID
Risk Log	Input	To be incorporated into the PID
Project controls	Input	To be incorporated into the PID
Communication Plan	Input	To be incorporated into the PID

Draft Project Initiation Document	Output	Final end product of *Assembling a* PID (IP6) and of initiation
Next Stage Plan	Output	Sent with the Project Initiation Document to the Project Board

5.9.6 Key criteria

- Is the Project Initiation Document going to provide all the information needs of the recipients?
- Is it easy to update those parts of the Project Initiation Document that are dynamic?
- Is the information compatible across all the sections?

Hints and tips

Make sure that the presentational aspects of the Project Initiation Document are thought through. The complete product can be large when all the detailed Product Descriptions and job descriptions are included. Use appendices to hold the detail and only publish these when requested. For example, if the Project Board prefers to keep the Project Initiation Document as slim as possible, just the project management team structure can be put in the Project Initiation Document, with the job descriptions retained in the project management filing.

Where the project is part of a programme, the Project Initiation Document must be created with the needs of the programme in mind. One way to ensure this is for programme management to play a part in developing the Project Initiation Document.

6

DIRECTING A PROJECT (DP)

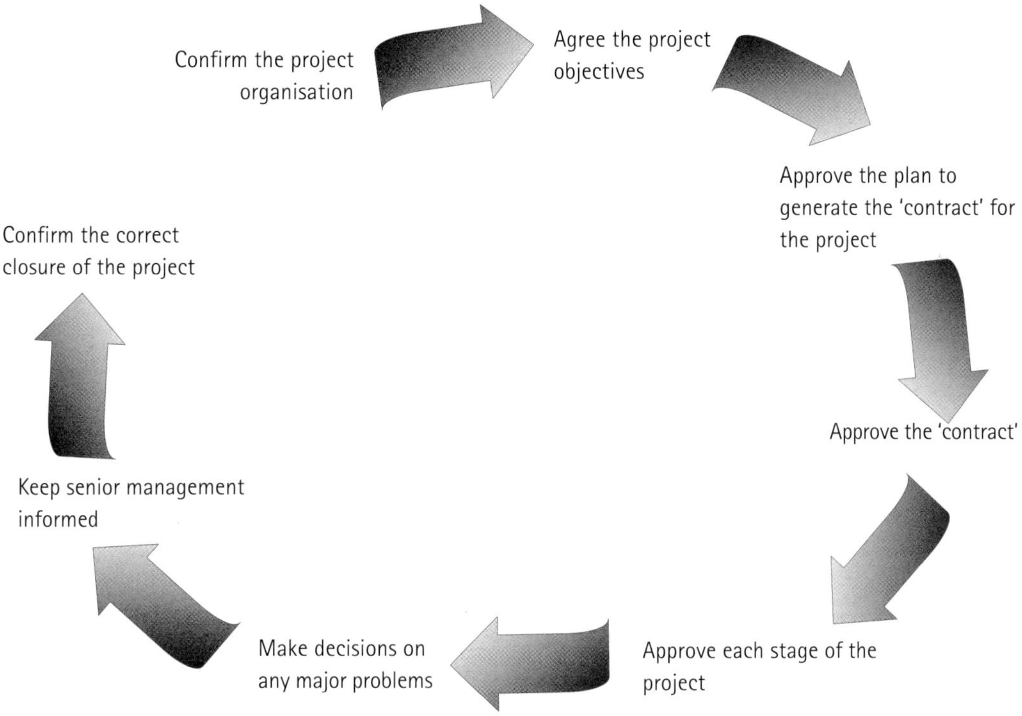

Figure 6.1 Overview of Directing a Project

6.1 Fundamental principles

Senior management who have the authority and responsibility for:

- Defining what is required from the project
- Authorising the funds for the project
- Committing the resources
- Communicating with external interested parties

will typically delegate day-to-day charge of the project to a Project Manager. However, the Executive must exercise overall control and be responsible for the key decisions. It is also important that levels of authority and decision-making processes are clearly identified.

6.2 Context

Directing a Project runs from after *Starting up a Project* until project closure and includes the work to:

- Authorise the initiation of the project
- Provide management direction and control throughout its life

- Liaise with corporate and programme management
- Confirm project closure.

It does not cover the day-to-day activities of the Project Manager.

This process is aimed at the level of management above the Project Manager, that is, the Project Board. The Project Board manages by exception. It monitors via reports and controls through a small number of decision points. There should be no need for other 'progress meetings' for the Project Board. The Project Manager will inform the Project Board of any exception situation.

There needs to be a flow of information from the Project Board to corporate or programme management during the project. This need and how it is to be satisfied should be documented in the Communication Plan, which is part of the Project Initiation Document.

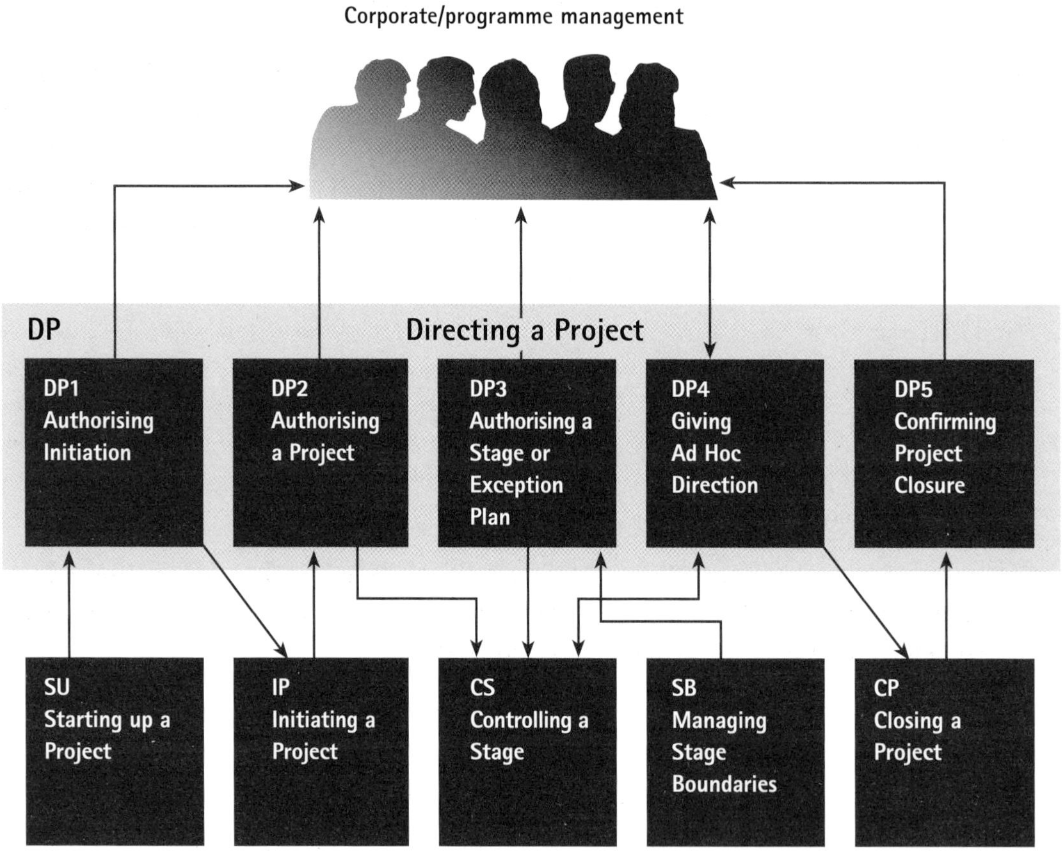

Figure 6.2 Directing a Project

6.3 Process description

The objectives of Directing a Project are to:

- Ensure the ultimate success of the project, judged by:
  - the ability of the products of the project to deliver the business benefits set out in the Business Case
  - delivery to agreed time, cost and quality parameters

- Manage the identified risks to the project
- Ensure the effective management of all people and resources concerned with the project
- Commit the required resources
- Make decisions on any changes when requested by the Project Manager
- Provide overall direction and guidance throughout the project
- Make decisions on exception situations
- Ensure that the project and the products remain consistent with business plans and the external environment
- Ensure that the necessary communications mechanisms are in place
- Sponsor appropriate external communication and publicity about the project.

This process covers the direction of the project throughout its life cycle. The Project Board proactively manages the project's response to the external environment. Within the project the Project Board should 'manage by exception'. The Project Board members are normally busy executives with a range of responsibilities, and demands on their time should be kept to a minimum, while fulfilling their responsibilities to the project. The key responsibilities are:

- Overall direction and decision making
- Resource commitment.

Where the project is part of a programme, the authority to direct the project is delegated to the Project Board by programme management. Where decisions are required that are outside the defined authority of the Project Board, these must be referred to programme management for a decision.

The key processes for the Project Board are predominantly event driven and focus the Project Board members on a small number of key decision points, plus informal discussions where required. These key processes break into four main areas:

- Initiation (starting the project off on the right foot)
- Project re-evaluation at stage boundaries or following an exception situation (commitment to further work after checking results so far)
- Ad hoc direction (monitoring progress, providing advice and guidance)
- Project closure (confirming the project outcome and bringing the project to a controlled close or premature closure of the project should the Business Case no longer be valid).

6.3.1 Scalability

As this process covers the activities of the Project Board and describes its control over the project direction, it is in the hands of the Project Board how formally or informally it wishes to handle its controls. For medium-sized or large projects and all those dealing with external suppliers, it is recommended to use this process formally with meetings, written reports and stage approvals signed by the Project Board.

For small projects, the Project Board may decide to:

- Receive some or all reports orally
- Have an oral exchange of information and decisions instead of formal meetings.

As a minimum, all decisions should be documented, so that they are auditable at a later date. Three points contained within the process are strongly recommended:

- A check (at the end of initiation) to ensure there is clear understanding of what is needed, preferably in writing
- The establishment of tolerances and the exception procedure
- Confirmation at the end that an acceptable product has been delivered and that there are no loose ends.

Hints and tips

The Project Board needs to keep the balance of management by exception between the two extremes of, on the one hand, interfering and, on the other, deserting the Project Manager once the project is under way.

The success of the process depends to a large extent on performing *Setting up Project Controls* (IP4) well; therefore that process needs active Project Board participation.

6.3.2 Initiation

Corporate or programme management should confirm the appointment of the Project Board and other project management team members. This is done in *Appointing a Project Board Executive and a Project Manager* (SU1) and *Appointing a Project Management Team* (SU3). It is important to ensure that everyone is committed to the work that is to be done.

At the outset the Project Board approves a plan for the initiation stage only, which should be relatively short. The purpose of the initiation stage is to produce a high-level plan for the entire project, document its Business Case, examine the risks involved, make management decisions about them and approve the plan for the next stage. *Planning an Initiation Stage* (SU6) is where the initiation Stage Plan is prepared.

At the end of the initiation stage, the Project Board must agree whether it makes sound business sense to continue with the project. If so, and if it approves the Project Plan and the next Stage Plan, the Project Board gives the go-ahead for the next stage.

6.3.3 Stage boundaries

As part of the initiation stage the Project Board and Project Manager will agree on the division of the project into stages. The division is normally proposed by the Project Manager and approved by the Project Board during informal discussions after production of a draft Project Plan.

Basically the Project Board only authorises the Project Manager to proceed with one stage at a time. At the end of each stage the Project Board reviews the whole project status and approves the next Stage Plan only if it is satisfied that the Business Case still stands and the project will deliver what is required.

If major problems occur during a stage, the Project Manager may ask the Project Board to approve an Exception Plan, which will bring the stage (or project) back under control. This is as part of 'management by exception'.

6.3.4 Ad Hoc Direction

The Project Board's main objectives are to provide overall direction and guidance throughout the project and to ensure that the project and the products remain consistent with business plans. Activities to achieve these objectives are formally defined as part of the Stage Plans, but the Project Board will want to monitor these activities by receiving appropriate reports on key elements from the Project Manager.

There may also be a need for the Project Board to provide advice and guidance to the Project Manager or to confirm some of the decisions he/she needs to make, for example, regarding potential problems.

The Project Board must maintain a feedback on project progress to corporate or programme management during the project.

The Project Board must also be mindful of any changes to corporate strategy or the external environment and reflect the impact of such changes when directing the Project Manager.

6.3.5 Project Closure

The project ends with confirmation by the Project Board that everything expected has been delivered to the correct level of quality and that, where applicable, it is in a state where it can be used, operated, supported and sustained.

There may be follow-on actions as a result of the project, about which the Project Board must make decisions and refer to the appropriate bodies.

A date and plan for a post-project review can be agreed. This is a point in the future when the benefits and performance of the end product can be assessed.

Any lessons learned that may be of benefit to other projects are also directed to the relevant body.

Finally, the project's support infrastructure can be disbanded.

The closure process will be modified in situations where the project is terminated prematurely. It is likely that there will be follow-on actions, but not all products may have been produced and there may be little or nothing to support. It is unlikely that there will be a post-project review, but the review of the End Project Report and Lessons Learned Report may be very important to understand why the project has been prematurely terminated and how we can best go forward.

6.4 Authorising Initiation (DP1)

6.4.1 Fundamental principles

No one should commit to large expenditure on the project before verifying that it is sensible to do so.

6.4.2 Context

Authorising Initiation is the first major activity for the Project Board. After the process, *Starting up a Project* (SU), it must decide whether to allow the project to enter the initiation stage. This may be done at a formal Project Board meeting. The Project Board can, however, choose to make the decision without the need for a formal meeting, as long as all members are in agreement.

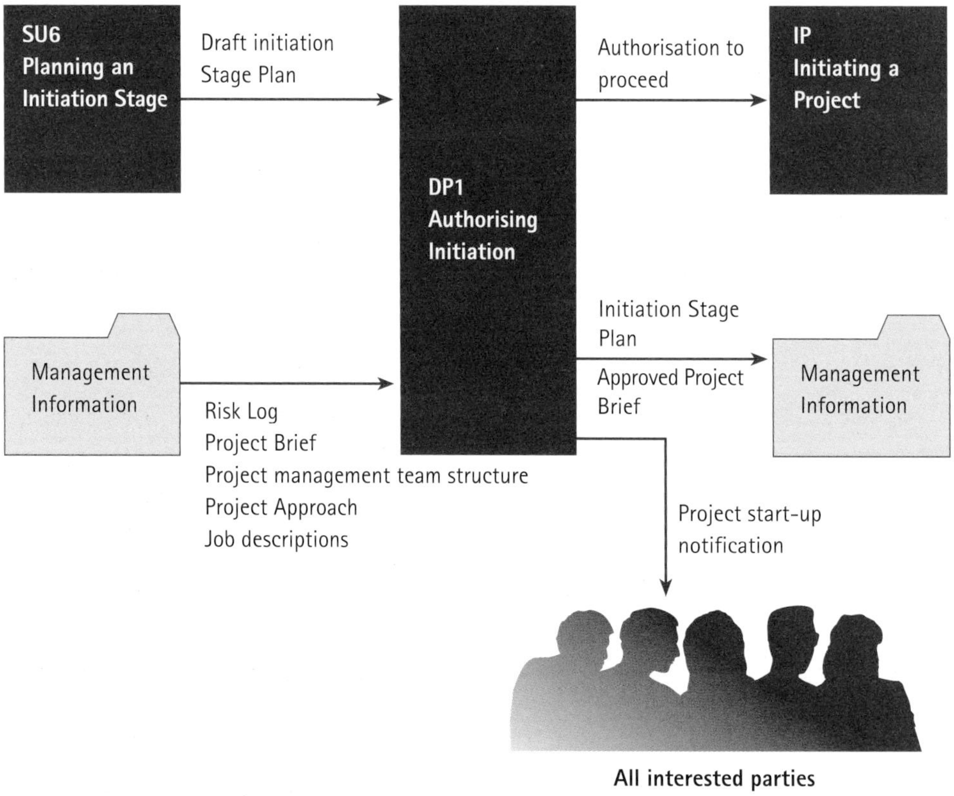

Figure 6.3 Authorising Initiation

6.4.3 Process description

The objective is to ensure that the project is properly initiated by:

- Formally confirming the appointments to the project management team
- Ratifying the Project Brief with corporate or programme management
- Approving a plan to develop the Project Initiation Document
- Obtaining or committing the resources needed by the initiation Stage Plan

- Requesting the necessary logistical support via the project start-up notification to the host organisation (the location where the work is to be done).

The Project Board must ensure that adequate reporting and control mechanisms are in place for the initiation stage. A tolerance level should be set for initiation, just as for the later Stages.

The Project Board is responsible for obtaining resources and providing a support infrastructure for the project in line with those requirements identified in the initiation Stage Plan. The support infrastructure may include accommodation, communication facilities, equipment and any Project Support.

6.4.4 Responsibilities

Responsibility for the process rests with the Project Board, based on input provided by the Project Manager and those with Project Assurance responsibilities. Corporate or programme management is responsible for ratifying the Project Brief for the Project Board.

6.4.5 Information needs

Table 6.1 DP1 information needs

Management information	Usage	Explanation
Risk Log	Input	Are there risks that affect the decision to authorise the initiation stage?
Job descriptions	Input	Details of job responsibilities
Project management team structure	Input	Details of who is to be involved in the management of a project
Project Approach	Input	Information needed as part of the decision to go ahead. Does it fit with corporate or programme strategy?
Project Brief	Update	Baselined after approval by corporate or programme management
Draft initiation Stage Plan	Update/ Output	Contains the 'what' and 'why' of the project and is the document that specifies the Project's terms of reference for approval by the Project Board
Project start-up notification	Output	Formal notification to those that need to know that the project has started
Authorisation to proceed	Output	Confirmation to the Project Manager that the work defined in the initiation Stage Plan may start

6.4.6 Key criteria

- Is there adequate funding for the project?
- Does the Project Brief demonstrate the existence of a worthwhile project and hence justify the investment involved?
- Are external support and facility requirements available and committed?

- Have the most appropriate standards been applied, particularly if the customer and supplier standards differ?
- Are Project Assurance responsibilities allocated and accepted?
- Are the known risks acceptable at this point in the project?

Hints and tips

The Project Board should expect to be involved extensively during the initiation stage, as this is the stage where the infrastructure of the project is laid down – the foundation for the project's success.

Apart from requesting any staff to support the Project Manager, the process also has to formally agree with the host organisation the logistical support requirements of the forthcoming project. This would include any accommodation, equipment, access, security arrangements, tools and administrative support.

Initiation should be a fast-moving process; hence the need for frequent ad hoc discussions between Project Board and Project Manager. Avoid smothering the initiation process with excessive formality of reporting.

Where a third party is funding the project, it may be necessary for the financier to be extensively involved in the management of the project. Project Board roles should reflect this, but also emphasise the user's role in specifying what is needed and monitoring the project to ensure that the solution is going to satisfy those needs.

Where the supplier is funding the project, the Executive and Senior Supplier roles will need tailoring to reflect the financial responsibilities.

Where the project is part of a programme, the programme may have already prepared the Project Initiation Document, thus shortening the normal project initiation process. In such cases, the project may start with *Authorising a Project* (DP2). It is still the responsibility of the Project Board to ensure that all necessary steps have been taken and documented.

6.5 Authorising a Project (DP2)

6.5.1 Fundamental principles

No project should commit to significant expenditure without:

- Management approval that an acceptable Business Case exists for the project
- Checking that it fits with any relevant corporate and programme strategy
- Assessment and acceptance of the risks involved
- An estimate of the time and cost involved
- Checking that the project will be appropriately controlled.

A benchmark should be established against which the project can be judged and which can be used to control change.

6.5.2 Context

The process is undertaken at the same time as approving the Stage Plan for the stage to follow initiation. This process will be combined with *Authorising a Stage or Exception Plan* (DP3) to approve both the Project Plan and the next Stage Plan.

The approved Project Initiation Document triggers the start of the next stage of the project and forms the benchmark for the rest of the project.

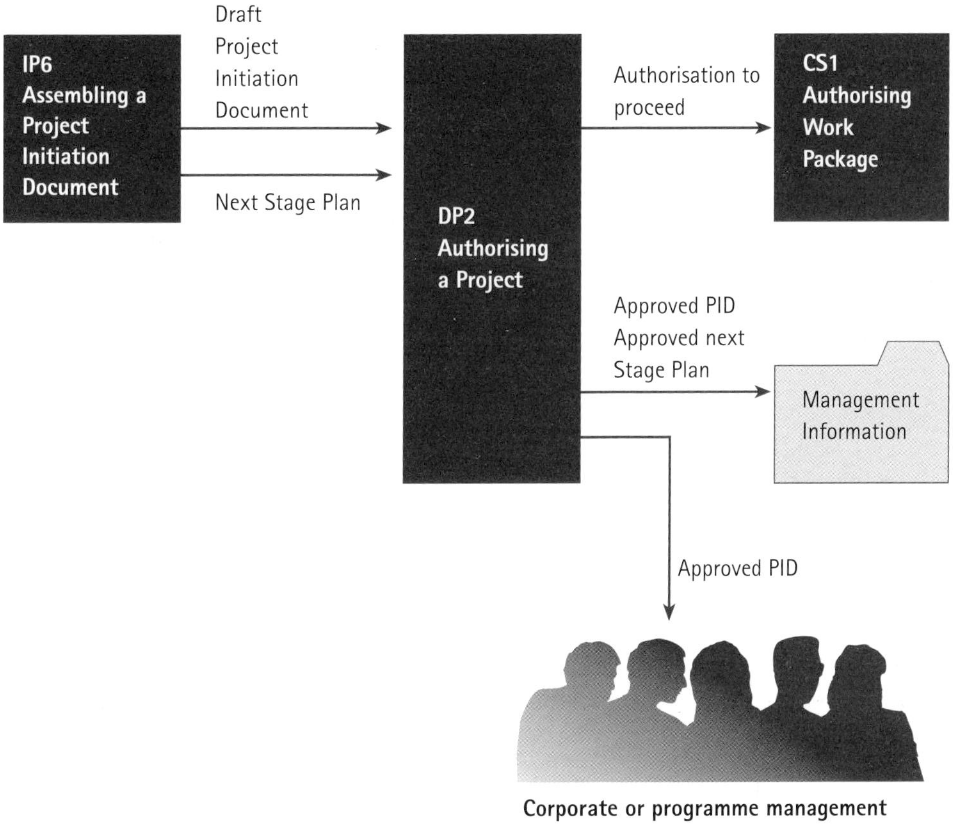

Figure 6.4 Authorising a Project

6.5.3 Process description

The objective of this process is to decide whether to proceed with the project.

This is based on approval or rejection of the Project Initiation Document. The decision-making process is best understood by highlighting the key elements of the Project Initiation Document (see Appendix A, *Product Description outlines* for detailed contents). The Project Initiation Document contains all the important management information about the project. Once the Project Initiation Document is accepted by the Project Board, it is 'frozen' so that a record is preserved of the project's original intentions. Later reviews of how successful the project has been or whether it diverged from its original aims can be measured from the Project Initiation Document.

It is important to recognise the difference between 'freezing' the Project Initiation Document at this point and the subsequent updating of the dynamic parts of it (see the Product Description outline of the Project Initiation Document). A record is needed of what the situation was when we started the project. The 'frozen' Project Initiation Document gives that. As the project moves on, events occur that may change the situation. New risks may emerge or old risks die away. The customer may make changes to the specification. Project costs or time constraints may change. The Business Case may improve or lessen. These dynamic parts of the Project Initiation Document need to be kept up to date to give the Project Board the latest information on which to base decisions on the continuation of the project. New versions of them are created, but the original basis is still preserved.

If the fixed parts of the Project Initiation Document need to be changed, such as the project definition, thought should be given to closing the project and restarting with a new Project Initiation Document.

The Project Initiation Document should contain the following items.

The project definition

The Project Board must satisfy itself that the project objectives are still achievable. The remainder of this section would be a refinement of the Project Brief and Project Approach.

Business Case

The Project Board has to confirm that an adequate and suitable Business Case exists for the project and that it shows a viable project. Information on the expected benefits and savings should be supplied and approved by the customer. The project costs should come from the Project Manager and match the Project Plan (see *Business Case*, Chapter 13).

Project Quality Plan

The Project Quality Plan must state how the project intends to meet the customer's quality expectations and where quality responsibilities have been allocated. The Project Board must satisfy itself that the quality expectations have been correctly translated from the Project Brief and that the Project Quality Plan will deliver them.

Risk Log

The project management team should identify any risks (see *Management of Risk*, Chapter 17) facing the project's products. The Project Board should ensure that there is an assessment of the risks, plus appropriate countermeasures and, where appropriate, contingency plans.

Project Approach

This indicates what method will be used to provide a solution to the Project's objectives. A full description can be found in *Defining Project Approach* (SU5).

Project Plan

The Project Plan gives an overall view of the major products, timescale and cost for the project. Any wide variation between this and any previous forecast for the project (for example, one done as part of a feasibility study) should be examined and the Project Board should assure itself of the continued validity and achievability of the plan and reasons for the variation. The Project Plan needs to be co-ordinated with any relevant strategic and programme management plans.

Project organisation

Most, if not all, of the appointments of the project management team will have been finalised during *Starting up a Project* (SU). These now have to be formally confirmed and any late appointments negotiated. Each member of the team should have agreed their role (as described in *Organisation*, Chapter 14) and this agreement is one of the items that the Project Board has to confirm.

Controls

The Project Initiation Document will include details of the controls that will enable the Project Board to keep overall control of the project. This will include step-by-step approval for the project to proceed via a series of end stage assessments, confirmation of the tolerance level for the project and the stage after initiation, and details of what will happen if any stage exceeds its agreed tolerance. There should be information on the frequency and content of reports from the Project Manager to the Project Board, together with details of how the Project Manager intends to control the project on a day-to-day basis. The Project Board must satisfy itself that these controls are adequate for the nature of the project.

Communication Plan

This should reflect the information needs and timing between the Project Manager, the Project Board and any other interested parties. It includes communication in both directions between the parties.

External interfaces

The Communication Plan will contain details of any required co-operation from outside the project, plus links to corporate or programme management. It is the responsibility of the Project Board to obtain this and confirm the availability as part of this process.

6.5.4 Responsibilities

The Project Board is responsible for this process. Most of the input will come from the Project Manager.

6.6.5 Information needs

Table 6.3 DP3 information needs

Management information	Usage	Explanation
Next Stage Plan or Exception Plan	Input	Plan for which the Project Manager is seeking approval
Project Plan	Input	To allow the Project Board to review the whole project status
Business Case	Input	To allow the Project Board to check that the project is still justified
Project Initiation Document	Input	Used to provide a benchmark against which to assess the advisability of any deviations
Project management team changes	Input	To allow the Project Board to ratify any appointment changes
Risk Log	Input	Check that the risks are still acceptable
End Stage Report	Input	Report of stage just completed. Helps assessment of current situation. There would not be one of these for the initiation stage
Request for authorisation to proceed	Input	Usually a stage approval form for the Project Board to sign
Authorisation to proceed or trigger for premature close	Output	Authorisation to proceed with the submitted plan. During project initiation, the Project Board decides how formal or informal it wishes the approval to be. The Project Board, of course, has the authority to reject the plan. It may ask for a resubmission or decide to close the project. The Project Board also defines the levels of tolerance for the next plan – or Instruction from the Project Board to the Project Manager to close the project down before its expected end
Approved Stage Plan or Exception Plan	Output	Approved by the Project Board
Progress information	Output	The Communication Plan may indicate the need to advise an external group of progress

6.6.6 Key criteria

- Was everything expected of the current stage delivered? If not, was this with the approval of the Project Board?
- Are there clear statements about what is to be done about anything not delivered? Does a Project Issue cover it? Is its delivery included in the next Stage Plan (or Exception Plan)?
- Is the project still viable and does it remain focused on the same business need?
- Are the risks still acceptable?

- Are the countermeasures still valid, including any contingency plans?
- Does the Project Board want to, and is it able to, commit the resources needed for the next stage of work?
- In projects that have a different supplier for each stage, is it documented and agreed by all suppliers that the key project information will be made available to subsequent suppliers?

Hints and tips

The Project Board members are likely to be busy people. Setting dates for any end stage assessments can be difficult because of diary commitments. Get these meetings into diaries as early as possible (at the previous end stage assessment) and accept that, in the event, they may not fall exactly at stage end. Make sure that the stage boundary issues are discussed somewhere near the end of stage rather than risk that no discussion is held because people are not available.

Make sure that there are 'no surprises' from the outset; that is, the project situation should be discussed informally between the Project Manager and Project Board and any problems sorted out before any formal request for authorisation of the next stage.

Where the project is part of a programme, careful co-ordination with programme management may be necessary to ensure the timely achievement of programme-level approvals.

Although a stage may stay within its tolerances, information may be produced within a stage that shows that at some time in the future the project will exceed its tolerances. An example would be information that the cost of equipment to be bought a year down the line will exceed the project budget tolerance. It is important that these types of issue are discussed as early as possible, so they should still be raised with the Project Board as exceptions.

Where the project deviates significantly from its tolerances, it may be better to stop the current project and restart with a Project Initiation Document that reflects the new situation.

In small projects, the Project Board and Project Manager may agree to an informal end stage assessment and authorisation to proceed to the next stage. But a formal sign-off and authorisation by the Project Board is a useful document to have in the management file if problems come along later and the Project Manager is asked why a stage was undertaken.

It is essential to ensure that the project is not adversely affected by delays in customer or supplier management chains.

6.7 Giving Ad Hoc Direction (DP4)

6.7.1 Fundamental principles

Even when a stage is proceeding according to plan and within tolerance, there may be a need for the Project Board to be consulted. Such occasions might be:

- For advice on direction when options need clarifying
- When the impact of events external to the project needs to be considered
- To resolve resourcing issues that would affect tolerance
- To resolve areas of conflict
- Organisational changes within the project.

It is also possible that, during a stage, the Project Board itself will need to pass information to the Project Manager about external events and its own changing requirements or pass information to external interested parties.

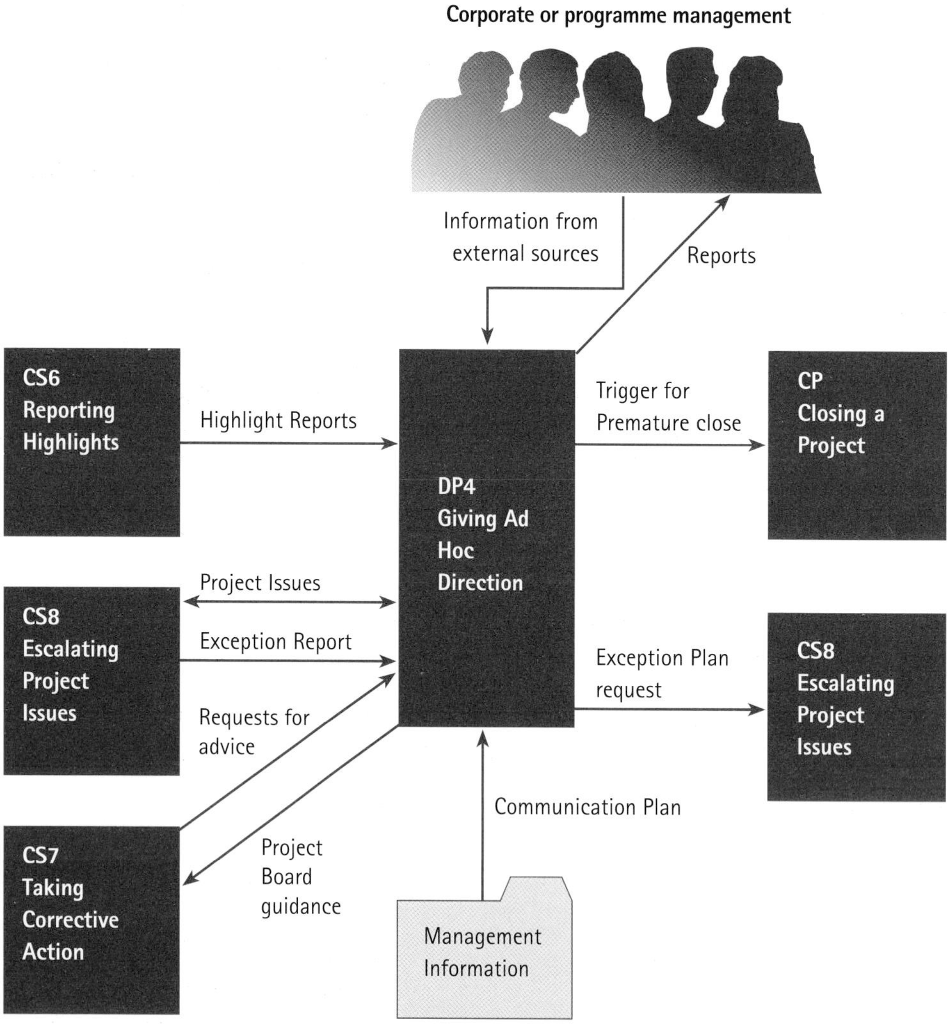

Figure 6.6 Giving Ad Hoc Direction

6.7.2 Context

This is a process that may be needed at any point during the project. It could be prompted by an external event or by information or circumstances arising from within the project.

6.7.3 Process description

The objectives are for the Project Board to:

- Ensure that the project remains focused on the business objectives set and remains justified in business terms
- Ensure that the stage is progressing according to plan
- Ensure that changes in the corporate or programme environment that may impact on the project are notified to the Project Manager and appropriate action is taken
- Ensure that the project is kept informed of external events that may affect it
- Make decisions on Project Issues or Exception Reports that are beyond the Project Manager's authority
- Advise the Project Manager of any change to Project Board personnel
- Keep corporate or programme management and other interested parties informed about project progress.

These objectives should be achieved without the need for the Project Board to interfere in the project beyond the controls and reports it has agreed with the Project Manager.

The Project Board should receive regular Highlight Reports from the Project Manager with a frequency agreed for the current stage.

The Project Board should ensure that any serious risk situations are being monitored sufficiently regularly to keep the risks under control. The Project Manager will refer situations to the Project Board via an Exception Report where a stage or the whole project is forecast to exceed its tolerances.

Within its delegated limits of authority, there may be occasions when the Project Board may choose to:

- Ask the Project Manager to submit an Exception Plan for the remainder of the stage to reflect the new situation (see *Producing an Exception Plan* (SB6))
- Reduce the scope of stage or project expectations to bring it back within tolerance using change control (see *Producing an Exception Plan* (SB6))
- Abandon the project (see *Decommissioning a Project* (CP1)).

Project Issues may arise on which the Project Manager needs guidance. The Project Board provides this guidance based on the impact of the Project Issue in question on the Business Case and risks. Project Issues include all Requests for Change and Off-Specifications raised. As these represent changes to the agreed Project Initiation Document, it is a Project Board function to approve or reject any changes. Agreed changes may need extra time and/or funds.

Where a Project Issue goes beyond the brief held by the Project Board, the Project Board has the responsibility of seeking a decision from corporate or programme management.

The Project Board has the responsibility to obtain any extra or changed resources that occur as a result of agreements with the Project Manager on issues raised.

The Project Board must ensure that external events that could impact the project are monitored adequately and dealt with effectively.

The Communication Plan may contain details of external interested parties, such as programme management, who need to receive (or are required to provide) information on project matters at given frequencies from/to the Project Board. The Project Board must make itself aware of any such requirements and how, when and by whom such information is to be either given or received.

There will be times when a Project Board has to be changed. This may be because a current member changes job or extra customers or suppliers may be found and they need representation on the Project Board. It is the Project Board's job to notify the Project Manager. The Project Board must then agree a job description with the new member(s).

6.7.4 Responsibilities

This is a Project Board responsibility. It may look to share some of the activities with those with Project Assurance responsibilities.

6.7.5 Information needs

Table 6.4 DP4 information needs

Management information	Usage	Explanation
Highlight Report	Input	Regular feedback on progress from the Project Manager
Exception Report	Input	Early warning of a deviation. May trigger the creation of an Exception Plan
Request for advice	Input	Situations where a decision is needed that is beyond the authority of the Project Manager
Communication Plan	Input	Details of any interested parties
Information from external sources	Input	Collection of information pertinent to the project from outside sources
Corporate or programme management reports	Output	Feedback on project progress to outside sources
Project Board guidance	Output	Guidance and instruction to the Project Manager following request for advice or as a result of information from corporate or programme management

Exception Plan request	Output	Request in reaction to the inputs noted above, particularly the Exception Report
Trigger for premature close	Output	Possible closure of the project before its expected end

6.7.6 Key criteria

- Does the Project Manager know how to contact Project Board members in the event of problems arising?
- Are Project Board members aware of the need to react quickly to issues raised?
- Are Project Board members committed to prompt reading of Highlight Reports and to a timely response to them?

Hints and tips

There are projects that are so dynamic that there will be many Requests for Change. The Project Board and Project Manager should agree change authority responsibilities, a procedure and possibly a separate budget to handle these.

Expected external changes that can pose a threat to the project should be documented as risks.

The Project Board may delegate among its members responsibility for monitoring particular external sources for any potential impact on the project. Each individual Project Board member will have prime responsibility for monitoring a particular area to which the project might be sensitive – for example, changing interest rates.

The Project Manager may seek Project Board guidance if any risks materialise.

Where the project is part of a programme, if there is to be a change in the composition of the Project Board, the advice and approval of programme management should be sought.

6.8 Confirming Project Closure (DP5)

6.8.1 Fundamental principles

There needs to be a formal hand-over of responsibility and ownership of the project's products to the ultimate user(s).

For most final products there must be a reliable operational and support environment in place.

Every effort should be made to pass on any lessons that have been learned from the project.

6.8.2 Context

The process is triggered by the Project Manager carrying out the activities and producing the management products of *Closing a Project* (CP). It is the last work done by the Project Board prior to its disbandment.

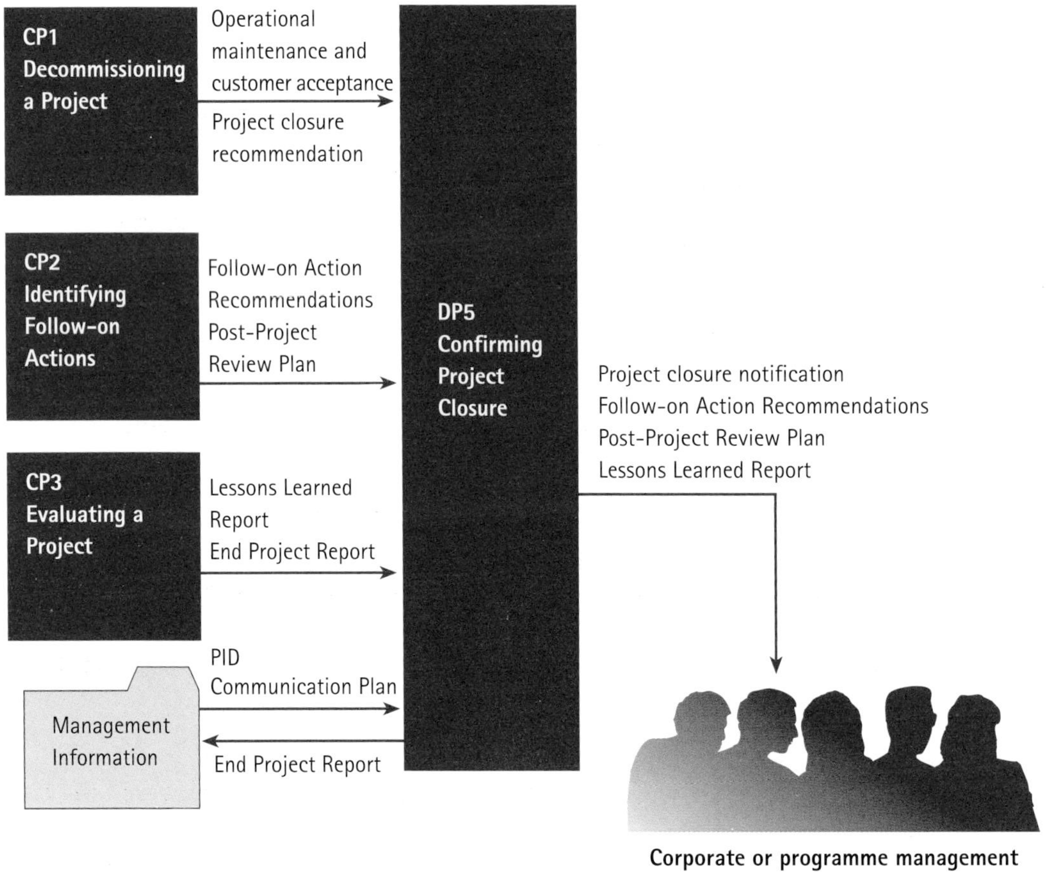

Figure 6.7 Confirming Project Closure

6.8.3 Process description

The project needs to be closed down in an orderly manner.

The objectives of this process are to:

- Ensure that the project has a clearly defined end and an organised hand-over of responsibility to the group(s) who will use, support and sustain the products
- Release the resources provided to the project
- Gain formal acceptance from the customer that the Acceptance Criteria set down at the outset have been met adequately
- Direct any changes that have not been implemented to an appropriate authority for attention and any lessons learned to the people who best benefit from them
- Establish a future method for verifying that the product has produced the desired benefits
- Recommend closure of the project to corporate or programme management.

To achieve these objectives, various steps need to be undertaken:

- Ensure that all the completed products have been approved by the customer or are covered by approved concessions (if there have been any concessions, these may also be covered in Follow-on Action Recommendations)
- Ensure that, where appropriate, the resulting changes in the business are supported and sustainable
- Ensure Follow-on Action Recommendations have been recorded correctly and that the appropriate groups are responsible for taking them forward. These recommendations will have listed all the follow-on actions from the project, those Project Issues that were classified as pending by the Project Board, and any proposals for new work emanating from the project. These have to be directed to the appropriate body. They may be given to the support team to implement, or they may go to programme management or a strategy group for consideration as projects in their own right
- Where applicable, ensure the hand-over of the products and configuration management method to the appropriate support group for ongoing control
- Approve the Lessons Learned Report for distribution. A number of lessons may have been learned during the project about weaknesses or strengths of the processes, procedures, techniques and tools used, when they were used, how they were used and by whom. If there is anything that could benefit other projects within the remit of the corporate body, the Project Board has the responsibility of ensuring that this information is passed on to the relevant people, such as quality assurance
- Prepare a project closure notification. The Project Board advises those who have provided the support infrastructure and resources for the project that these can now be withdrawn
- Publish and distribute the plans for the post-project review.

6.8.4 Responsibilities

This process is the responsibility of the Project Board, supported by those with Project Assurance responsibilities.

It is the responsibility of the Executive to ensure that the person responsible for conducting the post-project review is properly briefed and that accountability is passed to that person.

Where the project is part of a programme, it may be necessary to obtain programme management approval for project closure.

Programme management may also wish to direct the hand-over of any follow-on work from the project.

6.8.5 Information needs

Table 6.5 DP5 information needs

Management information	Usage	Explanation
Project Initiation Document	Input	Used as the baseline against which to assess how far the project deviated from its initial basis. Also contributes some of the information against which to judge the success of the project
Communication Plan	Input	Used to identify all recipients of information on project closure
Operational and maintenance acceptance	Input	Confirmation that the final product can be used and supported
Customer acceptance	Input	Confirmation that the customer accepts the products
Project closure recommendation	Input	Assurance from the Project Manager that everything has been done
End Project Report	Input/Output	More information on which to judge the success of the project
Follow-on Action Recommendations	Approval	Recommendations for all issues classified as pending and other future actions
Post-Project Review Plan	Approval	Suggested plan for assessing the achievement of project benefits. Ratified by the Project Board to be passed on to the people responsible for carrying it out
Lessons Learned Report	Approval	Project lessons that have been learned that might be useful to pass on to other projects
Project closure notification	Output	Notification that facilities and support can be withdrawn

6.8.6 Key criteria

- Have the results and products been accepted and are they no longer dependent on work that is part of this project?
- Is the business ready to support, sustain and further develop the environment and products delivered?
- Are the customers content with the results and products?
- Have any necessary programme management requirements been met?

Hints and tips

Give recognition to teams and individuals for significant project achievements and success.

Even if it is not obligatory, it is a sensible precaution to have written confirmation of acceptance from those who will be responsible for the operation and maintenance support of the delivered product.

7 CONTROLLING A STAGE (CS)

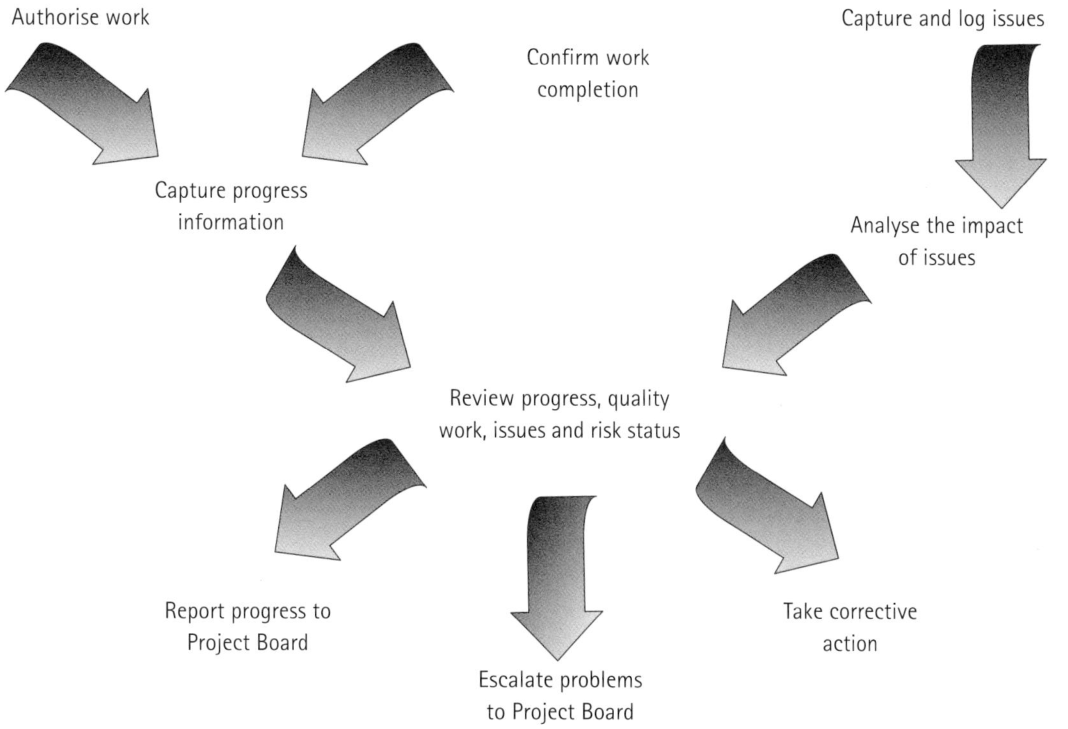

Figure 7.1 Overview of Controlling a Stage

7.1 Fundamental principles

Once a decision has been taken to proceed with work, and resources have been committed, the project management team must be focused on delivery within the tolerance laid down.

This means controlled production of the agreed products:

- To stated quality standards
- Within cost, effort and time agreed
- Ultimately to achieve defined benefits.

To achieve this success, the project must:

- Focus management attention on delivery of the stage's products
- Focus the resources used during the stage towards this end
- Keep the risks under control
- Keep the Business Case under review

- Carefully monitor any movement away from the direction and products agreed at the start of the stage to avoid 'scope creep' and loss of focus.

7.2 Context

This process describes the work of the Project Manager in handling the day-to-day management of the project. It starts after the Project Board approves the Stage Plan in *Authorising a Stage or Exception Plan* (DP3).

Controlling a Stage (CS) drives *Managing Product Delivery* (MP); the interfaces being the authorisation of a Work Package, any specified reports, and the return confirmation that the Work Package has been completed satisfactorily.

There is a 'natural' pattern of events to ensure that all necessary actions are carried out on a regular basis. However, project management is of an ad hoc nature, driven by problems and circumstances as they arise. This means that any or all of *Controlling a Stage* may be used in an event-driven manner as well as on the regular basis indicated.

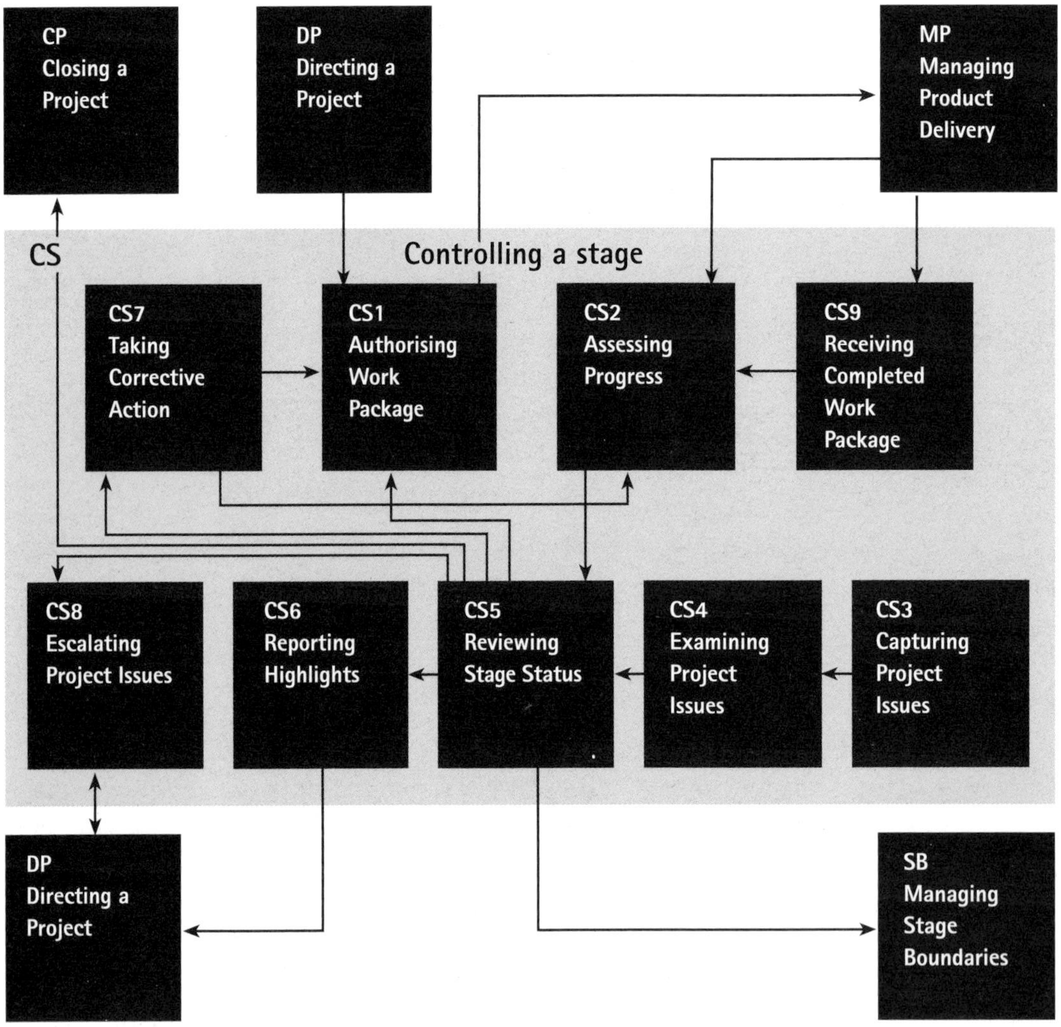

Figure 7.2 Controlling a Stage

7.3 Process description

The objectives of *Controlling a Stage* are to:

- Deliver the right products
- Ensure that quality is achieved as planned
- Deliver products on time and to cost within agreed tolerances
- Correctly direct and conduct work on products
- Keep control of products via configuration management
- Properly direct and utilise resources
- Update plans with actuals, enabling progress to be checked against the plan
- Correctly cost resource usage
- Correctly manage any deviations from Stage or Project Plans
- Inform all interested parties about project progress in a timely manner
- Ensure that projects are stopped or redirected if the reasons for setting them up have been invalidated by internal or external events.

Central to the ultimate success of the project is the day-to-day control of the work that is being conducted. Throughout a stage, this will consist of a cycle of:

- Authorising work to be done (CS1)
- Monitoring progress information about that work (CS2 and CS9)
- Watching for and assessing changes (CS3 and CS4)
- Reviewing the situation and triggering new Work Packages (CS5)
- Reporting (CS6)
- Taking any necessary corrective action (CS7).

If changes are observed that are forecast to cause deviations beyond agreed tolerances, *Escalating Project Issues* (CS8) covers the activities of bringing the situation to the attention of the Project Board.

Other factors that must be borne in mind are as follows:

- The current stage contains work and involves resource expenditure that has been authorised by the Project Board. It is therefore important to give the Project Board feedback on progress against its expectations
- All individual items of work in a stage should be authorised (see the format of the Work Package in Appendix A, *Product Description outlines*)
- Project work can be adequately controlled only against a plan
- If the project is to be successful, the Project Manager and Project Board must react quickly to changes and deviations from the agreed Stage Plan.

7.3.1 Scalability

The core activities of the process can be summarised as:

- Allocate work
- Check on progress
- Ensure that the quality is appropriate for the project's needs
- Ensure that changes are controlled
- Monitor risks
- Report on progress
- Watch for plan deviations.

There should be nothing in this list to alarm the manager of a small project. In even the smallest of projects, the Project Manager must have sufficient time to manage the project activities and resource usage.

The process suggests a number of reports; the inference being that these should be written reports – for example, Work Packages, Highlight Reports and Exception Reports. In small projects a decision may be taken to make some or all of these oral. Even here the Project Manager must think of what events should be recorded in writing, in case of later disputes. Part of the reason for documenting events and decisions is continuity if the Project Manager is suddenly unavailable.

Some projects may have no separate Team Manager(s) and only one team whose members are directly responsible to the Project Manager. In this case the Project Manager and the Team Manager will be one and the same person and Work Packages will be negotiated between Project Manager and individual team members. This point should be borne in mind when reading the rest of the section, which will refer to a Project Manager/Team Manager interface.

Hints and tips

The emphasis within this process is on the processes and techniques of controlling a management stage. However, much of the ultimate success of the project will be just as dependent on the handling of the people and 'politics' of the project.

7.4 Authorising Work Package (CS1)

7.4.1 Fundamental principles

It would be chaotic to have the people who are working on the project starting activities whenever they think fit. There must be a level of autonomy within the project team(s), but there will be wider issues involved of which they cannot be expected to be aware. It is therefore important that, in broad terms, work only commences and continues with the consent of the Project Manager.

7.4.2 Context

The process will be running constantly throughout a stage. It interfaces with the process, *Managing Product Delivery* (MP), which handles the production of the products involved and provides plan updates to *Assessing Progress* (CS2) during the project.

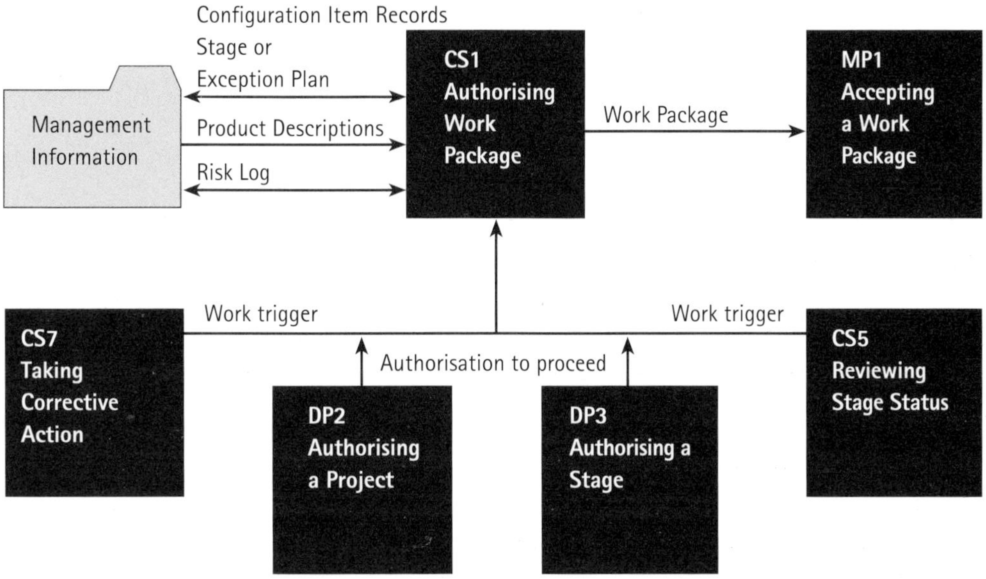

Figure 7.3: Authorising Work Package

7.4.3 Process description

The objective of this process is to keep control over the work of the team(s) by:

- Issuing work instructions (work trigger) to the Team Manager(s) to commence work
- Revising the instructions as required following management decisions.

The set of instructions issued to the Team Manager(s) is known as a Work Package.

In order to achieve these objectives, various steps have to be undertaken:

- Review the Product Description(s) for the product(s) to be delivered; ensure that they describe what is required and add any constraints and responsibilities required
- Brief the Team Manager(s) and hand out the Work Package with all relevant documentation and information, including terms of reference covering:
  - the cost and effort that the work is expected to consume
  - the timescale for completion
  - the progress reporting arrangements
  - any individuals, groups or products with whom it is necessary to interface in the performance of the work
  - Product Descriptions
- Update the status information to 'under development' in any affected Configuration Item Records
- Ensure that the Team Manager has the correct resources to carry out the work

- Identify any problems or risks associated with the work and incorporate any necessary changes or other measures to handle these
- Ensure the Team Manager is committed to completion of the work within the terms of reference laid down
- Instruct the Team Manager to proceed via an appropriate form of Work Package.

The 'work' discussed in this overview could be by people and resources within the customer organisation, by outside suppliers or by a combination of the two. It could also cover the supply of products or services that do not involve any actual effort. The objectives and steps outlined apply in all circumstances. The formality of the Work Package will depend on the project situation. The suggested contents of the Work Package are given in Appendix A, *Product Description outlines*.

This process must be done in conjunction with *Accepting a Work Package* (MP1). The overlap covers the negotiation with the Team Manager on dates and other parameters.

If this is the first Work Package agreed with the Team Manager, a check should be made to ensure that the Team Manager is aware of the project's change control procedure.

7.4.4 Responsibilities

The Project Manager is responsible, assisted by any Project Support roles, and in agreement with the relevant Team Managers. The Configuration Librarian will update the Configuration Item Records.

7.4.5 Information needs

Table 7.1 CS1 information needs

Management information	Usage	Explanation
Authorisation to proceed	Input	Authorisation from the Project Board to proceed with the stage
Product Description(s)	Input	Description of the required product(s), including quality criteria
Work trigger	Input	Information from *Authorising a Stage*, *Taking Corrective Action* or *Reviewing Stage Status* requiring the creation or modification of a new Work Package
Stage or Exception Plan	Update	The Stage Plan may need to be updated as a result of discussions between the Project Manager and the Team Manager during *Authorising Work Package* (CS1)
Configuration Item Records	Update	Change the status of any products allocated as part of the Work Package

Work Package	Output	Formal hand-over of responsibility for the detailed conduct of the work and delivery of any products from the Project Manager following agreement with the Team Manager
Risk Log	Update	Any new or modified risks after negotiation with the Team Manager

7.4.6 Key criteria

- Is the Team Manager clear as to what is to be produced and what has to be done to produce it?
- Is the Team Manager clear about the effort, cost and timescale expectations in connection with the work involved?
- Is the Team Manager clear about the expected quality of the work and products and also clear about how that quality is to be checked, as defined in the relevant Product Descriptions?
- Have the quality checking procedures been put in place and resourced?
- Is the work achievable within the terms of reference laid down?
- Is the Team Manager committed to the achievement of the work?
- Has the Stage Plan been updated as required, based on the agreement on the Work Package?
- Should any Project Assurance involvement be planned, especially in quality checking?

Hints and tips

In a simple, low-risk project, Work Package authorisation may be reasonably informal, although thought should be given to recording an individual's work and performance for appraisal purposes.

If a third party is involved, Work Package authorisation should always be formally documented.

A Work Package should ideally not spread over more than one stage. If there is any danger of this, it should be broken down so that its intermediate parts fit into one management stage or another.

It is good practice for the people who will receive the resulting products of a Work Package to be involved in writing the relevant Product Descriptions, especially the quality criteria. If this is done, other people should review the Product Descriptions.

If there is a contract in operation between customer and supplier, this may have an impact on the terms of the authorisation. The reverse is also true, so the authorisation of Work Packages should be considered during contract preparation.

When the first Work Package is negotiated with a Team Manager or a team member, the Project Manager should ensure that the change control process is understood.

7.5 Assessing Progress (CS2)

7.5.1 Fundamental principles

In order to make informed decisions and exercise rational control, it is necessary to know what has *actually* happened, to be compared with what it was *hoped* would happen. 'Fire fighting' and day-to-day problem solving can dominate project management. This can result in Project Managers losing sight of the overall goal. It is vital that this is countered by a steady flow of information that provides an overall view of progress and simple, robust monitoring systems to supply the information.

7.5.2 Context

Assessing Progress monitors the status of resource utilisation and product development as documented in the process *Executing Work Packages* (MP2), and reviews the Quality Log (as updated by the quality checks carried out by the team(s)). It also receives information on completed and approved products from *Receiving Completed Work Packages* (CS9), and keeps the Stage Plan up to date.

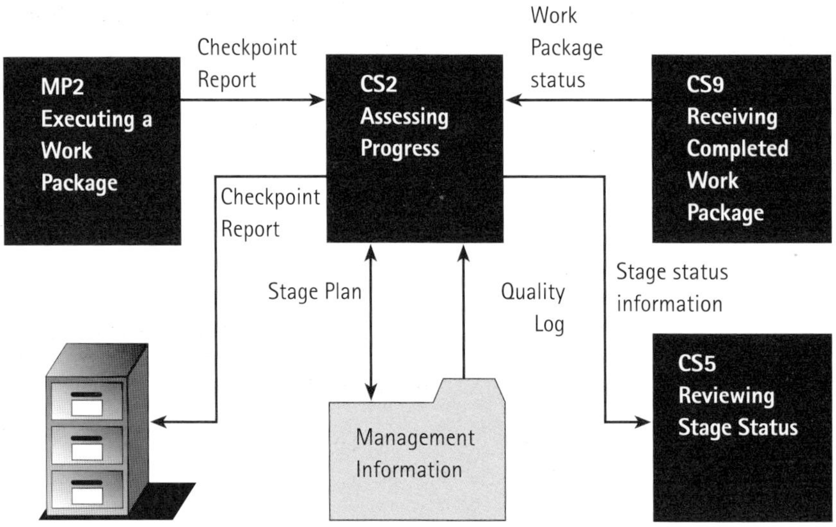

Figure 7.4 Assessing Progress

7.5.3 Process description

The objective of assessing progress is to maintain an accurate and current picture of:

- Progress on the work being carried out
- The status of resources.

The main data-gathering control for the Project Manager is the checkpoint, described in *Controls* (Chapter 16). The information is captured in a Checkpoint Report. A product status account may also be requested from configuration management to provide information on the status of the stage's products.

In order to achieve the objectives, various steps have to be undertaken:

- Collect in all of the progress information for all work currently being undertaken
- Collect feedback on recent quality-checking activities carried out
- Assess the estimated time and effort to complete any unfinished work (including that not yet started)
- Assess the utilisation of resources in the period under review and their availability for the remainder of the stage (or project)
- Review with the Team Manager(s) whether work will be completed on time and to budget
- Update the Stage Plan with actuals to date
- Identify any points that need attention in CS5, *Reviewing Stage Status*.

7.5.4 Responsibilities

The Project Manager is responsible for this process, assisted by any Project Support roles. The Configuration Librarian would provide any product status account required. If the Team Manager works for a supplier who does not use PRINCE2, the Work Package will still contain a requirement for Checkpoint Reports to be submitted.

7.5.5 Information needs

Table 7.2 CS2 information needs

Management information	Usage	Explanation
Checkpoint Reports	Input	Flows of information, either written or oral depending on the need for formality. The information will cover current status of Work Packages against plan
Quality Log	Input	Update from the Team Manager(s) on the quality-checking work done
Work Package status	Input	To update the Stage Plan
Stage Plan	Update	Updated with actuals to date, forecasts and adjustments
Stage Status Information	Output	Holds a summary of progress information

7.5.6 Key criteria

- Is the level and frequency of progress assessment right for the stage and/or Work Package?
- Is the information timely, useful and accurate?
- Are the estimates of outstanding work objective?

Hints and tips

Progress should be measured and reported in a manner that is suitably accurate and does not allow exaggeration of progress.

Measurement of progress and status is easier if the information collection is product based, as in *Planning* (PL).

The use of earned value analysis may be considered in order to obtain an accurate view of expenditure on more complex or critical projects.

Depending on project factors, such as size and geography, the process may be run formally or informally. The Project Manager may hold checkpoint meetings with Team Managers and the Team Managers may hold their own checkpoint meetings with the team.

Stage status information could consist of the Checkpoint Report/s, Work Package status, the Quality Log and any other such information, or could be a summary of these. In many instances it will be the contents of the Daily Log, especially on smaller projects.

7.6 Capturing Project Issues (CS3)

7.6.1 Fundamental principles

In the course of managing the project, various problems, queries and changes will occur. They will arrive in a haphazard manner and will need to be captured in a consistent and reliable way so that they can be assessed and managed properly.

It is also important that Project Issues are not forgotten, especially if there is no immediate solution.

7.6.2 Context

The process of capturing Project Issues is by its nature ad hoc, since it takes in details of problems, queries and changes as they occur. These details can come from a wide range of sources, both internal to the project and external.

Capturing Project Issues (CS3) produces information to go forward to *Examining Project Issues* (CS4). The process should be read in conjunction with the *Change Control Approach* defined in the techniques section of the manual (Chapter 23).

This process provides the entry point for all external stimuli, such as changes of scope.

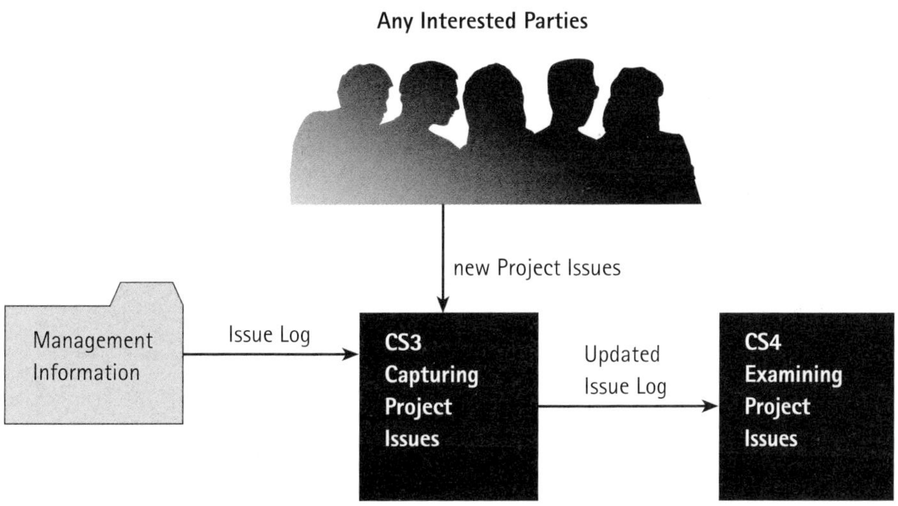

Figure 7.5 Capturing Project Issues

7.6.3 Process description

The objectives of this process are to capture, log and categorise all Project Issues. The stages involved in achieving this are:

- Enter all Project Issues in the Issue Log as soon as they are identified. See *Change Control Approach* (Chapter 23) for suggestions on how logging can be done.
- Assess whether the Project Issue is:
  - a Request for Change
  - an Off-Specification
  - a general issue.

See *Change Control* (Chapter 20) for an explanation of types of Project Issue.

Suggested structures for a Project Issue, Request for Change, an Off-Specification and an Issue Log are given in Appendix A, *Product Description outlines*.

7.6.4 Responsibilities

The Project Manager is responsible for this process, although a Project Support role (Configuration Librarian) may be nominated to act as the central focus for receiving and documenting Project Issues.

7.6.5 Information needs

Table 7.3 CS3 information needs

Management information	Usage	Explanation
New Project Issues	Input	Any Project Issues being raised against the project from whatever source, to be logged in the Issue Log and the type of Project Issue to be decided
Issue Log	Update	Repository of all Project Issues and their status

7.6.6 Key criteria

- Are all significant Project Issues being documented?
- Is this a new Project Issue or a previous one differently worded?
- Is the source of the Project Issue identified?
- Does the Project Issue affect the Project Plan as well as the Stage Plan?
- Is the Project Issue an enquiry that can be answered without changing the Stage Plan?

Hints and tips

Sometimes a Project Issue is so complex that it is better to split it into several smaller Project Issues.

Where the project is part of a programme, Project Issues must be copied to the programme support office for it to look for any impact on the programme as a whole or on other projects within the programme.

7.7 Examining Project Issues (CS4)

7.7.1 Fundamental principles

Before making a decision on a course of action, each Project Issue should be assessed for its impact and alternative actions considered.

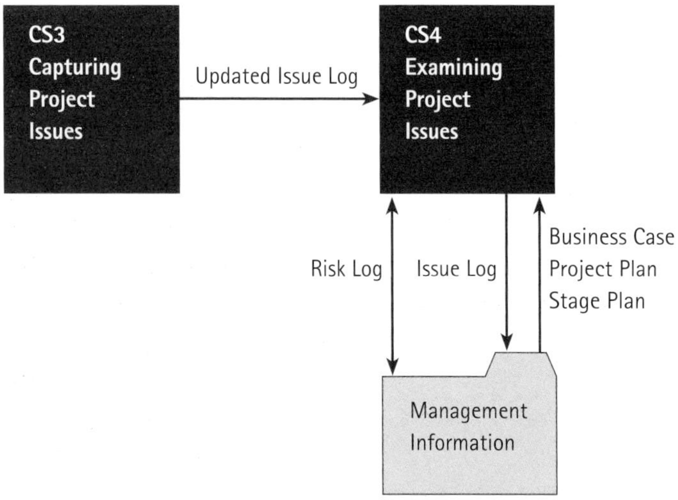

Figure 7.6 Examining Project Issues

7.7.2 Context

Capturing Project Issues (CS3) captures and catalogues all Project Issues. This process examines Project Issues that have not yet been resolved. All open Project Issues should be reviewed and courses of action be recommended for consideration during *Reviewing Stage Status* (CS5).

7.7.3 Process description

An initial examination of a Project Issue should be performed as soon as it is logged.

On a regular basis, all open Project Issues should be reviewed. Decisions on a course of action should not be taken until the Project Issue can be seen in the wider context of stage status, product delivery and progress against plan. The exception to this delay is where the Project Issue raises an urgent need for action. While most Project Issues will be directly related to the project, the process must allow for Project Issues that have an impact outside the project – for example, impact on a programme. Such issues need to be closed in the project Issue Log with a note that they have been transferred to the programme Issue Log.

In order to prepare Project Issues for review in *Reviewing Stage Status* (CS5), the following steps need to be taken:

- Assemble all available and relevant information about the Project Issue, including anything that pertains to the Project Issue's effect on:
  - costs
  - timescales
  - benefit achievement and/or value
  - risks
  - meeting the requirements of the project
  - meeting the stated quality standards
- Update the Risk log if the Project Issue relates to a previously identified risk or reveals a new risk
- Recommend a course of action. A recommendation may address a number of Project Issues.

7.7.4 Responsibilities

The Project Manager is responsible for this process. Members of the teams may be required to assess the impact of Project Issues on products, workload, cost, schedule and risk and devise alternative courses of action. Some of the administrative work may be delegated to an appointed Project Support role. Those with Project Assurance responsibilities should be involved in the examination of the impact of Project Issues on the products, risks and the Business Case. The Configuration Librarian, where appointed, will be responsible for maintaining the Issue Log. Who makes the decisions on actions to be taken about the Project Issues depends on decisions made during *Initiating a Project* (IP). The Project Manager will have discussed the likely volume of changes with the Project Board, which will have decided whether to make decisions on the Project Issues itself or delegate this to a change authority. (See Authority Levels in Chapter 20 for more information on this.)

7.7.5 Information needs

Table 7.4 CS4 information needs

Management information	Usage	Explanation
Business Case	Input	Reference back to the Business Case to evaluate the impact of the Project Issue
Stage Plan	Input	One of the bases for impact analysis
Project Plan	Input	To check whether an issue affects the project
Issue Log	Update	A list of all outstanding Project Issues and their status, updated with impact analysis information
Risk Log	Update	Current risks that may be affected by a Project Issue. To be updated if any action is recommended that will affect a risk or generate a new one

7.7.6 Key criteria

- Who would be best to evaluate the Project Issue?
- How urgent is the decision? Is it clear when a decision has to be taken?
- Is any special action needed to assure the customer's best interests during the evaluation?
- Was time and effort for Project Issue evaluation put in the Stage Plan?
- How do any relevant contracts handle changes?
- Is there a separate change budget?
- What products would the Project Issue affect?
- Who would be involved in taking any action?
- What alternative courses of action are there?
- What would the solution to the Project Issue cost in effort and money?
- What is the impact of the Project Issue on the Business Case?
- Would implementation change the current project objectives, as specified in the Project Initiation Document?
- What would the impact of the Project Issue be on anything in the Risk Log?

Hints and tips

The impact analysis for a new Project Issue should be done as soon as possible after receipt. Time should be built into the Stage Plan for people with the necessary expertise to do the analysis.

Reviews of open Project Issues should occur on a regular and frequent basis.

This process and *Reviewing Stage Status* (CS5) need not be formally separated in small-to-medium-sized projects, but information gathering/talking to the originator might be hard to do during a stage status review.

The urgency and the importance of a Project Issue are not the same thing. Deal with urgent Project Issues quickly. Deal with important Project Issues comprehensively.

Filter out the trivia as early as possible to allow concentration on the important issues.

Feed back information on actions to the authors of the Project Issues.

7.8 Reviewing Stage Status (CS5)

7.8.1 Fundamental principles

A Project Manager's job can easily become dominated by day-to-day problem solving. This can mean that overall progress is not checked regularly. If the project is not checked on a timely basis, there is a danger that it will get out of control. There needs to be a balance between planning ahead and reacting to events.

There will often be a need to incorporate unplanned activities.

A regular check must be kept on external events that could affect the project.

7.8.2 Context

This process brings together the information gathered in *Assessing Progress* (CS2) and *Examining Project Issues* (CS4) and decides what actions need to be taken.

If the stage and project are within tolerance, the next actions are *Reporting Highlights* (CS6) to the Project Board and *Authorising Work Package* (CS1) for any subsequent work.

If corrective actions are needed, and the stage and project are predicted to stay within tolerance, the next process will be *Taking Corrective Action* (CS7).

The Project Manager may seek guidance from the Project Board about any Project Issue (*Taking Corrective Action* (CS7)) and should always do so if the stage or project is predicted to go outside tolerance (*Escalating Project Issues* (CS8)). Another reason for reference to the Project Board would be that a Project Issue affects policy external to the project.

7.8.3 Process description

This process provides the means for a regular assessment of the stage status. The process decides whether:

- Further Work Packages should be proposed
- Any plan modifications are required.

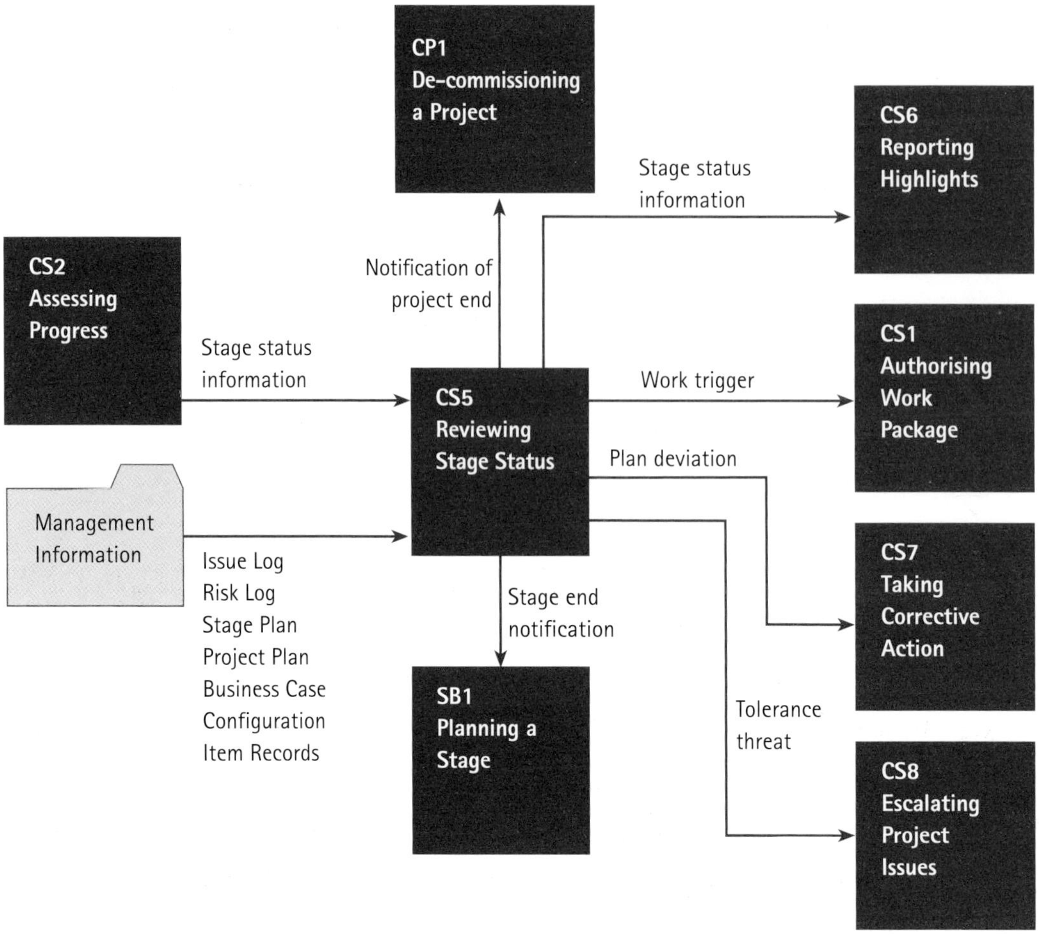

Figure 7.7 Reviewing Stage Status

The first objective of this process is to check periodically that the current stage is kept within the tolerances set down by the Project Board by:

- Reviewing progress against the Stage Plan
- Checking the Quality Log to see the state of quality checking
- Checking the Configuration Item Records to ensure that all products have been completed as stated and anticipated
- Reviewing resource utilisation and future availability
- Reviewing the effect of Project Issues on any change budget and Stage and Project Plans
- Establishing whether the stage will go outside the tolerances or not
- Passing Project Issues likely to cause tolerance to be exceeded to the Project Board – via *Escalating Project Issues* (CS8) – for consideration.

If corrective action is needed, but the stage is forecast to stay within tolerance, the action can be taken by the Project Manager, as described in *Taking Corrective Action* (CS7).

The second objective of the process is to review the project status, specifically:

- Checking that the Business Case is still valid
- Reviewing the Risk Log for possible changes
- Establishing whether or not the project will go outside the tolerances.

In order to achieve these objectives, various steps have to be undertaken:

- Identify any variation between plan and actual progress
- Check for any variation in the expected future resource availability
- Assess any current risk to the Stage Plan for any change to the exposure
- Check the updated Stage Plan for any new risks
- Review external developments for any impact on the project
- Check to see whether anything has happened within the project or externally that will impact the Business Case
- Assess whether the stage will stay within tolerances
- Use *Authorising Work Package* (CS1) to authorise any necessary new work required by the Stage Plan.

The Project Manager can use the Daily Log to note any of these checks that need to be done and many of the small actions that are needed after carrying the checks out.

7.8.4 Responsibilities

The Project Manager is responsible for this process, supported by any Project Support roles, including Configuration Librarian, and those with Project Assurance responsibilities. It may be necessary on occasion to consult Project Board members for guidance, especially with regard to Project Issues or resource shortfalls or external events that may impact the Business Case or Risk Log.

7.8.5 Information needs

Table 7.5 CS5 information needs

Management information	Usage	Explanation
Issue Log	Input	This product will show the current situation regarding all Project Issues. These may be needed for reference when deciding on appropriate action to deal with them
Risk Log	Input	This product shows the current understanding of the problems and threats to the project
Project Plan	Input	Check to establish whether any stage problem (or potential change) would have an impact on the Project Plan

7.10.3 Process description

The objective of this process is to select and (within the limits of the stage and project tolerances) implement actions that will resolve deviations from the plan. Decisions may be required from the Project Board via *Giving ad hoc direction* (DP4). The Project Manager has to decide when to seek the advice of the Project Board.

In order to achieve this objective, various steps have to be undertaken. If the input comes from *Examining Project Issues* (CS4), some of these steps may have already been taken. The steps are:

- Collect any pertinent information about the deviation
- Identify the full cause and effect of the deviation
- Identify the potential ways of dealing with the deviation
- Select the most appropriate option
- Where direction from the Project Board is sought, assemble all information about the problem (it may already be a Project Issue) plus any recommendation
- Update the Stage Plan
- Update any affected Product Descriptions/Configuration Item Records as appropriate
- Make available any baselined products from the configuration library
- Trigger corrective action.

Where the actions are small and the problem can be remedied without changing the plan or modifying a Work Package, the Daily Log can be used to note what actions are needed, by whom and by what date. The Project Manager can then use this to speak to the people involved and follow up to ensure that the actions are taken. Where this does not lead to the desired result, more formal action can be taken, such as plan and Work Package adjustments, Exception Reports or maybe just a note in the next Highlight Report.

7.10.4 Responsibilities

The Project Manager is responsible, supported by Project Assurance and Project Support roles and in consultation with Team Managers if appropriate. The Configuration Librarian, where appointed, will update the Configuration Item Records and make any necessary products available.

7.10.5 Information needs

Table 7.7 CS7 information needs

Management information	Usage	Explanation
Plan deviation	Input	The plan problem that requires corrective action
Issue Log	Update	This contains details of any Project Issues, Requests for Change or Off-Specifications that could be causing deviations from plan. Updated with details of the action taken
Configuration Item Records	Update	Amend the status of affected products and add links to the Project Issue. Create new versions of any baselined products that require changes
Risk Log	Update	The change in a risk may be causing the corrective action and its status may need updating with details of the action taken
Stage Plan	Update	Amended with the implications of the corrective action selected
Work trigger	Output	Corrective action
Request for advice	Output	Request for advice on corrective action
Project Board guidance	Input	Response to request for advice

7.10.6 Key criteria

- Have all sensible options for corrective action been considered?
- Is there confidence that, after the corrective action has been taken, the stage and project will still stay within tolerance?
- Were the impacts on the Business Case and risks fully considered?
- Has the Stage Plan been updated to reflect the corrective actions?

Hints and tips

Beware the cumulative effect on the budget, and the costs of small changes.

Beware the direction in which some small changes may be taking the project.

7.11 Escalating Project Issues (CS8)

7.11.1 Fundamental principles

A stage should not go outside the tolerances agreed with the Project Board.

The Project Manager should always present a recommendation when escalating Project Issues.

7.11.2 Context

This process can be an advance warning to the Project Board of a deviation that may lead to the need for an Exception Plan. The Project Manager can only take corrective action or maintain the status quo alone while the stage is forecast to stay within the tolerances set by the Project Board. *Escalating Project Issues* (CS8) applies where any corrective action would not save the stage or project from going beyond the tolerance margins.

The decision by the Project Board in response to the escalation may lead to the removal of the problem, the production of an Exception Plan, where cost and/or time targets are adjusted, the approval of a concession or to the premature close of the project.

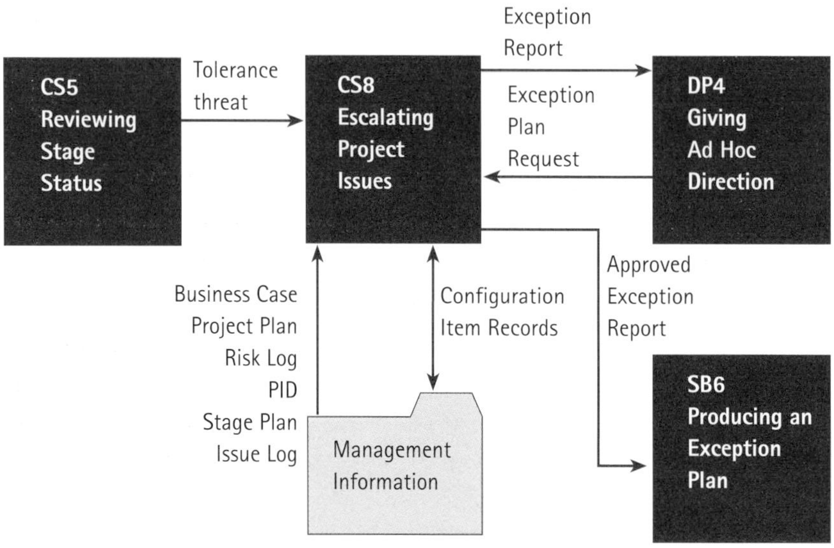

Figure 7.10 Escalating Project Issues

7.11.3 Process description

One of the major controls available to the Project Board is that it sets tolerances for each stage. (Tolerance is fully described in *Controls*, Chapter 16.) The Project Manager only has authority to proceed with a stage while it is forecast to stay within the tolerance margins. If the stage is forecast to go outside the tolerance margins (possibly as a result of a corrective action), the Project Manager must bring the situation to the attention of the Project Board.

One item likely to cause a deviation is a Project Issue. Project Issues are fully described in *Change Control* (Chapter 20). There may be one or more Project Issues, the implementation of which would take the stage (and possibly the entire project) beyond the agreed tolerances.

Other causes may be poor estimation, a change in resource availability, resources under or over performing, unplanned tasks, tasks not needed and rework.

The Project Board must make the decision on which (if any) changes to approve for action.

In order to retain the Project Board's overall control, the following steps are taken:

- Carry out a full impact analysis of the deviation; the analysis should cover specialist, user and business impacts (normally done in *Examining Project Issues* (CS4))

- Identify and evaluate options for recovery (or to take advantage of good news) (again, normally done in *Examining Project Issues* (CS4))
- Make a recommendation
- Put the situation, options and recommendation to the Project Board in an Exception Report
- The Project Board indicates support or otherwise for the Project Manager's recommendation (in *Giving ad hoc direction* (DP4))
- Update the information in the Configuration Item Records of any affected products.

The suggested content of an Exception Report is given in Appendix A, *Product Description outlines*.

Normally, where an exception situation has been identified, an Exception Plan has to be devised which either recovers a situation that is outside tolerance or proposes a new plan with a new target cost and time, plus new tolerances around that target. While the Project Board is considering the Exception Report, the Project Manager has to decide how to continue the stage, if this is possible. Is there work that would not be wasted, whatever the decision of the Project Board? Should some or all work be stopped?

The Project Board's advice should be sought before devising the Exception Plan. All current constraints should be investigated with the Project Board to see if they still stand in the light of the new situation. The Project Manager will advise the Project Board of the impact of the deviation on the Project Plan, Business Case and risks. Various options should be identified and a course of action recommended to the Project Board. The Project Board (in process DP4) may request an Exception Plan. The Exception Plan would then replace the remainder of the current Stage Plan.

The parts of a plan that can be varied in response to an exception situation are:

- Cost
- Delivery date
- Quality
- Scope.

Speed is an important factor in notifying the Project Board of an exception situation.

It will often be necessary to revise the Project Plan as described in *Updating a Project Plan* (SB2).

7.11.4 Responsibilities

The Project Manager is responsible for escalating Project Issues. Those with Project Assurance responsibilities should also be monitoring any situations that could cause a deviation and should bring the matter to the Project Manager's attention. The Configuration Librarian will update configuration records where necessary.

7.11.5 Information needs

Table 7.8 CS8 information needs

Management information	Usage	Explanation
Tolerance threat	Input	Trigger for the Exception Report
Project Initiation Document	Input	This baseline allows comparison of any change against original expectations
Business Case	Input	The latest version allows examination for impact of the Project Issue on the Business Case
Stage Plan	Input	Updated with the actuals so far, this shows the likely impact on the stage of the deviation in question
Project Plan	Input	This indicates the project status and the overall effect of any deviation
Issue Log	Input	Details of the change(s) that may have caused the exception situation
Risk Log	Input	Details of the risk exposure that may have caused the escalation
Exception Plan Request	Input	Request from Project Board to prepare an Exception Plan based on Exception Report findings.
Approved Exception Report	Input/ Output	May pass on to *Producing an Exception Plan* (SB6)
Configuration Item Records	Update	Fields such as status may be updated (plus the addition of links to the relevant Project Issue)
Exception Report	Output	Description of the exception situation, its impact, options, recommendation and impact of the recommendation

7.11.6 Key criteria

- Is the Project Issue within the remit of the project? If not, has guidance been given on how to progress it?
- Is the stage forecast to go outside its tolerance margins?
- Is there anything within the Project Manager's remit that would bring the stage back within its tolerances without reducing quality or project scope?
- Have the implications for the Business Case and risks been considered?
- Have all sensible alternatives been considered?
- Is there a recommended course of action for the Project Board to consider?
- Has the impact on the Project Plan been calculated?

Hints and tips

The approval of Project Issues for which work needs to be done in the current stage may be the factor that drives the stage outside its tolerances. The Project Board should be made aware of this likelihood when it is considering Project Issue requests.

Such potential deviations should be forecast as far in advance as possible without 'crying wolf'. The Project Manager is expected to try to contain any such situation.

Previous Highlight Reports might have set alarm bells ringing that the stage might exceed its tolerances.

One option available to the Project Board in response to an exception situation is to stop the project.

One cause of an exception might be a supplier going out of business.

It is necessary to undertake impact analysis on the options to counter a forecast deviation.

User input should be sought on the impact to the user community of the deviation and options.

Specialist input should be sought on the impact on the specialist of the deviation and options.

The business impact should cover the Project Plan, Business Case and risks.

The Project Board may decide to accept an Off-Specification without corrective action, turning the Off-Specification into a concession.

Consider the need for speed in notifying the Project Board. The process can be done in three steps: a brief statement, followed by supporting information, followed by exception planning.

7.12 Receiving Completed Work Package (CS9)

7.12.1 Fundamental principles

Where work has been allocated to individuals or teams, there should be a matching confirmation that the work has been completed and accepted.

7.12.2 Context

This process records the successful completion and return of Work Packages from *Delivering a Work Package* (MP3). This information is then passed to *Assessing Progress* (CS2).

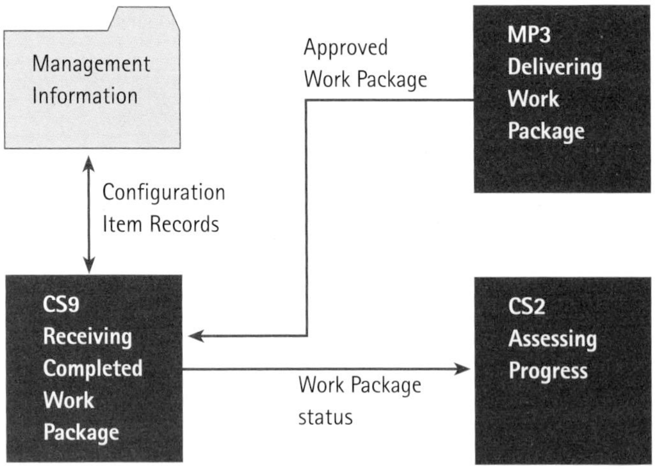

Figure 7.11 Receiving Completed Work Package

7.12.3 Process description

Confirmation is sought that the Work Package has been completed satisfactorily. This includes checking that:

- The recipient of the products has accepted them
- The Quality Log entries are complete
- The appropriate records have been put in the quality file
- The products have been transferred to configuration management.

Any approvals defined as part of the Acceptance Criteria are checked to ensure they are in order. The Configuration Item Record is updated to change the status to completed. The completed, accepted product is now baselined. Any subsequent changes to the product must pass through change control. This would be an automatic part of any configuration management method being used.

7.12.4 Responsibilities

The Project Manager is responsible for this process, assisted by any appointed Project Support staff. The team member or Team Manager responsible for completion of the Work Package will provide information. The Configuration Librarian will update all affected Configuration Item Records.

7.12.5 Information needs

Table 7.9 CS9 information needs

Management information	Usage	Explanation
Approved Work Package	Input	Signed-off confirmation that the Work Package is complete and acceptable
Configuration Item Records	Update	Change of product status
Work Package status	Output	To update the Stage Plan

7.12.6 Key criteria

- Are all individuals or teams whose work is to use or interface with the completed Work Package happy with the product(s)?
- Are the sign-offs sufficiently independent of the creator(s)?

Hints and tips

There is a close link between the management information requirements of this process and the technical requirements of any configuration management method being used in receiving and recording completion data. The configuration management method will also take charge of the product of the Work Package and be responsible for its storage – see Chapter 19, *Configuration Management.*

8
MANAGING PRODUCT DELIVERY (MP)

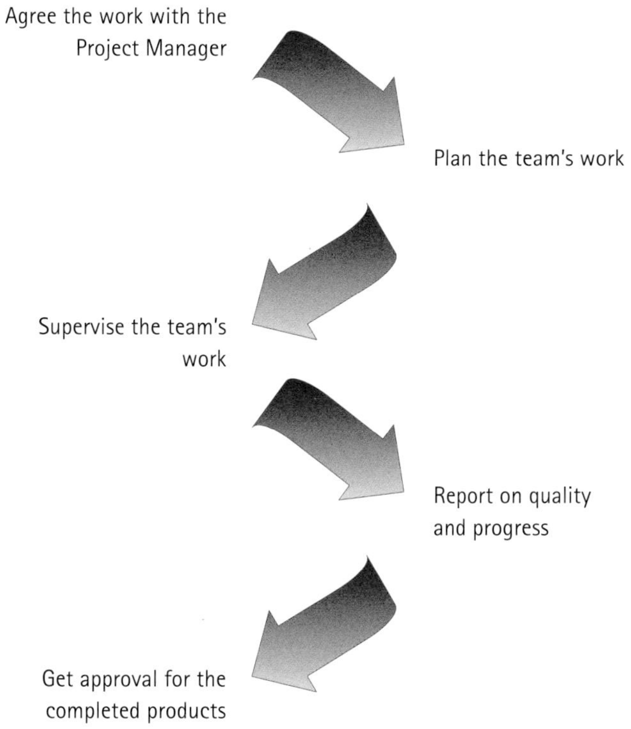
Agree the work with the Project Manager
Plan the team's work
Supervise the team's work
Report on quality and progress
Get approval for the completed products

Figure 8.1 Overview of Managing Product Delivery

8.1 Fundamental principles

Managing Product Delivery (MP) allows a controlled break between the Project Manager, Team Manager and product creation/provision by third-party suppliers. The process needs careful implementation to avoid being over-bureaucratic.

8.2 Context

This process interfaces with *Controlling a Stage* (CS) and may use the *Planning* (PL) process to create team plans. The third party may not be using PRINCE2, so this is a statement of the required interface between the Team Manager and the PRINCE2 method being used in the project.

In projects where there is only one team, reporting directly to the Project Manager, the team member who is to do the work will agree details with the Project Manager. The principles of this process will still apply, but will be implemented much more informally.

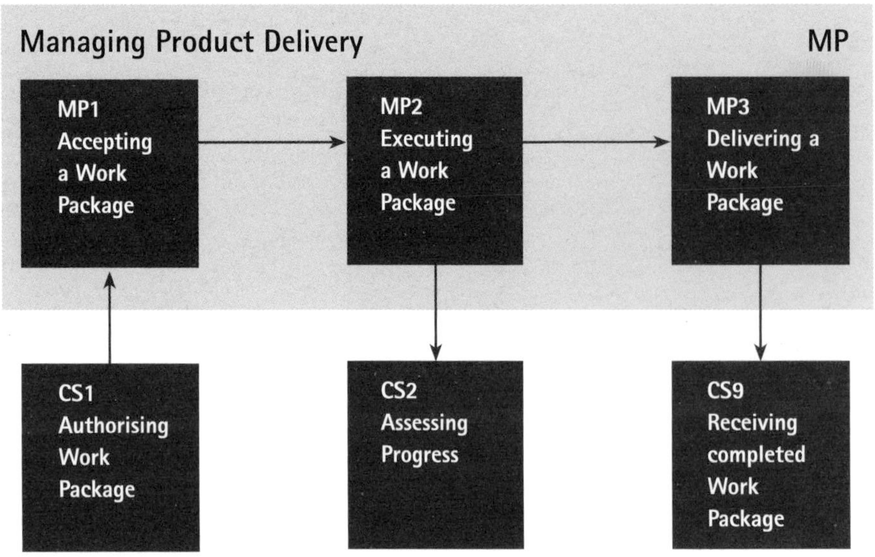

Figure 8.2 Managing Product Delivery

8.3 Process description

The objectives of this process are to allow a Team Manager to:

- Agree work with the Project Manager
- Get it done
- Hand it back to the Project Manager.

This agreement to do a defined amount of work is parcelled into Work Packages. Where external suppliers are involved, the acceptance of Work Packages will be affected by the terms of their contract.

The Team Manager ensures that planned products are created and delivered by the team to the project by:

- Accepting and checking authorised Work Packages from the Project Manager
- Making certain that work on products allocated to the team is effectively authorised and agreed
- Ensuring that work links to any interfaces identified in the Work Package
- Creating or revising a team plan for the work
- Ensuring that the work is done
- Ensuring that work progress and forecasts are regularly assessed
- Ensuring that completed products meet quality criteria
- Obtaining approval for the completed products.

8.3.1 Scalability

For small projects, or any with just one team reporting directly to the Project Manager, the link between this process and *Controlling a Stage* (CS) will be much less formal.

The process work can be summarised as:

- Negotiate work to be done
- Plan it
- Oversee it being done
- Keep track of progress
- Report progress
- Have products checked
- Make a record of quality checks
- Control changes
- Get the product(s) approved
- Return the completed Work Package to the Project Manager.

8.4 Accepting a Work Package (MP1)

8.4.1 Fundamental principles

The fundamental principle of this process is that before a Work Package is allocated to the team, there should be agreement with the Project Manager on:

- What is to be delivered
- What constraints apply
- Any interfaces to be recognised
- Whether the requirements of the Work Package are reasonable and can be achieved.

8.4.2 Context

This process is the management interface between the Team Manager and the Project Manager for the transfer to the team of work to be done.

The process is the Team Manager's counter to *Authorising Work Package* (CS1). There will be many instances of the two processes during the project.

8.4.3 Process description

The suggested content of a Work Package is given in Appendix A, *Product Description outlines*.

The Team Manager has to agree the Work Package with the Project Manager. The steps for this are:

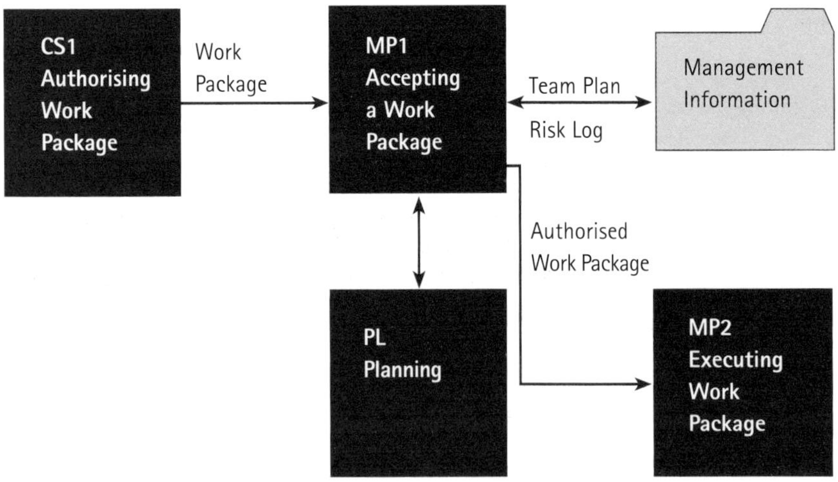

Figure 8.3 Accepting a Work Package Make a clear agreement with the Project Manager on what is to be delivered

- Negotiate with the Project Manager on behalf of the team the constraints within which the work is to be done
- Agree tolerance margins for the Work Package
- Understand the reporting requirements
- Understand how, and from whom, approval for the products is to be obtained
- Understand how the approved products are to be formally handed over
- Confirm how the Project Manager is to be informed of completion of the Work Package
- Produce or amend a team plan to show that the Work Package can be completed within the constraints. The common *Planning* (PL) process will be used to modify or create team plans
- Perform risk analysis, planning and resourcing.

The Work Package should contain Product Description(s) that describe the product(s) required, including the quality criteria. The Stage and team plan should indicate agreed constraints, such as time and effort.

8.4.4 Responsibilities

The Team Manager is responsible for the agreement with the Project Manager.

8.4.5 Information needs

Table 8.1 MP1 information needs

Management information	Usage	Explanation
Work Package	Input	Package put together by the Project Manager in *Authorising Work Package* (CS1) for the Team Manager's agreement. May be revised in coming to an agreement
Team plan	Update	Details of the Work Package are added to the team's workload
Risk Log	Update	The Team Manager adds any risks identified in the team plan to the Risk Log
Authorised Work Package	Output	The Work Package is agreed by the Team Manager

8.4.6 Key criteria

- Has there been full consultation on the Work Package between the Project Manager and Team Manager?
- Is there a cost and time allowance for the quality checking work and any rework that may be required?
- Are the reporting requirements reasonable?
- Are any interfacing requirements achievable within the constraints?
- Are any links to the project's configuration management method clear and consistent with the way in which the products will be controlled in the team?
- Has any required interface to Project Assurance been made clear and the interface with the team established?
- Are any risks and the means of managing them identified?
- What is the resource availability over the period covered by the Work Package?
- What skills and experience are needed by the Work Package elements?
- Does the individual or group agree with the work allocated?
- Is there adequate description of the quality required?
- Are any standards and techniques to be used defined?

Hints and tips

Where the project has no Team Managers and the Project Manager hands work directly to a team member, the individual can use this process informally. On small projects it may only be documented via the Daily Log.

This process 'matches' *Authorising Work Package* (CS1) and the two will be done together.

8.5 Executing a Work Package (MP2)

8.5.1 Fundamental principles

The fundamental principles of this process are that:

- Whatever the type of project, the actual task of creating the required products needs to be managed
- In the same way that work is delegated to a Team Manager, so the tracking of that work is also delegated.

8.5.2 Context

This process may occur at a level that is not using PRINCE2 – for instance when a non-PRINCE2 third party is involved. There is, therefore, no definition of specific standards or procedures to be used, just a statement of what must be done in order for the Team Manager to liaise within the project.

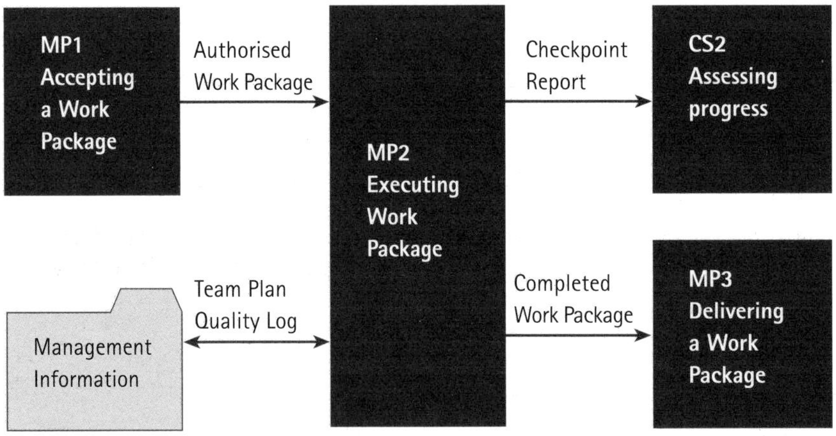

Figure 8.4 Executing a Work Package

8.5.3 Process description

The work on an authorised Work Package has to be monitored at the depth required to provide feedback to the Project Manager as defined in the authorised Work Package. The necessary steps are:

- Manage the development of the required products/services
- Capture and record the effort expended
- Determine the status of each product in the Work Package
- Monitor and control the risks associated with the Work Package
- Evaluate with the creator(s) the amount of effort still required
- Feed the progress and status information back to the Project Manager, in Checkpoint Reports, in the manner and at the frequency defined in the Work Package

- Ensure that the required quality-checking procedures are carried out and that the product(s) satisfy the quality standards defined in the Work Package
- Update the Quality Log with details of all quality checks carried out
- Advise the Project Manager of any problems that might impact the agreed tolerance levels for the Work Package. (Formally, this would be done via a Project Issue.)

It is useful for a Team Manager to use a Daily Log, as described in *Controls* (Chapter 16). It can be used to remind the Team Manager to follow up on quality checks still not done or those revealing too many errors or errors taking too long to remedy. Items on the critical path due to start or complete can also be put in the Daily Log to remind the Team Manager to check that everything is on course.

8.5.4 Responsibilities

The Team Manager is responsible for the process.

8.5.5 Information needs

Table 8.2 MP2 information needs

Management information	Usage	Explanation
Authorised Work Package	Input	Work agreed with the Project Manager
Team plan	Update	Record allocation, planned effort, actual effort and progress, plus any modifications required, are all used to update the team plan
Quality Log	Update	Details of the checks carried out on the product, to ensure conformance to quality standards, are added to the Quality Log
Checkpoint Reports	Output	Progress reports to the Project Manager at the frequency defined in the Work Package
Completed Work Package	Output	Completed Work Package

8.5.6 Key criteria

- Is the work divided into sufficiently small segments to facilitate the required level of control?
- How will progress be monitored?
- How will the final product(s) be checked?
- Does the team plan include the quality-checking work?
- Are the team members' progress recording and reporting procedures at the right level for the project reporting requirements?
- Is work being done to the requirements and constraints of the Work Package?

- Are progress recording and reporting in sufficient detail to give early warning of any threat to the tolerance margins?
- Were the quality checks fully carried out?

Hints and tips

The Team Manager may need to add extra information to the Work Package to indicate version control or configuration management methods to be used within the team.

Procedures must be put in place to keep the Project Manager up to date on progress.

Even if the team is not using PRINCE2, it must provide the Project Manager with the required information in the format stipulated in the Work Package. Therefore, it would be sensible to have recording and reporting procedures that match those of the project (or even use the respective PRINCE2 reports).

8.6 Delivering a Work Package (MP3)

8.6.1 Fundamental principles

Just as the Work Package was accepted from the Project Manager, notification of its completion must be returned to the Project Manager.

8.6.2 Context

The configuration management system used by the project may handle the return of the actual products of the Work Package. The essence of this process is that the Team Manager must ensure that the products are handed over correctly and advise the Project Manager that the hand-over has occurred.

The process may trigger *Authorising Work Package* (CS1) for the next Work Package or may overlap with it.

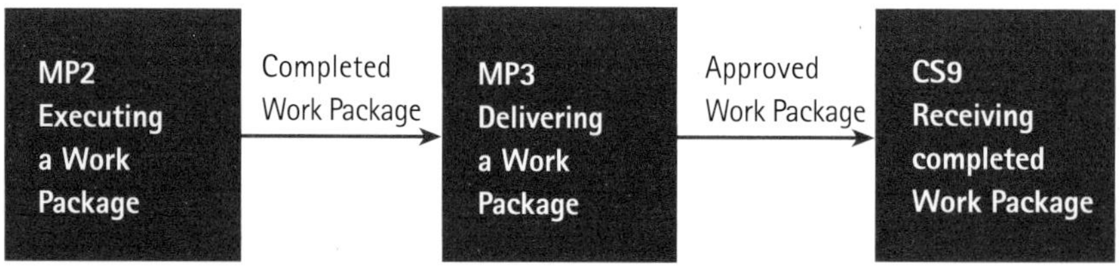

Figure 8.5 Delivering a Work Package

8.6.3 Process description

The process has three elements:

- Obtain acceptance for the products developed
- Hand over the completed products
- Advise the Project Manager of completion of the Work Package.

The methods of achieving these elements should have been defined as part of Work Package authorisation. The acceptance should come from two sources: the person or group identified as the recipient and the Configuration Librarian.

Before advising the Project Manager of the completion, the Team Manager should check that the Quality Log entries are complete for the product(s).

8.6.4 Responsibilities

The Team Manager is responsible for the process, liaising with the Configuration Librarian.

8.6.5 Information needs

Table 8.3 MP3 information needs

Management information	Usage	Explanation
Completed Work Package	Input	Details of the work agreed with the Project Manager
Approved Work Package	Output	Products approved as defined in the Work Package

8.6.6 Key criteria

- Has the identified recipient accepted the product(s)?
- Has hand-over been completed, including any configuration management aspects?
- Are any agreed statistics available for the Project Manager to record in the Stage Plan?
- Did anything happen during execution of the Work Package that is worthy of addition to the Lessons Learned Log?

Hints and tips

If the Work Package contains a number of products to be developed, they may be handed over to the project's configuration management system as they are approved. This may imply a period of time before the Project Manager is notified that the whole Work Package has been completed.

The level of formality required will vary according to the project: formal when third parties are involved, informal when the Project Manager manages the work directly.

9

MANAGING STAGE BOUNDARIES (SB)

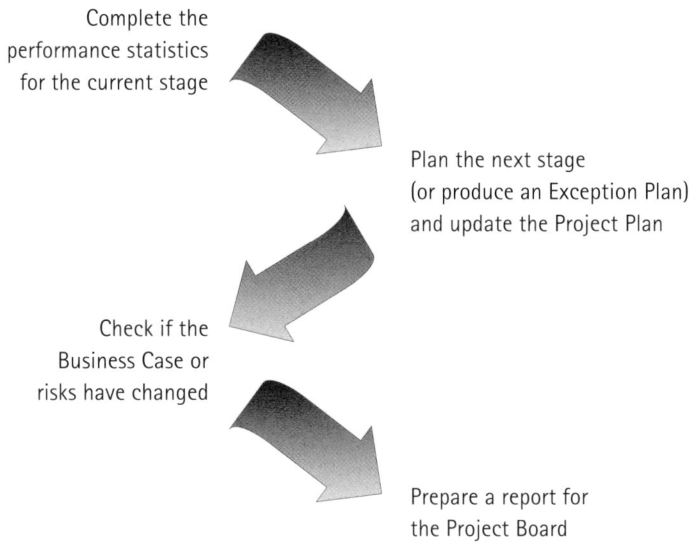

Complete the performance statistics for the current stage
Plan the next stage (or produce an Exception Plan) and update the Project Plan
Check if the Business Case or risks have changed
Prepare a report for the Project Board

Figure 9.1 Overview of Managing Stage Boundaries

9.1 Fundamental principles

Projects, whether large or small, need to be focused on delivering business benefit, either in their own right or as part of a larger programme. The continuing correct focus of the project should be confirmed at the end of each stage. If necessary, the project can be redirected or stopped to avoid wasting time and money.

9.2 Context

Before the end of each stage except the final one, the next stage is planned, together with a review and update of the Business Case, risk situation and overall Project Plan.

This process is normally triggered by *Reviewing Stage Status* (CS5), uses the *Planning* (PL) process to develop the next Stage Plan (or Exception Plan), and its output triggers the Project Board process, *Authorising a Stage or Exception Plan* (DP3).

The steps of this process will also be used when creating an Exception Plan.

9.3 Process description

The objectives of the process are to:

- Assure the Project Board that all products in the current Stage Plan have been completed as defined
- Prepare the next Stage Plan

- Provide the information needed for the Project Board to assess the continuing viability of the project
- Obtain authorisation for the start of the next stage, together with its delegated tolerance margins
- Record any information or lessons that can help later stages of this project and/or other projects.

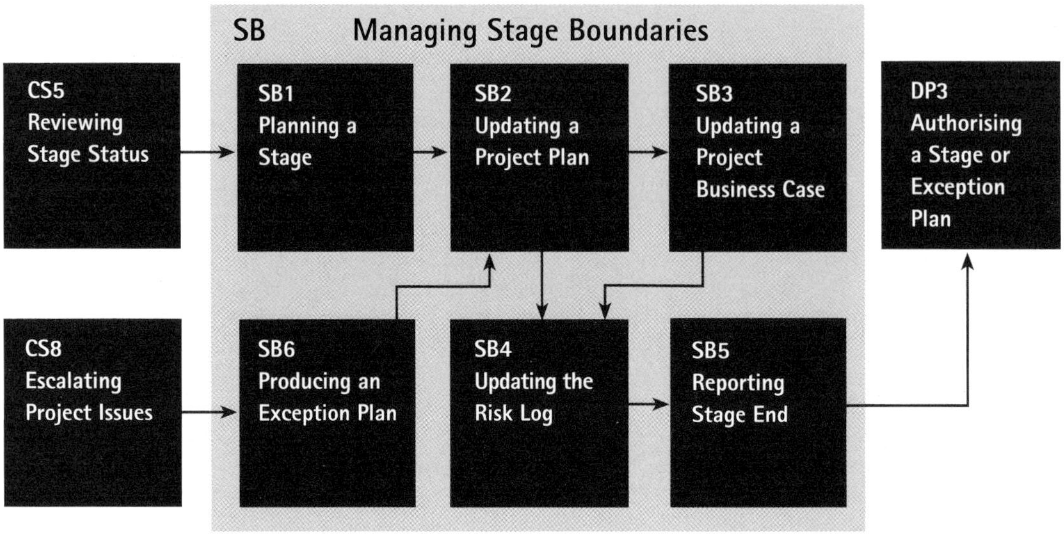

Figure 9.2 Managing Stage Boundaries

There could well be changes of personnel and management, necessitating changes to the project management team.

There is also a requirement to revisit the Project Quality Plan and Project Approach to check whether they need changing or refining.

The stage immediately post-initiation is normally approved at the same time as the Project Initiation Document. If so, this process would need customising for that situation.

9.3.1 Scalability

As can be seen from the following list, the process has a simple purpose and this can be done as informally as the Project Board and Project Manager wish. The reporting and approval may be informal, if the Project Board is agreeable. However, it is advisable to document the major decisions, even if it is only in the Project Manager's Daily Log.

- Gather the results of the current stage
- Plan the next stage
- Check the effect on:
  - the Project Plan
  - the justification for the project
  - the risks
- Report and seek approval.

9.4 Planning a Stage (SB1)

9.4.1 Fundamental principles

Planning each stage of the project ensures that:

- There is sufficient detail for day-to-day control to be exercised against the plan
- Each Stage Plan has the commitment of the Project Board and Project Manager
- The Project Board is fully aware of what it is approving at the start of each stage.

9.4.2 Context

The approaching end of the current stage triggers the process.

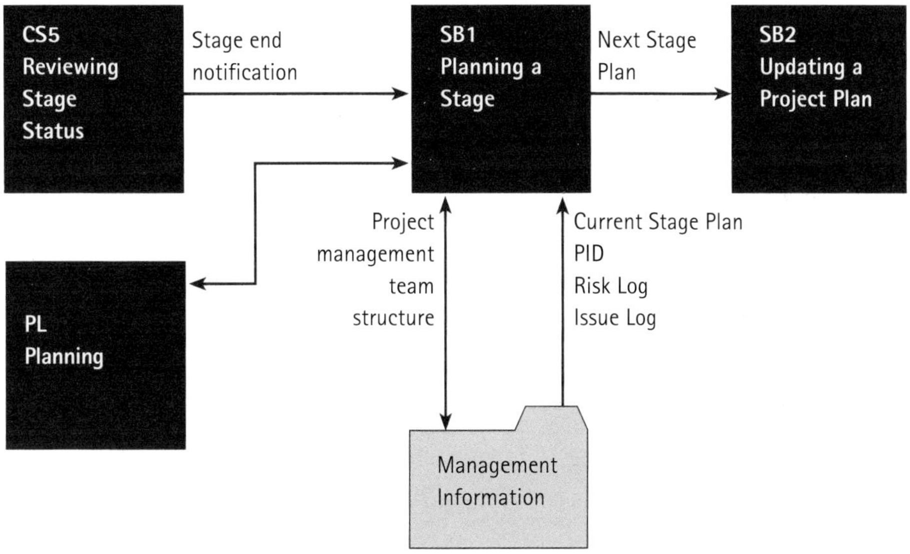

Figure 9.3 Planning a Stage

9.4.3 Process description

The main objective is to prepare a plan for the next stage of the project. The high-level summary of the next stage is expanded from the Project Plan into sufficient detail that the Project Manager will be able to control progress against it on a day-to-day basis. The *Planning* (PL) process is used to develop the plan.

The plan should include all products – not only the specialist ones but management products as well. A typical management product would be the next Stage Plan, which will require preparation towards the end of the stage. Quality activities and products should also appear in the plan. Whoever is providing Project Assurance should be consulted about the timing and resourcing of quality activities before the Stage Plan is presented to the Project Board.

The management structure of the next stage must be specified and any new or changed job descriptions prepared.

9.4.4 Responsibilities

The Project Manager is responsible for this process, assisted by Project Support. Those with Project Assurance responsibilities should check out the plan, with respect to continuing to meet customer and business expectations.

9.4.5 Information needs

Table 9.1 SB1 information needs

Management information	Usage	Explanation
Stage end notification	Input	Indication from CS5 that the end of a stage is approaching
Current Stage Plan	Input	The results of the current stage may affect the planning of the new stage activities
PID	Input	Contains the 'what' and 'why' of the project and is the document that specifies the Project Board's terms of reference
Issue Log	Input	May contain information that affects the next stage or issues marked for reassessment at stage end
Risk Log	Input	Current risks may affect the next Stage Plan and the next Stage Plan may create or modify risks
Project management team structure	Update	This should be updated with any changes for the coming stage
Next Stage Plan	Output	Produced via *Planning* (PL)

9.4.6 Key criteria

- Are the major products shown in the Project Plan for the next stage reflected in the next Stage Plan?
- Are all user, customer or other resources required to check the quality of products identified?
- Are the resources used to check quality in line with the requirements of the Project Quality Plan?

Hints and tips

Ensure that any externally produced products are shown in the Stage Plan, together with sufficient monitoring points to assure the Project Board that these products are both on schedule and to the required quality.

Check any external dependencies to ensure that there has been no change in the scope or constraints of products expected from them.

The Stage Plan will need to be prepared in parallel with any relevant team plans.

Ensuring that quality control procedures are used correctly is jointly the responsibility of the Senior Supplier and Senior User. Does the Stage Plan show how this responsibility will be carried out, particularly by the Senior User? The plan needs user involvement in checking products delivered by the supplier.

Where the project is part of a programme, it is unlikely that programme staff will want to record this level of detail, except for any inter-project dependencies. The Project Plan is a more appropriate level. However, the programme may wish to hold a copy of the Stage Plan for reference.

9.5 Updating a Project Plan (SB2)

9.5.1 Fundamental principles

The Project Board uses the Project Plan throughout the project to measure overall progress. As stages are completed or planned in detail, the Project Plan must be updated to reflect the latest understanding of the project and to allow the Project Board to revise its expectations.

9.5.2 Context

The Project Plan is updated from information in the Stage Plan for the stage that is finishing, the next Stage Plan (from SB1), and any Exception Plan (from SB6) triggered by *Escalating Project Issues* (CS8). Actuals are taken from the first and the forecast duration and costs from the last two. Details of any revised costs or end dates are passed to the next process, *Updating a Project Business Case* (SB3).

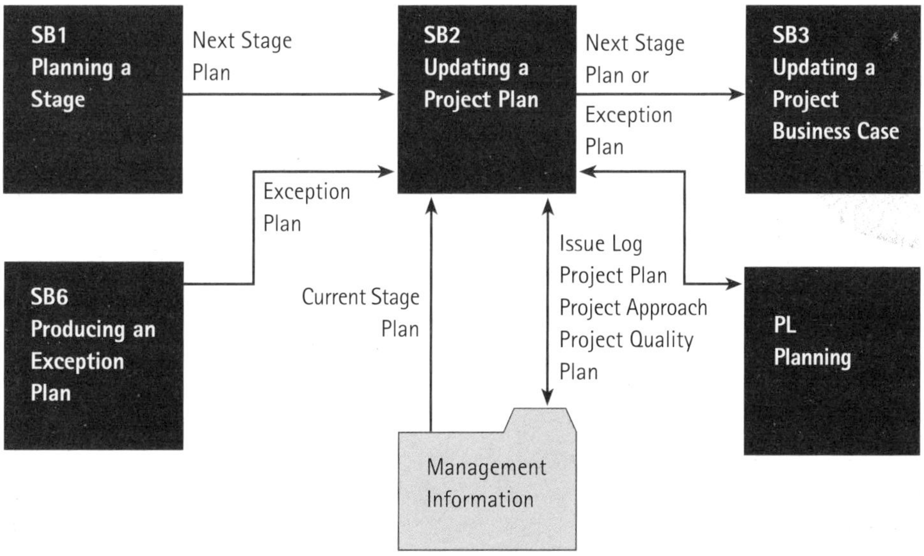

Figure 9.4 Updating a Project Plan

9.5.3 Process description

The Project Quality Plan and Project Approach are reassessed and refined to reflect the current understanding of the project and to form a basis for updating the Project Plan.

The Project Plan is updated based on the actual costs and schedule from a completed Stage Plan or Exception Plan, the new detail of activities and costs from the next Stage Plan and any acquired knowledge about the project. The last might be information about changes that have been agreed by the Project Board and that will cause activities in the next Stage Plan.

The Project Manager should describe in the End Stage Report why any change to the Project Plan has occurred.

9.5.4 Responsibilities

The Project Manager is responsible for this process, assisted by Project Support and the work checked out by those with Project Assurance responsibility.

9.5.5 Information needs

Table 9.2 SB2 information needs

Management information	Usage	Explanation
Current Stage Plan	Input	The results of the current stage may affect the project planning
Next Stage Plan or Exception Plan	Input/ Output	The extra detail in the Stage Plan or Exception Plan may reveal the need to modify the Project Plan
Project Approach	Update	Events may have occurred that modify the approach
Issue Log	Update	There may be issues that need to be addressed at this point
Project Quality Plan	Update	If quality results so far show the need to adjust the Project Plan
Project Plan	Update	Revised in the light of the actuals from the current stage and the forecast of the next Stage Plan. Also updated to reflect any changed or extra products sanctioned by the Project Board

9.5.6 Key criteria

- How reliable are the figures for cost and schedule for the stage just being completed (especially if fed information from team plans)?
- How do the results of the stage impact the Project Plan?
- How does the next Stage Plan impact the Project Plan, Business Case and risks?
- Did any other information come out of the last stage that will impact later stages of the project?

Hints and tips

If the Project Plan is being updated because the scope of the project has changed, make sure that there is an audit trail between cause and effect – for example, ensure that the changes are recorded as a Project Issue.

9.6 Updating a Project Business Case (SB3)

9.6.1 Fundamental principles

Projects do not take place in a static environment. The environment external to the project changes, as do the nature and timing of the project's products. The Business Case needs to reflect these changes and must be reviewed and amended to keep it relevant to the project.

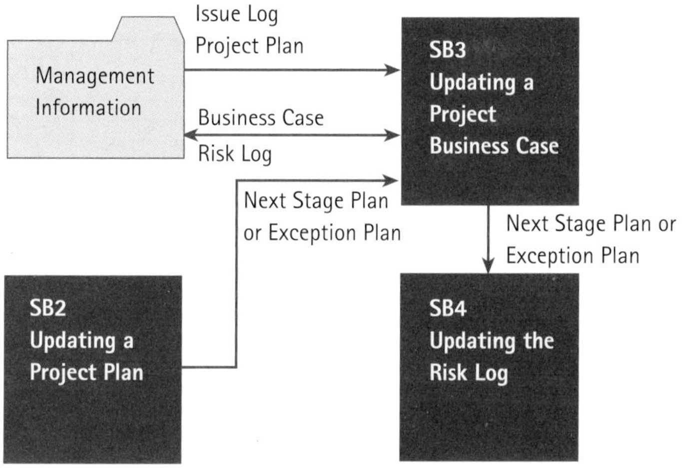

Figure 9.5 Updating a Project Business Case

9.6.2 Context

The update of the Business Case and the Project Plan is a cyclical process during stage-end activities throughout the project.

9.6.3 Process description

The objective is to revisit and revise, where necessary, the costs, benefits, key risks and timings stated in the Business Case. These may have been affected by internal or external events.

Various factors will affect this process:

- The final implementation date of the project may have changed, for better or worse, which might affect some or all of the benefits
- The cost of delivering the product might have changed, thus affecting the cost side of the cost/benefit analysis
- Approved changes will have affected products, hence benefits

- Externally the corporate or programme environment into which the product will be delivered may have changed
- The situation with regard to external resources or suppliers may have changed beyond the control of the project
- It may be an Exception Plan that has caused the Business Case to be revisited.

A revised version of the Business Case is created. The Risk and Issue Logs are examined to see if anything has changed that might affect the Business Case.

It is worth noting that changes may improve the Business Case, as well as weaken it.

The Project Board is ordinarily only authorised to continue while the project remains viable (that is, the benefits will be realised within the cost and time parameters set out in the currently agreed Business Case). If costs and/or time are to be exceeded or it becomes clear that benefits will be substantially lower than those set out in the Business Case, the Project Board needs to have the revised Business Case approved afresh by corporate or programme management.

9.6.4 Responsibilities

The Project Manager is responsible for this process, assisted by Project Support and those with Project Assurance responsibilities should check out the work.

The project's benefits are a prime responsibility of the customer.

9.6.5 Information needs

Table 9.3 SB3 information needs

Management information	Usage	Explanation
Project Plan	Input	Have any changes to the Project Plan been made that affect the Business Case?
Issue Log	Input	Are there any new issues that threaten (or could improve) the Business Case?
Next Stage Plan	Input/ Output	Does anything in the next Stage Plan affect the Business Case?
Exception Plan	Input/ Output	If the SB process has been triggered by an exception situation, does the Exception Plan affect the Business Case?
Business Case	Update	Revised to account for any changes to the project that may affect it
Risk Log	Update	Are there any new risks that threaten the Business Case?

9.6.6 Key criteria

- Has anything happened external to the project that affects the Business Case?
- Has the Project Plan changed such that it impacts the Business Case – for example, in terms of overall cost or the date of the scheduled outcome?
- Has it become impossible to achieve some or all of the identified benefits?

Hints and tips

Reviewing the Business Case is best done after the Project Plan has been brought up to date.

It is sensible to review the Business Case after any activities caused by reaction to risks have been added to the new Stage Plan. These activities or their cost may have an effect on the Business Case.

9.7 Updating the Risk Log (SB4)

9.7.1 Fundamental principles

Risks change during the life of the project. New risks arise. Old risks change their status. The exposure of the project to risk should be regularly reviewed.

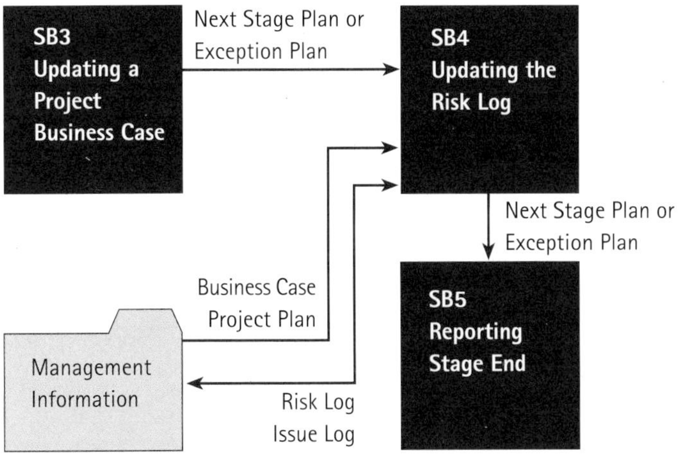

Figure 9.6 Updating the Risk Log

9.7.2 Context

The update of the Risk Log is a cyclical process during stage-end activities throughout the project. This is the minimum number of times to review risks. Lengthy or risky projects will need to review risks more frequently.

9.7.3 Process description

The objective is to revisit and revise, where necessary, the risks in the Risk Log. These may have been affected by internal or external events.

Hints and tips

Following the motto 'No surprises', the Project Manager should informally keep the Project Board aware of what the End Stage Report will say. Any problems should, wherever possible, be resolved before presentation of the report.

The level of formality or informality in the presentation of the End Stage Report depends on factors such as the project size and the desires of the Project Board.

Where the project is part of a programme, the programme support office must examine the End Stage Report, the next Stage Plan and the updated Project Plan to ensure that the project stays in tune with the programme.

9.9 Producing an Exception Plan (SB6)

9.9.1 Fundamental principles

A stage is deemed to be in exception as soon as current forecasts for the end of the stage deviate beyond the delegated tolerance boundaries. The project is in exception if the whole project is likely to go beyond tolerance boundaries.

If either stage or project is forecast to deviate beyond its agreed tolerance boundaries, it no longer has the approval of the Project Board. A new plan must be presented to take the place of the current plan.

9.9.2 Context

The deviation should have been recognised during *Controlling a Stage* (CS). The Project Manager will have brought the situation to the attention of the Project Board through an Exception Report. The Project Board will have requested the Project Manager to produce an Exception Plan. The Exception Plan will then be presented to the Project Board at an Exception Assessment.

9.9.3 Process description

If a stage or the project is forecast to go outside the tolerances agreed with the Project Board when the plan was approved and the situation cannot be rectified, the Project Manager has no further mandate to carry on with the work.

The Exception Plan will have the same structure as other PRINCE2 plans. It should run from the present time to the end of the plan that it replaces. If it is the Project Plan that is in exception, a revised Project Plan should be created, taking into account the actuals to date.

The configuration records of all products included in the plan being replaced must be checked. Where the status shows that work is outstanding, the Exception Plan should include this work.

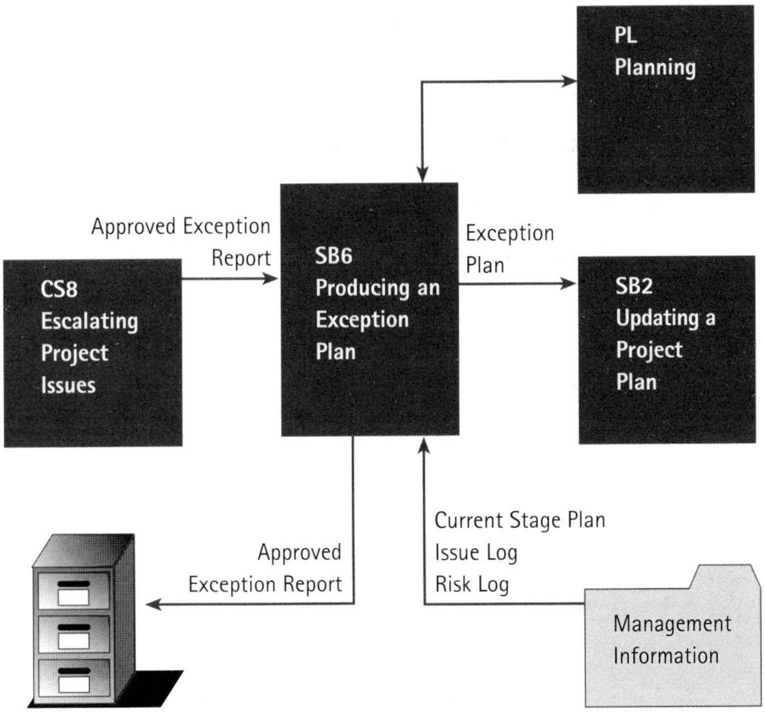

Figure 9.8 Producing an Exception Plan

9.9.4 Responsibilities

The Configuration Librarian will provide a product status account of the products in the plan that is to be replaced. The Project Manager is responsible for producing Exception Plans with the help of Project Support. The Project Manager would work with those responsible for Project Assurance to check it.

9.9.5 Information needs

Table 9.6 SB6 information needs

Management information	Usage	Explanation
Current Stage Plan	Input	This is the plan from which the deviation has occurred and that will define the tolerances and the extent of the deviation. It can also be used to extrapolate what would happen if the deviation were allowed to continue
Issue Log	Input	This may contain details of the reasons for the project or stage being forecast to deviate beyond its tolerances
Risk Log	Input	This may contain details of the reasons for the project or stage being forecast to deviate beyond its tolerances

Management information	Usage	Explanation
Approved Exception Report	Input/ Output	This warning should have been sent to the Project Board at the first indication of a probable deviation. It is the trigger from the process *Escalating Project Issues* (CS8) for the start of this process
Exception Plan	Output	The product of the process, a plan that replaces the current Stage Plan

9.9.6 Key criteria

- Has the deviation adversely affected the Business Case for the project?
- What extra risks does the approved option bring?

Hints and tips

If it is the project tolerances that are under threat, a revised Project Plan should be produced.

Where the project is part of a programme, the programme support office must examine the Exception Plan to ensure that the project remains consistent with the programme.

The Project Manager should be wary of overestimating the ability to recover from a forecast deviation.

10
CLOSING A PROJECT (CP)

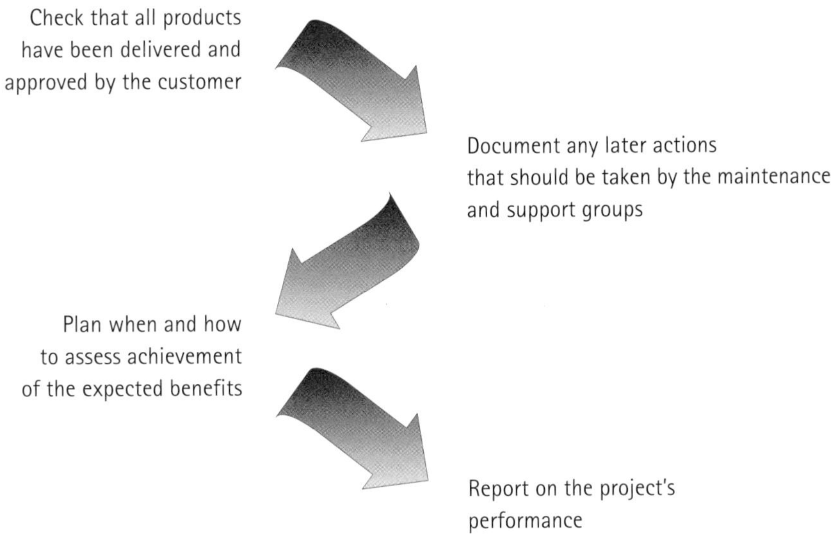

Check that all products have been delivered and approved by the customer
Document any later actions that should be taken by the maintenance and support groups
Plan when and how to assess achievement of the expected benefits
Report on the project's performance

Figure 10.1 Overview of Closing a Project

10.1 Fundamental principles

One of the defining features of a project is that it is finite – it has a start and an end. If the project loses this distinctiveness, it loses some of its effectiveness over purely operational management approaches.

A clear end to the project:

- Is always more successful than the natural tendency to drift into use and subsequent modification of the product. It is a recognition by all concerned that the original objectives have been met, that the current project has run its course and either the operational regime must now take over or the products from this project become feeds into some subsequent project or into some larger programme
- Helps to achieve business objectives by avoiding wasted time and by providing a useful opportunity to take stock of achievements and experience
- Provides an opportunity to ensure that all unachieved goals and objectives are identified, so that they can be addressed in the future.

10.2 Context

Preparation for closing the project is triggered by the approaching end of the final stage of the project or by it becoming apparent that the project is no longer viable for some reason. All the processes within *Closing a Project* (CP) may be done in parallel – or at least with considerable overlap. *Closing a Project* is not a stage.

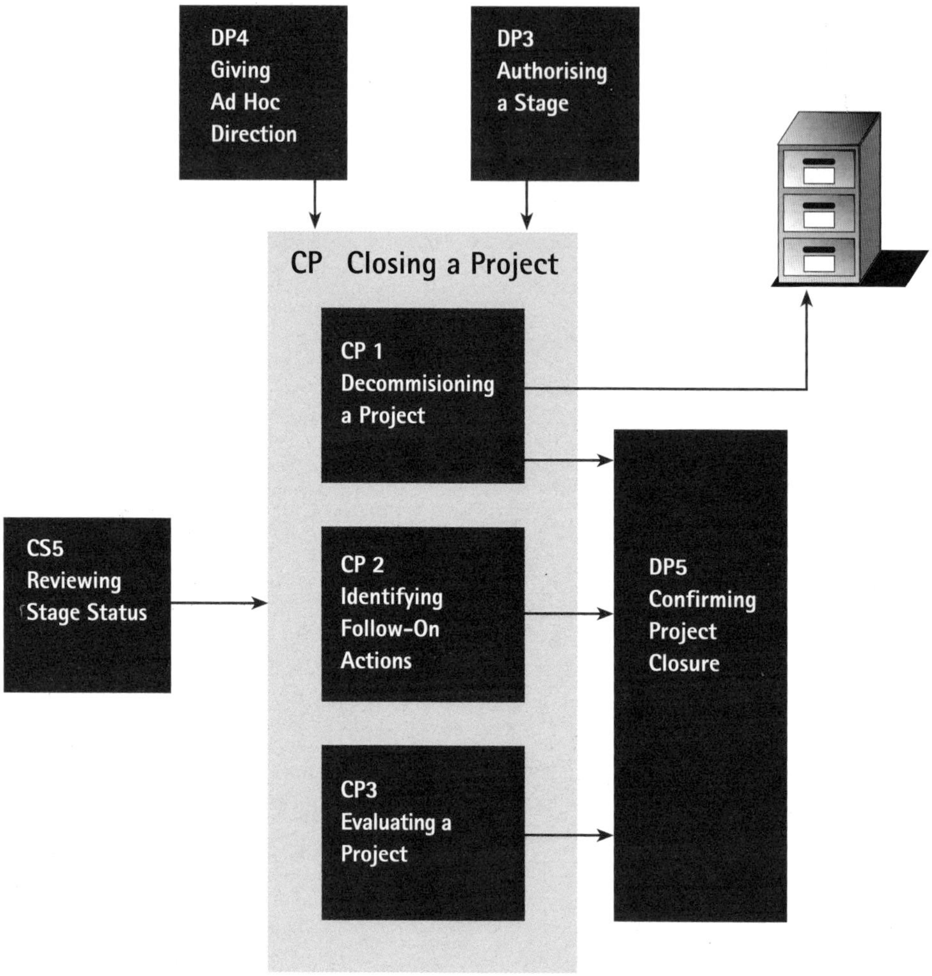

Figure 10.2 Closing a Project

10.3 Process description

The approach to *Closing a Project* (CP) has to be tailored to suit the needs of the particular project. For example, if the project is part of a programme or a series of projects, this may affect how some of the fundamental principles, such as follow-on actions, are handled. The project may be closely connected with a subsequent project and may have been planned ahead that way. All the results of the first project feed into the subsequent one, with no need to be concerned about maintenance, operational or other follow-on actions. As another example, if the project has delivered an intangible product – for example to bring about a change in philosophy – then the objective of ensuring that operational and support arrangements are in place may not be appropriate.

The following is an illustrative list of aims of the process to close the project. According to the type of project, they may not all be required:

- Ensure that the objectives or aims set out in the Project Initiation Document have been met
- Ensure that all expected products have been handed over and accepted by the customer or relevant subsequent project
- Ensure that the Acceptance Criteria have all been met and get the customer's confirmation of this
- Ensure that arrangements for the support and operation of project products are in place (where appropriate)
- Request formal acceptance of the products from the Project Board
- If the project has been closed prematurely, document what has been achieved and recommend the way forward
- Identify any recommendations for follow-on actions
- Capture and document lessons resulting from the project
- Prepare an End Project Report
- Plan any post-project review required
- Prepare notification to the host location of the intention to disband the project organisation and resources
- Arrange secure and orderly archiving of the project's records.

The process covers the Project Manager's work to wrap up the project either at its end or at premature close. Most of the work is to prepare input to the Project Board to obtain its confirmation that the project may close. If the project is being brought to a premature close, this process will have to be tailored to the actual project situation. It will be a case of what can be saved for use by another project or what remedial work is now required to fill any gaps left by the cancellation of this project.

The Project Initiation Document is examined to check the actual results of the project against the original expectations (or as modified by the Project Board). All planned products should have been approved and delivered to the customer or be ready for hand-over. There must be documented confirmation from the customer that all Acceptance Criteria, defined at the outset of the project, have been met.

The Project Manager prepares an End Project Report that comprehensively evaluates the actual project result versus that envisaged in the Project Initiation Document.

There may be a number of Project Issues that were held over by the Project Board. These may lead to new projects or enhancements to the products of the current project during its operational life. The Project Manager sorts these out into appropriate follow-on actions.

The Lessons Learned Log, which has been developed during the project, is now turned into a report and made available outside the project.

Notification to the host location that any provided facilities and resources will no longer be required is prepared for Project Board approval, including release dates.

Archiving of the management documents should be arranged, such that any later audit or retrieval can be done conveniently.

Suggested contents of the management products described in this process can be found in Appendix A, *Product Description outlines*.

10.3.1 Scalability

For small projects, the essentials of this process can be summarised as:

- Check that everything has been delivered
- Check that the product is accepted
- Make sure there are no loose ends
- Record any follow-on recommendations
- Store the project records for audit
- Release resources.

The last in the list may not be required.

10.4 Decommissioning a Project (CP1)

10.4.1 Fundamental principles

The main principles are that:

- Every project should come to an orderly close
- Customer and supplier should be in agreement that the project has delivered what was expected; this expectation should have been defined at the outset of the project
- Everyone who has provided support for the project should be warned of its close, so that they can plan for the return of the resources provided for that support
- Project records should be retained to assist with possible audits or the production of estimating metrics.

10.4.2 Context

The process is normally triggered by the process, *Controlling a Stage* (CS), when the Project Manager recognises that the project is nearing the end of the final stage. The process is part of the work leading to the Project Board process, *Confirming Project Closure* (DP5). There is no specific sequence in the three processes. *Closing a Project* (CP) will cycle round the three processes.

In exceptional cases the process may be used because the Project Board directs the Project Manager to close the project before its planned end.

10.4.3 Process description

The objectives of the process are to:

- Check that all Project Issues are closed or transferred to Follow-on Action Recommendations
- Ensure that all project products have been approved and handed over to the customer or user
- Confirm that the delivered products meet any needs defined in the customer's specification for operation and support (where applicable)

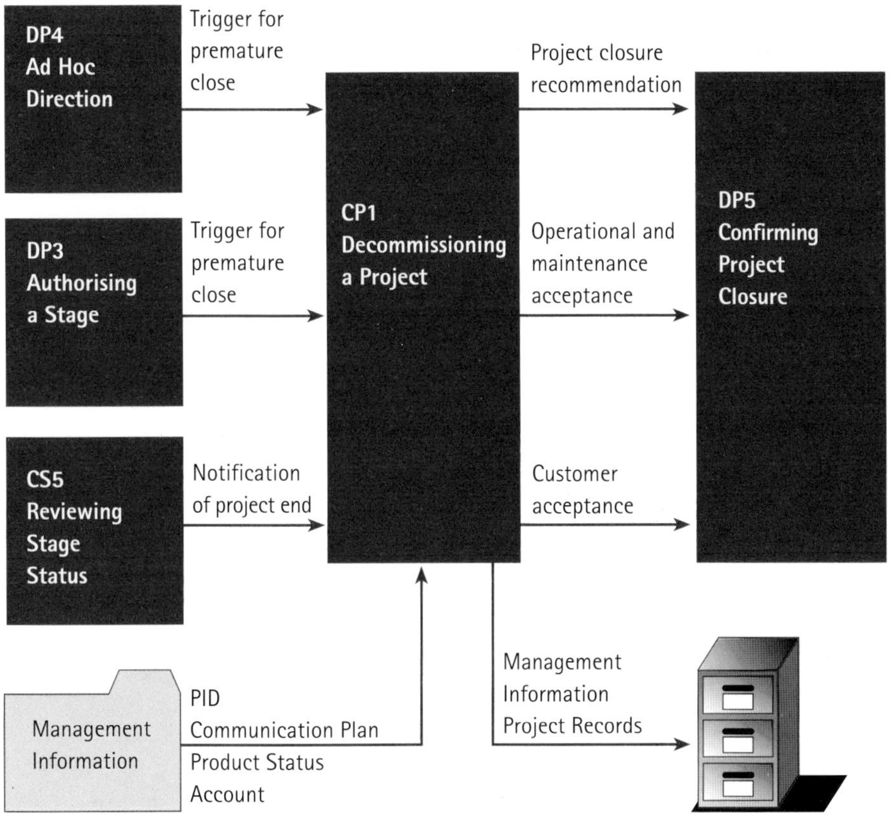

Figure 10.3 Decommissioning a Project

- Confirm that the correct operational and maintenance environment is in place (where applicable)
- Confirm that all Acceptance Criteria have been met
- Complete and store all project information
- Prepare a notification to all involved organisations and interested parties that the project is to be closed and facilities and resources disbanded.

The Project Manager prepares the project closure recommendation to the Project Board that the project resources and the support services can be disbanded and also prepares notification to any parties identified in the Communication Plan as needing to be told about the project closure. These have to be confirmed by the Project Board.

Before closure of the project can be recommended, the Project Manager must ensure that the expected results have all been achieved and delivered (or have been told by the Project Board that the project is to be closed prematurely).

A product status account (and possibly a configuration audit) is carried out to confirm that all products have been approved.

Where a product has to be supported and sustained during its useful life, there must be confirmation in the report by the people who will use and support it that they have received the product in a state that allows them to carry out their duties.

The Project Manager must go through the Acceptance Criteria with the customer and obtain agreement that all criteria have been met.

To permit any future audit of the project's actions and performance, the project files should be secured and archived. This entails an important task of weeding out documents that would not be useful to those who may need to access the archived files, e.g. audit, the project support office, future Project Managers (for planning models) and those who later carry out the post-project review. It is wise to have the weeding done by a group consisting of the Project Manager, Project Assurance and Project Support.

10.4.4 Responsibilities

The Project Manager has responsibility for the process, but may need assistance from Project Support (including the Configuration Librarian) to gather the necessary input and prepare elements of the report. The Project Manager should have informal contact with the Project Board during this time to ensure that there will be no problems with its confirmation of the project closure in *Confirming Project Closure* (DP5).

Those currently responsible for Project Assurance should also be consulted by the Project Manager for their views on the completeness of work, before making the recommendation.

10.4.5 Information needs

Table 10.1 CP1 information needs

Management information	Usage	Explanation
Project Initiation Document	Input	Contains a statement of the project's Acceptance Criteria
Product Status Account	Input	Confirmation from configuration management records that all products are approved
Trigger for Premature close	Input	Instruction from the Project Board to close the project before its expected end
Notification of project end	Input	The trigger from stage monitoring that the normal end of the project is near
Communication Plan	Input	Identification of any other interested party who needs to know

Customer acceptance	Output	Confirmation that the customer accepts the products
Operational and maintenance acceptance	Output	Confirmation that the product can be operated and supported
Project closure recommendation	Output	A note to be sent by the Project Board to the host location and any other relevant stakeholders that the project is about to close, and that supplied facilities and resources will no longer be needed
Project Records	Archive	Preserve the important and useful project records for future use by auditors or other enquirers

10.4.6 Key criteria

- Have all products in the Project Initiation Document been approved and delivered?
- Have the operational and support teams formally agreed that they are ready to accept hand-over (if appropriate)?
- Are the project resources and support services (if any were provided) no longer required?
- Are there any contractual implications when decommissioning the project?

Hints and tips

The configuration management system used on the project to control and record the status of products should check that all products are complete and handed over.

Where the final product will require a lot of potentially expensive maintenance, the Project Manager should ensure that a suitable service agreement or contract has been drawn up between the support group and the end users. In such instances, it may be correct to include the agreement as a project product. This will probably lead to a small team from the operations group being part of the final stages of the project, leading to the delivery of a signed agreement. The support group would need full information about the product, as it is developed (see the *Communication Plan*) to understand the support and maintenance implications of the product and its working environment.

10.5 Identifying Follow-on Actions (CP2)

10.5.1 Fundamental principles

If there is any unfinished business at the end of the project, it should be formally documented and passed to those who have the authority and responsibility to take action.

10.5.2 Context

Most of the input will be those items on the Issue Log that were held back by the Project Board.

The output is submitted to the Project Board as recommendations.

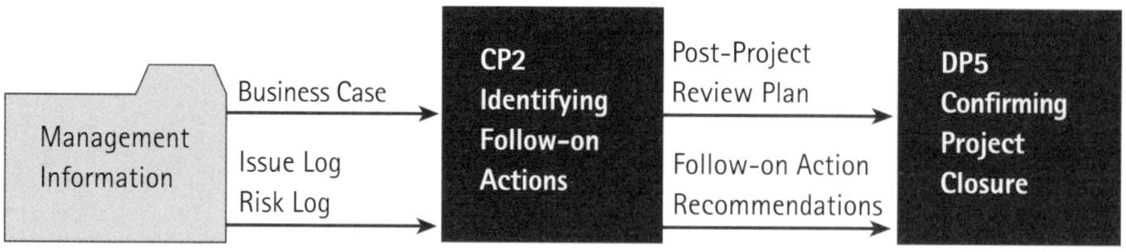

Figure 10.4 Identifying Follow-on Actions

10.5.3 Process description

The aims of the process are to:

- Establish actions required following the project
- Document any Follow-on Action Recommendations
- Recommend a date and plan for any post-project review(s) considered necessary.

A number of actions may be required after the project. The input will come mainly from those Project Issues that were put into 'pending' status by the Project Board during the project. The Risk Log may also contain risks that may affect the product in its useful life.

All unfinished work is documented in Follow-on Action Recommendations.

Many project products should be re-examined after a period of use to check on their quality, effectiveness in use and achievement of benefits. Examination of the updated Business Case will identify whether there are any expected benefits whose achievement cannot be measured until the product has been in use for some time. If this is the case, a recommended date and plan should be made for a post-project review, the benefits to be measured at that time and the measurements to be applied. These benefits should have been defined in the Business Case.

It is not a project activity to produce the post-project review, only to plan it. In summary the post-project review is to assess achievement of the benefits claimed in the Business Case. The following questions are a sample:

- To what level has the product achieved the benefits expected?
- Is there an identifiable trend of improving benefits?
- Are the user(s) happy with the product?
- Is the product proving to meet quality expectations?
- Is the product as well supported as was expected?
- Are the support staff happy with what they have been given to support the product?

- Have there been any unexpected problems in the introduction?
- Has the product caused new problems?

The Post-Project Review Plan will make use of the information contained in the Business Case (see its *Product Description outline* in Appendix A). This should have stated how the achievement of benefits was to be measured. The plan should be defining:

- What benefit achievements are to be measured
- When benefit achievement can be measured
- How the achievement can be measured
- The pre-delivery situation against which achievement is to be compared
- Who is needed to carry out the measurements (individuals or skill types).

10.5.4 Responsibilities

The Project Manager has responsibility for this process.

10.5.5 Information needs

Table 10.2 CP2 information needs

Management information	Usage	Explanation
Issue Log	Input	Unactioned Project Issues will form the basis of any follow-on actions
Business Case	Input	This will reveal benefits whose achievement cannot be measured immediately and will therefore need a post-project review
Risk Log	Input	Check for any risks to the operational use of the end product(s)
Post-Project Review Plan	Output	Suggested plan for a post-project review for ratification by Project Board
Follow-on Action Recommendations	Output	Recommendations for further work, which the Project Board must direct to the appropriate audience for attention

10.5.6 Key criteria

- Is a post-project review needed to measure achievement of business benefits and re-examine the quality of products after a period of use?
- How much time needs to elapse before these benefits can be measured?
- Are the benefits for this project alone or combined with the outcomes from other projects?

- Which 'pending' Project Issues should be recommended for follow-on action by the operations and support team?
- Which 'pending' Project Issues should be recommended to be turned into Project Mandates for potential enhancement projects or referred to programme management for further action?

Hints and tips

Arrangements for any post-project review should be discussed informally with the Project Board before making any recommendation, so as to avoid any disagreement in the subsequent process, *Confirming Project Closure* (DP5).

The date for the post-project review should be set as soon after the project closes as would allow adequate assessment. The quality of a product may have appeared fine during testing, but is it still good after a period in the working environment? Also, where some benefits will take much longer to come to fruition, it is worth considering a recommendation to the Project Board that these are the subjects of other, later post-project reviews.

Dependent on the type of project product, there may be contractual issues to be resolved for the operational and maintenance support of the products.

A copy of the follow-on actions should always be sent to the operational support group to keep it informed.

Where the project is part of a programme, the Project Board's recommendation to close the project should be reviewed by programme management in the light of the list of follow-on actions recommended.

If the project is part of a programme, the follow-on actions should be assigned by programme management, where appropriate.

10.6 Project Evaluation Review (CP3)

10.6.1 Fundamental principles

Successful organisations learn from their experiences with projects. This is more likely if the lessons learned are somehow preserved beyond the end of the project.

10.6.2 Context

This is the internal project evaluation. The aim here is to assess how successful the project has been, not how successful the end product is. There may be a separate external evaluation – for example, from a quality assurance group.

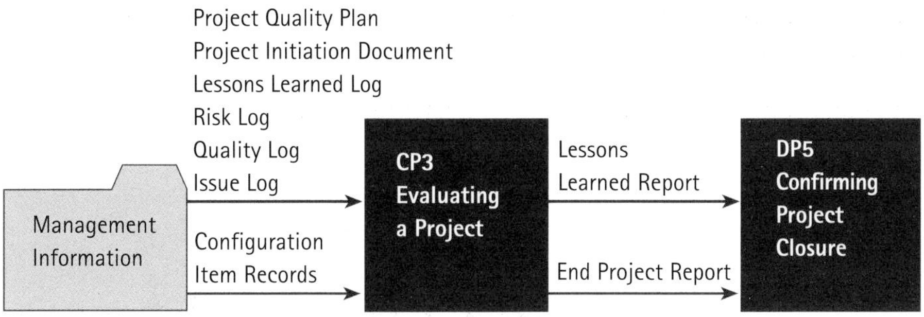

Figure 10.5 Project Evaluation Review

The comments gathered over the project in the Lessons Learned Log are arranged into a Lessons Learned Report. The log is created at the outset of the project and incremented as the project progresses with observations on what aspects can usefully be noted to help future projects. It should include observations on management, specialist and quality procedures.

Again, the results are to be input to the Project Board process, *Confirming Project Closure* (DP5).

10.6.3 Process description

The objectives of the process are to:

- Update the Project Plan with actuals from the 'final' stage
- Assess the results of the project against what it was intended to achieve
- Examine the records of the completed project to assess the quality of its management, especially quality and risk management
- Identify lessons to be learned from the project and applied on future projects.

End Project Report

The updated Project Plan allows the Project Manager to document in the End Project Report the effectiveness of the project management processes, and how well the project has performed against its Project Initiation Document, including the original planned cost, schedule and tolerances.

Not all benefits will have been achieved by the time of project closure. Any achievements or non-achievements that can be defined should be part of the report. A note of any benefits that need to be measured after operational use of the final product is passed to *Identifying Follow-on Actions* (CP2).

The report should also take into consideration the effect on the original Project Plan and Business Case of any changes that were approved. The End Project Report should give final statistics on changes received during the project and the total impact of approved changes. Any outstanding ones should match up with follow-on actions defined in *Identifying Follow-on Actions* (CP2). Statistics may also be appropriate for all quality work carried out.

The End Project Report is concerned with how well the project fulfilled its objectives. This includes the performance of all the project management team, the success of any scaling, use of the specialist processes and any tailoring of them, change control and quality results. The

Lessons Learned Report, by way of contrast, is concerned with how well the project was managed, and with the project's use of the project management processes and techniques – that is, PRINCE2 and any local standards used and what can be learned from this implementation.

Lessons Learned Report

At the start of the project a Lessons Learned Log should be created. A note should be added to this every time the project management team spot something about the management, specialist or quality processes and procedures that either made a significant contribution to the project's achievements or caused a problem.

In this process, all the notes should be correlated and turned into a report, including any views with hindsight on the project's management. The report should be aimed at answering the question 'What should be done differently next time?' As part of this process a configuration audit should have been done at the end of the project, as part of process CP1, to look for discrepancies. The cause of any discrepancies might justify an entry in the Lessons Learned Report.

The report is also the repository of any useful measurements and quality statistics collected during the project that will help in the planning and estimation of subsequent projects.

It is important to identify at the beginning of the project who should receive the Lessons Learned Report and make sure that the Project Board knows where it should go. There is little point in preparing the report, only to find that it will not be used.

10.6.4 Responsibilities

The Project Manager bears overall responsibility for this process, but additional information could come from anyone involved in the project.

10.6.5 Information needs

Table 10.3 CP3 information needs

Management information	Usage	Explanation
PID	Input	Original statement of project objectives, scope and constraints
Issue Log	Input	The reasons for Off-Specifications may provide lessons for future projects
Risk Log	Input	What risks were considered and what happened to them may provide lessons for future projects
Project Quality Plan	Input	This will indicate whether the quality policy and procedures were adequate, and correctly stated

Quality Log	Input	Statistics of the number of quality checks made and the errors found are useful to a quality assurance function
Configuration Item Records	Input	Are there any discrepancies between the records and reality? These may inform the conduct of future products
Lessons Learned Log	Input	This should be an ongoing document from the start of the project, completed with relevant notes on the good and bad lessons learned about management and specialist procedures, forms, other documents, tools and techniques
Lessons Learned Report	Output	This takes the Lessons Learned Log and writes it up into a report to be passed via the Project Board to the group charged with maintaining such quality standards
End Project Report	Output	Evaluation of the management, quality and specialist performance of the project and achievement of objectives as defined in the PID

10.6.6 Key criteria

- Which management processes or procedures have worked well?
- Which management processes have had problems?
- Was it easy to achieve the required quality?
- Which quality procedures have worked well?
- Were there any weaknesses in quality procedures for specific types of product?
- How well did risk strategies work?
- Were there any unforeseen risks?
- How well were the risks managed?
- Was the contingency used?
- Was training in the management, quality and delivery processes and procedures adequate? Were there recognisable benefits from the level of training given or recognisable problems caused by lack of training?
- How well did any support tools work?
- Could anything have been done to improve skill levels before the relevant work was done?
- If there has been deviation from the Project Initiation Document, is the Project Board still prepared to accept the project closure? Are those deviations reflected in the End Project Report and Lessons Learned Report? Where appropriate, are any deviations reflected in the Follow-on Action Recommendations?

Hints and tips

Concentrate on items that can be of use to future projects.

Observations on successful elements can be as useful as identification of failures and omissions.

Deviations documented in the End Project Report, the Lessons Learned Report and the Follow-on Action Recommendations should, as far as is sensible, avoid overlap – in other words, the same deviations should not be unnecessarily recorded in several places.

Consider whether there are any lessons about the quality procedures that should be directed to any quality assurance function. These might be weaknesses in current standard practices, new quality testing requirements from the products of the project that are not currently covered by standards or new ways of testing quality that the project has pioneered.

Where the project is part of a programme, the programme support office should review the Lessons Learned Report for applicability to the programme or to individual projects within the programme.

There are a number of possible recipients of the Lessons Learned Report. The aim is to identify the group that will distribute the report to other projects, not just current ones but any that may be starting up in the future. Ideally, this should be a group that has the responsibility to maintain project management standards. Some organisations have a project management office; others make the responsibility part of the duties of a quality assurance group. Elsewhere it may be known as management services or the central Project Support Office.

11
PLANNING (PL)

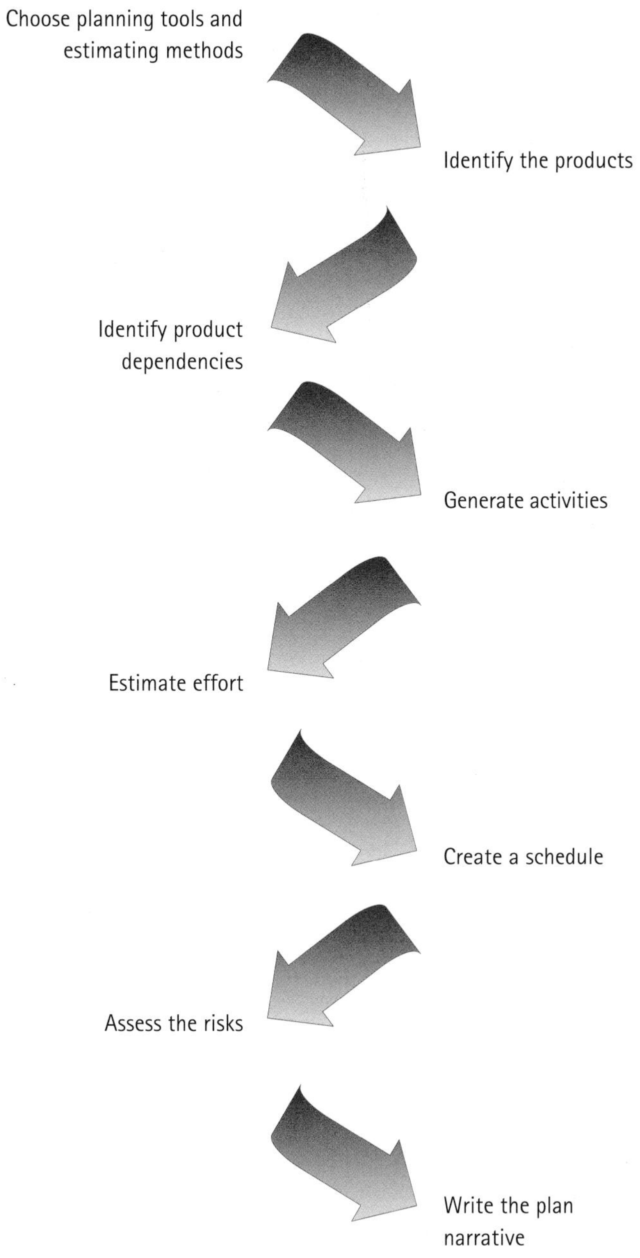
Choose planning tools and estimating methods
Identify the products
Identify product dependencies
Generate activities
Estimate effort
Create a schedule
Assess the risks
Write the plan narrative

Fig 11.1 Overview of Planning

11.1 Fundamental principles

Effective project management relies on an effective planning and control process. Even small projects require planning.

Planning provides all personnel involved in the project with information on:

- What is required
- How it will be achieved and by whom, using what specialist equipment and resources
- When events will happen.

The *Planning* (PL) process is where the technique of product-based planning is used. Product-based planning is a key technique of PRINCE2 and provides a comprehensive platform for effective planning. It is the technique that enables the Project Manager to:

- Define what the project has to deliver
- Provide descriptions of the required products, the skills needed to develop the products, plus measurable statements of the quality required and how the presence of that quality is to be tested
- Objectively monitor and control progress.

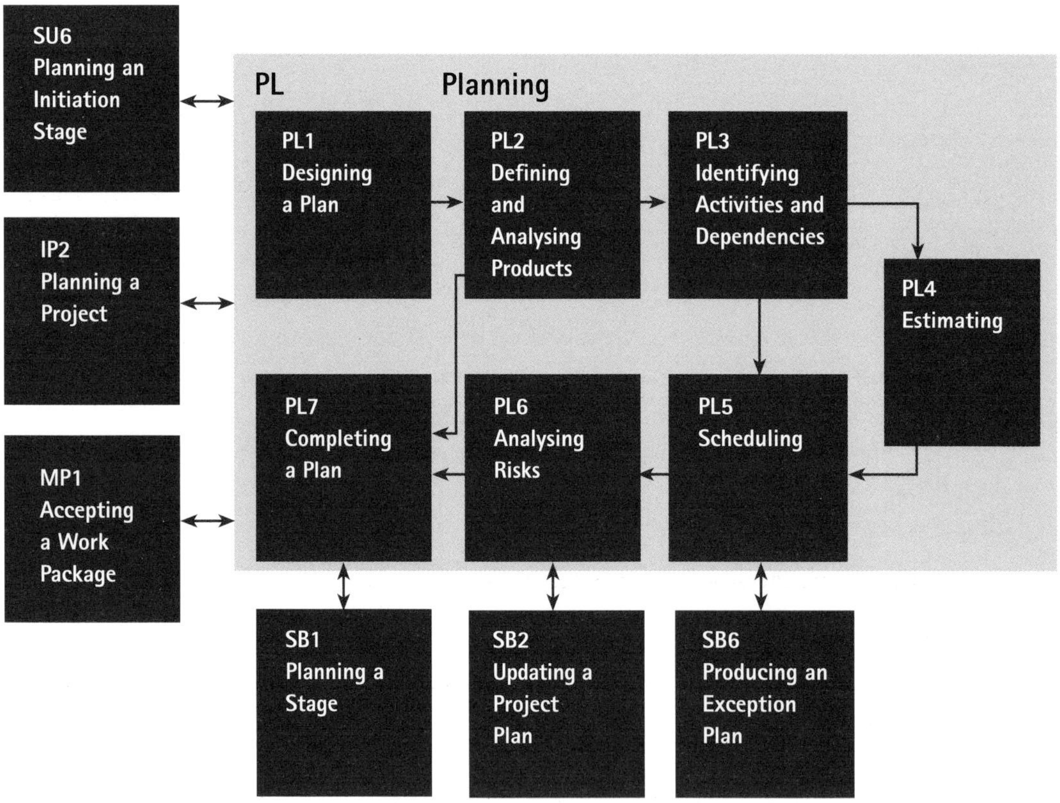

Figure 11.2 Planning

11.2 Context

Planning is a repeatable process and plays an important role in other processes, the main ones being:

- *Planning an Initiation Stage* (SU6)
- *Planning a Project* (IP2)
- *Planning a Stage* (SB1)
- *Updating a Project Plan* (SB2)
- *Accepting a Work Package* (MP1)
- *Producing an Exception Plan* (SB6).

Planning is also an iterative process. There will be a series of loops through the planning steps as extra information becomes available or adjustments are made.

11.3 Process description

The philosophy behind producing plans in PRINCE2 is that:

- Plans are constructed by identifying the products required, and then the activities and appropriate resources necessary to deliver them
- Plans should cover management needs as well as the customer's products
- There should be assurance that all activities are thought through in advance and to a level consistent with the control requirements identified in the Project Initiation Document.

The product-based planning technique provides a start to the planning activity and a planning framework. It involves:

- Establishing what products are needed for this plan
- Describing those products and their quality criteria
- Determining the sequence in which each product should be produced and any dependencies.

After these initial steps, the normal steps of planning are:

- Deciding when the activities should be done and by whom
- Estimating how much effort each activity will consume
- Estimating how long the activities will take
- Agreeing what quality control activities and resources are needed
- Producing a time based schedule of activities
- Calculating how much the overall effort will cost

- Producing the budget from the cost of the effort plus any materials and equipment that must be obtained
- Assessing the risks contained in the plan
- Identifying the management control points needed
- Agree tolerance levels for this plan.

The steps involved are the same for all levels of plan.

Several iterations of the *Planning* process are normally needed.

The Project Approach is a prerequisite for planning. This should have been defined as part of *Starting up a Project* (SU).

11.3.1 Scalability

Planning is essential, regardless of type or size of project. The amount of detail varies according to the needs of the project.

The Product Checklist is optional in a small project. People might prefer its tabular form to a Gantt chart, but the choice should be one or the other, not both.

The first process *Designing a Plan* (PL1) is done only once in a project. Where the project is part of a programme, all the design decisions will probably have been taken at programme level. In a small project it may be just a matter of deciding on a planning tool (if any).

Hints and tips

Keep plans relevant. Be aware of the audience for the prepared set of plans and aim to provide an appropriate level of detail.

Time must be allowed for planning because it is a time-consuming exercise. Planning for the next stage should start towards the end of the current stage.

It is easier and more accurate to plan short stages than long ones.

Past Lessons Learned Reports are an excellent source of information and guidance for planning at all levels, and should be referenced where appropriate.

Where the project is part of a programme, programme staff should be involved or referenced during planning to ensure that any questions that affect the programme are resolved. This will help avoid rework following presentation of the plan.

Involve those with Project Assurance roles in proposing quality-checking resources. This should happen in team plans as well as Stage Plans.

11.4 Designing a Plan (PL1)

11.4.1 Fundamental principles

A plan is the backbone of every project and is essential for a successful outcome. Good plans cover all aspects of the project, giving everyone involved a common understanding of the work ahead.

Designing a plan will ensure that all aspects are adequately covered. It is important that all involved can easily assimilate the plan.

11.4.2 Context

This process includes decisions on the approach to planning for the project and therefore needs to be used early in the project. These decisions must be made before any of the other PL processes can be used.

It may be sensible to have one plan format for presentation in submissions seeking approval and a more detailed format for day-to-day control purposes.

The strategies for tackling the project and ensuring quality of the products will already have been defined during *Defining Project Approach* (SU5) and *Planning Quality* (IP1).

11.4.3 Process description

Choices need to be made for presentation and layout of the plan, planning tools, estimating methods, levels of plan and monitoring methods to be used for the project. Any recipients of plans and their updates should be identified. There may be a central function that consolidates all plans for senior management, particularly if the project is part of a programme.

Presentation and layout

Decisions need to be made about how this plan can best be presented given the audience for the plan, and how it will be used. This will include the use of diagrams versus text, and will be driven in part by any standards adopted by the Project.

Planning tools

One of the first decisions will be to identify any planning and control aids to be used by the project. There may be a company standard or the customer may stipulate the use of a particular set of tools. The choice of planning tool may in part, however, depend on the complexity of the project. If so, the choice may need to be deferred until after some of the other planning processes.

Estimating

The method(s) of estimation must be chosen. Each facet of the project may need its own estimation method. Estimating may be done by:

- Using computer tools

- A group of experienced planners
- Top-down or bottom-up methods
- Discussion with those who will do the work
- Any combination of these.

The methods chosen should be evaluated and comments about their effectiveness made in the End Project Report and Lessons Learned Report when the project ends.

The estimating methods to be used in the plan may affect the plan design, so decisions on the methods to be used should be made as part of plan design.

Allowances

There are two possible allowances that may have to be considered for inclusion within the project's plan structure, a change budget and a contingency plan. These are not mandatory and their use depends on each project's circumstances.

11.4.4 Responsibilities

Ultimately, the responsibility for the decisions in designing a plan rests with the Project Board, but in practice the Project Manager would produce recommendations for informal Project Board approval. Local standards may pre-empt some of the decisions, and where third parties are being used the Team Manager will usually expect to use their own standards. The Project Assurance roles have a responsibility to check the designs.

11.4.5 Information needs

Table 11.1 PL1 information needs

Management information	Usage	Explanation
Project Approach	Input	The approach may impact on the number of stages and plan levels required
Project Quality Plan	Input	The contents of plans, level of detail and monitoring needs will be affected by the Project Quality Plan
Company planning standards	Input	These may identify the planning and estimating tools and methods to be used
Project Brief (or PID)	Input	Scope of the work to be planned
Plan design	Output	A statement of the planning approach, levels of plan, tool set to be used and major monitoring methods

11.4.6 Key criteria

- What planning, estimating, monitoring and risk assessment methods will be used?
- What tool set should be used to help with planning, estimating, monitoring and risk assessment?
- What level of detail about the products, their creation, quality checks and plan monitoring does the Project Manager require for day-to-day control?
- What level of detail does the Project Board need:
  - before commitment to a plan?
  - to monitor progress against a plan?
- How many levels of plan are suitable for this project?
- To what level of detail does each plan need to go?
- How will any quality checks be shown on the plans?
- How will tolerances be assigned?
- Should there be a change budget?
- What level of productivity for team members should be used?
- How will contingency allowances be handled (if appropriate)?

Hints and tips

A lot of time can be wasted in producing a very good plan to achieve the wrong objective.

The use of planning tools is not obligatory, but it can save a great deal of time if the plan is to be regularly updated and changed. A good tool can also validate that the correct dependencies have been built in and have not been corrupted by any plan updates.

The Project Manager should decide what level of efficiency is to be taken for project members when planning their work. No one is 100 per cent efficient. The estimator must know how to treat non-planned time such as telephone calls, ad hoc meetings and sickness.

Watch out for 'double counting' – for example, adding in allowances both when estimating and when scheduling.

It may be sensible to consider different levels of presentation of the plan for the different levels of readership. Most planning software packages offer such options.

When working with sub-contractor companies, a copy of their plan(s) may form part of the overall plan. A decision will need to be taken on whether sub-contractor plans are shown separately or built into the Project and/or Stage Plans.

Not all projects need a 45-page plan, but equally a half-sheet of paper is likely to be insufficient for most Project Plans.

Where the project is part of a programme, the programme may have developed a common approach to project planning. This may cover standards (for example, level of planning) and tools. These will be the starting point for designing any Project Plans. Any project-specific variations should be highlighted and the agreement of the programme management sought.

11.5 Defining and Analysing Products (PL2)

11.5.1 Fundamental principles

By defining a plan in terms of the products to be delivered, the creation, quality and suitability of those products can be managed and controlled more easily. In addition, by defining the required products, everyone involved can see and understand the required outcome.

11.5.2 Context

Once the decisions have been made in *Designing a Plan* (PL1), this process will be the normal starting point for producing the plan.

11.5.3 Process description

This process is divided into three steps:

- Identify the specialist products and the management products to be produced
- Describe each of them in terms of their quality requirements and ensure that they are fully understood and agreed by everyone involved (this requires the creation of the necessary configuration records)
- Sequence them in their logical order of creation.

These steps are described in more detail in *Product-Based Planning* (Chapter 22).

11.5.4 Responsibilities

The Project Manager is responsible for the process for Project and Stage Plans. Team plans may well be produced by Team Managers for agreement by the Project Manager. There should be consultation with the customer, user(s) and specialists to ensure that all the required products are covered. Those with Project Assurance responsibilities should vet the results. The Configuration Librarian is responsible for the creation of Configuration Item Records for all necessary products, as specified in the Configuration Management Plan.

11.5.5 Information needs

Table 11.2 PL2 information needs

Management information	Usage	Explanation
Plan Design	Input	This defines the level of plan required, the tools to be used, estimating techniques and the approach to contingency allowances
Project Quality Plan	Input	This will guide the selection and placement of quality control activities. Also contains the Configuration Management Plan. This will identify products which will require Configuration Item Records
Product Breakdown Structure	Output	A hierarchical table of all the products required to be created in the plan
Product Descriptions/ Configuration Item Records	Output	A description of each product plus its quality criteria. This is also the initial creation of the Configuration Item Records for the products
Product Checklist	Output	A draft list of the major products of the plan
Product Flow Diagram	Output	A diagram showing the sequence in which the products should be produced

11.5.6 Key criteria

- Has the plan reached the agreed level of detail?
- Are all management products identified, as well as specialist products?
- Are the management products/activities added correctly to the sequence of work?
- Does the plan need any products from external sources?
- Have these been shown correctly in the sequence of work?
- Have known risk factors been identified?
- Does the management of risks require any extra products?
- Have these been shown correctly in the sequence of work?

Hints and tips

A decision point can be associated with one or more intermediate products on which the decision will be based.

The list of products, their required sequence and their descriptions should all be quality reviewed for accuracy and completeness.

Required quality is a criterion against which the product will be accepted. When working in a customer/supplier relationship, this may form the basis of project acceptance.

The definition of the major end products or results required to satisfy the business needs should be documented within the Project Initiation Document as part of the project objectives.

11.6 Identifying Activities and Dependencies (PL3)

11.6.1 Fundamental principles

Simply identifying products may be insufficient for scheduling and control purposes. The activities implied in the delivery of each of the products need to be identified to give a fuller picture of the plan's workload.

11.6.2 Context

This process is done when the Product Flow Diagram from process (PL2) has been agreed. Identification of activities may reveal that extra products are needed, causing a reiteration of PL2. As with the other *Planning* (PL) processes, *Identifying Activities and Dependencies* (PL3) will be performed iteratively. Activities and extra products may be required in response to identified risks, so the Risk Log should be checked.

11.6.3 Process description

This process is divided into three steps:

- Identify all activities necessary to deliver the products
- Establish the interdependencies between activities
- Ensure that dependencies both internal and external to the project are covered.

All the activities required to create or change the planned products have to be identified (see Figure 11.3). After a Product Flow Diagram has been created, the activities are most easily identified by using a transformation process. Transformation identifies the activities needed to take one product or set of products and turn it into the next product or set of products in the sequence. There may be only one activity or there may be a group of activities, depending on the level of detail required for the plan.

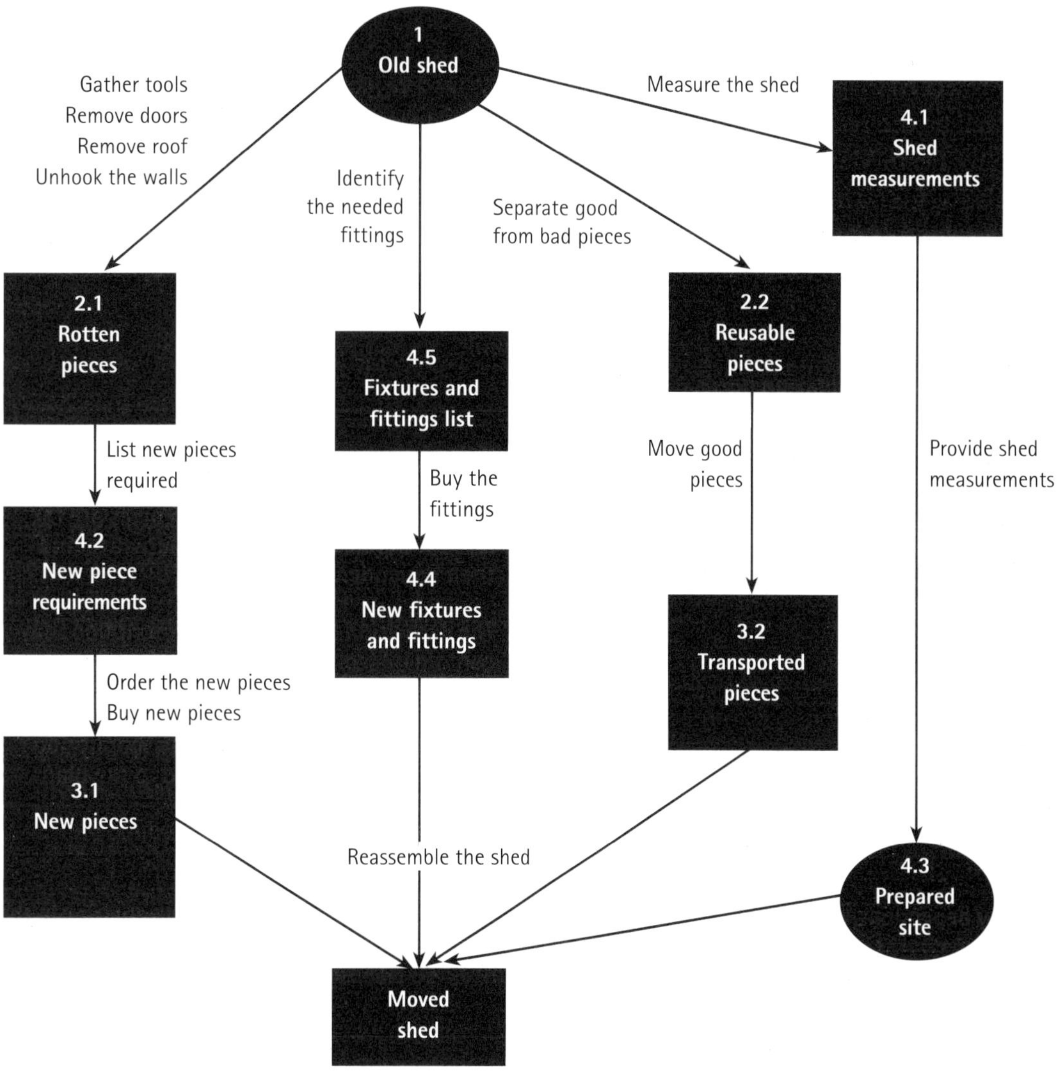

Figure 11.3 Product Flow Diagram

The list of activities should normally include management activities as well as the activities needed to develop the specialist products.

Any constraints should also be identified. External constraints may be:

- The delivery of a product required by this project from another project
- Waiting for a decision from programme management.

Wherever possible, external constraints should be described as a dependency on the availability of an external product. Resource-based constraints (for example, 'Is the resource available to do the work?') are not considered here. They are a question for the scheduling process.

The activities should include any that are required to interact with external parties – for example, obtaining a product from an outside source or converting external products into something that the plan requires.

	Activity	Duration in hours	Dependency
1	Measure the shed	0.25	–
2	Provide shed measurements	0.5	1
3	Gather tools	0.5	–
4	Remove doors	1	3
5	Remove roof	2	4
6	Unhook the walls	1	1, 5
7	Separate good from bad pieces	1	6
8	List new pieces required	0.5	7
9	Order the new pieces	2	8
10	Buy new pieces	1	9
11	Move good pieces	2	7
12	Identify the needed fittings	0.5	7
13	Buy the fittings	2	12
14	Prepared site	(external)	–
15	Re-assemble the shed	4	14, 11, 13, 10

Figure 11.4 List of activities

11.7.4 Responsibilities

The Project Manager is responsible for estimation on Project and Stage Plans. The Team Manager will be responsible for team plan estimates. It is a difficult job and, wherever possible, extra help should be sought. It requires previous experience in the subject matter of the plan as well as training in the job of estimation. This is where expertise from Project Support can help greatly.

11.7.5 Information needs

Table 11.4 PL4 information needs

Management information	Usage	Explanation
All planning information so far	Input	Products and activities that require estimation
Activity estimates	Output	Estimated activities are passed to *Scheduling* (PL5)

11.7.6 Key criteria

- Is the estimation to be made against known resources or general requirements for skill and experience?
- What level of productivity should be taken for the resources?
- Should allowance be made for different levels of productivity in the resources?

- What supporting infrastructure does the estimate assume is in place? Are these assumptions documented in the plan text?
- Has allowance been made for quality checking products?

Hints and tips

There may be a computerised estimating tool, written text, tables, graphs or formulae available for the type of work identified in the plan. These tools are normally based on information of actual time taken by identical or similar activities to the ones required in the plan. The figures can generally be tailored to some extent to reflect more closely the environment for which the plan in question applies.

Estimation is best performed by a group of two or three people experienced in both the subject matter and estimating. This number tends to balance out any individual over-optimism or pessimism in estimation.

Where possible, estimating should include discussion with the people who will be responsible for doing the work.

In large projects or difficult areas of work, it is prudent to estimate at least twice, either by using two distinct approaches or by allowing two different sets of people to estimate independently.

When resources have been estimated it may become clear that resource constraints cannot be met. If this should happen, the matter should be referred to the Project Board.

More uncertainty should be expected in a Project Plan than in a Stage Plan. A Stage Plan is for a shorter timeframe, in the near future and planned in much greater detail.

Refer to the Lessons Learned Reports from earlier similar projects. Understanding past estimation successes and failures by reading the Lessons Learned Reports of other projects can assist with estimating.

Any assumptions made during the estimation process should be documented under the heading of 'Assumptions' in the plan text. If the assumption refers to a risk, the risk should be documented in the Risk Log.

11.8 Scheduling (PL5)

11.8.1 Fundamental principles

A plan can only show the ultimate feasibility of achieving its objectives when the activities are put together in a schedule that defines when each activity will be carried out.

11.8.2 Context

Scheduling follows estimates of the time for each activity and is then followed by an assessment of the risks inherent in the plan. The schedule may need to be revisited during the planning process to refine and improve the way in which the plan will be carried out.

11.8.3 Process description

The objectives of scheduling are to:

- Match available resources to the identified activities
- Schedule work according to the defined sequence and dependencies
- Smooth resource usage within the bounds of the identified dependencies and any overall time constraints
- Identify surplus resource effort or additional resource effort needed and negotiate with the Project Board to resolve these
- Calculate total requirements for human and other resources and produce a cost for these.

There are many different approaches to scheduling. The steps can either be done manually, or a computer-based planning and control tool can be used.

Typical scheduling steps are:

- *Draw a planning network*: take the list of activities and their durations and produce a network of the activities, based on the dependencies, from beginning to end. This provides useful information, such as what the total duration might be, given no resource constraints. Figure 11.5 is a network of the listed activities from 'Gather tools' onwards for moving the garden shed shown in Figure 11.4.

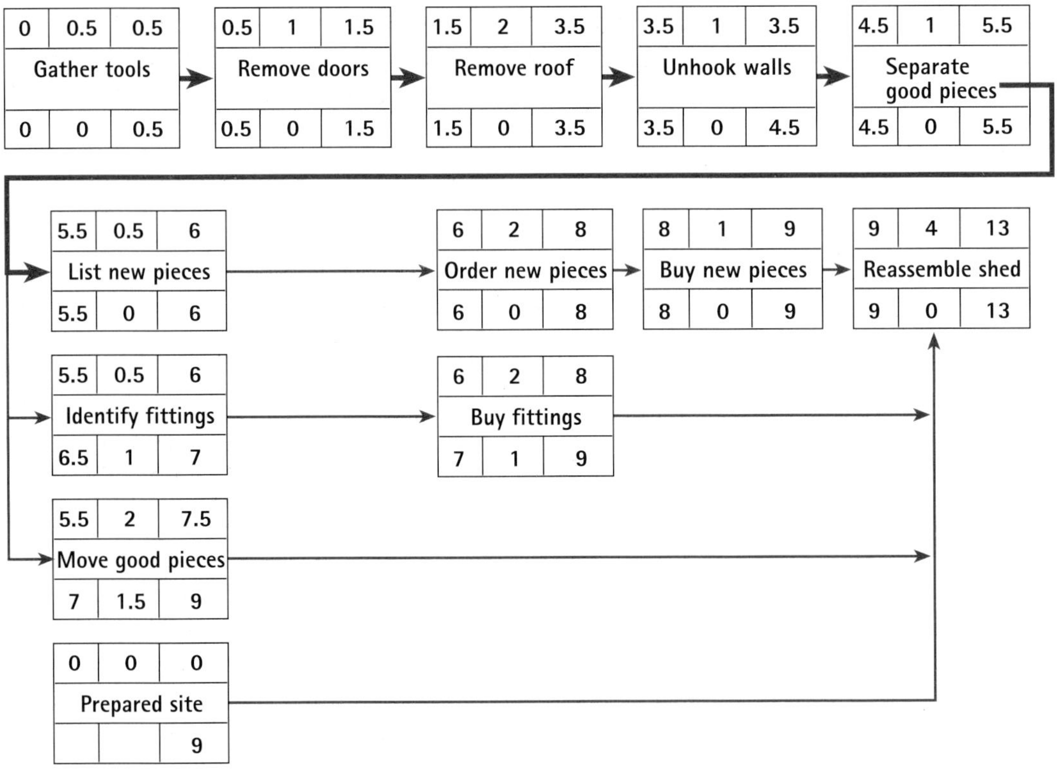

Figure 11.5 Planning network

The number in the top centre column of each box is the duration time for that activity. The number on the top left is the 'earliest start time' for the activity. The number on the top right of each box is the 'earliest finish time' for that activity. For example, the 'earliest finish time' for 'remove roof' is after 3.5 hours. The bottom set of columns in each box are, from left to right, the 'latest start time', the 'float' and the 'latest finish time' for the activity.

- *Assess resource availability*: the number of people who will be available to do the work (or the cost of buying in resources) should now be established. Any specific information should also be noted - for example, names, level of experience, percentage availability, dates available from and to, external or internal resource. The project may also require non-human resources; this availability must also be assessed.
- *Produce a draft schedule and assign responsibilities*: using the resource availability and the information from the activity network, resources are now allocated to activities. The rule is 'allocate resources in order of ascending float', that is, allocate resources first to activities with zero float (which, by definition, are on the critical path). Those activities with the greatest amount of spare time (float) are lowest in priority for resource allocation.

  The result will be a schedule that shows the loading of work on each person and the usage of non-people resources. The duration of each activity can be amended, based on knowledge of the resource effort required and the availability of the appropriate resource type.

The schedule is often displayed as a Gantt chart. Figure 11.6 illustrates a Gantt chart for the shed move.

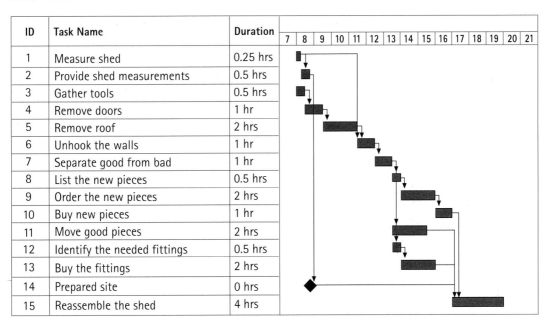

ID	Task Name	Duration
1	Measure shed	0.25 hrs
2	Provide shed measurements	0.5 hrs
3	Gather tools	0.5 hrs
4	Remove doors	1 hr
5	Remove roof	2 hrs
6	Unhook the walls	1 hr
7	Separate good from bad	1 hr
8	List the new pieces	0.5 hrs
9	Order the new pieces	2 hrs
10	Buy new pieces	1 hr
11	Move good pieces	2 hrs
12	Identify the needed fittings	0.5 hrs
13	Buy the fittings	2 hrs
14	Prepared site	0 hrs
15	Reassemble the shed	4 hrs

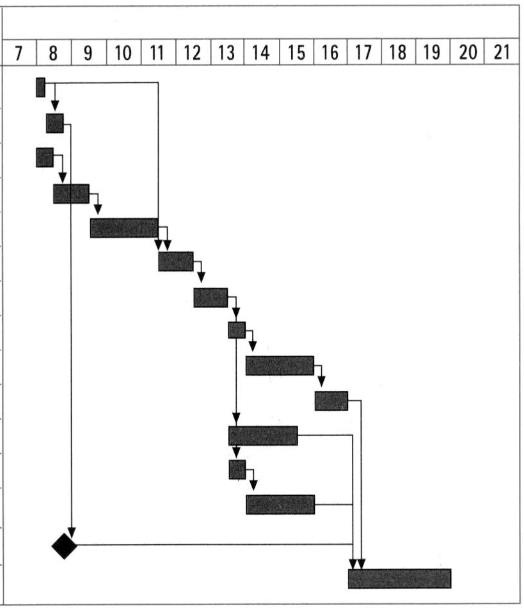

Figure 11.6 Gantt chart example

- *Level resource usage*: the scheduling of any allowances should be considered and built into the plan.

  The first allocation of resources may result in uneven resource usage, maybe even over-utilisation of some resources at certain times. Responsibilities are reassigned, activities moved about within any 'float' they may have, and activity duration changed from the original estimate to reflect resource constraints. The end result of this step is a final schedule in which all activities have been assigned and resource usage equates to resource availability

- *Confirm control points*: the first draft schedule enables the control points identified earlier (in the Product Flow Diagram, Figure 11.3) to be confirmed by the Project Board. End of stage activities (for example, drawing up the next Stage Plan, producing an End Stage Report) should be added to the activity network and a new schedule produced
- *Calculate resources and costs*: the resource requirements can now be tabulated and the cost of the resources and other costs calculated to produce the plan budget. Remember to consult Project Assurance personnel in case they wish to add specific resources to quality-checking activities.

11.8.4 Responsibilities

The Project Manager is responsible for scheduling. For team plans, the Project Manager would involve the person responsible for the work contained in the plan – for example, a Team Manager. Help may be provided by Project Support staff allocated to the Project.

11.8.5 Information needs

Table 11.5 PL5 information needs

Management information	Usage	Explanation
Activity estimates	Input	When studied with the resource numbers, these give the activity duration
Activity dependencies	Input	These give the required sequence of work in the schedule
Resource availability	Input	The start and end dates of resource availability, plus the amount of time they are available in this period, are required
Schedule	Output	A list of activities and their allocated resources, plus the dates over which the activities will take place

11.8.6 Key criteria

- Have all types of required resource been considered?
- Has the critical path been identified?
- Has sufficient monitoring been planned for activities on the critical path?
- Have any training requirements been incorporated?
- Has resource availability been realistically assessed?

Hints and tips

At project level, resources need not be identified by name, but the type of skills required to carry out an activity should be identified.

The availability of the resources required (including those required for quality reviews) should be checked with the relevant line managers.

Be realistic about the availability of resources. Allowance should be made for holidays and time that people will spend on non-project activities. The average working week is only 4 days after allowing for holidays, training, sickness, etc. Of those 4 days, at least another half-day will be spent on other duties, even by dedicated staff – for example, quality reviewing for other projects, line management and meetings.

The use of a skills matrix may assist a scheduler when using internal resources. This will allow appropriate people to be pinpointed, as well as giving an overall view of the skills available to the project.

When the availability of resources has been discussed with line managers, any agreement reached with them should be documented immediately.

11.9 Analysing Risks (PL6)

11.9.1 Fundamental principles

Commitment to a course of action without consideration of the risks inherent in that course is courting disaster. Risks should be considered and modifications made to the course of action in order to remove or lessen the impact of those risks.

11.9.2 Context

Once the plan has been produced, it should still be considered a draft until the risks inherent in the plan have been identified, assessed and the plan possibly modified.

11.9.3 Process description

Analysing risks runs parallel to all other planning work. It is an iterative process and the results of analysing risks may result in returning to previous steps and repeating the process as necessary.

An overview of the management of risk is given in the Components section of this manual (see Chapter 17).

Any planning assumptions create a risk. Is the assumption correct?

Each resource should be examined for its potential risk content. Is the resource a known quantity? Is the quality of work required and the ability to meet deadlines known? Is the level of commitment known? Will the resource be totally under the control of the Project Manager? Where the answer is 'No', there is a risk involved. Countermeasures would include tighter and more frequent monitoring until confidence in the resource is achieved. It might be better to allocate work that is either easy to do or less critical to the schedule until the skill level has been checked.

Each activity should be checked for risk. Is there any spare time or does the entire schedule depend on no slippage for the activity? Everything on the critical path therefore represents a risk. At the very least the countermeasures should include more frequent monitoring to give early warning of any problem.

The planning information produced so far should be examined for risks. All identified risks should be entered into the Risk Log.

Examples of risk that might be inherent in a plan are:

- A sub-contractor might fail to deliver a needed product on time
- A product to be delivered by a third party might be of poor quality
- A resource may not perform at the required level
- A specific resource, on which the plan is dependent, might be removed from the project
- External events may create a crisis
- The timetable is very tight and depends on the timely delivery of several products, any of which might be delayed.

11.9.4 Responsibilities

The Project Manager is responsible for the analysis and monitoring of risks, with assistance from those with Project Assurance responsibilities. There may be risks outside the control of the Project Manager. These fall within the responsibilities of the Project Board. The Project Manager should discuss any such risks with the Project Board to ensure that the risks are being adequately monitored. They should also discuss risks with Team Managers and subject experts.

11.9.5 Information needs

Table 11.6 PL6 information needs

Management information	Usage	Explanation
All previously planned information	Input	Basis of the risk assessment
Risk Log	Update	Any new risks should be added to this

11.9.6 Key criteria

- Are there any dependencies on products or other support from external sources that have not been listed as risks?
- When does the cost of risk avoidance or reduction approach the cost of the risk if it occurs?

- Has a range of means of addressing each risk been considered?
- Are the risks so great that they put the viability of the project in question?

Hints and tips

There are various risk management and analysis methods and tools available to assist with these aspects of the process.

Allocate to each high risk or critical activity a resource in which management has confidence.

Monitor the schedule and quality of any external product to be delivered on which any activities in the plan are dependent.

Check items such as holidays and training to make sure that they don't have an impact on the schedule.

In case of illness consider the actions needed for any resource that cannot be replaced. Train other resources as back-up for any critical and scarce skills.

The addition of risk management activities will elongate the schedule and require extra resources. The benefit of the protection against risks is valuable, but remember to allow for the 'cost' of these activities in the plan.

Where the project is part of a programme, any risks identified at programme level should be examined for impact on the project. Where there is an impact, the risk should be added to the project's Risk Log. Careful consideration should be given to whether further project-specific risk analysis is required. Similarly, any project risks should be examined for programme impact.

11.10 Completing a Plan (PL7)

11.10.1 Fundamental principles

A plan is not simply a diagram. It is incomplete without certain supporting narrative sections.

11.10.2 Context

Having completed the schedule and assessment of the risks satisfactorily, the plan, its costs and its supporting text need to be consolidated.

11.10.3 Process description

Narrative needs to be added to explain the plan, any constraints on it, external dependencies, assumptions made, the risks identified and their required countermeasures. Suggested texts for a Project Plan and a Stage Plan are given in Appendix A, *Product Description outlines.*

The format of plans presented for approval should be a summary and should show the major products and activities that will occur throughout the plan and describe the resource and cost requirements. Project Board approval will 'freeze' the plan as a baseline.

The graphical presentation of the plan is normally a Gantt or bar chart. Most computerised planning-and-control packages provide a report in this format. Such packages also provide a report on cost and resource requirements, typically in the form of a spreadsheet.

The majority of the material for the narrative sections of the plan will evolve as the previous steps in the planning cycle are undertaken. Some of it will already be known because of adherence to local standards.

Tolerance margins for the plan should be agreed with the next level of management. Depending on such factors as size, complexity and risk there must be agreement on what amount of deviation from planned cost and timescale is to be allowed before the plan is considered to be out of control. Tolerances are discussed more fully in *Controls* (Chapter 16).

The products of the planning cycle should be checked for completeness and reasonableness by people experienced in planning and who know the project subject.

Amend the plans as required by the quality check.

The Product Checklist is now completed with the planned start and end dates added from the plan.

11.10.4 Responsibilities

The Project Manager is responsible for completing each plan, assisted by Team Managers where appropriate, and by Project Support staff where available.

11.10.5 Information needs

Table 11.7 PL7 information needs

Management information	Usage	Explanation
Assessed plan	Input	Basics of the final planning package
Product Checklist	Update	Start and end dates added to the list
Completed plan for approval	Output	For approval by the Project Board

11.10.6 Key criteria

- When considering a suitable level of tolerance, what level of confidence is there in the plan?
- Has consideration been given to the business risks and constraints when setting tolerance levels?
- Has the format of the plan's presentation material been agreed with the Project Board?
- Will the planning tool produce acceptable formats and quality for the presentation?

Hints and tips

Keep plans simple. It is a good discipline to try to keep all graphical plans presented to the Project Board to one sheet of paper. In this way the plan is easily prepared, easily read and therefore more likely to be understood. Anything that cannot be displayed in this way should be summarised and the detail included in a lower level of plan. Similarly, do not use complex symbols, or present plans that require education or too much explanation for them to be understood.

It might be worth considering the replacement of the graphical Project Plan with the Product Checklist.

Do not rely on pictures alone. As far as planning is concerned, it is not necessarily true that 'a picture paints a thousand words'. Although a Gantt chart can show what is intended to happen and then what actually happened, it does not show why it should happen that way or why something is different from the plan.

The narrative of a plan describes the thought that went into it, the assumptions made in preparing the plan, and any inherent risks. This is particularly important when presenting plans for approval. The readers are then able to accept both the plans and the assumptions and risks behind them and the planner obtains informed approval and commitment to the plans from senior management.

If the layout of the report produced by a software package is not satisfactory, the data can usually be transferred to a spreadsheet or graphical package, where the required presentation can be constructed.

The Project Manager should discuss the plan informally with the Project Board and any assurance responsibilities appointed by the Project Board before formally presenting it for approval.

The presentation of the plan should be appropriate for the audience. In some circumstances it may be necessary to break down into further detail areas of a plan for the use of teams or individuals.

Be wary of producing an over-complex plan, containing lots of detail that might be better supplied in narrative form. A confusing or too detailed plan may 'switch off' the reader.

It helps if assumptions are consistent across all the projects of a programme.

12 INTRODUCTION TO THE PRINCE2 COMPONENTS

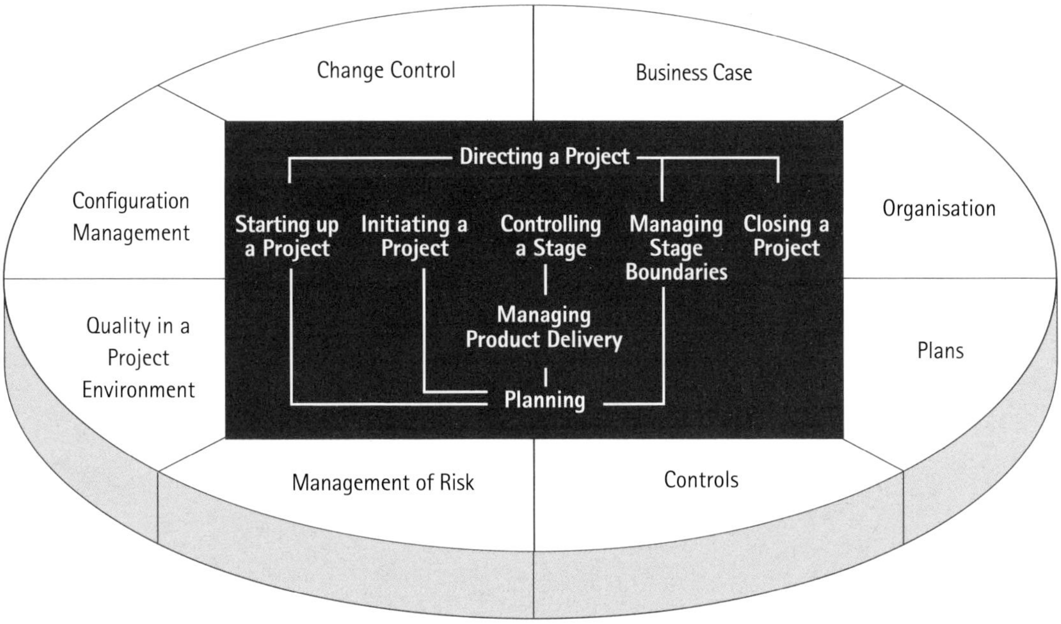

Figure 12.1 The PRINCE2 template

As shown in Figure 12.1, PRINCE2 has a number of components that are used by the processes:

- Business Case
- Organisation
- Plans
- Controls
- Management of risk
- Quality in a project environment
- Configuration management
- Change control.

The following chapters of the manual explain the philosophy of these components and how they should be used.

There are also hints and tips on using and tailoring the components to suit various situations and types of project.

13 BUSINESS CASE

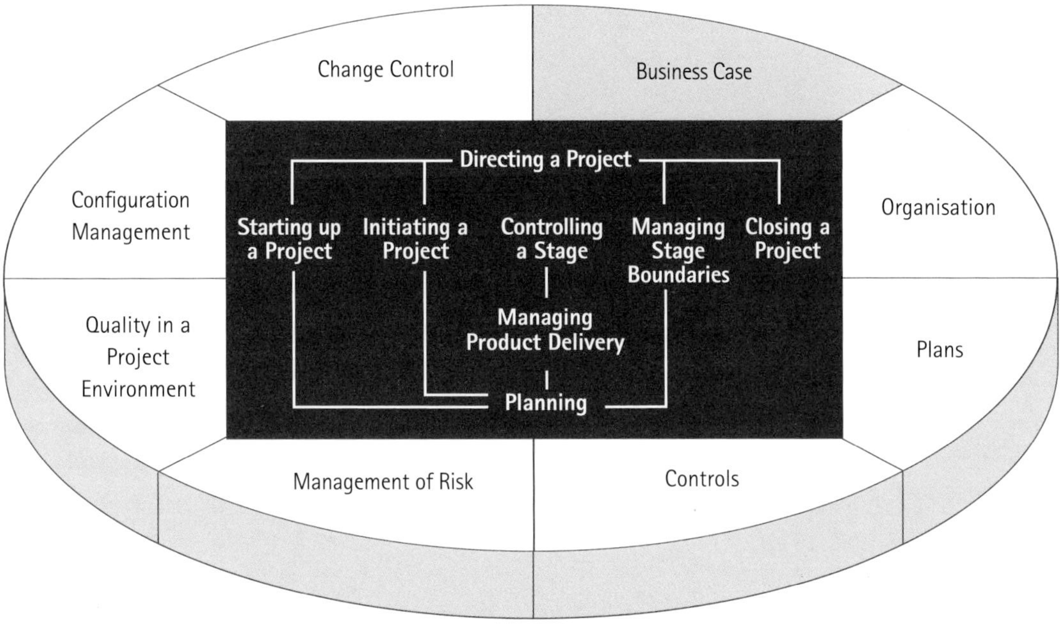

Figure 13.1 The Business Case

This chapter outlines an approach to the development of a project's Business Case. PRINCE2's key philosophy is that its Business Case must drive the project. If a satisfactory Business Case does not exist, a project should not be started. If a Business Case is valid at the start of a project, but this justification disappears once the project is under way, the project should be stopped. The focus of the Business Case should be on the *totality* of business change, not just one element of it, e.g. the cost of buying new equipment should take into account the impact on personnel, training, changed procedures, accommodation changes, relationships with the public, etc.

In PRINCE2, the Business Case is developed at the beginning of the project and maintained throughout the life of the project, being reviewed by the Project Board at each key decision point, such as end stage assessments.

13.1 What is a Business Case?

- The Business Case is a description of the reasons for the project and the justification for undertaking the project, based on the estimated costs of the project, the risks and the expected business benefits and savings.
- The Business Case covers the entire scope of change to the business that is affected by the project.

- The Business Case is the most important set of information for the project. It drives the decision-making processes and is used continually to align the project's progress to the business objectives that are defined within the Business Case.
- Business Cases need to be developed according to any organisational standards that might exist and the nature of the project. Some Business Cases will require significant effort in their development and approval because the project will have a major impact on the organisation. Others will require less effort and involvement as the project is self-contained and has minimal impact on other parts of the organisation. Also the level of investment required will influence the rigour with which the Business Case is developed.

13.2 What should a Business Case contain?

There are many different Business Case formats. Each Business Case should contain sufficient management information such that it can be used effectively throughout the project. The Business Case in PRINCE2 is supported by other documentation such as the Risk Log, which will contain the detailed information underpinning the Business Case. As a minimum in PRINCE2, the Business Case should contain information under the following headings. These are the ones that appear under 'composition' in the Business Case *Product Description outline* in Appendix A.

13.2.1 Reasons

This section provides an explanation of the reasons why the project outcome is needed. This information should be in the Project Mandate. If not, the area needs further investigation during *Starting up a Project* and the rationale for the project established.

13.2.2 Options

This section should describe in outline the various options that have been considered to deliver the required outcome. The chosen option should be indicated, together with a summary of the reasons why. This information provides assurance that alternatives were considered.

13.2.3 Benefits

This section should identify each benefit that is claimed would be achieved by the project's outcome. Each one should be described clearly in measurable terms. It is important to define the current status of each benefit in quantifiable terms so that measurable improvements can be assessed after the project has completed. Consideration should be given to defining how and when the measurement of improvement can be made. The Executive has the responsibility for defining benefits.

A 'negative' way of assessing benefits may be useful as part of the overall justification for the project. This describes what will happen if the project is not done, e.g. the loss of market share, large maintenance costs, heavy legal penalties for non-compliance with new laws.

13.2.4 Risks

This section contains a summary of the key risks facing the project that, if they happen, would seriously affect delivery of the outcome. Details of how these risks will be managed are contained in the Risk Log.

13.2.5 Cost and timescale

This information comes from the Project Plan. If the Project Plan is not yet completed, it may be necessary to outline the project's costs and timescales in the Business Case and refine them when the Project Plan is completed.

13.2.6 Investment appraisal

This illustrates the balance between the development, operational, maintenance and support costs against the financial value of the benefits over a period of time. This period may be a fixed number of years or the useful life of the product.

The baseline for investment appraisal is the 'do nothing' option, i.e. what will the picture of costs and benefits be if the project is not undertaken? This is compared to the picture expected from completing the project.

Wherever possible, benefits should be expressed in tangible ways. To start with, the customer, user or Executive may define many benefits as intangible, e.g. 'happier staff'. It is worth making the effort to think carefully about intangible benefits to see if they can be expressed in more tangible ways. For example, 'happier staff' may translate into less staff turnover and/or less time off for stress-related problems. Both of these can be converted into a likely monetary saving.

Evaluation

There are many ways to evaluate the claimed benefits and investment appraisal. For example, sensitivity analysis can be used to determine whether the Business Case is heavily dependent on a particular benefit. If it is, this may affect project planning, monitoring and control activities and risk management, as steps would need to be taken to protect that benefit.

Another example is to define three views of the achievement of the benefits, i.e. what are we really expecting, what might we achieve if things went well, what might be the worst-case scenario? The latter might be affected by building into the costs an allowance for estimating inaccuracies, tolerances and risks. This usually reveals if benefit expectations are reasonable or are really over-optimistic. The result of this analysis can lead to revision of the decision to go ahead with the project which would form a basis for setting any benefit tolerance. This technique is sometimes referred to as GAP analysis (good, average, poor).

13.3 Developing a Business Case

- The Executive is the 'owner' of the project's Business Case. It is the Executive's responsibility to ensure the project's objectives, costs, benefits, etc. are correctly aligned with the business strategy or programme objectives

- The Executive may delegate the development of the Business Case to the Project Manager. However, the data upon which the case will be developed will be largely provided by the business and responsibility for an accurate and effective Business Case remains with the Executive. On large projects, the Business Case may require a small team of experts to develop the contents. On small projects, the Business Case may only require one person to develop the information
- During start-up, the information from the Project Mandate is used to develop the information required for the Business Case. Where the project is part of a programme, much of the required information should be available within programme-level documentation. Projects operating within a programme environment may not in themselves deliver business benefits. They may be required to deliver products that are prerequisites for other projects. The Business Case should reflect this
- During initiation, the Business Case is updated to provide more detailed information on the benefits, risks, options and costs. The Project Plan, once completed, gives a much clearer view of risks and costs. This information is used to refine the investment appraisal or GAP analysis. The detailed information on risks is kept in the Risk Log for formal monitoring during the project
- Formal approval of the Business Case is required from the Executive to ensure there is senior management commitment to the project. This approval is part of the formal review done at the end of *Initiating a Project* (IP)
- During each stage of the project, the Business Case is reviewed to confirm that the project remains on track and to check that the Business Case remains valid within the business context. The Business Case requires formal change control and configuration management to ensure any changes to the project's environment are accurately reflected and approved before revising the Business Case. The Business Case remains a 'live' document during the project and all decisions regarding project progress are made using the Business Case as the 'driver'
- The project's Business Case provides all stakeholders with basic information about the project. The Communication Plan for the project should cover how and when the Business Case information is to be communicated to stakeholders and how they can provide feedback and raise issues concerning the Business Case
- At project closure, the Business Case is used to confirm that the project has delivered the required products and that the benefits expected can be realised in an appropriate timeframe by the business. The Business Case provides the basis for the Post-Project Review Plan, to ensure that the later assessment of whether the outcome was successful or not is firmly linked to the Business Case.

13.4 Development path of the Business Case

Figure 13.2 shows the PRINCE2 management products that affect the Business Case or use its contents.

The Project Mandate should contain some basic elements at least of the Business Case. At this point there may be only some reasons why a solution is being sought. If the project is part of a programme, the Project Mandate may be just a pointer to the programme's Business Case. If the project were preceded by a feasibility study or something similar, the Project Mandate would contain a copy of the Business Case for the preferred option.

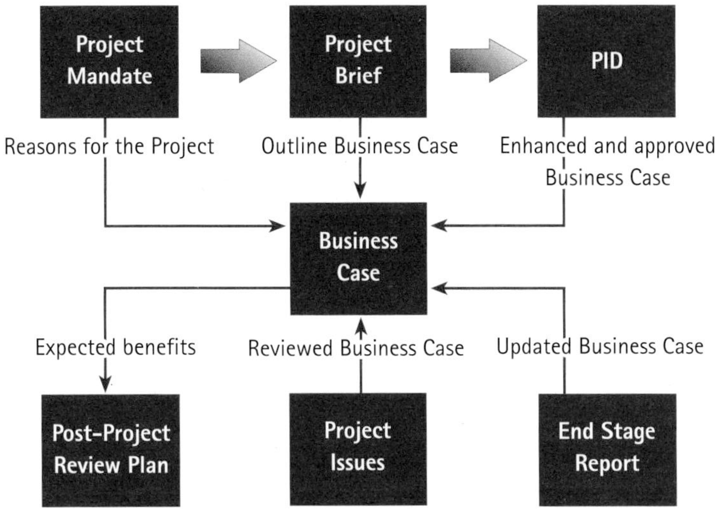

Figure 13.2 Business Case development path

Depending on how much information there was in the Project Mandate's Business Case, *Starting up a Project* (SU) might be required to bring it up to a basic level, containing sufficient justification for the Project Board's *Authorising Initiation* (DP1).

Initiating a Project (IP) is the process that fully develops the Business Case as part of the Project Initiation Document. It now contains the latest information on the costs and time to develop the product, taken from the Project Plan. If not done before, this is also where all benefits will be defined (or revised) and, wherever possible, put into measurable terms. This is needed for the Project Board's *Authorising a Project* (DP2) and also in readiness for the post-project review.

As part of *Managing Stage Boundaries* (SB) the Business Case is revised for each End Stage Report with information from the stage that is closing and the next stage's plan. This revision is a major input to the Project Board in its decision in *Authorising a Stage or Exception Plan* (DP3).

As part of *Examining Project Issues* (CS4) each Project Issue is reviewed for any impact that it might have on the Business Case.

At the end of a project the Business Case provides the agenda for much of the creation of the Post-Project Review Plan, submitted by the Project Manager as part of *Closing a Project* (CP).

Hints and Tips

It can be useful to hold a stakeholder workshop to help clarify the business objectives and impact of the project. Capturing input from stakeholders to inform the Business Case will help achieve greater commitment to the project.

14 ORGANISATION

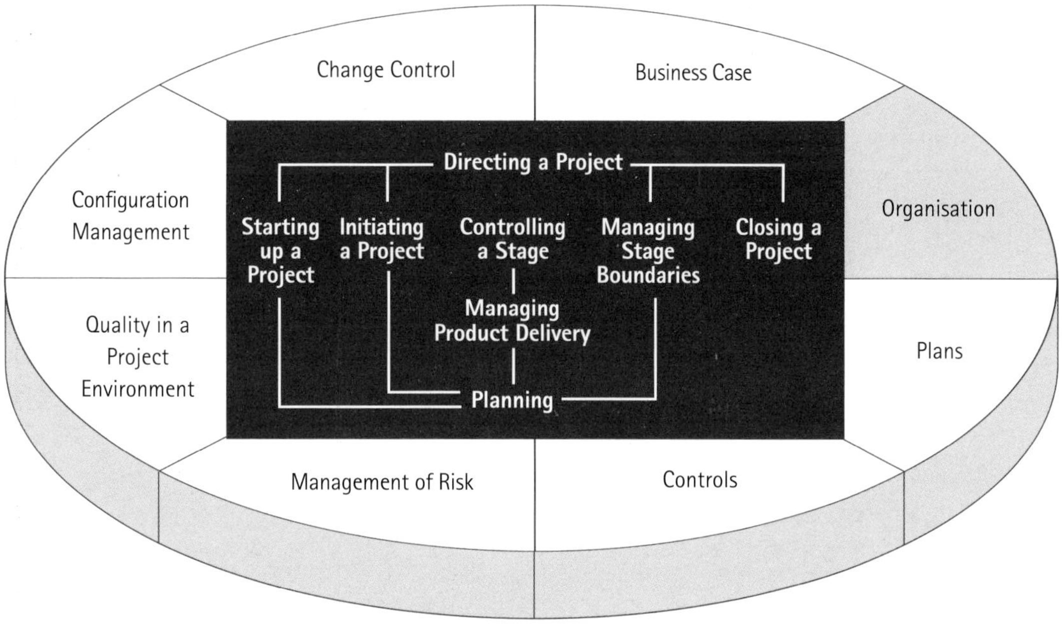

Figure 14.1 Organisation in the PRINCE2 template

14.1 Overview

The PRINCE2 project management structure is based on a customer/supplier environment. The structure assumes that there will be a customer who will specify the desired outcome, make use of the outcome and probably pay for the project and a (prime) supplier who will provide the resources and skills to create that outcome. This assumption has a bearing on how the project is organised.

The customer and supplier may be part of the same corporate body or may be independent of one another.

Establishing an effective organisational structure for the project is crucial to its success. Every project has need for direction, management, control and communication. PRINCE2 offers an approach that provides these elements and is sufficiently flexible to be mapped to any environment.

A project needs a different organisational structure from line management. It needs to be more flexible and is likely to require a broad base of skills for a comparatively short period of time. A project is normally cross functional, an involved partnership.

The project organisation may combine people who are working full time on the project with others who have to divide their time between the project and other duties. The Project

Manager may have direct management control over some of the project staff, but may also have to direct staff who report to another management structure.

The management structure of those with a problem to be solved will very often be different from that of those providing the solution. They will have different priorities, different interests to protect, but in some way they must be united in the common aims of the project. The management level that will make the decisions and the commitments on behalf of their interests may be too busy to be involved on a day-to-day basis with the project. But projects need day-to-day management if they are to be successful.

14.1.1 Four layers

PRINCE2 separates the management of the project from the work required to develop the products and concentrates on the former.

A fundamental principle is that the project organisation structure has four layers, illustrated in Figure 14.2, which undertake:

- Corporate or programme management
- Direction of the project
- Day-to-day management of the project
- Team management.

The first of these instigates a project and defines overall constraints. The project management team performs the next three layers

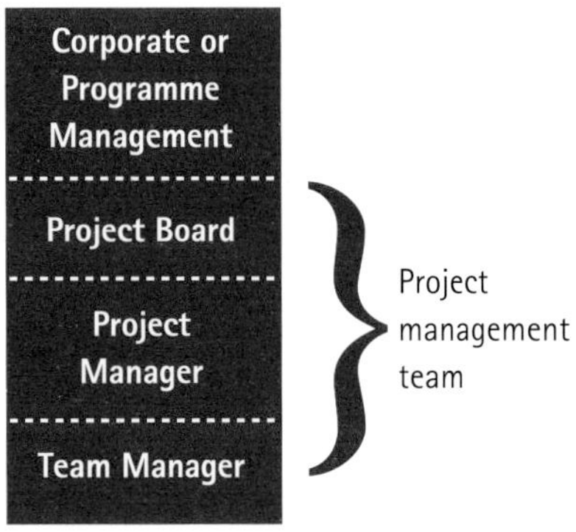

Figure 14.2 The four layers of a project

14.1.2 Project management structure

PRINCE2 provides a structure for a project management team that supports:

- Roles for decision makers
- Management by exception for the decision makers
- Full or part-time project management
- Controlled delegation of some day-to-day management responsibilities, where required, to Team Managers

- Roles for the independent inspection of all aspects of project performance
- Administrative support, as required, to the Project Manager and Team Managers
- Agreement by all concerned on what the various roles and responsibilities are
- Lines of communication between the project management team members.

The PRINCE2 project management structure (Figure 14.3) consists of roles and responsibilities that bring together the various interests and skills involved in, and required by, the project. For the project to be successful, it is important to define these roles at the outset.

A project management structure is a temporary structure specifically designed to manage the project to its successful conclusion to meet the requirements defined in the Project Brief. The structure allows for channels of communication to decision-making forums and should be backed up by job descriptions that specify the responsibilities, goals, limits of authority, relationships, skills, knowledge and experience required for all roles in the project organisation.

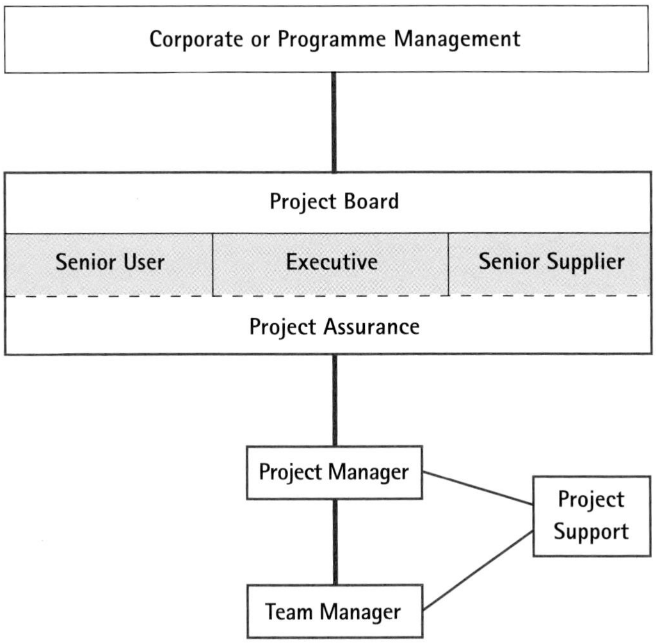

Figure 14.3 Project management structure

All the roles set out in Figure 14.3 need to be accommodated within job descriptions. In addition, the relationship between people's authority and responsibility within the project and their normal management responsibility and authority needs to be understood by those concerned and documented.

In order to be flexible and meet the needs of different environments and different project sizes, PRINCE2 does not define management *jobs* to be allocated on a one-to-one basis to people. PRINCE2 defines *roles*, which might be allocated, shared, divided or combined according to the project's needs. Associated with this is the concept that some responsibilities for a role can be moved to another role or delegated, but they should not be dropped. If a responsibility is dropped, the risks of doing so must be addressed.

Some of the PRINCE2 roles cannot be shared or delegated if they are to be undertaken effectively. The Project Manager role cannot be shared, neither can the Project Manager or Project Board decision-making roles be delegated. The Project Board may, however, delegate some or all of its Project Assurance responsibilities (see section 14.2.4), but it still remains accountable for these.

Corporate cultures differ, PRINCE2 can be used whatever the culture or corporate organisation structure.

Hints and tips

Contractual and commercial arrangements will often influence the ideal project management organisation.

The project organisation structure should include links with the more permanent, functional or line management structures within both the customer and supplier communities.

14.1.3 Three project interests

Figure 14.4 represents the structure and composition of the Project Board. Three interests must be represented on the Project Board at all times.

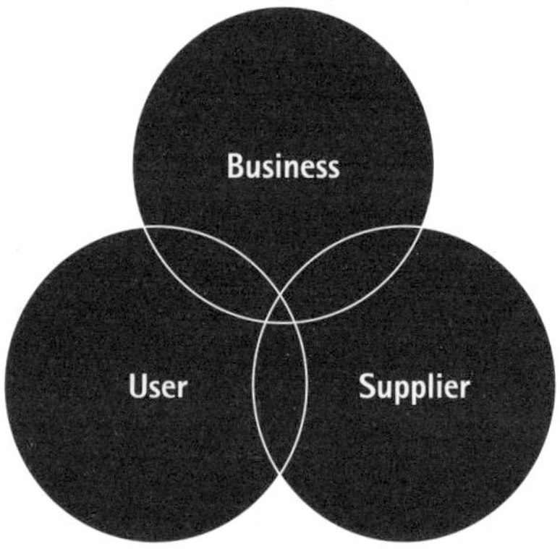

Figure 14.4 The three project interests

Business

The product(s) of the project should meet a business need. The project should give value for money. There should, therefore, be representation from the business viewpoint to ensure that these two prerequisites exist before commitment to the project is made and remain in existence throughout the project. PRINCE2 makes a distinction between the business and the requirements of those who will use the final product(s). The Executive role is defined to look after the business interests (representing the customer).

User

There will be an individual, group or groups for whom some or all of the following will apply:

- They will use the final product
- The product will achieve an objective for them
- They will use the end result to deliver benefits
- They will be impacted by the project outcome.

The user presence is needed to specify the desired outcome and ensure that the project delivers it. User management should therefore be represented on the Project Board. They will typically form part of the customer representation.

Supplier

The creation of the end product will need resources with certain skills. Representation is needed from the supplier who will provide the necessary skills. The project may need to use both in-house and external supplier teams to construct the final outcome.

14.1.4 The customer/supplier environment

PRINCE2 is defined in terms of a customer/supplier environment. There are many combinations of customer and supplier that may affect the organisation and control of the project, including:

- A customer with an in-house 'supplier'. Even here they may have separate budgets and therefore need separate 'Business Cases'.
- Projects sponsored by a single customer versus those supporting multiple customers
- Those projects that are supplied by a single source versus those with multiple suppliers
- Situations that involve a consortium of equal customers and/or suppliers versus those that involve a 'legal' hierarchy of either:
  - projects supplied by an in-house source (part of the parent organisation)
  - those with a mixture of in-house and external suppliers.

The project's direction set by the Project Board must reflect the agreements and decisions of the three interests as defined in section 14.1.3. It may be difficult in certain business environments to contemplate having the supplier represented on the Project Board, but there must be a common platform for decisions that affect all parties. The Senior Supplier role is needed if the Project Board is to enable full decision making.

At times there may be questions of confidentiality or conflicts of interest. The customer representatives on the Project Board may not wish to discuss everything in front of the supplier and vice versa. There is nothing to prevent either party having private meetings to make internal decisions and/or discuss their position before meeting with the other party. The main objectives are full communication and agreed decisions by all three parties and the Project Board composition including the Senior Supplier is a powerful aid to achieving these.

If there are problems in identifying an external contractor who could take the role of Senior Supplier (for example, the project involves procurement and the supplier has not yet been identified) the customer's procurement manager or contracts manager could take on the role. Whoever is in the Senior Supplier role must have the appropriate authority to deploy supplier resources.

In customer/supplier situations there will always be two Business Cases: the customer's and the supplier's. Unless otherwise stated, in this manual any references to the Business Case mean the customer's Business Case.

14.2 The PRINCE2 project management team

The following is a summary of the project management team. A full description of each role is provided in Appendix B, *Project Management Team Roles*.

14.2.1 Project Board

The Project Board represents at managerial level the business, user and supplier interests of the project. The Project Board members must have authority because they are the decision makers and responsible for the commitment of resources to the project, such as personnel, cash and equipment.

The level of manager required to fill the roles will depend on such factors as the budget, scope and importance of the project. This will often result in people in senior management positions sitting on Project Boards. Their Project Board responsibilities will be in addition to their normal work, which makes it important that PRINCE2 offers them 'management by exception', keeping them regularly informed but only asking for joint decision making at key points in the project.

The Project Board consists of three roles:

- Executive
- Senior User
- Senior Supplier.

These roles should ideally be assigned to individuals who can stay with the project throughout its life.

The Project Board is appointed by corporate or programme management to provide overall direction and management of the project. The Project Board is accountable for the success of the project and has responsibility and authority for the project within the remit (initially contained in the Project Mandate) set by corporate or programme management.

The Project Board approves all major plans and authorises any major deviation from agreed Stage Plans. It is the authority that signs off the completion of each stage as well as authorising the start of the next stage. It ensures that required resources are committed and arbitrates on any conflicts within the project or negotiates a solution to any problems between the project and external bodies. In addition, it approves the appointment and responsibilities of the Project Manager.

The Project Board is responsible for assurance that the project remains on course to deliver products of the required quality to meet the Business Case defined in the Project Initiation Document. According to the size, complexity and risk of the project, the Project Board may decide to introduce specific additional resources to address some of its Project Assurance activities. Project Assurance is discussed in section 14.2.4.

The Project Board is the project's 'voice' to the outside world and is responsible for any publicity or other dissemination of information about the project.

The Project Board is not a democracy controlled by votes. The Executive is the key decision maker with advice and commitments from others.

Executive

The Executive is ultimately accountable for the project, supported by the Senior User and Senior Supplier. The Executive is responsible for the following key aspects of the project:

Development and continuation of the project Business Case

Overseeing the development of a viable Business Case is part of ensuring that the aims of the planned change continue to be aligned with the business and establishing a firm basis for the project during its initiation and definition. The Executive should be responsible for securing the necessary investment for the business change.

The Executive has the responsibility throughout the project to ensure that the business benefits will be achieved.

Project organisation structure and plans

The Executive ensures that there is a coherent organisation structure and logical plan(s). This will involve being actively engaged with the work of project initiation.

Monitoring and control of progress

Monitoring and controlling the progress of the business change at a strategic level (at an operational level this is the responsibility of the Project Manager). The Project Manager is responsible for regular reports (Highlight Reports) to the Executive on progress of the business change. There will be inevitable issues that arise, requiring the Executive's advice, decision making and communication with senior stakeholders.

Problem referral

Referring serious problems upwards to top management as necessary, in a timely manner. Regular consultation will be required between those delivering the change and its stakeholders and sponsors. The Executive is responsible for ensuring the communication processes are effective and linkages are maintained between the project and the organisation's strategic direction.

Formal closure

Formally closing the project and ensuring that the lessons learned are documented: closure requires formal sign-off by the Executive that the aims and objectives have been met and that lessons learned are documented and disseminated. Some benefits may already be delivered. However, the activities at closure include the planning of the post-project review when the entire benefits realisation process will be assessed.

Post-project review

Ensuring that the post-project review takes place, whose purpose is to find out if the benefits, as stated in the Business Case, have been realised. The Executive is responsible for commissioning and chairing these reviews and ensuring that the relevant personnel are consulted and involved in the review process. The output is forwarded to the appropriate stakeholders.

Senior User

The Senior User is accountable for any products supplied by the user(s), such as making sure that requirements have been clearly and completely defined, that what is produced is fit for its purpose and for monitoring that the solution will meet user needs.

The role represents the interests of all those who will use the final product(s) of the project, those for whom the product will achieve an objective, those who will use the product to deliver benefits or those who will be affected by the project. The Senior User role is responsible for:

- Providing user resources
- Ensuring that the project produces products that meet user requirements
- Ensuring that the products provide the expected user benefits.

The Senior User is responsible for Project Assurance from a user perspective. Other resources may be assigned to undertake these Project Assurance activities on behalf of (and reporting to) the Senior User.

The Senior User role may require more than one person to cover all the user interests. For the sake of effectiveness, the role should not be split between too many people. The *Hints and tips* section gives guidance on solutions to the problem of too many contenders for the Senior User role.

Senior Supplier

The Senior Supplier needs to achieve the results required by the Senior User. The Senior Supplier is accountable for the quality of all products delivered by the supplier(s). Part of this is to ensure that proposals for designing and developing the products are realistic. The Senior Supplier aims to achieve the results required by the Senior User within the cost and time parameters for which the Executive is accountable. The role represents the interests of those designing, developing, facilitating, procuring and implementing. The Senior Supplier role must have the authority to commit or acquire the required supplier resources. The Senior Supplier has responsibility for the supplier's Business Case. The Senior Supplier role is responsible for assurance of the quality of supplied products. According to the volume and/or complexity of delivered products the Senior Supplier may delegate some or all of the Project Assurance activities while still remaining accountable.

In some environments the customer might share design authority for specialist solutions, or have a major say in it, along with the suppliers.

Hints and tips

Project Board members are normally very busy outside the project. There is a danger in larger projects that if they don't delegate their Project Assurance responsibilities these will not get done. If the Project Assurance activities are not delegated, Project Board members must seriously consider how the work associated with these responsibilities will get done, when they will find the time and how well those responsibilities will be carried out.

Roles may be combined but never eliminated.

It is advisable to avoid combining the roles of Senior User and Senior Supplier if there would be a potential conflict of interest.

Project Boards are the major decision makers. It is important that the business, user and supplier are represented, because they all need to make commitments to the project.

NOTE: Customer specialists may also be involved in setting the approach and direction of the project, especially in cases where the project is part of a programme.

Both the customer and the supplier may wish to appoint their own Project Assurance roles. In particular, the customer may feel the need for assurance about the specialist aspects of the project, independent of the supplier.

The Senior Supplier may wish to appoint a business assurance role to monitor the supplier's Business Case.

A large Project Board can become unwieldy and inhibit the decision-making process. If there are too many candidates for a Project Board role, they should be encouraged to appoint a spokesperson to carry out that role. In particular, if there are too many wanting to share the Senior User role, a user committee can be formed with a chairperson. The chairperson represents them as Senior User, reports back to the committee and takes direction from it before Project Board meetings.

The involvement of multiple suppliers may necessitate more than a single Senior Supplier representative on the Project Board.

Suppliers should not be in a position to overwhelm the business/user representatives by sheer weight of numbers.

Other interests can be invited to attend Project Board meetings to provide advice, etc. but not to take part in the decision making.

All Project Board members need training in Project Board procedures and responsibilities.

Where the project is one of a string, a decision is needed on who is the user. Is it an end user or is it the next project in the string?

Don't confuse the need for an organisation to manage the project with the need for a communication vehicle.

Project Board members should sign up to their agreed roles and responsibilities before taking the job on.

The authority levels required of Project Board members should match the needs of a project.

Where the project is part of a programme, the programme appoints the Project Board Executive and has the option of appointing the other Project Board members. Alternatively the Project Board Executive may be asked to select the other Project Board members. Where the latter is the case, the advice and approval of the programme should be sought.

There may sometimes be a lack of confidence between a programme and its projects. In order to ensure that a project that forms part of a programme maintains the focus required to fulfil the programme objectives, it will often be appropriate to have programme representation on the Project Board. This may be done either by appointing a programme representative into a Project Board role or by having a representative of programme management attend the Project Board meetings without taking a formal project role. In such cases project decisions that have a programme impact can be made more quickly. The programme representative is more likely to be able to make a decision on the spot, rather than the project having to wait until the programme's managers are consulted. This should lead to a reduction in delays or rework caused by having to wait for crucial decisions.

14.2.2 Project Manager

PRINCE2 provides for a single focus for day-to-day management of the project, namely the Project Manager, who has well-defined responsibilities and accountability. Figure 14.5 gives an idea of the many facets to the role of Project Manager. The Project Manager needs a project organisation structure that will take responsibility for or provide support in addressing these facets and provide support in performing some of the other facets.

The Project Manager is given the authority to run the project on a day-to-day basis on behalf of the Project Board within the constraints laid down by the board.

The Project Manager's prime responsibility is to ensure that the project produces the required products, to the required standard of quality and within the specified constraints of time and cost. The Project Manager is also responsible for the project delivering an outcome that is capable of achieving the benefits defined in the Project Initiation Document.

The Project Manager is responsible for the work of all the PRINCE2 processes except *Directing a Project* (DP)and the pre-project process *Appointing a Project Board Executive and Project Manager* (SU1). The Project Manager would delegate responsibility for the process *Managing Product Delivery* (MP), to the Team Manager(s) in projects using this role. The Project Manager manages the Team Managers and Project Support and is responsible for liaison with Project Assurance and the Project Board.

In a customer/supplier environment the Project Manager will normally come from the customer organisation, but there will be projects where the Project Manager comes from the supplier. In this case, the customer may appoint a 'project director' or 'controller' to be its day-to-day liaison with the Project Manager.

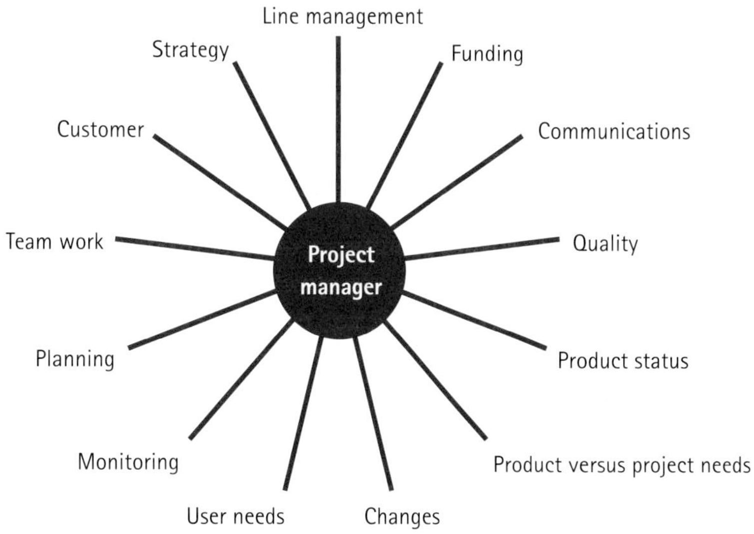

Figure 14.5 The many facets of the Project Manager role

Hints and tips

It may be beneficial to employ high-quality people part time rather than lesser quality people full time.

It is important to remember that this manual assumes that the Project Manager will be from the customer. It is possible that the Project Manager may be from the supplier – in such cases the customer/supplier interface moves from Project Manager/Team Manager to Project Board/Project Manager.

Where the Project Manager does not have direct authority over personnel required to work on the project, it is essential that the agreement of the appropriate managers is obtained (and maintained throughout the project) for the commitment of their personnel.

Remember that the Project Manager's role is to manage the work, not to do it.

The Project Manager must avoid becoming involved in low-level detail to the extent that sight is lost of the 'big picture', that is, what is going on in every part of the project.

Different Project Manager attributes are needed for different types of project.

In tailoring the Project Manager and Team Manager roles in a customer/supplier environment, consideration must be given to whether it is acceptable for customer resources to be managed by a supplier or supplier resources to be managed by the customer representative. If such a situation is permitted, the division of management responsibilities for human resource management should be made clear – for example, appraisals, promotion and training.

- Gaining commitment from the contributors and recipients
- The provision of personal targets.

Planning is not a trivial exercise. It is vital to the success of the project. A plan must contain sufficient information and detail to confirm that the targets of the plan are achievable.

It is essential to allocate time for the planning activity. Every project should have an initiation stage, in which time is allocated to identify and agree the scope of the project and to plan it in terms of management, resourcing, products, activities, quality and control. Time should also be allocated for the refinement of the Business Case. The initiation stage may or may not be formal, depending on the nature and complexity of the project. In addition, during the initiation stage and towards the end of every stage in the project except the last one, time should be allowed for planning the next stage in detail.

Without effective planning, the outcome of complex projects cannot be predicted in terms of scope, quality, risk, timescale and cost. Those involved in providing resources cannot optimise their operations. Poorly planned projects cause frustration, waste and rework.

15.2 What is a plan?

A plan is a document, framed in accordance with a predefined scheme or method, describing how, when and by whom a specific target or set of targets is to be achieved. A plan is a design of how identified targets for products, timescales, costs and quality can be met.

Plans are the backbone of the management information system required for any project. It is important that plans are kept in line with the Business Case at all times.

A plan requires the approval and commitment of the relevant levels of the project management team, i.e. the Project Board and Project Manager for the Project Plan and all Stage Plans, the Project Manager and a Team Manager for a team plan.

15.3 What are the elements of a plan?

When asked to describe a plan, many people think only of some sort of bar chart showing timescales. A PRINCE2 plan is more comprehensive. It should contain the following elements (making maximum use of charts, tables and diagrams for clarity):

- The products to be produced
- The activities needed to create those products
- The activities needed to validate the quality of products
- The resources and time needed for all activities (including project management and quality control) and any need for people with specific skills
- The dependencies between activities
- External dependencies for the delivery of information, products or services
- When activities will occur

- The points at which progress will be monitored and controlled
- Agreed tolerances.

The plans need to have the endorsement and approval of the Project Board. This endorsement should relate to the latest version and will emphasise the importance of the plan to the project. Plans should be presented as management reports, with key information documented in a way that the audience can understand, interpret and question. A Stage Plan might, therefore, be held in two forms: a summary plan suitable for presentation to the Project Board (the basis for authorisation) and the more detailed one used for day-to-day control of the stage.

The statement of activities and breakdown of resource requirements must be backed up by text that explains to the reader:

- What the plan covers (for example, delivery of specific products)
- The intended approach to implement the plan
- How adherence to the plan is to be monitored and controlled
- What management reports will be issued

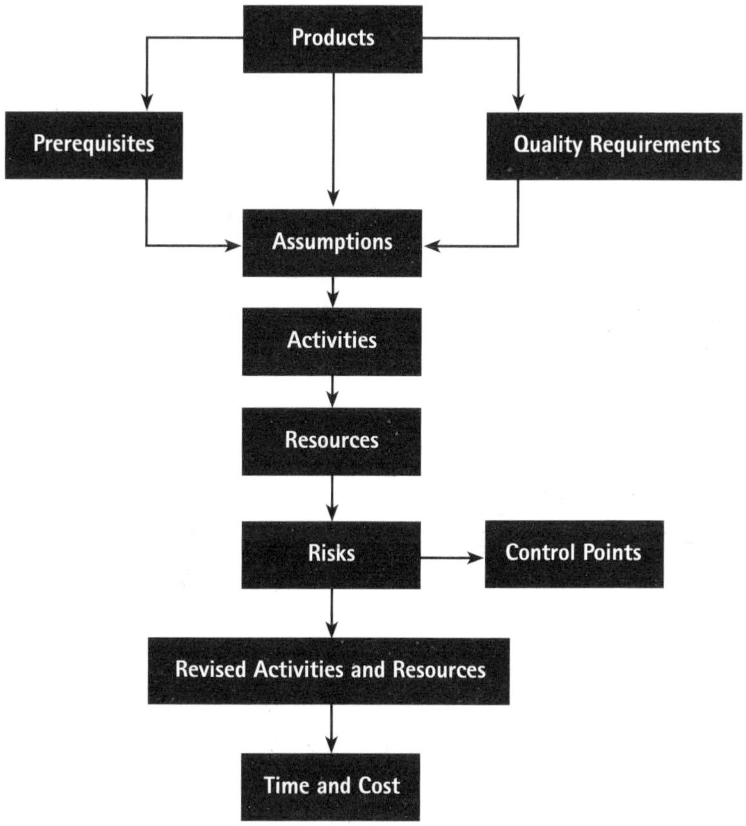

Figure 15.2 The elements of a plan

- The quality control methods and resources to be used
- Any assumptions on which the plan is based
- Any prerequisites that must be in place on day one of the plan

- What risks there are that may prevent the plan being achieved and what measures should be (or have been) taken to address these risks.

Figure 15.2 shows the elements of a plan and illustrates how it might be built up, starting from a list of the products to be produced. Any prerequisites are identified, together with the quality requirements of the products. These three elements lead to consideration of what assumptions are being made. The next consideration is to define the activities required to generate the products.

The dependencies between the activities are identified and then resources to carry out the activities are added. Risks are then considered, followed by the addition of control points. The last two steps might add to the activities and resources required. Finally, the overall time and cost are calculated.

15.4 The PRINCE2 approach

The PRINCE2 planning structure allows for a plan to be broken down into lower level plans containing more detail. But all plans have the same overall structure and are always matched back to the planned requirements, including quality and benefits, before approval.

15.5 Levels of plan

PRINCE2 proposes three levels of plan, the Project Plan, the Stage Plan and the team plan, to reflect the needs of the different levels of management involved in the project. Use of the team plans illustrated in Figure 15.3 will depend on the needs of the individual project. Team plans are explained in more detail later in this chapter, but, briefly, a Stage Plan may be broken down into a number of team plans (where, for example, a number of teams may be contributing to the work) or a set of sub-contractors' team plans may be assembled into a Stage Plan.

Where a Stage or Project Plan is forecast to exceed its tolerances, an Exception Plan will often be put forward that will replace the plan. Where a team plan is forecast to exceed its tolerances, a similar procedure should be followed between Project and Team Managers.

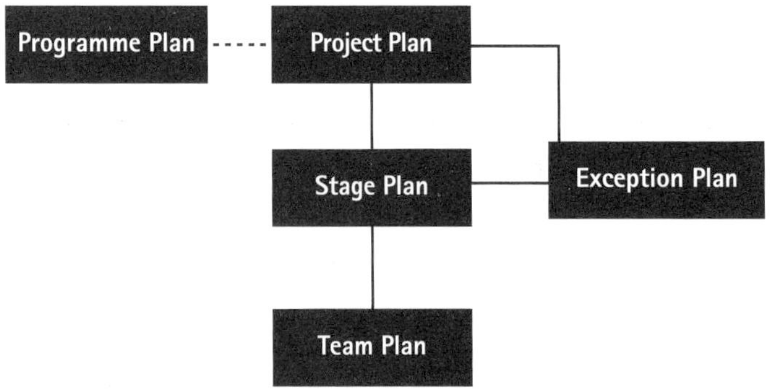

Figure 15.3 Plan levels in PRINCE2

The principal idea behind the levels is that the lower the level, the shorter the plan's timeframe and the more detail it contains. The project chooses the levels and, therefore, the number of plans it needs according to its size and extent of risk exposure. Activity durations and resource requirements become more difficult to estimate accurately the further into the future they extend. Regardless of this problem, there is still a need to provide a provisional estimate of the duration and cost of the project as a whole in order to gain approval to proceed.

It is seldom desirable, or possible, to plan an entire project in detail at the start. The reasons for this include:

- Uncertainty about the detailed nature of later elements of work
- A changing or uncertain environment
- Risk factors that could change the situation
- Difficulty in predicting resource availability well into the future
- Difficulty in predicting business conditions in the future.

However, if the current elements of work are to be controlled, detailed plans containing firm estimates are needed for the realistically foreseeable future. For these reasons, plans need to be produced at different levels of scope and detail.

Where a project forms part of a programme, the Project Plan will exist within the context of the programme plan. The programme plan may place constraints that will need to be considered as the Project Plan is being prepared or reviewed. There needs to be uniformity between project and programme plans to ensure that the project is working to meet programme objectives and products, especially if the Project Plan is revised to meet issues and risks as they develop.

15.5.1 Project Plan

An overview of the total project is needed. This is the Project Plan. It forms part of the Project Initiation Document. The Project Plan is the only mandatory PRINCE2 plan. It provides the Business Case with project costs and is used by the Project Board as a basis against which to monitor actual costs and project progress stage by stage. The Project Plan identifies key products, resource requirements and the total costs. It also identifies major control points within the project, such as stage boundaries. The Project Quality Plan (see Chapter 18, *Quality in a Project Environment*) for the project is documented separately in another part of the Project Initiation Document.

Once the Project Initiation Document has been accepted, the initial Project Plan is 'baselined' and shows the original plan on which the project was approved. As the project moves through its stages subsequent versions of the Project Plan are produced at the end of each stage to reflect:

- Progress already made
- Any agreed changes in circumstances
- Any revised forecast of cost and/or duration of the total project.

The initial and current versions of the Project Plan form part of the information used by the Project Board to monitor how far the project is deviating from its original size and scope.

If the Project Plan is likely to exceed the agreed tolerance levels (see *Controls*) the deviation must be referred upwards by the Project Board to get a decision on corrective action.

15.5.2 Stage Plan

For each stage identified in the Project Plan, a Stage Plan will normally be required. Each Stage Plan is produced near the end of the previous stage. It will be the basis of the Project Manager's day-to-day control. For a very small project of only two stages (initiation plus the rest) the Project Manager may choose to put all the detailed requirements for day-to-day control into the Project Plan.

It is frequently the case that much of the work in a stage will be done by specialist teams or suppliers, who will have their own plans for the work they are doing. These plans will not necessarily integrate comfortably with the stage concepts (see *Controls*). This means that the Project Manager will need to construct the Stage Plan from the various specialist development plans to establish overall resource and timing elements and interdependencies for the work through to the next assessment by the Project Board.

The Stage Plan is similar to the Project Plan in content, but each element will be broken down to the level of detail required to be an adequate basis for day-to-day control by the Project Manager. The validity of assumptions and risk analyses should be reassessed for the stage, as these may have changed since they were previously considered or new risks may have arisen or become apparent when looking in more detail.

Each Stage Plan is finalised near the end of the previous stage as part of *Managing Stage Boundaries* (SB). This approach should give more confidence in the plan because:

- The Stage Plan is produced close to the time when the planned events will take place
- The Stage Plan is for a much shorter duration than the Project Plan
- After the first stage, the Stage Plan is developed with knowledge of the performance of earlier stages.

15.5.3 Team plan

Team plans are optional and the need for them will be determined by the size and complexity of the project and the number of people involved. They will often be needed if there are separate teams from different skill groups or from external contractors.

The plans are prepared in parallel with the Stage Plan, either by subdividing the activities of the stage into the tasks for which the teams are responsible or by taking the plans prepared by each of the teams and assembling a Stage Plan from them. The latter will be the case where there are large elements of sub-contracting of the work of the project. The Team Manager would create a team plan for input into *Managing Stage Boundaries* (SB) or revise an existing one as part of *Accepting a Work Package* (MP1).

15.5.4 Stage and team quality plans

Stage Plans and team plans should contain a quality plan, which will identify the method(s) to be used to check the quality of each product created/updated during the activities covered by the plan and the resources to be used for the checks. The user and supplier Project Assurance roles have a key part to play here in:

- Identifying products of key interest to their role
- Specifying who should be involved in quality checking these products
- Specifying at what points in the product development quality checking should be done.

For example, for any quality reviews the names of the review chairperson and the reviewers would be given. The timing and resource effort will be shown in the graphic plan (typically a Gantt chart). The Stage and team quality plans will not be separate documents, but an integral part of the relevant plans.

15.5.5 Exception Plan

When it is predicted that a plan will no longer finish within the agreed tolerances, an Exception Plan is normally produced to replace that plan. An Exception Plan is prepared at the same level of detail as the plan it replaces. An Exception Plan picks up from the current plan actuals and continues to the end of that plan. Most Exception Plans will be created to replace a Stage Plan, but the Project Plan may also need to be replaced.

An Exception Plan has the same format as the plan it will replace.

If a Stage Plan is being replaced, this needs the approval of the Project Board. Replacement of a Project Plan because of a deviation beyond project tolerances must be referred by the Project Board to corporate/programme management.

Hints and tips

When planning, it is easy to forget to add the resources needed to do impact assessment on change requests. Even if a change is subsequently rejected, the assessment will still consume time and effort, probably from the senior team members.

It is important to identify for which products the customer and supplier are responsible. An extra heading can be added to the Product Description to record this information.

Plans need to be at an appropriate level to facilitate control. Will the supplier's and customer's plans be written at the same level of detail?

16
CONTROLS

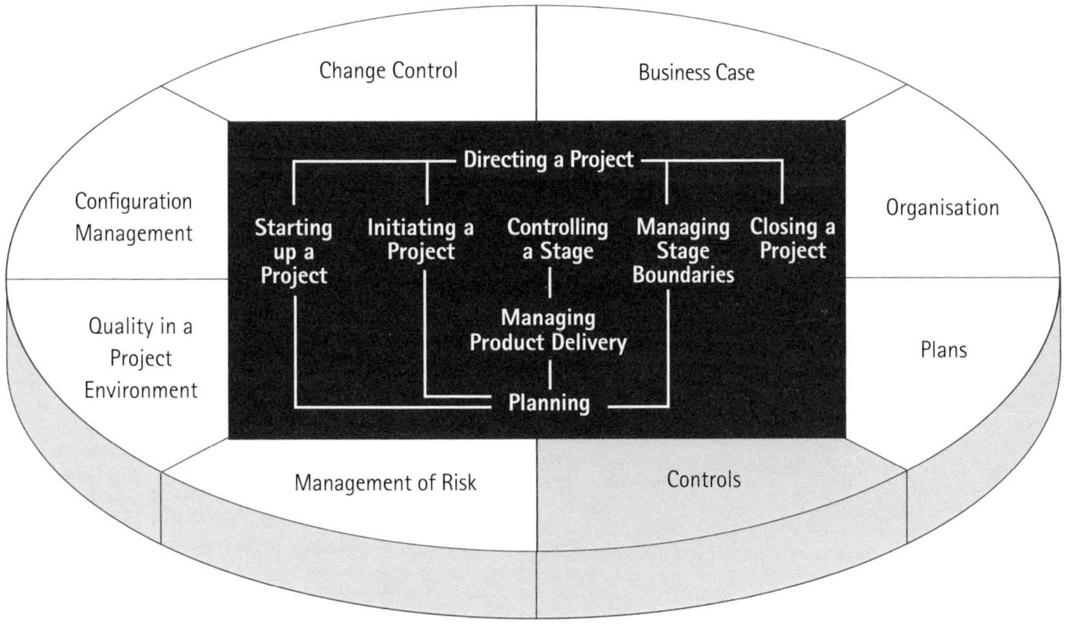

Figure 16.1 Controls in the PRINCE2 template

16.1 Purpose of control

Control is all about decision making and is central to project management.

The purpose of control is to ensure that the project:

- Is producing the required products, which meet the defined quality criteria
- Is being carried out to schedule and in accordance with its resource and cost plans
- Remains viable against its Business Case.

Figure 16.2 illustrates the control loop where monitoring activities facilitate the checking and reporting on progress against the plan. Control activities promote revisions to be made to the plan in response to problems discovered during monitoring.

Controls ensure that, for each level of the project management team, the next level up of management can:

- Monitor progress
- Compare achievement with plan
- Review plans and options against future situations
- Detect problems

- Initiate corrective action
- Authorise further work.

Controls must also cover capturing information on changes from outside the project and taking the necessary actions.

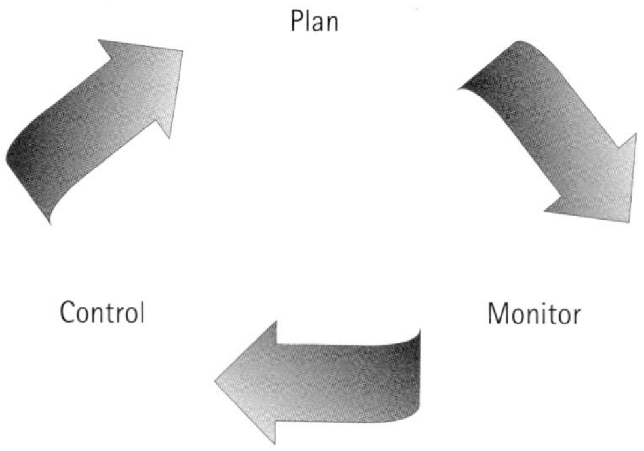

Figure 16.2 The control loop

16.2 Controls overview

There are various levels of control in the project. Many controls in PRINCE2 are event driven, including all the decision-making ones. 'Event driven' means that the control occurs because a specific event has taken place. Examples of these events are the end of a stage, the completion of the Project Initiation Document, the creation of an Exception Plan. There are some time-driven controls such as regular progress feedback. At the project level there is overall control by the Project Board, which receives information from the Project Manager (and any Project Assurance roles appointed) and has control over whether the project continues, stops or changes direction or scope.

PRINCE2 applies the concept of 'management by exception' where the Project Board is concerned. That is, having approved a Stage Plan with the Project Manager, the Project Board is kept informed by reports during the stage. There is no need for 'progress meetings' during the stage unless the situation deviates from the plan. The Project Board knows that the Project Manager will inform them immediately if any exception situation is forecast.

The major controls for the Project Board are:

- Project initiation (Should the project be undertaken?)
- End stage assessment (Has the stage been successful? Is the project still on course? Is the Business Case still viable? Are the risks still under control? Should the next stage be undertaken?)
- Highlight Reports (Regular progress reports during a stage)
- Exception Reports (Early warning of any forecast deviation beyond tolerance levels. The Project Board jointly considers what action to take in response to the forecast deviation)
- Exception assessment (The Project Board meets to review and approve an Exception Plan)

- Project closure (Has the project delivered everything expected? Are any follow-on actions necessary? What lessons have been learned?).

The Project Board must also monitor the environment outside the project and bring to the notice of those concerned, such as the Project Manager, any changes that affect the project.

The Project Manager has control on a day-to-day basis within a stage and can make adjustments as long as the stage and project stay within the tolerances defined by the Project Board and the adjustments do not change the Business Case. The Project Manager is responsible for monitoring progress and may be assisted by Project Support roles if these have been appointed.

Work Package authorisation is a control that the Project Manager uses to allocate work to individuals or teams. It includes controls on quality, time and cost and identifies reporting and hand-over requirements. The individuals or teams monitor progress through the Work Package and report back to the Project Manager via Checkpoint Reports or other identified means, such as risk 'triggers', and by updating the Quality Log.

PRINCE2 is designed for a variety of customer/supplier situations. For clarity, the PRINCE2 manual has been written on the assumption that the project will be run for a customer with a single (prime) supplier involved throughout. This has a bearing on not only the organisation of the project, but also the controls.

Planned achievement includes the required quality of products. The aim is to detect problems early while they can be corrected at least cost. Action should be taken in respect of any deviation from plan that is forecast to be outside tolerance.

Progress is monitored against plans, with control actions if adjustments are needed. The project management team is kept informed at its various levels by reports and assessments.

A controlled close ensures that the project does not drift on for ever but does not finish until the Project Manager can satisfy the Project Board that the objectives specified in the Project Initiation Document have been achieved.

16.3 Project start-up

Project start-up is an important prerequisite of project control. Project start-up contains the work that PRINCE2 requires to be done before the project can begin. Its functions are to:

- Set up the project management team so that the Project Board and Project Manager can make the necessary initial decisions about the project
- Develop what *may* be a rudimentary Project Mandate into the Project Brief
- Plan the initiation stage.

The establishment of a suitable project management team is discussed in *Organisation* (Chapter 14).

Project initiation is likely to be a short stage in comparison with the other project stages, but the approval of the Project Board is needed before it can be done. Project start-up must, therefore, create a plan for the initiation stage that the Project Board can examine in order to understand the required commitment more clearly. The plan should include a statement of any controls to be applied and reports that the Project Board is to receive, so that the Project Board is assured in advance that the stage will be under its control.

As the creation of the Project Mandate is out of the control of the project, it often falls short of providing all the information that the project needs. Project start-up gives the Project Manager the opportunity to flesh it out into a full Project Brief and thus present the objectives of the project for the Project Board's agreement.

Where the project is part of a programme, the programme should provide a complete Project Brief, thus removing the need to produce it during project start-up.

16.3.1 Authorising Initiation (DP1)

After the process *Starting up a Project* (SU), the Project Board approves progress to the initiation stage, which is the official 'start' of the project.

It needs the documented approval of all members of the Project Board identified so far, but depending on the project size, risk status, importance and environment, obtaining this approval may be done with or without a formal meeting.

After project initiation is authorised, a copy of the Project Brief should be sent to all stakeholders, including the group responsible for the operational support of the final product. This is to give early warning of the need to prepare for that support.

16.3.2 Project Initiation

The purpose of project initiation is to ensure that before significant resource is spent on the project, everything involved in the project is agreed:

- The project objectives
- What products will be delivered
- The reasons for the project
- Who the customer is
- Who has which responsibilities and authority
- Project boundaries and interfaces to the outside world
- How the objectives will be met
- What assumptions have been or can be made
- What major risks exist that might prevent the project from achieving its objectives
- When the major products will be delivered
- How much the project will cost
- How the project will be controlled
- The division of the project into stages
- How the acceptability of its products will be assessed.

These questions are answered in the Project Initiation Document, which is the main product from the stage. A suggested outline of the contents of the Project Initiation Document is included in Appendix A, *Product Description outlines*.

Another product of the initiation stage is the next Stage Plan, so that if the Project Board is satisfied with the Project Initiation Document, it can also approve progress into the next stage without further delay.

Once approved at the end of the project initiation stage, the Project Initiation Document is 'frozen'. It is now a reference document to show the original basis of the project. At the end of the project it can be measured against final expectations and results to assess the success of the project and to check, for example, that any changes to the Project Plan were made in a controlled manner. It is an essential part of the audit trail on how the project has been managed.

But changes do occur and it would be wrong not to record the impact of those changes and keep the project management team up to date and so further versions of the most volatile parts of the Project Initiation Document are created as changes occur. Again, this forms part of the audit trail, showing any moves away from the information in the Project Initiation Document, when and why this happened and what the impact of the change was. The most volatile parts of the Project Initiation Document are:

- The Project Plan
- The Business Case
- The Risk Log.

As later versions of these are created, they are kept in the management section of the project filing. A suitable structure for project filing is illustrated in Appendix E of the manual.

These volatile parts will be updated throughout the project, at least at the end of each stage.

To summarise, the main purpose of the Project Initiation Document is to pull the information together to answer the questions: 'What?', 'Why?', 'Who?', 'When?' and 'How?'

Hints and tips

Under the 'Project Control' section of the Project Initiation Document, it is useful to mention the development of the Lessons Learned Log (see later in this chapter). This alerts readers to the fact that it should be a document ongoing throughout the life of the project. Otherwise it may be left until project closure, when memories of some lessons may have faded.

16.3.3 Stage selection

According to the size and risk of a project, the Project Board will decide to break the project down into a suitable number of stages. This is agreed during the initiation stage. Reasons for the breakdown of the project into stages are discussed in the Stages section of this chapter (Section 16.6).

The end of each stage is a major control point for the Project Board (see End stage assessment, section 16.4.11), and thus the selection of the number of stages and their timing in the project life cycle is an important control for the Project Board.

16.3.4 Communication Plan

One entry in the Project Initiation Document will be the Communication Plan. It plays an important part in control by identifying who needs to give and receive information about the project. A suggested description of its contents is given in Appendix A, *Product Description outlines*. Briefly, it shows:

- Who needs information
- What information they need
- When they need it
- The format in which it should be presented.

It should include senior or programme management, stakeholders and other interested parties, such as those who will have to support the product in its operational life.

16.4 Controlled progress

During the project there is a need to ensure that the project stays in line with the expectations defined in the Project Initiation Document and the current Stage Plan.

16.4.1 Tolerance

No project ever goes 100 per cent to plan. Even with a good plan, some things will go a little slower than planned or cost a little more; other things will go more quickly, cost a little less. Such variations will occur all the way through a plan. Although the Project Board agreed a plan with the Project Manager, it doesn't want the Project Manager to be constantly running back to it, saying 'I've spent a pound or a dollar more than I planned this week' or 'I'm a day late this week'. On the other hand, the Project Board doesn't want progress to deviate wildly from the plan without being told and being able to react. So where is the dividing line between differences that are permissible and those that require Project Board intervention? The dividing line is called tolerance.

Tolerance is the permissible deviation from a plan without bringing the deviation to the attention of the next higher authority.

The allocation of tolerances follows the four layers of project organisation discussed in the *Organisation* chapter. Tolerances for the project as a whole are given to the Project Board by corporate or programme management in the Project Mandate (or ascertained by the Executive during project start-up, to be entered into the Project Brief). Based on these overall figures, the Project Board agrees with the Project Manager a tolerance for each stage once the Stage Plan has been produced. The Project Manager may agree tolerance levels for a Work Package with a Team Manager.

Where the allocated tolerance is forecast to be exceeded, that level of management must refer the matter to the next higher level, i.e. if the tolerance allocated by the Project Manager to a Team Manager is likely to be exceeded, the Team Manager reports this to the Project Manager. If there is a forecast that the tolerance for a stage is to be exceeded, the Project Manager must refer the matter to the Project Board. The Project Board may set new tolerances around the new forecast as long as these are within the constraints of the overall project figures. Where the forecast is for the project tolerance to be exceeded, the Project Board must refer the matter back to corporate or programme management for a decision. Figure 16.3 illustrates this cascading effect.

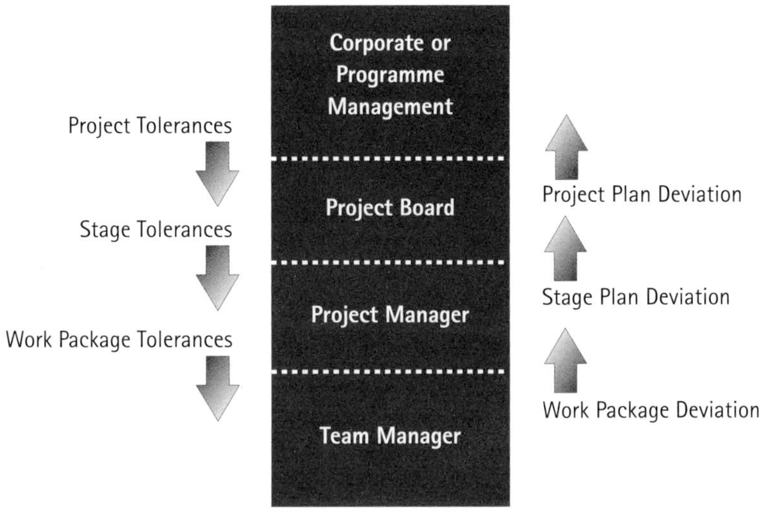

Figure 16.3 The use of tolerances across the four layers of management

The two standard elements to tolerance are:

- Time
- Cost.

Separate tolerance figures should be given for time and cost. Tolerance figures need not be the same for over and under cost and time. A tolerance of, say, +5% to -20% may be more realistic than +/-10%. It may be more realistic to quote tolerances as 'real' figures, rather than percentages; for example, ten days or a defined amount of money. The setting of these tolerances is done as part of *Planning* (PL).

Figure 16.4 illustrates stage level cost and time tolerances and the Project Manager's freedom of decision within the tolerances. The central line (A) is the plan. Lines B and C show the limits of the tolerance in cost and time given by the Project Board. Line B illustrates that the plan may cost a little more than forecast or take a little longer. Line C illustrates that the plan may cost a little less or take a shorter time. Within the box enclosing these two limits the plan is judged to be under control. Line D illustrates how things might be progressing. Although it is deviating from the plan, it is within the tolerance margins. If at any time the Project Manager can forecast that line D will break through either of the tolerance lines and therefore finish outside the tolerance box, a special procedure is invoked (see the Exception Report and Exception Plan later in this chapter) that brings in the Project Board to 'manage by exception'.

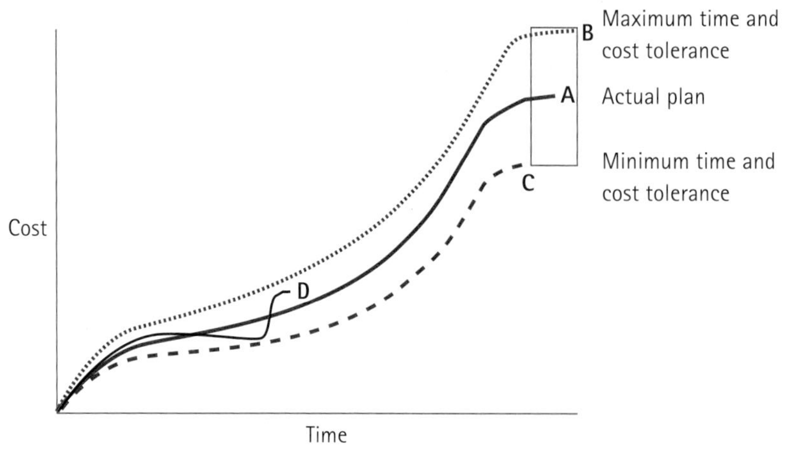

Figure 16.4 Cost/time tolerance graph

Other normal tolerance elements are as follows.

Scope tolerance

Scope tolerance may be used where there is no tolerance available in either time or money. There may be agreement to meet time and money limits by delivering reduced functionality. Examples of scope tolerance might be 'Yes, you can have the house by that date, but the shower won't be fitted' or 'We can afford to go out for a meal, but we will have to do without a dessert'.

Quality tolerance

The last tolerance a project would want to invoke is quality, but sometimes limits on the other types of tolerance may force this upon a project. Examples of quality tolerance would be 'You can have the car in any colour, as long as it's black' or 'We can afford a bottle of wine, but it will have to be the house red, rather than a vintage Burgundy'.

Risk tolerance

A different view of tolerance is taken when considering risks. Sometimes this is called a project's 'risk appetite', i.e. how much risk is the Project Board prepared to take? This may vary according to the area of risk, e.g. a company in financial trouble might have very little financial risk tolerance, but allow a lot of risk tolerance in terms of quality.

Benefit tolerance

The Project Board may wish to consider another aspect of tolerance – benefit tolerance. This implies setting boundaries on either side of a benefit. As long as the benefit is forecast to fall within these boundaries, the benefit would contribute to a viable Business Case.

Contingency, tolerance and change budget

There is a difference between contingency and tolerance. Contingency, in PRINCE2 terms, is a plan including the time and money set aside to carry out that plan, which will only be invoked if a linked risk actually occurs. Tolerance is built into a plan to allow for small problems (plus or minus), such as those described earlier.

Tolerance, especially in terms of cost, should not be confused with a change budget. Tolerance is not there to pay for when the users change their minds. If no change budget is set aside during initiation, there will always be the temptation to use up any tolerance to pay for changes to the specification. The alternative is that the Project Manager has always to go back to the Project Board to ask for more money to pay for the changes. This can be irritating and time wasting, especially if the Executive then has to go back to corporate/programme management for the extra money.

Hints and tips

Where there is a tight or non-existent time tolerance – for example, the end product must be delivered by date X – the Project Manager would normally look for extra tolerance in one or more of the other elements, such as cost (for example: 'Can more resources or overtime be used to ensure that the time tolerance is not exceeded?'). Where there is little or no tolerance on time, cost and scope, the Project Manager must watch out for the temptation for individuals or teams to reduce the quality of work unofficially as a means of saving time.

16.4.2 Product Descriptions

A description of each product is written down before that product is developed or obtained, even before it is planned, to ensure that the individual people know:

- Why it is needed
- What it will look like
- From what sources it will be derived
- The quality specification to which it must be built.

The Product Description is a control document. It is written as part of the planning process. It defines the product, the standards to be used in its creation and the quality criteria to be applied to ensure it is fit for its purpose. Not only is this information essential for the creator, but the Product Description also forms the initial checklist for checking the quality of the finished product.

When a product has been identified in a plan's Product Breakdown Structure, its Product Description should be drafted. Outline Product Descriptions of standard PRINCE2 management products (such as plans, reports, approvals) are provided in Appendix A, *Product Description outlines*.

All Product Descriptions must be approved. In formal terms, the Project Board approves them. If the Project Assurance roles of the Project Board members are delegated, the assurance of the Product Descriptions may be one of the authorities delegated to them.

The relevant Product Description forms part of a Work Package given to an individual or team responsible for creation of that product.

Hints and tips

Product Descriptions should be written by staff who know the proposed product. Users should be involved in setting quality criteria.

Product Descriptions may not be needed for every level of product. The Project Board can make a decision as to which are the major products for which a Product Description is necessary.

16.4.3 Work Package

A Work Package is the trigger from the Project Manager to an individual or group to undertake a piece of work during a stage. The implication is that work cannot be undertaken unless the Project Manager has specifically authorised it.

Work is released to a team member or Team Manager in an agreed Work Package. The Work Package will contain the Product Description(s), constraints such as time, cost and interfaces, reporting and product hand-over requirements and any other documentation or products necessary for understanding and implementing the Work Package. Work Package authorisation is particularly useful when dealing with contractors or sub-contractors. The two sides to it (giver and receiver) are described in *Authorising Work Package* (CS1) and *Accepting a Work Package* (MP1).

16.4.4 Quality Control

Every project needs procedures and techniques to control the quality of the products being produced. The ideal quality controls will vary according to the type of product and project and PRINCE2 makes no effort to define all the possibilities. It does, however, include a generic quality check, which has been found to be effective in checking the quality of documents. The check is called a quality review.

The quality review is one type of quality check. It is a team method of assessing product quality by a review process. The purpose of the review is to inspect the product for errors in a planned, independent, controlled and documented manner. Quality review documentation, when filed in the quality section of the project filing, provides a record that the product was inspected, that any errors found were corrected and the corrections themselves were checked. Knowing that a product has been checked and declared error free provides a more confident basis from which to move ahead and use that product as the basis of future work.

A quality review can be used to control the quality of documents, including those created by the specialists. A quality review provides feedback to the Project Manager on the status of a document. The quality review technique is fully described in Chapter 24.

There are many other types of quality check, depending on the type of product to be tested. PRINCE2 is compatible with all types of check. They need to be specified in the Product Description for the product(s) to which they apply.

16.4.5 Project Issues and Change Control

Every project must have a procedure to handle change. Without change control there is no project control.

As part of control there must be a procedure that caters for unexpected deviations from specification. These deviations occur for many reasons:

- The user's requirement changes
- Government legislation changes and the product's specification must be revised to accommodate these changes
- The user or supplier wants to change or add an acceptance criterion
- During the development, extra features suggest themselves for inclusion
- There are organisational or business changes that alter the scope and objectives of the project
- The supplier finds that it will be impossible to deliver everything within the agreed cost or schedule
- A question arises on whether the supplier can meet a particular part of the specification or acceptance criterion
- A sub-contractor or interfacing project (activity) fails to meet its planned commitment
- Resource availability changes.

Apart from deviation possibilities, there will also be a need for an avenue into the project for questions or concerns. All of these need a procedure to control them and their effect on the project. In PRINCE2 all such inputs are handled by the Project Issue procedure.

This procedure ensures that all such questions, problems, concerns or suggestions are answered, but that nothing is undertaken without the knowledge of the appropriate level of management, including the Project Board. Apart from controlling possible changes, it provides a formal entry point through which all questions or requests can be raised.

The Project Issue procedure logs and handles all Project Issues raised during the life of the project. The procedure provides knowledge of the status of all Project Issues, control over their processing and a feedback to the originator on any actions taken. This is explained in more detail in Chapter 20 (*Change Control*).

16.4.6 Risk Log

The management of risk is an important control throughout the project.

A Risk Log is kept of all identified risks, their analysis, countermeasures and status. This begins at the start of the project and continues until the project closes. All risks are frequently reviewed. As a minimum, risks are reassessed at the end of each stage, but they should also be reviewed as part of the assessment of stage progress.

There is a separate chapter (Chapter 17) on the management of risk.

16.4.7 Checkpoint

A checkpoint is a time-driven control when the status of work in a team is ascertained. It involves the people doing the work and is carried out by the Team Manager. It may or may not be a formal meeting and the frequency would be made clear in the Work Package.

One specific aim of a checkpoint is to check all aspects of team work against the plan to ensure that there are no nasty surprises. Useful questions are 'What is not going to plan?' and 'What is likely to fail to go as planned?'

The information gathered at a checkpoint is recorded on a Checkpoint Report for submission to the Project Manager. Again, this may be formal or informal according to the project or team circumstances. Checkpoint Reports are collated by the Project Manager and used to assess the current status of the stage. Checkpoints should be taken as frequently as the Project Manager requires in order to maintain control over progress. They may coincide with the Project Manager's need to consider re-planning.

A checkpoint can also be used for the downward dissemination to team members of information from the Project Board, or from corporate or programme management.

The suggested content of a Checkpoint Report is given in Appendix A, *Product Description outlines.*

16.4.8 Planning and replanning

Plans are, to a certain extent, guesswork. Activities do not always go as planned. Resources do not always perform as expected. Unplanned activities may emerge. The Project Manager needs to compare the plan regularly against latest information and be ready to replan. Failure to replan, or replanning too seldom, can leave it too late to recover from problems. There is, however, a danger of reacting too early or too frequently to the status of non-critical activities. Small deviations may correct themselves and the Project Manager may spend too much time in replanning rather than in monitoring. When and how often to replan will depend on the size and criticality of the project and is a matter for the Project Manager's judgement.

Replanning is needed at stage boundaries, when exceptions arise and may be needed as part of *Taking Corrective Action* (CS7).

16.4.9 Highlight Report

A Highlight Report is a time-driven report from the Project Manager to the Project Board. The Project Manager sends it to the Project Board during a stage at a frequency dictated by the Project Board. The frequency depends on such factors as the length and perceived risk of the stage. Typically, the report might be sent fortnightly or monthly.

The Project Board should define the content of the Highlight Report. Minimally, it should contain statements about:

- Achievements in the current period
- Achievements expected in the next period
- Actual or potential problems and suggestions concerning their resolution.

The Project Board may also ask for a copy of the Stage Plan (or parts of it), showing actual progress to date in terms of activities and cost, plus reports on any other item in the stage that it feels is important. Whatever the content, the style should be concise. Instead of a copy of the Stage Plan the Project Board may prefer to receive an updated copy of the Product Checklist, showing status and any revised dates.

Often the frequency of Highlight Reports is defined for the whole project in the Project Initiation Document, but the frequency can be varied for different stages. For example, the initiation stage is normally very short and the Project Board may request no Highlight Reports and a higher frequency for later stages.

A Highlight Report's purpose is to allow the Project Board to 'manage by exception' between end stage assessments. The Project Board is aware of the Stage Plan to which it is committed and of the tolerance margins that it agreed with the Project Manager. The Highlight Reports confirm that progress is being made within those tolerances. Early warning of any possible problems may be reported to the Project Board via the Highlight Report. The Project Board can react to any problems that are reported, as formally or informally as it feels is necessary.

The Project Board can request that copies of the Highlight Report are sent to other interested parties. This should be documented in the Communication Plan.

Appendix A, *Product Description outlines*, contains a suggested outline for a Highlight Report.

Hints and tips

The Project Manager can use the Highlight Report to convey concern about items that are under the control of any member of the Project Board. As the report is provided to all members of the Project Board, any member whose commitment is the source of the concern will feel pressure from the other members to put the matter right.

The Senior User has part of the responsibility for monitoring project deliverables. This may be difficult to do where a remote supplier or third party is developing or procuring the product. Monitoring can be assisted by Checkpoint and Highlight Reports and by user involvement in checking the quality of such products.

16.4.10 Exception Report

An Exception Report is a warning from the Project Manager to the Project Board that the Stage (or Project) Plan will deviate outside its tolerance margins. It is a wise precaution for the Project Manager to document the report.

There are situations where it is the tolerance for the whole project that is at risk and not just that for the stage. For example, information may be found that shows that a major equipment expenditure, which is to be made much later in the project, will greatly exceed current expectations and take the project outside tolerance.

An Exception Report describes a forecast deviation, provides an analysis of both the exception and the options for the way forward and identifies the recommended option. There is a suggested content for the Exception Report in Appendix A, *Product Description outlines*. The Project Board considers an Exception Report as part of process *Giving Ad Hoc Direction* (DP4).

Where the project is part of a programme, exception situations may occur because of changes or problems at the programme level. Examples would be a business change or the late delivery of an externally purchased product, which may impact the whole programme or just a single project. Changes to end dates or to the specification of products to be delivered by the project are likely to have a knock-on effect on the programme. To avoid duplication of effort and to save time, those exception situations likely to impact more than a single project within a programme should be co-ordinated at programme level.

16.4.11 End stage assessment

Part of the philosophy of breaking the project into stages is that the Project Board only commits to one stage at a time. At the end of each stage the Project Board takes a good look at the project to decide if it wishes to proceed to the next stage. This review is called an end stage assessment. According to such factors as project size, criticality and risk situation, the end stage assessment may be formal or informal.

However it is done, the end stage assessment is a mandatory control point at the end of each stage. The assessment approves the work to date and provides authority to proceed to the next stage. A stage should not be considered complete until it has received this formal approval.

The specific objectives of an end stage assessment are to:

- Check that the need for the project has not changed
- Review the results of the stage against the Stage Plan
- Satisfy the Project Board about the quality of the products delivered
- Establish that the current stage has been completed satisfactorily
- Check whether any external event has changed the project's assumptions
- Perform a risk analysis and management review of the project and the next Stage Plan and incorporate the results into the next Stage Plan and Project Plan
- Review overall project status against the Project Plans (which may now have been revised)
- Review the next Stage Plan against the Project Plan
- Ensure that a complete and consistent baseline is established for the next stage
- Review the tolerances set for the next stage
- Ensure that the specialist aspects of the project are still sound
- Review the project against its Business Case and ensure that the project is still viable
- Authorise the passage of the project into the next stage (if the Business Case continues to be viable).

The Project Board has the right to refuse to approve the next Stage Plan if it is unhappy with any of the aspects mentioned in this list. It can either ask the Project Manager to rethink the next Stage Plan, force closure of the project or refer the problem to corporate or programme management if the problem is beyond its remit.

16.4.12 End Stage Report

The End Stage Report is the vehicle through which the Project Manager informs the Project Board of the results of a stage. The Project Board can compare the results in terms of products, cost and time against the Stage Plan that it approved.

The End Stage Report contains all the information described for an end stage assessment, except the approval to proceed to the next stage. It forms a record that can be audited at any time in the project, giving a summary of what happened in a stage, the impact on the Project Plan, Business Case and risks and why decisions about the future of the project were made.

16.4.13 Exception assessment

An exception assessment is held between the Project Board and Project Manager to approve an Exception Plan. If any of the Project Board's assurance responsibilities have been delegated, the people to whom assurance has been delegated would also participate. Its purpose is for the Project Manager to present an Exception Plan to the Project Board and obtain its approval for implementation of the plan. As with the end stage assessment, it may be formal or informal according to the size, criticality and risk of the project.

The content of an Exception Plan is the same as that of other PRINCE2 plans.

Every exception has an impact on the Project Plan, Business Case and risks. The recommended option will also have an impact on the same items. The Project Board must consider both sets of impact.

16.4.14 Daily Log

A Daily Log can help a Project Manager in controlling the project. It is normally a notebook whose pages consist of the items listed in the *Product Description outlines* in Appendix A.

These can be tailored to the Project Manager's own preferences or needs. Entries can be made at any time. One key time would be when the Project Manager reviews the stage status. Another way of getting into a regular habit to make entries would be to sit down at the end or beginning of a week. Consideration of all the stage documents may lead to entries in the Daily Log. Typical entries might be:

- Check with a risk owner on the current state of a risk
- Note what is on the critical path and check with the producer on the work status
- Note any products due for completion in the next few days and check their status
- Review the Quality Log for any checks that are late in being done
- Make a note to check on any outstanding Project Issue's impact analysis
- Make a note to follow up on any outstanding item on the last Highlight Report that should have caused action from one or more Project Board members
- See if action can be taken on activities that are slipping before the plan has to be modified
- Check on the status of tolerances.

Other entries may come from discussions with Team Managers, team members or Project Board members; phone calls to be made, Communication Plan changes, Work Packages to be adjusted.

It is sensible for the Project Manager always to have the Daily Log at hand. Relying on memory is a recipe for disaster.

16.5 Controlled close

Before the Project Board allows the project to close (unless the project has been prematurely terminated), it has the control to ensure that:

- All the agreed products have been delivered and accepted
- Arrangements are in place, where appropriate, to support and maintain the product in its useful life
- Any useful statistics or lessons for later projects are passed to the relevant body
- A plan has been made to check the achievement of the benefits claimed in the project's Business Case.

At project closure the Project Board must confirm in writing (for the project management file) its acceptance that the project has been completed. If necessary, these statements can be qualified, for example, that the products have been delivered with minor deficiencies that can be rectified later.

The following information is generated at the close of the project, which leads to control actions by the Project Board.

16.5.1 End project notification

The end project notification advises all those who have provided resources, facilities or services to the project that the project is coming to an end. 'Officially' the Project Manager provides an end project recommendation to the Project Board. If the Project Board agrees with it, it releases the end project notification. In practice, there may be agreement that these are one and the same document.

16.5.2 Lessons Learned Report

The Lessons Learned Report is created at the end of the project from the Lessons Learned Log to disseminate useful lessons learned during the project for the benefit of other projects.

It covers management and specialist processes, techniques and tools, what worked well and what caused problems. It is a useful control as part of the functions of an independent quality assurance or similar group. A suggested content is included in Appendix A, *Product Description outlines*.

16.5.3 Follow-on Action Recommendations

At the close of the project there may be a number of actions left undone. For example, there may have been a number of Requests for Change that the Project Board decided not to implement during the project but that were not rejected; not all expected products may have been handed over or there may be some known problems with what has been delivered.

The Follow-on Action Recommendations document any 'unfinished business' and allow the Project Board to direct them to the person or group whose job it will be to have the recommendations considered for action after the current project has ended.

16.5.4 End Project Report

The End Project Report is similar to the End Stage Report, but covers the entire project. A suggested content is included in Appendix A, *Product Description outlines*.

The End Project Report reviews how well the project has achieved the objectives of the Project Initiation Document. Where the Lessons Learned Report concentrates on the good and bad points in the project management standards and conduct, this report concentrates on the performance of the project management team.

Where possible at this point, the achievement by the project of benefits anticipated in the Business Case is reviewed. (Most of this measurement will have to wait until the post-project review.) Any changes made after the Project Initiation Document was agreed are identified and their impact on the Project Plan, Business Case and risks is assessed.

The report provides statistics on Project Issues and their impact on the project, plus statistics on the quality of work carried out.

If the project is part of a programme, the programme will require a copy of the End Project Report. The programme management may provide details of extra statistics and information that it needs from the report. This should be covered in the Communication Plan.

16.5.5 Post-project review

The post-project review occurs outside the project. Its main aim is to review the benefits achieved by the project's products.

Normally many products need time in use before the achievement of their expected benefits can be measured. This measurement after a period of use is an activity called a post-project review. At project closure a plan is agreed on when and how achievement of benefits can be measured.

A post-project review occurs after the project has closed. Any corrective work identified by the post-project review would be done during product use and maintenance. Any problems may not be with the product, but organisational ones, needing such solutions as retraining.

Where a project is part of a programme, the project may simply contribute to the realisation of programme-level benefits.

A suggested content for a Post-Project Review Plan is given in Appendix A, *Product Description outlines*.

16.6 Stages

Stages are partitions of the project with decision points. A stage is a collection of activities and products whose delivery is managed as a unit. As such it is a subset of the project and in PRINCE2 terms it is the element of work that the Project Manager is managing on behalf of the Project Board at any one time. The use of stages in a PRINCE2 project is mandatory; the number of stages is flexible and depends on the needs of the project.

PRINCE2 stages are often described as 'management stages' in order to differentiate them from a different use of the word 'stages' in some specific project environments.

16.6.1 Phases and stages

In some methods the word 'phase' is used as an equivalent to the PRINCE2 stage. This is not in itself a problem.

It would become a problem if people thought of product life span phases, such as:

- Conception
- Feasibility
- Implementation (or realisation)
- Operation
- Termination

as PRINCE2 stages. These are phases for the product life span, not the project. The last two are outside the project. While a product is 'operational' it may be the subject of any number of projects to enhance or revise it. Most of what in PRINCE2 terms will be stages will be divisions of 'implementation' in the product life span. There are various reasons for breaking the project into stages. They include the following.

16.6.2 Review and decision points

Within any project there will be key decisions, the results of which will have fundamental effects on the direction and detailed content of the project. There is, thus, a need to review direction and ongoing viability on a regular basis.

PRINCE2 uses stages to deal with these decision points. The decisions form the basis of the end stage assessments carried out in *Authorising a Stage or Exception Plan* (DP3). The benefits that these end stage assessments bring to the project are:

- Providing a 'fire break' for the project by encouraging the Project Board to assess the project viability at regular intervals, rather than let it run on in an uncontrolled manner
- Ensuring that key decisions are made prior to the detailed work needed to implement them. The nature of these decisions can be varied and will include:
  - whether to commit major resources such as capital investment
  - what the impact is of major risk elements

  - the clarification of a previously unknown or ill understood part of the project's direction or products
- Clarifying what the impact will be of an identified external influence such as the corporate budget round or the finalisation of legislation
- Reviewing a risky project at key moments when new information about those risks appears.

Many people will have heard of the terms 'peer review' and 'gate review' in project work and wondered how they related to PRINCE2 controls.

Peer reviews are specific reviews of a project or any of its products where personnel from within the organisation and/or from other organisations carry out an independent assessment of the project. The purpose of peer reviews is to introduce a fresh perspective to the project and to encourage shared learning across other projects. Peer reviews can be done at any point within a project but are often used at stage-end points.

Gate review is a term often used in project management. Gate reviews are effectively formal end stage assessments where external scrutiny is applied to the assessment of the project and recommendations of whether the project should continue or not are given to the Project Board.

16.6.3 Planning horizons

Uncertainty can often mean that it is only possible to plan in detail the activities and products of a limited amount of the work of the project. The rest of the project's work can only be planned in broad outline. The adoption of stages handles this situation by having two different but related levels of plan that is, a Stage Plan and a Project Plan.

16.6.4 Scalability

Every PRINCE2 project should consist of at least two stages. The initiation stage is mandatory. It may last only a matter of hours but is essential to ensure that there is a firm basis for the project, understood by all parties. A small project may need only two stages: an initiation stage with the remainder of the project as the second stage.

Most projects need to be broken down into more manageable stages to enable the correct level of planning and control to be exercised.

16.6.5 Management versus technical stages

One method of grouping work together in stages is by the set of techniques used or the product created. This results in stages covering elements such as design, build and implementation. Such stages are *technical* stages and are a separate concept from the *management* stages already introduced.

Technical stages are typified by the use of a particular set of specialist skills. Management stages equate to commitment of resources and authority to spend. Often the two types of stage will coincide; for instance, where the management decision is based on the output from the technical stage. An example of this might be where the output from the technical stage is a set of design options.

However, on other occasions the stages will not coincide. There might be more than one technical stage per management stage. For example, the Project Board might decide to combine all the technical stages that investigate a need and produce a specification into one management stage. One plan would be approved to cover all the work, with Project Board commitment before the work started and a review at the end. In a risky project – for example, one that is (technically) innovative – a long technical stage might be divided into more than one management stage.

The PRINCE2 approach is to concentrate the management of the project on the *management* stages since these will form the basis of the planning and control processes described throughout the method. To do otherwise runs the risk of the project being driven by the specialist teams instead of the customer's management.

Where the desired management stages do not coincide with the technical stages, technical work can be broken down so that its products can be divided over two or more management stages. Figures 16.5 and 16.6 give an example of this break. Figure 16.5 shows four management stages with two technical products spreading across more than one management stage.

Figure 16.6 shows that design has been broken into three products. The overall design now falls within stage 1. Detailed design and training syllabus form the second management stage and periphery design is planned to be done in stage 3, together with the creation of trained staff.

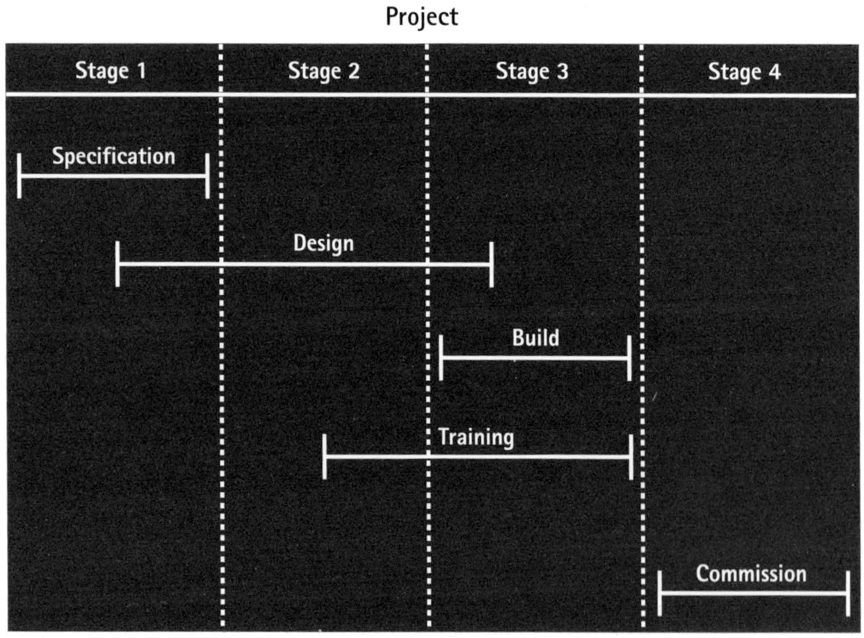

Figure 16.5 Technical products crossing management stage boundaries

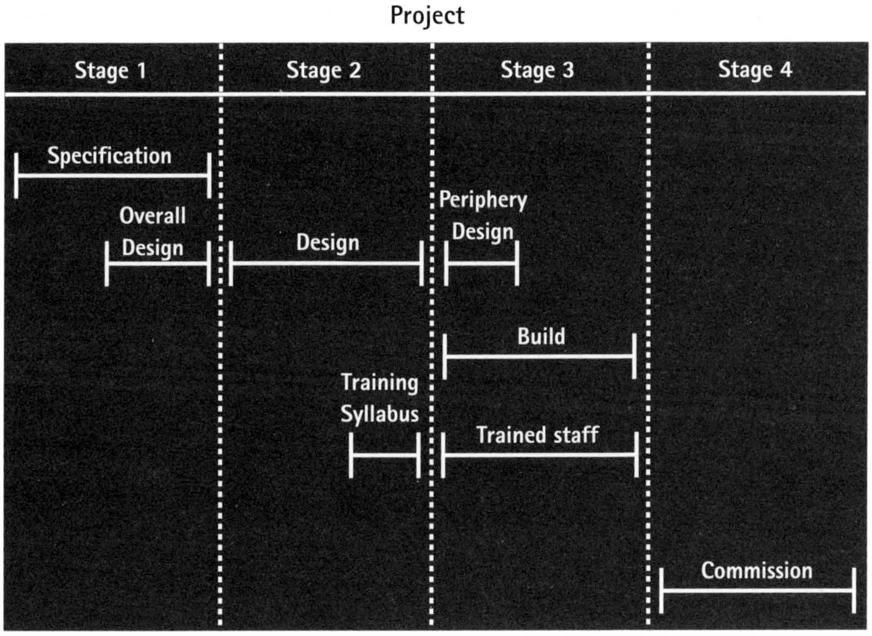

Figure 16.6 Technical products broken down to fit within management stages

16.6.6 How to define stages

The process of defining stages is fundamentally a process of balancing:

- How far ahead in the project it is sensible to plan
- Where the key decision points need to be on the project
- Too many small stages versus too few big ones.

This will be a balance of the factors identified earlier and will be influenced by any team plans. However, the Project Manager will have to reconcile these two types of plan. This is discussed in *Plans* (Chapter 15).

16.6.7 How to use stages

The primary use of stages is as a basis for dictating the timing of the stage boundary processes covered by *Managing Stage Boundaries* (SB), and by the associated *Authorising a Stage or Exception Plan* (DP3). These processes are used to make decisions regarding the continuation or otherwise of the project.

One element of this decision-making process is whether the stage that has just been completed has been completed successfully. This can be problematic where the management stage ends partway through one or more elements of specialist work, since it can be difficult to establish whether the specialist work is under control. The PRINCE2 technique of *Product-Based Planning* (see Chapter 22) is invaluable here, since by using it the Project Manager can identify the detailed products involved in any element of specialist work and can hence identify all the products that are due to be produced within the confines of any given management stage. This can then be used to assess completion or otherwise of the stage.

Stages can be very useful as a means of bringing Project Board control to risky projects. Stage breaks can be inserted at key points when risks to the project can be reviewed before major commitments of money or resources. Driving this will be *Planning a Project* (IP2).

17
MANAGEMENT OF RISK

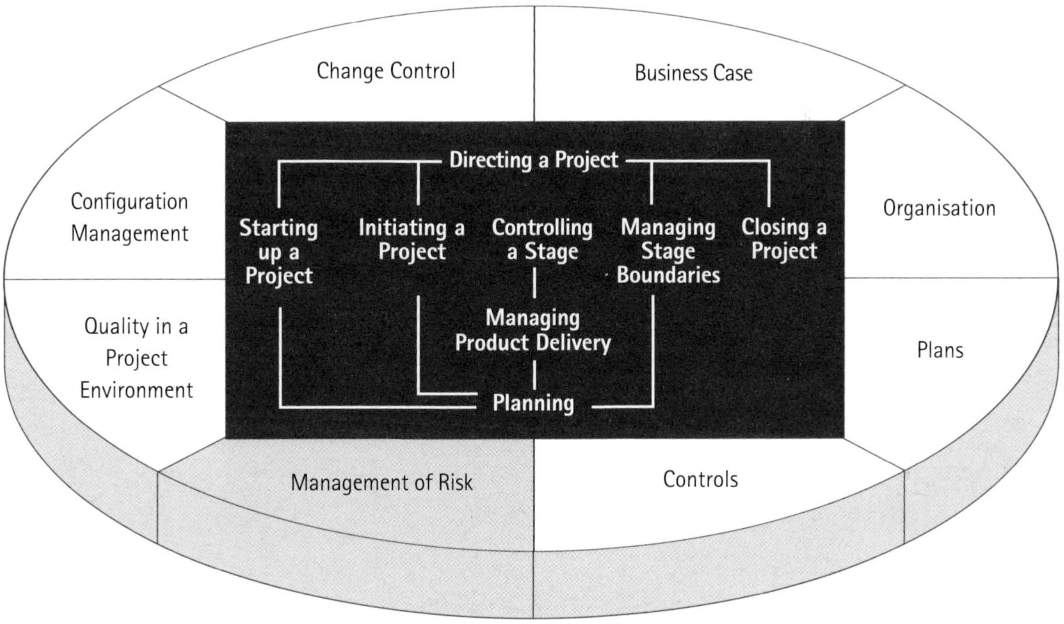

Figure 17.1 The management of risk in the PRINCE2 template

17.1 What is risk management?

Risk is a major factor to be considered during the management of any project. Project management must control and contain risks if a project is to stand a chance of being successful.

Risk can be defined as uncertainty of outcome (whether positive opportunity or negative threat). Some amount of risk taking is inevitable if the project is to achieve its objectives.

The task of risk management is to manage a project's exposure to risk (that is, the probability of specific risks occurring and the potential impact if they did occur). The aim is to manage that exposure by taking action to keep exposure to an acceptable level in a cost-effective way.

Risk management involves having:

- Access to reliable, up-to-date information about risks
- Decision-making processes supported by a framework of risk analysis and evaluation
- Processes in place to monitor risks
- The right balance of control in place to deal with those risks. (This is explained later in the chapter under the heading of 'Risk tolerance'.)

Risk management at the project level focuses on keeping unwanted outcomes to an acceptable minimum. Decisions about risk management at this level form an important part of the Business Case. Where suppliers and/or partners are involved, it is important to gain a shared view of the risks and how they will be managed.

17.2 Risk principles

Projects bring about change and change incurs risk. Change is usually about moving forward and this often means the use of new methods or new technology. These aspects can increase the risks. There are some essential elements that need to be in place in a project if risk management is to be effective and innovation encouraged, i.e. that:

- The Project Board supports and promotes risk management, understands and accepts the time and resource implications of any countermeasures
- Risk management policies and the benefits of effective risk management are clearly communicated to all staff
- A consistent approach to risk management is fully embedded in the project management processes
- Management of risks is an essential contribution to the achievement of business objectives
- Risks through working with programmes and other projects are assessed and managed
- There is a clear structure to the risk process so that each element or level of risk identification fits into an overall structure
- Where the project is part of a programme, changes in the state of any project risks that are also identified as programme risks must be flagged to programme management or the designated risk management function in the programme.

17.2.1 Risk tolerance

Another name for this is 'risk appetite'. Before determining what to do about risks, the Project Board and Project Manager must consider the amount of risk they are prepared to tolerate. This will vary according to the perceived importance of particular risks. For example, the view of financial risks and how much the project team is prepared to put at risk will depend on a number of variables, such as budgets, the effect on other parts of the programme or organisation or additional risks such as political embarrassment. A project team may be prepared to take comparatively large risks in some areas and none at all in others, such as risks to health and safety. Risk tolerance can be related to other tolerance parameters; risk to completion within time scale and/or cost and to achieving product quality and project scope within the boundaries of the Business Case.

Perceptions of risk tolerance have to be considered in detail to establish the optimum balance of a risk occurring against the costs and value for money of limiting that risk. The organisation's overall tolerance of exposure to risk must also be considered as well as a view of individual risks.

17.2.2 Risk responsibilities

The management of risk is one of the most important parts of the job done by the Project Board and the Project Manager. The Project Manager is responsible for ensuring that risks are identified, recorded and regularly reviewed. The Project Board has four responsibilities:

- Notifying the Project Manager of any external risk exposure to the project
- Making decisions on the Project Manager's recommended reactions to risk
- Striking a balance between the level of risk and the potential benefits that the project may achieve
- Notifying corporate or programme management of any risks that affect the project's ability to meet corporate or programme objectives.

The Project Manager modifies plans to include agreed actions to avoid or reduce the impact of risks.

Risk analysis requires input from the management of the organisation. The organisation's management, in turn, is kept informed by the Project Board of the risk analysis results.

Communication is particularly important between the project and programme levels within the organisation. Where the project is part of a programme, the management of risk procedures used by the project must be consistent and compatible with those of the programme unless there are valid reasons not to do so. Where a risk is uncovered in the programme, any affected projects should be involved in the analysis of that risk. Similarly, project risk evaluation should include staff from the programme.

Project risks that threaten programme milestones or objectives must be escalated to programme management.

17.2.3 Risk ownership

An 'owner' should be identified for each risk, who should be the person best situated to keep an eye on it. The Project Manager will normally suggest the 'owner' and the Project Board should make the decision. Project Board members may be appointed 'owners' of risks, particularly risks from sources external to the project. Allocating ownership of the risk process as a whole and the various components is fundamental from the outset. When describing who owns the various elements of risk, it is important to identify who owns the following:

- The risk framework in totality
- Setting risk policy and the project team's willingness to take risk
- Different elements of the risk process, such as identifying threats, through to producing risk response and reporting
- Implementation of the actual measures taken in response to the risks
- Interdependent risks that cross organisational boundaries, whether they be related to business processes, IT systems or other projects.

Overall ownership of the Risk Log is likely to lie with the Executive. However, the Executive will need to ensure that the people who own the various parts of the risk process are clearly defined, documented and agreed, so that they understand their various roles, responsibilities and ultimate accountability with regard to the management of risk.

Normally the risk 'owner' will have the responsibility of monitoring each risk. If the owner is a Project Board member, the actual task of monitoring may be delegated, but the responsibility stays with the owner. The Executive, for example, has ultimate responsibility for monitoring any risks or opportunities facing the Business Case, particularly any external ones, such as changes in company policy. The Project Manager has the job of keeping a watching brief over all risks and checking that the defined actions, including monitoring, are taking place and are having the desired effect.

Risks owned at team level should be reported on in the Checkpoint Reports. The Project Manager includes some form of report on any significant risks in the Highlight Report. The End Stage Report also summarises the risk status.

Where a risk or opportunity actually occurs, the Project Manager will either instigate contingency action, or deal with the issue under *Change Control* (Chapter 20).

17.3 The risk management cycle

Every project is subject to constant change in its business and wider environment. The risk environment is constantly changing too. The project's priorities and relative importance of risks will shift and change. Assumptions about risk have to be regularly revisited and reconsidered, for example at each end stage assessment.

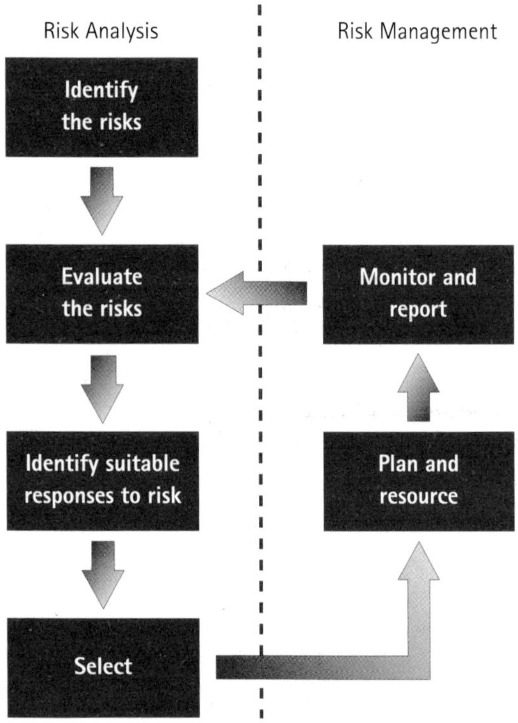

Figure 17.2 The risk management cycle

Figure 17.2 shows the main steps through the risk management cycle. The steps are described in more detail below.

17.3.1 Risk analysis

Risk identification

This step identifies the potential risks (or opportunities) facing the project. Appendix C lists various categories of risk that make a useful start point for risk identification. It is important not to judge the likelihood of a risk at this early time. This is done in a controlled manner in a later step. Attempting to form judgements while 'brainstorming' a list of potential risks may lead to hurried and incorrect decisions to exclude some risks.

Once identified, risks are all entered in the Risk Log. This contains details of all risks, their assessment, owners and status. A suggested list of contents is given in Appendix A, *Product Description outlines*. The Risk Log is a control tool for the Project Manager, providing a quick reference to the key risks facing the project, what monitoring activities should be taking place and by whom. Reference to it can lead to entries in the Project Manager's Daily Log to check on the status of a risk or associated activities.

Evaluation

Risk evaluation is concerned with assessing probability and impact of individual risks, taking into account any interdependencies or other factors outside the immediate scope under investigation:

- Probability is the evaluated likelihood of a particular outcome actually happening (including a consideration of the frequency with which the outcome may arise). For example, major damage to a building is relatively unlikely to happen, but would have enormous impact on business continuity. Conversely, occasional personal computer system failure is fairly likely to happen, but would not usually have a major impact on the business
- Impact is the evaluated effect or result of a particular outcome actually happening
- Impact should ideally be considered under the elements of:
  - time
  - quality
  - benefit
  - people/resources.

Some risks, such as financial risk, can be evaluated in numerical terms. Others, such as adverse publicity, can only be evaluated in subjective ways. There is a need for some framework for categorising risks, for example, high, medium and low.

When considering a risk's probability, another aspect is when the risk might occur. Some risks will be predicted to be further away in time than others and so attention can be focused on the more immediate ones. This prediction is called the risk's proximity. The proximity of each risk should be included in the Risk Log.

Identify suitable responses to risk

The actions break into broadly five types, as shown in Table 17.1.

Table 17.1

Prevention	Terminate the risk – by doing things differently and thus removing the risk, where it is feasible to do so. Countermeasures are put in place that either stop the threat or problem from occurring or prevent it having any impact on the project or business
Reduction	Treat the risk – take action to control it in some way where the actions either reduce the likelihood of the risk developing or limit the impact on the project to acceptable levels
Transference	This is a specialist form of risk reduction where the management of the risk is passed to a third party via, for instance, an insurance policy or penalty clause, such that the impact of the risk is no longer an issue for the health of the project. Not all risks can be transferred in this way
Acceptance	Tolerate the risk – perhaps because nothing can be done at a reasonable cost to mitigate it or the likelihood and impact of the risk occurring are at an acceptable level
Contingency	These are actions planned and organised to come into force as and when the risk occurs

Any given risk could have appropriate actions in any or all these categories. There may be no cost-effective actions available to deal with a risk, in which case the risk must be accepted or the justification for the project revisited (to review whether the project is too risky), possibly resulting in the termination of the project.

The results of the risk evaluation activities are documented in the Risk Log. If the project is part of a programme, project risks should be examined for any impact on the programme (and vice versa). Where any cross-impact is found, the risk should be added to the other Risk Log.

Selection

The risk response process should involve identifying and evaluating a range of options for treating risks and preparing and implementing risk management plans. It is important that the control action put in place is proportional to the risk. Every control has an associated cost. The control action must offer value for money in relation to the risk that it is controlling.

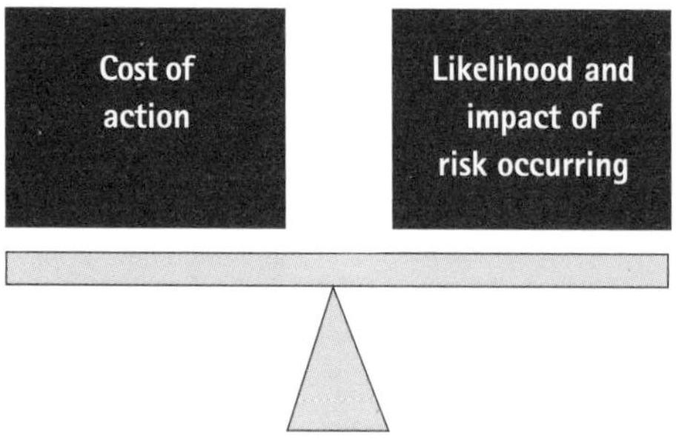

Figure 17.3 Balancing the risk

Selection of the risk actions to take is a balance between a number of things. For each possible action it is, first, a question of balancing the cost of taking that action against the likelihood and impact of allowing the risk to occur as shown in Figure 17.3. As an example, if a charity carnival is arranged, is it worth taking out insurance for £3,000 guaranteeing £6,000 if the carnival is rained off? Or, since the carnival date is in summer, do we take the risk and not spend the insurance money?

But the selection is usually more complex than that. As Figure 17.4 shows, there are many elements to be taken into consideration.

There may be several possible risk actions, each with different effects. The choice may be one of these options or a combination of two or more. We then have to consider the impact of (a) the risk occurring and (b) the risk action on:

- The team, Stage and/or Project Plans
- The business or programme
- The Business Case
- Other parts of the project.

The consideration has to be done in the light of the risk tolerances.

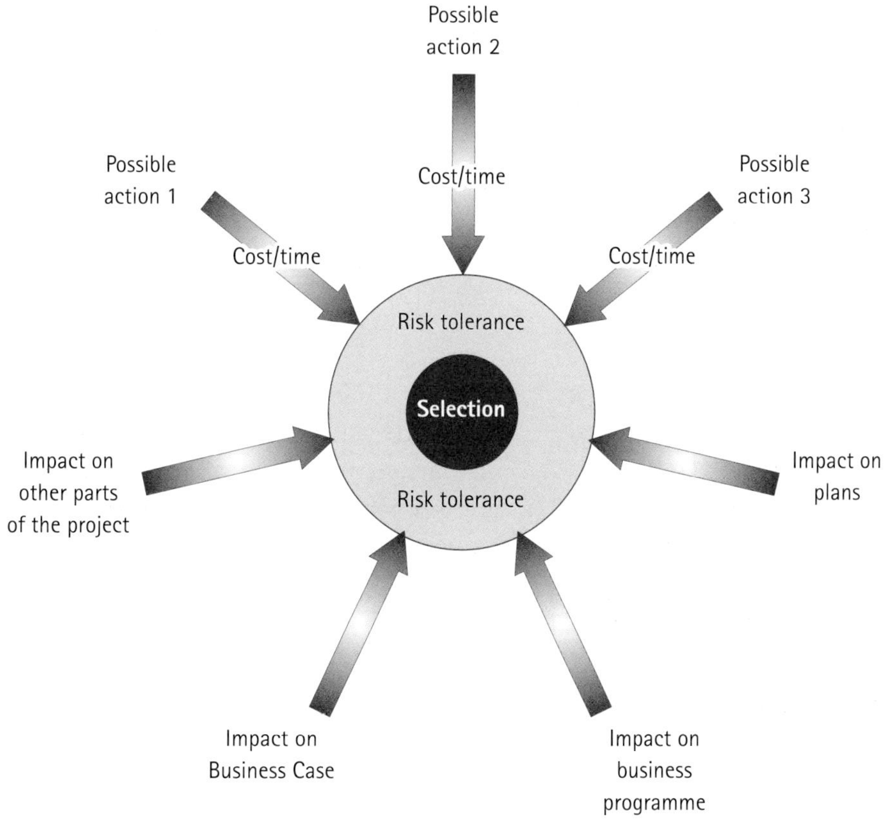

Figure 17.4 Risk action selection

17.3.2 Risk management

Planning and resourcing

Having made the selection, the implementation of the selected actions will need planning and resourcing and is likely to include plan changes, new or modified Work Packages:

- Planning, which, for the countermeasure actions itemised during the risk evaluation activities, consists of:
  - identifying the quantity and type of resources required to carry out the actions
  - developing a detailed plan of action; this will be included in Project and Stage Plans either as additional activities or as a contingency plan
  - confirming the desirability of carrying out the actions identified during risk evaluation in light of any additional information gained
  - obtaining management approval along with all the other aspects of the plans being produced
- Resourcing, which will identify and assign the actual resources to be used to conduct the work involved in carrying through the actions; these assignments will be shown in Project and Stage Plans; note that the resources required for the prevention, reduction and transference actions will have to be funded from the project budget since they are actions that we are committed to carry out; contingent actions will normally be funded from a contingency budget.

Monitoring and reporting

There must be mechanisms in place for monitoring and reporting on the actions selected to address risks.

Some of the actions may have only been to monitor the identified risk for signs of a change in its status. Monitoring, however, may consist of:

- Checking that execution of the planned actions is having the desired effect
- Watching for the early warning signs that a risk is developing
- Modelling trends, predicting potential risks or opportunities
- Checking that the overall management of risk is being applied effectively.

17.4 Risk profile

This is a simple mechanism to increase visibility of risks and assist management decision making. It is a graphical representation of information normally found in existing Risk Logs. It is only one possible representation of a project's risk status. The Project Board may choose to have an easy-to-read diagram as shown in Figure 17.5, for example, included in the Highlight Report.

The profile shows risks, using the risk identifier, in terms of probability and impact with the effects of planned countermeasures taken into account. The Project Manager would update this matrix in line with the Risk Log on a regular basis. In the example, we can see that risk 5 is currently considered to be of high probability and high impact. In particular, any risk shown above and right of the 'risk tolerance line' (the thick black line) should be referred upwards. This line is set for the project by agreement between the Executive and Project Manager.

As risks are reviewed, any changes to their impact or probability which cause them to move above and to the right of the 'risk tolerance line' need to be considered carefully and referred upwards for a management decision on the action to take.

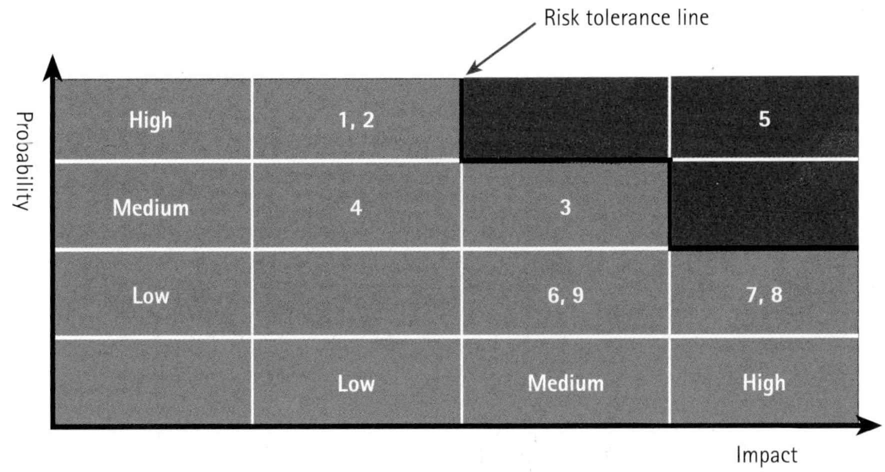

Figure 17.5 Summary risk profile

17.5 Budgeting for risk management

A project needs to allocate the appropriate budget, time and resources to risk management. The risk process must be embedded in the project environment, rather than being tacked on as an afterthought. The cost of carrying out risk management and the level of commitment and time, such as contingency plans, risk avoidance or reduction, needs to be recognised and agreed. While the budget may be allocated to actions relating to risk treatment, there is often a failure to provide sufficient budget to the earlier parts of the process, such as risk assessment that can require a diverse range of skills, tools and techniques. Experience has shown that allocating the correct budget to the risk management process early on will pay dividends later.

17.6 Mapping the risk management process to the PRINCE2 processes

At key points in a project, management of risk should be carried out (Figure 17.6).

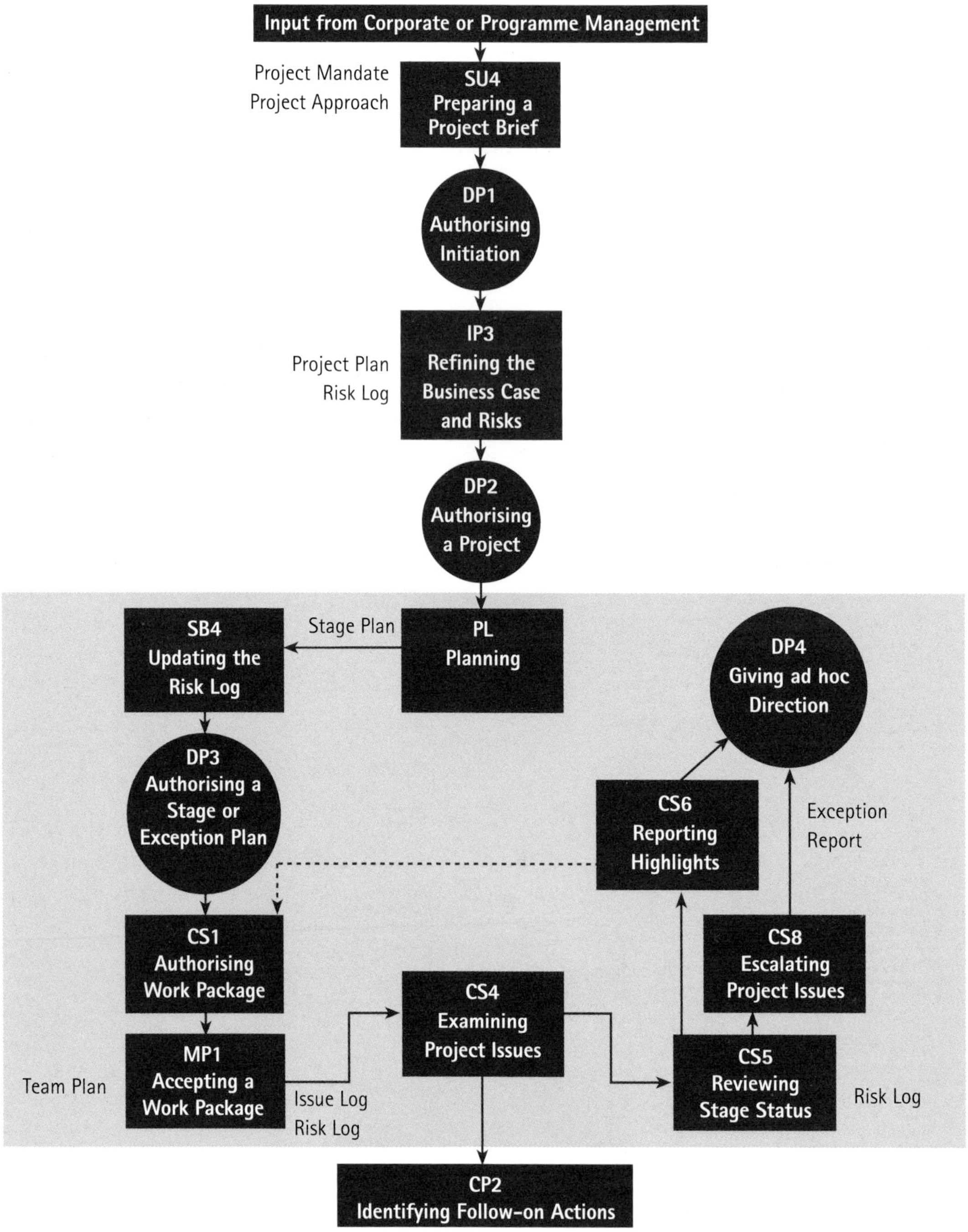

Figure 17.6 Risk flow, showing key points in a project when management is necessary

17.6.1 Preparing a Project Brief (SU4)

The Risk Log needs to be created by this time. A suggested structure for this is given in Appendix A, *Product Description outlines*. The Project Mandate may have referred to a number of risks facing the potential project. These may be such risks as competitor action, impending or mooted legislation, company policy changes, staff reorganisation or cash-flow problems. Certainly, the preparation of the Project Brief should give rise to an early study of such risks. Creation of the Project Approach (see *Defining Project Approach*, SU5) may also have introduced some extra risks.

17.6.2 Authorising Initiation (DP1)

This is the first formal milestone when the Project Board can examine the Risk Log as part of deciding whether project initiation can be justified. Pragmatically, the Project Manager should have discussed informally with board members any known risks that seem to threaten the project viability.

17.6.3 Refining the Business Case and Risks (IP3)

The Project Manager examines risks again as part of preparing the Project Initiation Document. At this time the Project Plan will be created and this may identify a number of risks, such as unknown performance of resources, contractor ability and any assumptions being made in the plan. New risks may also come to light as a result of adding detail to the Project Brief. At the same time all existing risks are reviewed for any new information or change in their circumstances.

17.6.4 Authorising a Project (DP2)

The Project Board now has an updated Risk Log to examine as part of its decision on whether to go ahead with the project. As a result of refining the Business Case, a number of risks may have been identified. Very often the 'owners' of these risks will be members of the Project Board and they should confirm their ownership and the actions required of them.

17.6.5 Planning (PL6)

Each time a plan is produced, elements of the plan may identify new risks, modify existing ones or eliminate others. No plan should be put forward for approval before its risk content has been analysed. This analysis may lead to the plan being modified in order to take the appropriate risk action(s). The Risk Log should be updated with all such details.

17.6.6 Updating the Risk Log (SB4)

As part of the preparation for a new stage, the Project Manager updates the Risk Log with any changes to existing risks.

17.6.7 Authorising a Stage or Exception Plan (DP3)

Before authorising a plan, the Project Board has the opportunity to study the risk situation as part of its judgement of the continuing viability of the project.

17.6.8 Authorising Work Package (CS1)

Negotiation with the Team Manager or team member may identify new risks or change old ones. It may require the Project Manager to go back and amend some part of the original Work Package or change the Stage Plan. Examples here are the assignee deciding to use new technology or needing to find special/rare resources.

17.6.9 Accepting a Work Package (MP1)

This is the point when the Team Manager makes out a team plan to ensure that the products of the Work Package can be delivered within the constraints of the agreed Work Package. Like any other plan, it may contain new risks or modify existing ones.

17.6.10 Examining Project Issues (CS4)

Assessment of a new Project Issue may throw up a risk situation. For example, a proposed change may produce a risk of pushing the stage or project beyond its tolerance margins.

17.6.11 Reviewing Stage Status (CS5)

This brings together the Stage Plan with its latest actual figures, the Project Plan, the Business Case, open Project Issues, the tolerance status and the Risk Log. The Project Manager (in conjunction with the Project Assurance roles) looks for risk situation changes as well as any other warning signs.

17.6.12 Escalating Project Issues (CS8)

As well as Project Issues, a risk change may cause the Project Manager to raise an Exception Report to the Project Board.

17.6.13 Reporting Highlights (CS6)

As part of this task, the Project Manager may take the opportunity to raise any risk matters with the Project Board. Examples here would be notifying the board of any risks that are no longer relevant, warning about new risks and reminders about risks that board members should be keeping an eye on. The suggested format of a Highlight Report is included in Appendix A, *Product Description outlines*.

17.6.14 Giving Ad Hoc Direction (DP4)

The Project Manager advises the Project Board of exception situations via the Exception Report. It has the opportunity to react with advice or a decision – for example, bringing the project to a premature close, requesting an Exception Plan or removing the problem. The Project Board may also instigate ad hoc advice on the basis of information given to it from corporate or programme management or another external source.

17.6.15 Identifying Follow-on Actions (CP2)

At the end of the project a number of risks may have been identified that will affect the product in its operational life. These should be transferred to the Follow-on Action Recommendations for the information of those who will support the product after the project.

17.7 Interdependencies

Risks may have additional factors relating to them that increase the complexity of assessing your overall exposure to risk. These include interdependencies. It is essential to understand the interdependencies of risks and how they can compound each other. For example, a skills shortage combined with serious technical problems and a requirement to bring the delivery date forward are common examples of risk compounding. Interdependencies can occur at all levels and across different levels.

A project may have interdependencies with other projects. A project may be dependent upon a supplier delivering products or services that have a further interdependency upon another internal project delivering its objectives and so on in the supply chain. These need to be explicitly identified and assessed as part of the process of risk management. Interdependencies often cross different boundaries, such as ownership, funding, decision making, organisational or geographical boundaries. You must be able to assess risk and communicate across these boundaries.

17.8 Further risk management considerations

The relationship between benefit and delivery risks

Often the risk management process is focused primarily on delivery rather than benefit. Changes to delivery dates, costs, quality, etc. are not related back to the benefits. The drive to deliver may continue long after the potential benefits have been significantly reduced or lost. A common cause of this is that the owners of benefit objectives are not the same as the owners of delivery. Decisions taken with regard to delivery must be related back to benefit and vice versa.

Internal versus external risks

Much is made of the difference between internal and external risks. The major differences, however, relate to the ability to apply the risk process to them. Internal risks can be just as difficult to identify, assess and evaluate as external risks and thus just as complex to manage. The same broad principles of risk management apply to both.

Hints and tips

The cost of setting up a management of risk process for a project depends on the technical, political and organisational complexity involved. There are some general guidelines that can be applied, however. Planners for projects should expect to spend 1–3 per cent of their budget on an initial risk management effort and an additional 2 per cent on monitoring and updating this throughout the development life cycle.

Checklist on assignment of risk ownership:

- Have owners been allocated to all the various parts of the complete risk process and the full scope of the risks being catered for? For example, suppliers may be tasked with ownership of assessing and evaluating risk as part of their contracts.

- Are the various roles and responsibilities associated with ownership well defined?
- Do the individuals who have been allocated ownership actually have the authority in practice to fulfil their responsibilities?
- Have the various roles and responsibilities been communicated and understood?
- Are the nominated owners appropriate?
- In the event of a change, can ownership be quickly and effectively reallocated?
- Are the differences between benefit and delivery risks clearly understood and, if required, do they have different owners?

The Project Manager's Daily Log can be very useful in monitoring risks. Entries can be made in it for the Project Manager to check on the status of any risks where he/she is the owner. Other entries can be made to remind the Project Manager to check that other owners are monitoring and controlling their risks and feeding the information back.

Where the project is part of a programme:

- Programme management is responsible for ensuring the management of those risks with interdependencies between projects and programme.
- Where appropriate, the programme should take part in the risk management activities at the project level. This can normally be done by attendance at end stage assessments by either a member of programme management or a designated risk management function.
- Risks are frequently common across projects and would benefit from being centralised at programme level. The cost of corrective action can be reduced if it is planned, agreed and actioned only once. Also, problems can result from an inconsistent approach being taken by projects.

18
QUALITY IN A PROJECT ENVIRONMENT

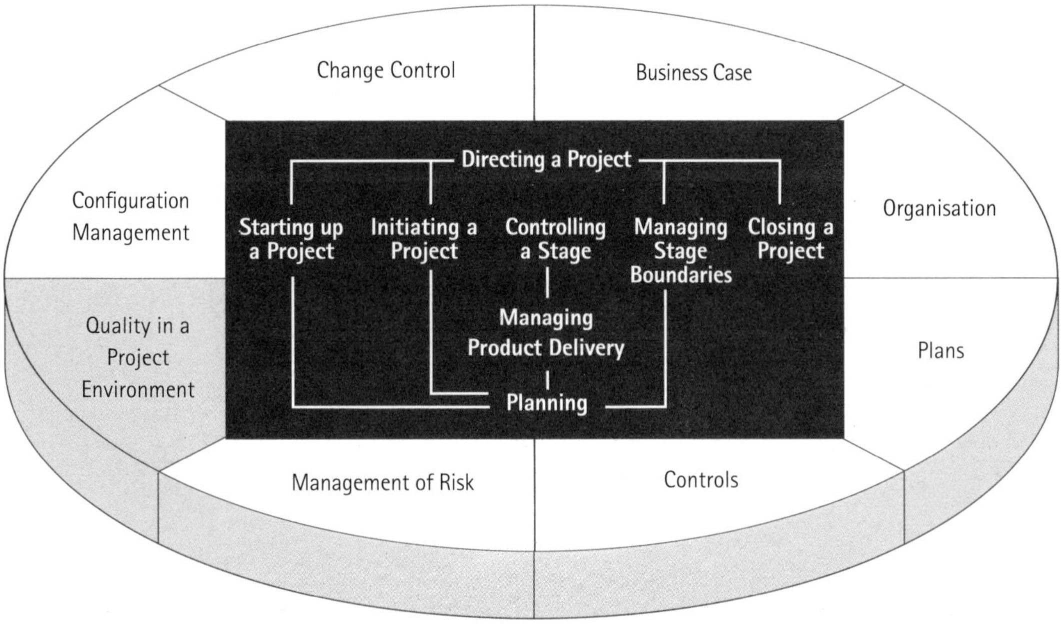

Figure 18.1: Quality in the PRINCE2 template

18.1 Purpose

The purpose of this chapter is to outline the main elements of quality as they apply to a project and to put project quality in context with ISO (International Organisation for Standards) quality standards.

18.2 What is quality?

Quality is defined in ISO 8402 as the:

totality of characteristics of an entity which bear on its ability to satisfy stated and implied needs

Within projects, quality is a question of identifying what it is about the project's products or services that makes them fit for their purpose of satisfying stated needs. Projects should not rely on implied needs. These lead to uncertainty and, as such, are of little use.

18.3 Quality management

Quality management is the process of ensuring that the quality expected by the customer is achieved. It encompasses all the project management activities that determine and implement the Project Quality Plan. The various elements of an organisation's quality management interrelate and are as follows:

- A *quality system,* which has an organisation structure, procedures and processes to implement quality management. Both the customer and the supplier may have quality systems. The project may have to use one of these systems or an agreed mixture of both. PRINCE2 itself will typically form part of a corporate or programme quality system where it has been adopted as a corporate or programme standard
- *Quality assurance,* which creates and maintains the quality system and monitors its application to ensure that the quality system is operated and is effective in achieving an end product that meets quality and customer requirements. A quality assurance function should be separate from and independent of the organisation's project and operational activities to monitor use of the quality system across all projects within the corporate body. If such an independent body does not exist, the Project Assurance function will assume the quality assurance role within the project
- *Quality planning,* which establishes the objectives and requirements for quality and lays out the activities for the application of the quality system. In the Project Initiation Document the quality methods for the whole project are defined in the Project Quality Plan. It is important that the customer's quality expectations are understood and documented prior to project commencement. This is done in *Starting up a Project* (SU). Each Stage Plan specifies in detail the required quality activities and resources, with the detailed quality criteria shown in the Product Descriptions. Product Descriptions define the required quality criteria for a product and the quality control method to be used to check for the existence of that quality. The Product Description may need to be updated if a change to the product is agreed. Once approved, a Product Description should not be changed without passing through change control
- *Quality control,* which is the means of ensuring that products meet the quality criteria specified for them. Quality control is about examining products to determine that they meet requirements. Quality reviews are the primary PRINCE2 technique in making project quality work and are fully described in Chapter 24.

18.4 The quality path

The path to quality in PRINCE2 is shown in Figure 18.2. Each element in this figure is explained in the following sub-sections, with cross-references to the areas of PRINCE2 that relate to it.

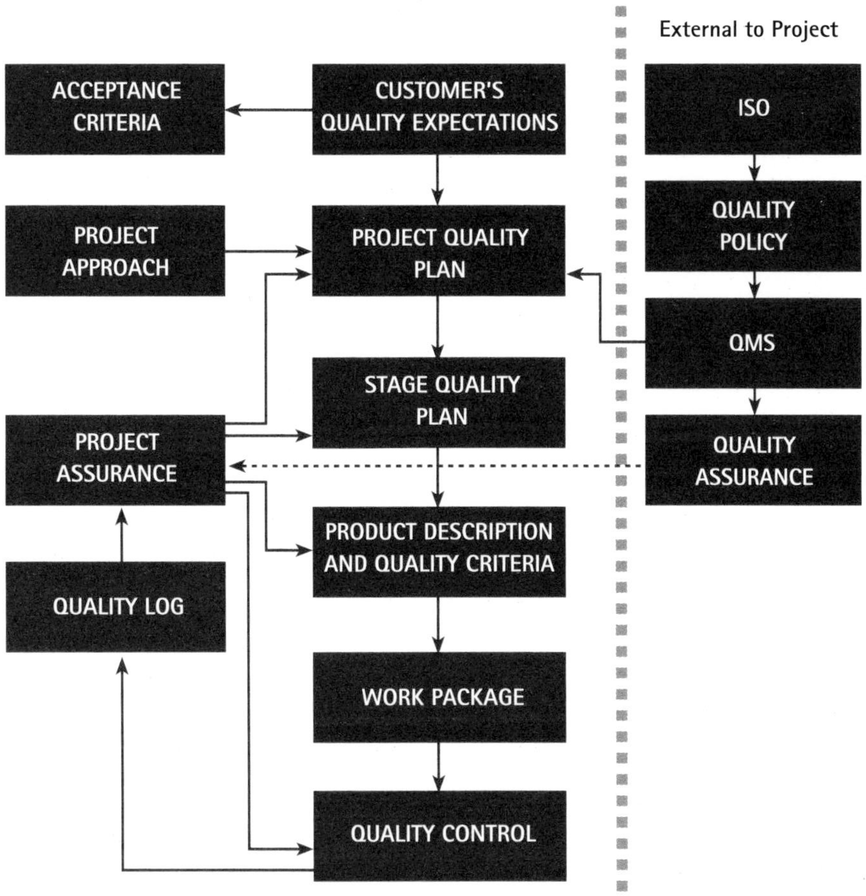

Figure 18.2 The path to quality

18.4.1 Elements of the quality path

Customer's quality expectations

In PRINCE2, quality considerations begin with discovering what the customer's quality expectations are. This should be done in the process *Starting up a Project* (SU). No realistic plan can be made to provide the customer with a quality product until both customer and supplier understand and agree what that quality should be. The customer and supplier need a common understanding of the link between quality, cost and time and must balance these while ensuring that the end product is fit for its purpose and built within the other constraints.

The colloquial use of the word 'quality' implies 'high quality', i.e. the use of the best materials, expert craftsmanship, inspection at all points of the product's development, and thorough testing beyond all its expected limits, but this may not be the case. All products do not have the same quality expectations. Is the product designed to 'last a lifetime' or is it 'use once, throw away'? Compare the time and effort spent in ensuring that the Oxford dictionary is free from spelling mistakes with that spent on your daily newspaper.

Quality expectations can be considered under many headings, such as:

- Functional requirement
- Performance

- Accuracy
- Practicability
- Security
- Compatibility
- Reliability
- Maintainability
- Expandability
- Flexibility
- Clarity
- Comparison to another product
- Cost
- Implementation date.

These elements need to be identified and, as far as possible, quantified for each project.

ISO

ISO issues an international range of standards including those for quality management systems. There is a specific standard covering quality management system requirements in the design/development, production, installation and servicing of a product, including project management. It is a standard used by many organisations as the basis for their quality management system (QMS). The use of PRINCE2 can help to meet this quality standard.

A company can use the ISO quality standard when:

- Setting up a quality management function
- Examining the quality assurance system of a supplier.

It therefore may have several impacts on the quality considerations for a project:

- The customer and/or the supplier when creating its quality management system may have used it as a checklist
- The supplier's development methods may be accredited under an ISO standard
- The customer may wish to match a supplier's quality methods against the requirements of an ISO standard or insist on a supplier who holds an ISO standard accreditation
- It may have been used as the basis for the corporate quality policy of the supplier.

Quality policy

The customer and/or the supplier may have a quality policy, laying down the company's attitude towards the quality of anything that it makes or uses. It should direct and influence the supplier's attitude in construction, testing and reaction to any customer complaints about quality.

If both customer and supplier have quality policies, it is sensible to check that they are in harmony. If not, there will need to be an agreed compromise, driven by the needs and best interests of the customer.

Where the project is part of a programme, the programme should provide guidance or direction to the project.

Quality Management System (QMS)

Two things should support a quality policy; a quality management system and a quality organisation structure.

The QMS is a set of standards covering all the normal work done by that company. Each standard will cover the techniques, tools, required expertise and steps to be used in the creation of a specific type of product. If the product is a document, the standard will also cover its format or appearance.

If both the customer and supplier have quality management systems, there must be agreement on which QMS or what amalgamation of standards from both sets of standards will be used.

The quality organisation structure indicates the responsibilities for quality – that is, who sets the quality policy, who sets the standards to meet the policy, any external body imposing quality constraints, who monitors use of the standards and any quality training group. Much of this work is often done by a central quality assurance function.

Acceptance Criteria

The customer's quality expectations should be linked with the overall Acceptance Criteria of the final outcome. Other possible Acceptance Criteria are given in the *Product Description outlines* in Appendix A.

Quality assurance

Site-wide responsibility for setting and monitoring quality standards is often given to a quality assurance group. The Project Quality Plan should indicate where this responsibility for setting the quality standards lies. It may be that the independent quality assurance group has a representative take a Project Assurance role in order to monitor the use and effectiveness of agreed standards. If so, this should be stated in the Project Quality Plan.

Project Approach

How the project aims to meet the customer's quality expectations will be affected by the approach chosen for the provision of the end result. Typical approaches would include:

- The product is built from scratch by the customer's staff
- An external supplier builds the product from scratch
- The product is built from scratch with contributions from many external organisations

- An existing product is modified to meet new needs
- An off-the-shelf product is bought.

Quality control methods and responsibilities will vary according to the approach chosen.

The Project Approach is confirmed as part of *Starting up a Project* (SU). Therefore it is in place and can be used by the initiation process *Planning Quality* (IP1).

It is normally impossible to be involved in the testing of an off-the-shelf product. A privileged customer might be asked to participate in an early test of a product, but this typically only happens when the organisation is already a customer. Checks on the quality of such products can be made with existing customers. Sometimes for more expensive products there is a trial period when testing can be done.

Project Assurance

PRINCE2 offers a good means of checking quality where a product is to be developed by external contractors. This is through use of the Project Assurance function. Each time an external Team Manager plans work for the project, the Project Assurance role should review and approve the draft plan. The purpose is to identify products being developed in the plan that are of interest to the Project Assurance function. Project Assurance then verifies that quality checking arrangements for these products are satisfactory. This covers the method of inspection, the points in the products' development when inspections are to be held and the people to be involved in the inspection. Project Assurance should have the option to specify people to be included in inspections. This is particularly relevant and important for the customer's assurance of an external contractor's work. This requirement to inspect and modify the contractor's plans should be included in the contract.

Project Quality Plan

This is created in *Initiating a Project* (IP). It forms part of the Project Initiation Document. It defines in general terms how the project will meet the customer's quality expectations.

It will identify the techniques and standards to be used. If there is a QMS in existence, it is normally sufficient simply to reference the QMS manual that contains the standards. If necessary, the Project Quality Plan will identify any standards in the QMS that will not be used or any extra standards not in the QMS that will be used.

The plan should also identify quality responsibilities for the project. For example, if the customer or the supplier has a quality assurance function, the plan would explain how that function would play a part in the project. This links with the *Organisation* component of PRINCE2, where the external quality assurance function may take part of the Project Assurance role.

The Project Quality Plan should mention the quality responsibilities of the Project Manager and Configuration Librarian, and define how the assurance responsibilities of each Project Board member are to be handled.

Stage or team quality plan

Stage Plans or team plans should contain a quality plan that will identify the method(s) and resources to be used to check the quality of each product. The Project Assurance roles have a key part to play here in identifying products of key interest to their role and in specifying who should be involved in quality checking these products. For example, for any quality reviews, the names of the chairperson and reviewers would be given. The Stage or team plan should show in diagrammatic form (typically a Gantt chart) when the review will take place and how long it will take.

This is particularly important where work is being allocated to an external team. Rather than wait until the 'finished' product is handed over for acceptance trials, it may be better for the customer to have people checking the product all the way through its design and development. Finding out that a product doesn't meet requirements during its acceptance trials is expensively late – maybe fatally so.

Stage and team quality plans will not be separate documents, but an integral part of the Stage and team plans.

Where external teams are to be used, it is important to define in the contract that the Project Assurance function has the right to see draft plans and insist on its people being part of quality checks whenever it wishes.

Product Descriptions and quality criteria

As part of a Stage Plan there should be a Product Description for each major product to be created during that stage. This indicates, among other things, the quality criteria that the product must meet and the method of checking that those criteria exist in the finished product.

It is sensible, often essential, to involve the customer's staff in defining the Product Descriptions, including the quality criteria. Not only are they the people who should know best, but also the product needs to meet their quality expectations.

An inherent quality criterion for every product is that the product should satisfy all the elements of the Product Description. For example, it should contain those elements mentioned under 'composition' and be capable of satisfying the defined purpose of the product.

Quality control

PRINCE2 identifies a specific technique for quality control called quality review. The detailed steps of a quality review are explained in Chapter 24. Basically it is a structured review of a document by a group of people in a planned, documented and organised fashion. The people involved should have been identified when creating the Stage Plan. The technique links with the configuration management part of the project organisation, which will be responsible for releasing copies of the document to be reviewed, freezing the original copy and updating the status of the product.

There is also a link with Project Support, which might undertake the organisation of the review and the dissemination of the documentation.

Quality Log

The Quality Log is created during *Initiating a Project* (IP). It is the record of all the quality checking done in the project.

Details of all quality checking activities are entered in the log as they are planned in either Stage or team plans.

The Team Manager or individual team member charged with the development and testing of a product subsequently updates the log with the results and dates of that quality checking. It forms an audit trail of the quality work done in the project.

18.4.2 Project Issues

Project Issues have many potential impacts on quality. A Project Issue may be reporting a quality problem. Normally such problems would be found during quality control. But a quality problem may be found in a product that has already been approved or a review might discover a problem in a product that is not the one being inspected. There is also the possibility that a problem may be found during quality control that requires a lot of time and/or resource to fix. It may even be decided, because of time constraints, to approve a product that contains an error. In both these cases the error may be accepted as a concession. This will be raised as a Project Issue (as an Off-Specification), so that a record exists and the error will not be overlooked.

If a Project Issue requires changes to one or more products, the relevant Product Descriptions should be checked to see if they also need changing.

18.4.3 What is special about quality in the project environment?

It is very difficult, if not impossible, to achieve the business benefits of a product if that product does not meet the customer's quality expectations.

By its nature, a project is a temporary environment created for a particular purpose. As such, any required quality management for the project may have to be created for that project if the organisation does not already have a quality system in place.

18.5 Making project quality work

Project quality planning should cover the following aspects to ensure that the project delivers to an acceptable level of quality:

- *How* each product will be tested against its quality criteria
- *When* each product will be tested against its quality criteria
- *By whom* each product will be tested against its quality criteria
- How acceptance will be notified.

The first aspect is actioned by *Planning Quality* (IP1) at the outset of the project, during *Initiating a Project*. The next two aspects are actioned in the relevant Stage Plans, created in *Planning a Stage* (SB1).

Quality is achieved by a combination of actions. The quality criteria for all levels of product are stated in measurable terms in the Product Descriptions (this is described in Chapter 22 *Product-Based Planning*). The process of producing the products and services is controlled via *Authorising Work Package* (CS1) and *Assessing Progress* (CS2).

The final aspect is the process of using all the quality-checking techniques defined in the quality system. These split largely into two groups:

- Objective methods, where, after applying them, there is a largely definitive 'yes' or 'no' answer to whether the product is 'to quality'. Examples of these methods are the use of gauges and meters, testing and checklists.
- Subjective methods, where the criteria involve either judgement or opinion, such as user friendliness, conformance to business strategy and market acceptability. To control the process of checking conformance to quality in these areas, the quality review technique is available.

Hints and tips

It is almost always possible to define objectively measurable criteria. But it is sometimes not worth it – that is, not cost or time effective.

The Daily Log can be used by either the Project Manager or the Team Manager to note down a check that needs to be made about quality, such as finding out why a planned quality check has not been done (or not recorded in the Quality Log), why so many errors were discovered in a quality check and so on.

Customers and Suppliers may have different Quality standards. It is important to ensure that appropriate measures are agreed with/between all parties.

19
CONFIGURATION MANAGEMENT

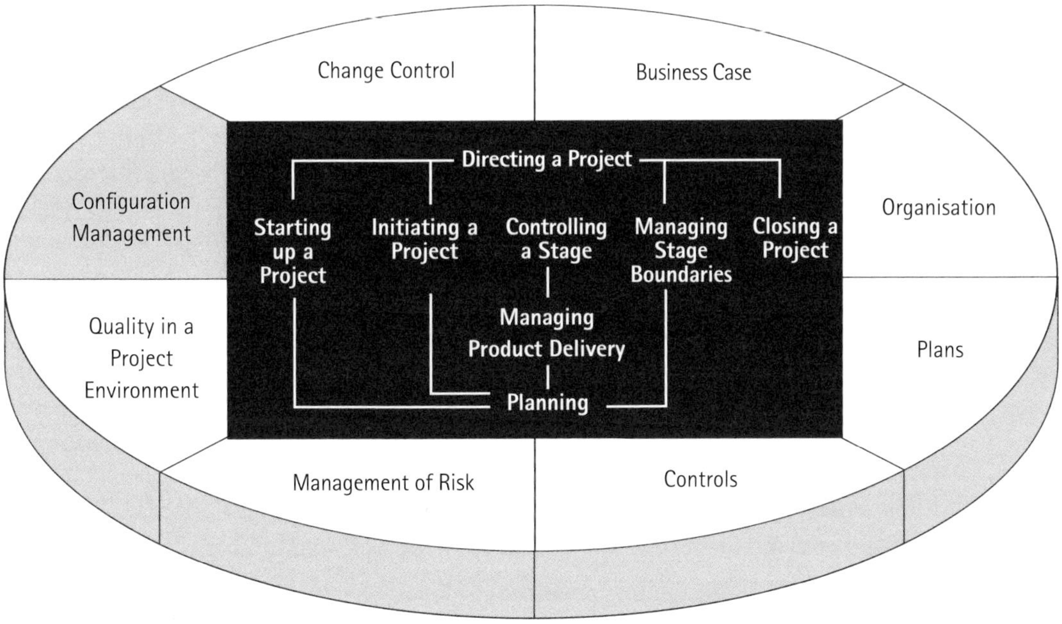

Figure 19.1 Configuration management in the PRINCE2 template

19.1 Purpose

No organisation can be fully efficient or effective unless it manages its assets, particularly if the assets are vital to the running of the organisation's business. The assets of the project are the products that it develops and these also have to be managed. The name for the combined set of these assets is a configuration. The configuration of the final outcome of a project is the sum total of its products.

Within the context of project management, the purpose of configuration management is to identify, track and protect the project's products.

19.2 Definition

Configuration management may be thought of as asset or product control. It is a discipline that gives precise control over the project's products by allowing management to:

- Specify the versions of products in use and in existence and hold information on:
  - their status (e.g. in live use, archived, ready for quality checking)
  - who owns each product (the individual with prime responsibility for it)
  - the relationships between products

does the stated person indeed have the item out for change, or an incorrect status, such as a product shown to be baselined that is in fact being changed. The audit also checks that the configuration management process is being done to standards. They are normally carried out at the end of each stage.

Normally, someone with Project Assurance responsibility is responsible for configuration audits, with help from the Configuration Librarian. If the Project Board is carrying out its own Project Assurance, the Project Manager may appoint someone else to carry out the audit.

19.5 Configuration management method

A configuration management method may be manual or automated; whichever is available and most appropriate for the project and the organisation.

Configuration management covers the following functions:

- Identifying the individual sub-products of the final product
- Identifying those products that will be required in order to produce other products

(These first two bullet points offer a clear link to the information coming from PRINCE2's Product-based planning technique)

- Establishing a coding system that will uniquely identify each product
- Identifying the 'owner' of a product
- Identifying to whom creation or amendment of a version of a product has been delegated (this information would normally come from *Authorising Work Package* (CS1))
- Recording, monitoring and reporting on the current status of each product as it progresses through its own specific life cycle
- Filing all documentation produced during the development life of the product
- Retention of master copies of all relevant completed products within the configuration library
- Provision of procedures to ensure the safety and security aspects of the products and to control access to them
- Distribution of copies of all products and recording of holders of product copies
- Maintenance of the record of relationships between products so that no product is changed without being able to check for possible impact on related products
- Providing administrative support for change to all products
- Establishment of baselines (described in 19.3)
- Performance of configuration audits.

Many of these functions could be incorporated into the role of Configuration Librarian. Apart from the configuration management work, the Configuration Librarian also creates and maintains the project and stage files.

Items can only be amended or deleted through submission of an authorised Project Issue to the Configuration Librarian.

19.5.1 Configuration management coverage

The amount and formality of configuration management needed by a project depends on the type and size of the project and the project's environment. It is a question that needs to be faced at the outset of a project.

The configuration management method should cover all products once they have reached the stage of draft completion.

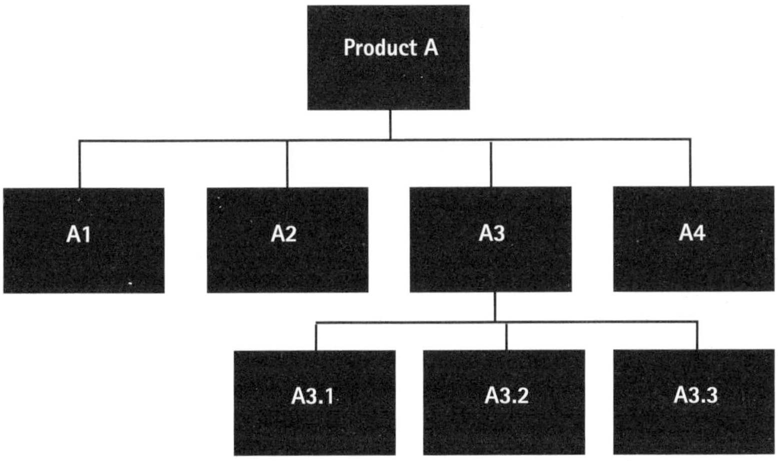

Figure 19.2 Configuration breakdown

19.5.2 Choosing the level of product

An important part of configuration management is deciding the level at which control is to be exercised – with top-level products broken down into components that are themselves products and so on. Figure 19.2 shows Product A, which consists of components A1, A2, A3 and A4. Each of these components can be broken down into smaller components. In this example A3 is made up of A3.1, A3.2 and A3.3. Each of the components shown is called a product, including the total product.

Normally, products are defined down to the lowest level at which a component can be independently installed, replaced or modified. Each project has to decide on the level at which to stop breaking products down to further levels. As another example, if the product is a training manual, does it make sense to break this product down into sub-products, such as contents page, index, overview chapter, glossary of terms, etc.? Would such a breakdown be better and more simply shown as the 'composition' part of the training manual's Product Description?

Apart from the construction of a car example quoted at the beginning of this chapter, other considerations are cost and effort. A more detailed breakdown gives greater control, but also increases the cost and effort of configuration management.

19.6 Configuration management and change control

There must be a close liaison between configuration management and change control. A key element is the ability to identify and control different versions of a product.

A baseline product can only be changed under formal change control. This means that a Project Issue has been authorised and presented to the Configuration Librarian. Once a product has been approved, that version of it never changes. If a change is required, a new version of the product is created that will encompass the change. The new version should be associated with documentation of the project issue that caused the need for the new version.

A product should not be issued for change to more than one person at a time. Where there are multiple changes to be applied to one product, they must be combined in some way and the completion of the product encompassing all changes must be delegated to one person. Alternatively, subsequent changes must wait until the current change has been implemented. Then, after approval of this change, the next version can be issued for the next change.

Where possible, the master copy of any product should never be issued, only a copy.

19.7 Configuration management and a Project Support Office

Because most final products will exist in operational use long after the project to create them has finished, configuration management is usually carried out on an organisation-wide basis, the same approach being used to look after both project and operational products. This is a good reason for providing configuration management expertise to all projects from a central Project Support Office, which will continue to control the products throughout their operational life.

There may be a requirement for a project to fit in with existing methods of configuration management used by the customer. Most end products from projects will have a long, useful life and will be modified many times during that life. Configuration management is essential to keep track of the changes. If the project has been outsourced, the configuration management method used by the supplier needs to be compatible with that of whichever group will look after the product during its operational life.

20 CHANGE CONTROL

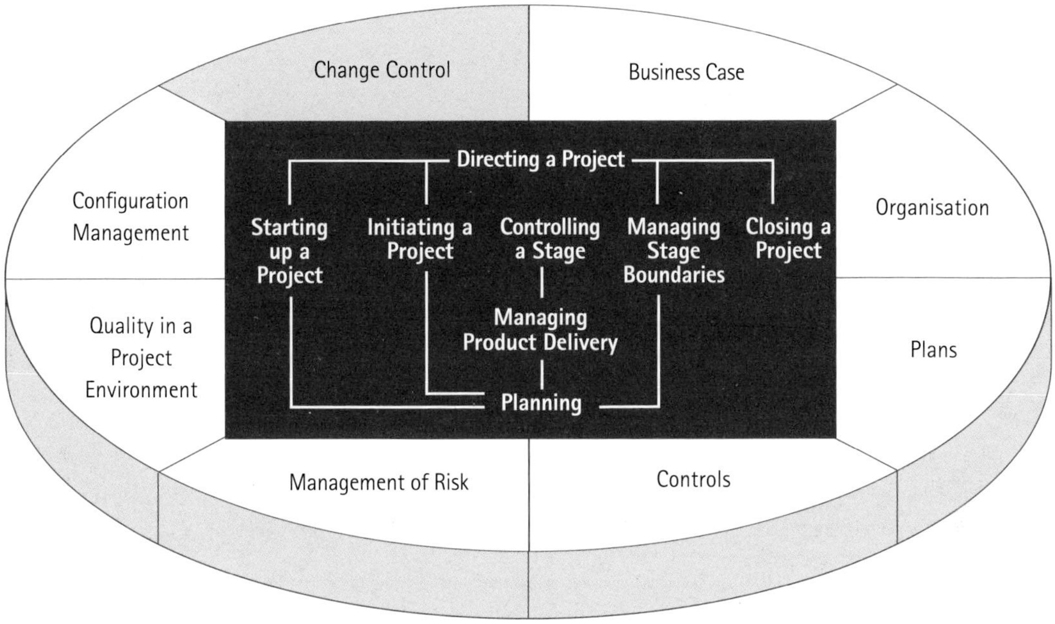

Figure 20.1 Change control in the PRINCE2 template

20.1 Purpose

Changes to specification or scope can potentially ruin any project unless they are carefully controlled. Change is, however, highly likely. The control of change means the assessment of the impact of potential changes, their importance, their cost and a judgmental decision by management on whether to include them or not. Any approved changes must be reflected in any necessary corresponding change to schedule and budget. An approach to the control of change is given in Chapter 23.

There is a need in any project to manage all the documents input to it. These documents may be change requests, suggestions or good ideas, documents relating to problems in fulfilling the requirements, recording external changes to the Business Case or risks or simply asking questions or making observations about some aspect of the project, such as the likely transfer of someone on the project management team. PRINCE2 uses change control as a common procedure to capture all these issues. All such input is recorded as a Project Issue.

20.2 Project Issue management

The objective is to capture, log and categorise all Project Issues. Project Issues may be raised at any time during the project, by anyone with an interest in the project or its outcome.

A Project Issue is anything that could have an effect on the project (either detrimental or beneficial). Project Issues include:

- A change in requirements, however minor (even apparently very minor changes can have major long-term implications)
- A change in the environment applicable to the project, for example:
  - a legislative change
  - a corporate change of direction
  - a new customer
  - a new supplier
  - an unexpected change to a member of the project management team
  - actions by a competitor
  - a programme management directive
  - a corporate reorganisation
- A problem occurring or being identified that was not anticipated during risk analysis
- An anticipated, but unavoidable, risk occurring
- A problem or error occurring in work completed or currently under way
- A query about any aspect of the Project.

Managing Project Issues will involve:

- Capturing and formally logging the issue (in the Issue Log)
- Assessing the issue to decide on the type and therefore what action is required
- Investigating the required actions
- Documenting the actions and confirming their completion
- Reviewing the Issue Log on a regular basis to monitor progress on outstanding issues.

Project Issues can arise from a very wide range of sources, including other project processes, can come in many forms and can show themselves in many ways. The first requirement of this process is, therefore, to provide a consistent and reliable method of capturing all Project Issues. All Project Issues should be entered into the Issue Log as soon as they are identified.

An initial assessment needs to be made as to the nature of each issue. Apart from general problems and questions, two specific types of change can result:

- A Request for Change, which, for whatever reason, will cause a change to the specification, or Acceptance Criteria, of the project or one of the project's products. Any additional cost to carry out the change will normally have to be funded by the customer
- An Off-Specification, covering errors or omissions found in work already conducted or planned for the future, which will result in agreed specifications or Acceptance

Criteria not being met. Additional costs to carry out this work will normally fall on any suppliers involved.

The funding implications make it important that the distinction between these two outcomes is made. There is usually more motivation to fix mistakes (i.e. Off-Specifications) than make changes (Request for Change). It is for these reasons that the distinction is made, although they are both processed in the same way.

20.3 Authority levels

One consideration at project initiation should be who is permitted to authorise changes (Project Issues) to what the project is to produce. Because this is a potential change to what the Project Board originally committed to at the start of the project, it is the Project Board's responsibility to agree to each change before it is implemented. In a project where few changes are envisaged, it may be reasonable to leave this authority in the hands of the Project Board. But projects may be in a dynamic environment, where there are likely to be, for example, many requests to change the initial agreed scope of the project. Remember, a Project Issue may be a notification of a failure to meet the specification, not just a request for change by the user:

- Is the Project Board prepared to make the time available to review all Project Issues?
- Does it wish to consider only the top priority Project Issues and delegate decisions on minor issues to another body?

The Project Board needs to decide before the project moves out of project initiation where the authority for approving or rejecting Project Issues lies and these responsibilities must be written into the appropriate job descriptions. In some projects the Project Board may choose to delegate decisions on Project Issue action to a group, here called a 'change authority'.

For projects that exist within a programme, programme management will define the level of authority that the Project Board will have to approve changes.

20.3.1 Change budget

As well as considering where authority for decision lies, the Project Board must consider:

- How will changes be funded?
- Will the Project Board go back to corporate or programme management to vary funding, timetable or scope each time a change is desired?

Unless the anticipated level of change on a project is low, it is advisable for the change authority to be given a budget to pay for changes. This arrangement can avoid a number of in-stage assessments by the Project Board in projects where the frequency of Project Issues is forecast to be high. Where a change budget has been allocated, there must be agreement on how it is to be used, where the responsibilities lie and what constraints there are on its use.

20.4 Integrity of change

Project Issues should not be considered in isolation. Some other considerations are as follows.

20.4.1 Benefit/Business Case driven

The Project Issues should be viewed against the benefits they offer and their impact on the Business Case.

20.4.2 The Risk Log

Project Issues should be considered in two ways under the 'risk' heading:

- Would the issue impact an existing risk?
- Has this issue already been anticipated as part or the risk management processes, and hence the mechanism for handling it already identified?
- Would the issue create a new risk?

20.4.3 Time/cost/risk function balance

There must be a balance between the advantage achieved by incorporating the change and the time, cost and risk of implementing it. This is illustrated in Figure 20.2. Can the project afford the delay? Can the extra funds be found? (Or will the change save time and money?) Is this a good way of spending the extra funds? Is it too risky? Should (and can) the change wait until after the current project ends?

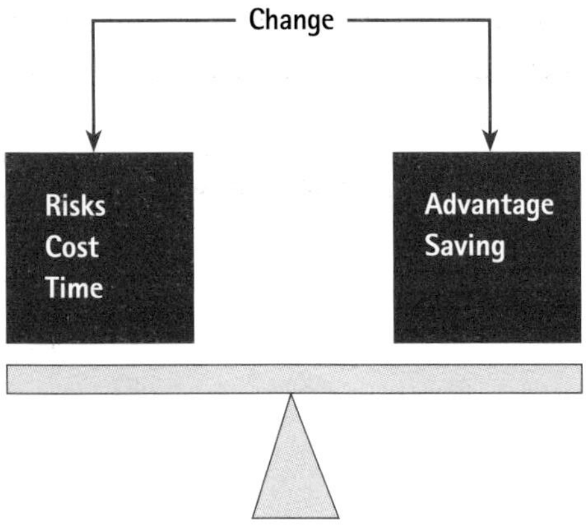

The balance act between risks, costs and time and what the customer gets out of it

Figure 20.2 Balancing the decision to change

20.4.4 Where the project is part of a programme

If the project is part of a programme, the impact of the change on the programme as a whole should also be considered. There may also be effects on other projects not necessarily part of the programme. The change control procedures for project and programme need to work in harmony.

20.5 Management of change and Configuration Management

The procedure used to control Project Issues must be integrated with the configuration management approach as identified in the Configuration Management Plan. If the project is not in an environment that already has procedures for change control, the change control approach in Chapter 23 can be used.

Project Managers should constantly be looking for ways to take advantage of events to improve on project costs, schedule or performance. These ways should also be recorded as Project Issues (as well as the final outcome being recorded in the Lessons Learned Log).

Hints and tips

Where a change budget is given to a change authority, the Project Board may wish to put a limit on (a) the cost of any single change and (b) the amount spent on change in any one stage – without reference to the Project Board.

Where a project involves third party suppliers, it is important that change processes are agreed as part of the contract negotiations. It is particularly important to agree how the distinction between Requests for Change and Off-Specifications will be made, by whom, and what arbitration processes may be needed.

Very often the people with delegated Project Assurance responsibilities may act as the change authority.

21 INTRODUCTION TO TECHNIQUES

PRINCE2 is capable of working with most techniques that implement project management best practices.

There are three techniques specifically described by PRINCE2 :

- Product-based Planning
- Change control
- Quality reviews.

Product-based planning is a key feature of PRINCE2, providing a focus on the products to be delivered and their quality. It forms an integral part of the *Planning* (PL) process and leads into the use of other generic planning techniques such as network planning and Gantt charts.

Change control is an essential part of any project management. PRINCE2 can integrate with any existing change control technique but a simple approach is offered here for those projects that do not already have one.

The quality review technique is useful for reviewing document-based products, and can be used in conjunction with other quality checking and testing techniques. Its use is not mandatory. Organisations may already have a similar technique, but quality reviews are recommended as a well-proven technique where there is not a satisfactory standard approach for document inspection.

22
PRODUCT-BASED PLANNING

PRINCE2 provides a product-based framework that can be applied to any project to give a logical sequence to the project's work. A 'product' may be a tangible one such as a machine, a document or a piece of software, or it may be intangible, such as a culture change or a different organisational structure. Within PRINCE2 these will all be called 'products'.

The use of the product-based planning technique is recommended for all levels of plan required in a project. The technique is closely allied to *Defining and Analysing Products* (PL2) in *Planning* (PL).

There are three steps to the product-based planning technique:

- Producing a Product Breakdown Structure
- Writing Product Descriptions
- Producing a Product Flow Diagram.

22.1 Product-based planning examples

Three examples of product-based planning are given to illustrate the technique. The first example is an extremely simple one whose purpose is to illustrate the various steps and parts of the technique without any complexity in the plan's subject. The second example is a Project Plan of a procurement project. The third example is a Stage Plan from the procurement project. Short scenarios explain the background to each of the examples.

22.1.1 Simple example

There is a shed in a garden. The project is to dismantle the shed and reassemble it in the garden of a close neighbour. The shed has some rotten pieces. When the shed has been dismantled, these rotten pieces must be identified and replacements ordered from the company that supplied the original shed. New fixtures and fittings (screws, nuts and bolts, glue, etc.) for all pieces will be needed, so a list of the requirements is to be made as the shed is dismantled. The neighbour has said that he will prepare the site for the shed's new location as part of his own, separate project.

22.1.2 Procurement Project Plan

A product is to be obtained and introduced into a company's method of working. After specifying its needs, the project has to find potential suppliers, create an Invitation To Tender (ITT) and evaluate the responses. Sites already using the offered products are to be visited as an early part of the evaluation process. Measurement criteria will be needed to complete the evaluation before a selection is made and a contract signed.

The company has never used such a product before, so staff will need to be trained in its use. Training cannot commence until the product has been installed. This will need a training strategy. The product supplier will be expected to provide training material. The environment will need to be prepared for the new product. A test strategy will be needed to show how the product, once installed, will be tested and accepted.

22.1.3 Procurement Stage Plan

The first specialist stage of the project has been taken down to the level of a Stage Plan. This covers the work required to issue an Invitation To Tender (ITT) to selected suppliers. The scoring chart is to be included in the ITT to tell potential suppliers how their bid will be evaluated.

22.2 Producing a Product Breakdown Structure (PBS)

This is the first step in product-based planning. Breaking down a product into its constituent sub-products helps clarify and identify all necessary work for its creation.

The objectives of the step are:

- Identify the products required by the customers
- Identify additional products needed to build and support the customer products
- Build a consensus on the best product groupings that should be used to generate ideas on what products have to be created or obtained.

A PRINCE2 project has two types of product:

- The specialist products whose development is the subject of the plan
- The management 'products' that will be required as part of managing the project (e.g. Highlight Reports, End Stage Reports, Project Issues) and as part of establishing and maintaining quality.

All the products of the project need to be drawn up in a hierarchical structure, known as a Product Breakdown Structure. At the top of the chart is a single box that summarises the overall project, e.g. 'fully operational product' or 'Delivered ITT'.

It is useful to have an initial breakdown into management and specialist products. This decomposition into two types of product is purely a device to remind the planner to think of the management products that will be needed and will require effort and time to produce. Most of these are not added until later in the planning process, such as during creation of a Gantt chart.

Figure 22.1 shows the standard PRINCE2 management products as a Product Breakdown Structure. This stays fairly constant, whatever the type of project, and can be used as it is or with any relevant additions, for all projects.

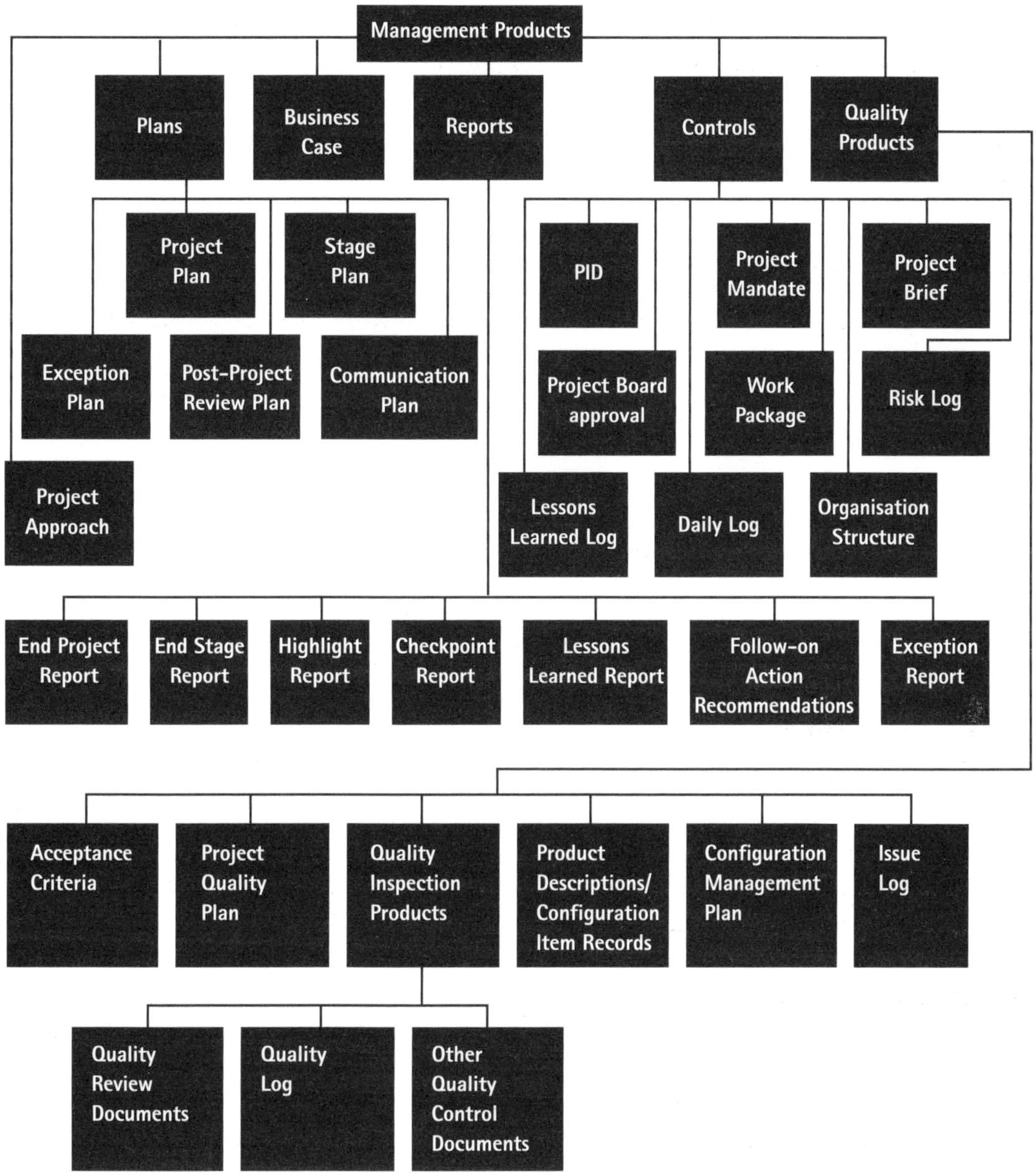

Figure 22.1 Management Product Breakdown Structure

During a project there will be many versions of such products as the Issue Log. A new version is created every time that a Project Issue is added or amended. There is no value in trying to illustrate multiple versions in a Product Breakdown Structure.

The topmost product in a Product Breakdown Structure is the final product and represents the outcome of the project, stage or Work Package. The specialist box is then decomposed into its major specialist products or product groups to form the next level of the structure. Each of these is then further decomposed until an appropriate level of detail for the plan in question is reached. Products at the lowest level on any leg are simple products, so called because they have not been broken down into more detail in a particular Product Breakdown Structure. Products on higher levels in a Product Breakdown Structure are known as intermediate products. They represent major specialist products or product groups.

22.2.1 Levels

It would be wrong to break a product down into only one lower level product. This is not decomposition. It would be the equivalent of saying 'this product consists of only one product', in which case the breakdown is unnecessary and incorrect.

When a team is creating a Product Breakdown Structure, there is likely to be a discussion on which intermediate products will be identified, i.e. how products will be grouped. For example, if the outcome of a project were an accounts system, users might want to break the system down into intermediate products called Accounts Payable, Accounts Receivable, General Ledger, etc. The suppliers might want intermediate products called Screens, Reports, Database, etc. Neither breakdown is wrong, but the project team must reach a consensus on which approach will be used in the Product Breakdown Structure and hence in the project. Agreement on a common language for use throughout the project will help with team building.

The lowest level on a Product Breakdown Structure is not fixed. It depends on the level of detail required in the plan to allow the Project or Team Manager to exercise an appropriate level of control. Simple products on a Project Product Breakdown Structure may become intermediate products on a Stage Plan.

Higher level products must be completely defined by the lower level products to which they are attached. The implication in breaking a product down to a lower level is 'this product consists of these products'. It should not be 'this product is followed by these products'.

22.2.2 External Products

The key to producing the breakdown of the specialist products is that it should show the scope of the plan. The Product Breakdown Structure should include not only the products to be delivered by the project, but also any products to be supplied from external sources, over which the Project Manager may have no control (e.g. planning permission from the local town council), plus any required products that already exist.

A different symbol should be used in the Product Flow Diagram (see section 22.4, Producing a Product Flow Diagram) to identify products upon which the project is dependent, but are outside the scope of the project, or that already exist. These products are termed external products. In this manual an ellipse is used for this purpose. A product in an ellipse, therefore, means that the Project Manager is not accountable for its provision. It should be noted that it is the product that is shown, not the source of the product. For example, if a product needs planning permission from the local authority, 'planning permission' would be the external product, not 'local authority'.

In the simple example, the Product Breakdown Structure for the specialist products might be constructed as shown in Figure 22.2. 'Old shed' is an external product because it has to exist at the start of the project. 'Prepared site' is an external product because the neighbour is providing that from a separate project.

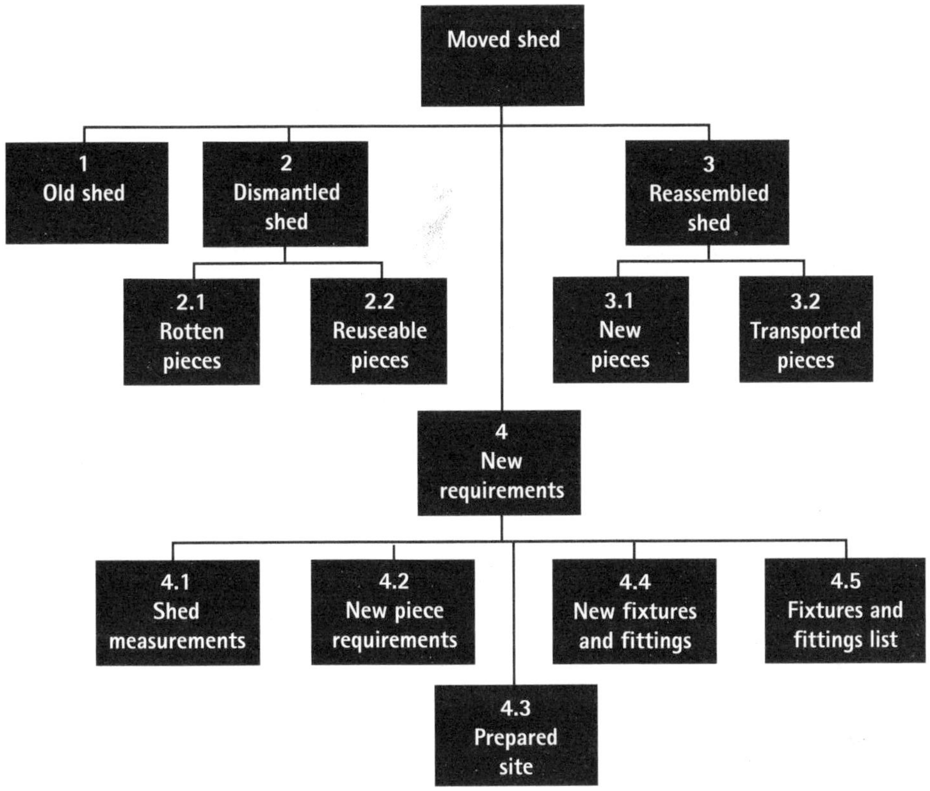

Figure 22.2 Simple example – Specialist Product Breakdown Structure

22.2.3 Key criteria

- Have all products required to solve the business need been identified?
- Have all management products that must be generated during the project to ensure audit or quality assurance, guidance and control been identified?
- Does the plan rely on products that are outside the scope of this project? If so, have they all been identified?
- Is responsibility for these external products clearly identified and agreed?
- How will progress on external products be monitored by this project?

Hints and tips

The products in a plan include not only those that will be developed within the plan but any 'products' external to the plan (and possibly outside the project) that are required as input to the work identified in the plan.

If the Product Breakdown Structure is being created manually, a numbering system may be devised that will indicate each product's level in the hierarchy and its parent. The easiest way to do this is to enter each product immediately into the project's configuration management system, then use the product identifier from that.

If a product is further decomposed in the PBS, there should be a match between the composition content of its Product Description and the breakdown of that product in the PBS.

The delivery of each external product also represents a risk.

22.3 Writing Product Descriptions

A clear, complete and unambiguous description of products is a tremendous aid to their successful creation.

A documented and agreed Product Description ensures that all personnel affected by that product have the same understanding. A Product Description should be written for each significant product to ensure that it is understood, to provide a pointer to the way in which the product is to be presented and to define its quality expectations.

A Product Description should be written for a product as soon as possible after the need for the product has been identified. This may only be a 'skeleton' with little more information than the title and identifier. It will be refined and amended as the product becomes better understood and the later planning steps are done. A Product Description should be baselined when the plan containing its creation is baselined. If it needs to be updated because of a change to the product, the Product Description must also pass through change control.

22.3.1 Product Description contents

Detail of the contents of a Product Description can be found in Appendix A, *Product Description outlines*. A Product Description carries important information about the product. It is a key element in the quality work of a project. It is given to the creator to explain what quality is required of the product when built. It is later given to the quality checkers to establish if the required quality has been built into the product.

If there are any relevant checklists covering the product's development, these should also be added to the Product Description.

Although responsibility for writing Product Descriptions rests officially with the Project Manager, it is wise to involve representatives from the area with expertise in the product and those who will use the product in question. The latter should certainly be asked to define the quality they expect.

An example of a Product Description for one of the products in the simple example is shown in Figure 22.3.

Title: Fixtures and Fittings List

Purpose
To identify all the fixtures and fittings that will be required in order to re-assemble the shed.

Composition
A list with entries for the required:
- Nails
- Screws (showing quantity and size)
- Nuts and bolts (showing quantity and size)
- A sample of each type of screw, nail, nut and bolt required
- Hinges
- Adhesive
- Preservative stain
- Clear plastic bag

The list should be divided into columns with space for type, size, and quantity or amount

Derivation
Existing shed
Count of any reusable fixtures and fittings after the shed is dismantled

Format and Presentation
A4 white paper with lines and columns. Entries in ink. Samples should be in a clear plastic bag.

Quality criteria
- List must identify everything apart from the shed panels, windows and doors that will be required to reassemble the shed
- Screws, nuts and bolts and nails should be rust-resistant
- Plastic bag should be big enough and strong enough to hold all the samples
- Adhesive should be suitable for sealing roof panels
- Preservative stain must match colour of neighbour's other shed
- Amount or quantity must be sufficient to do the job.

Quality Method
One check of the list before the shed is dismantled
A confirmation of quantity after the old shed has been dismantled
Discussion with neighbour on the colour of stain required
Manual test of the strength of the plastic bag.

People or skills required
Shed owner or the neighbour taking the shed.

Figure 22.3 Sample Product Description

22.3.2 Key criteria

- Are the products clearly and unambiguously defined?
- Have all types of quality check for the products been specified, i.e. ones that will check the presence of the quality criteria?
- Are there centrally held standards to which the description can point when it comes to defining the quality criteria and have they been applied?
- Where there are conflicting customer and supplier standards, has a sensible compromise been reached?
- Does the user/customer want any specific standards used?
- Have the right people been involved in writing each Product Description?
- Are suitable checklists available to help check the products?

Hints and tips

Writing down the purpose and composition in a Product Description helps clarify how much work is needed to create the product. This can be a big help in estimation.

Concentrate the writing of Product Descriptions on any products in the project with which the Project Manager is not familiar and those that in past projects have been done badly.

Appendix A, *Product Description outlines,* contains outlines of the standard key management products. It should not be necessary for each project to redefine these unless there are changes to them.

Writing good Product Descriptions is not a trivial undertaking. In particular, quality criteria, aimed at separating an acceptable product from an unacceptable one, need careful thought.

It is a good start to get the user or customer involved in the writing of Product Descriptions, defining quality expectations and deciding how the product can be checked against these expectations.

Test the setting of quality criteria by asking the question 'How will I know when work on this product is finished as opposed to stopped?'

Listing the composition of a product can often remind the planner of another product that is needed.

Very often the same products are created in many plans. Standard Product Descriptions can be written which can be used by many plans.

Are there any standard checklists that can be used?

Be careful not to over-engineer the Product Description. It exists to help and support the production and planning processes and is not an end in itself.

Don't try to replace the requirements specifications with a Product Description.

If the quality criteria for a product are agreed with the customer, this may assist in the ultimate acceptance of the project.

If Product Descriptions are used as control documents, then additional information, such as estimated and actual dates and effort, may be added.

Identifying who will accept a particular product and making sure that they agree to the Product Description can reduce the potential for conflict at later stages of the project.

Assistance could be sought from a 'quality specialist' when defining quality, particularly when adherence to recognised standards is part of the Acceptance Criteria.

22.4 Producing a Product Flow Diagram (PFD)

The Product Flow Diagram is created from the Product Breakdown Structure and precedes the identification of activities in *Identifying Activities and Dependencies* (PL3).

Every planner needs to know the answer to the question 'What comes next?'. The Product Flow Diagram shows the sequence of development of the products of the plan and any dependencies between them. It also identifies dependencies on any products outside the scope of the plan.

22.4.1 Creating a Product Flow Diagram

A Product Flow Diagram needs very few symbols. Time flows in one direction only, usually from top to bottom but, depending on the shape of the medium on which the diagram is drawn, it may be more convenient to draw the flow from left to right. Each product to be developed within the plan is enclosed in a box. Arrows connect the boxes, showing the sequence in which they are to be created. Any products that should already exist or that come from work outside the scope of the plan should be clearly identified by using a different type of enclosure, for example, an ellipse.

The diagram begins with those products that are available at the start of the plan (perhaps many of these are documents, such as statements of requirements or designs) and ends with the final product(s) of the plan.

It is sensible to create the PFD from the specialist products and then add any relevant management products. For example, when the project PFD is done, it can be a useful basis for deciding where the stage boundaries should go. The management products may be added to the Gantt chart later in the planning process.

Creation of a Product Flow Diagram may reveal new products that are required. These should also be added to the Product Breakdown Structure and Product Descriptions should be written for them when the need for them is recognised.

Although the Project Manager or Team Manager is responsible for creation of the Product Flow Diagram, it is sensible to use the help of those who are to develop or contribute the products contained in the plan.

Figure 22.4 illustrates the Product Flow Diagram for the simple example project.

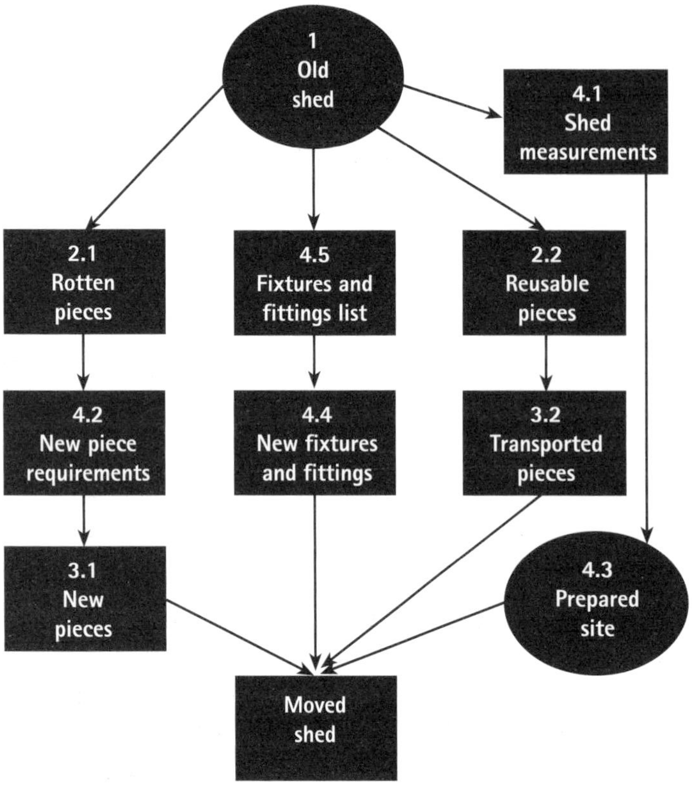

Figure 22.4 Simple example – Product Flow Diagram

22.4.2 Product Checklist

A draft of the Product Checklist can be created at this time from the information in the Product Breakdown Structure. There is a Product Description of the checklist in Appendix A. It is a table that shows all the products of the plan with entries for the planned and actual dates when the product reaches key moments in its creation, such as 'Draft Ready', 'Quality Check Done' and 'Product Approved'. These are suggested events and can be varied according to the needs of the project.

The planned dates are added at the end of *Planning* (PL) after scheduling and any adjustments for risk actions. The Project Manager adds the actual dates as they are achieved and this can form a useful addition to the Highlight Report.

22.4.3 Key criteria

- On what other products is each product dependent?
- Is any product dependent on a product developed outside the scope of this plan?
- Which products can be developed in parallel?

Hints and tips

At project level, the dependencies can be rather crude – for example, not all elements of major product 1 need to be done before any elements of major product 2 can start. To try to break those major products down so that the dependencies can be refined is likely to confuse the diagram. It is better to accept the crude dependencies and resolve them at Stage Plan level.

The easiest way to create a Product Flow Diagram is to put all the specialist products in their required sequence and then add the management products to the correct point in the flow.

It is often easiest to fill in the middle of the flow by working back from the final product and asking the question 'Which products should be available in order to create this product?'. Self-adhesive notelets on a whiteboard can be an effective way of developing a Product Flow Diagram, particularly where there is likely to be a lot of modification.

A useful way to get started with the flow of specialist products is to 'top and tail' the diagram – that is, put the final product at the bottom of a sheet of paper and any products that are prerequisite to starting the work at the top (in ellipses). Take each product in the list and match it to every other product to establish if there is any particular dependency between them. Work through all the products in this way. Use this information to connect all the products in their appropriate sequence from such prerequisites as there are to the final product.

If Project Board approvals are listed as management products, their later placement in the sequence will show where the stage ends should come, if this is not already known.

The derivation section of a Product Description gives useful information about dependencies. The key question to ask is 'From where do I get this information?'

The Project Board may find that the Product Flow Diagram and Product Checklist are easy to use to check on plan progress.

22.5 Further examples

Two further examples of a more realistic project to procure a product follow. The first is at the level of a Project Plan. The second is the first Stage Plan of this project.

22.5.1 Project Plan example

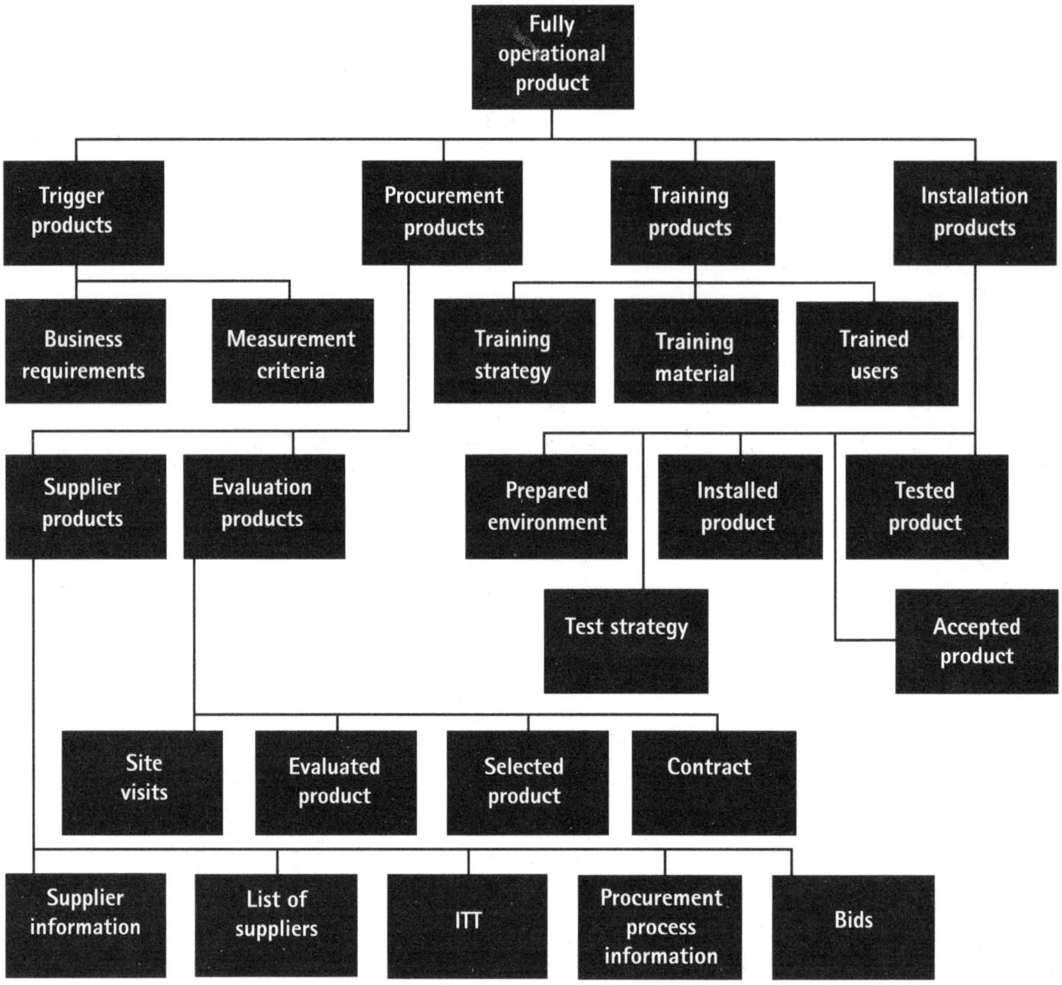

Figure 22.5 Project Plan Product Breakdown Structure

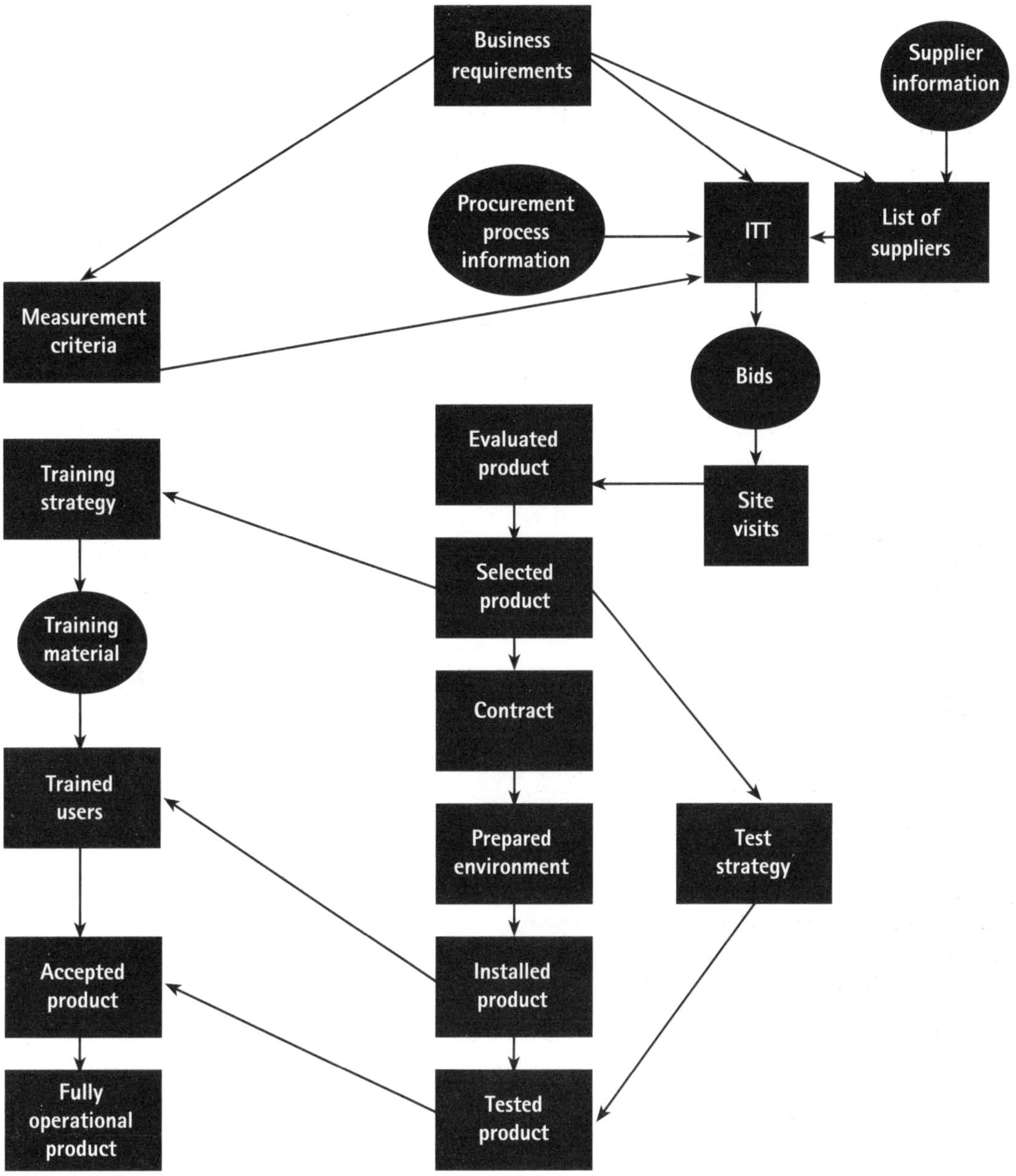

Figure 22.6 Project Plan Product Flow Diagram

22.5.2 Stage Plan example

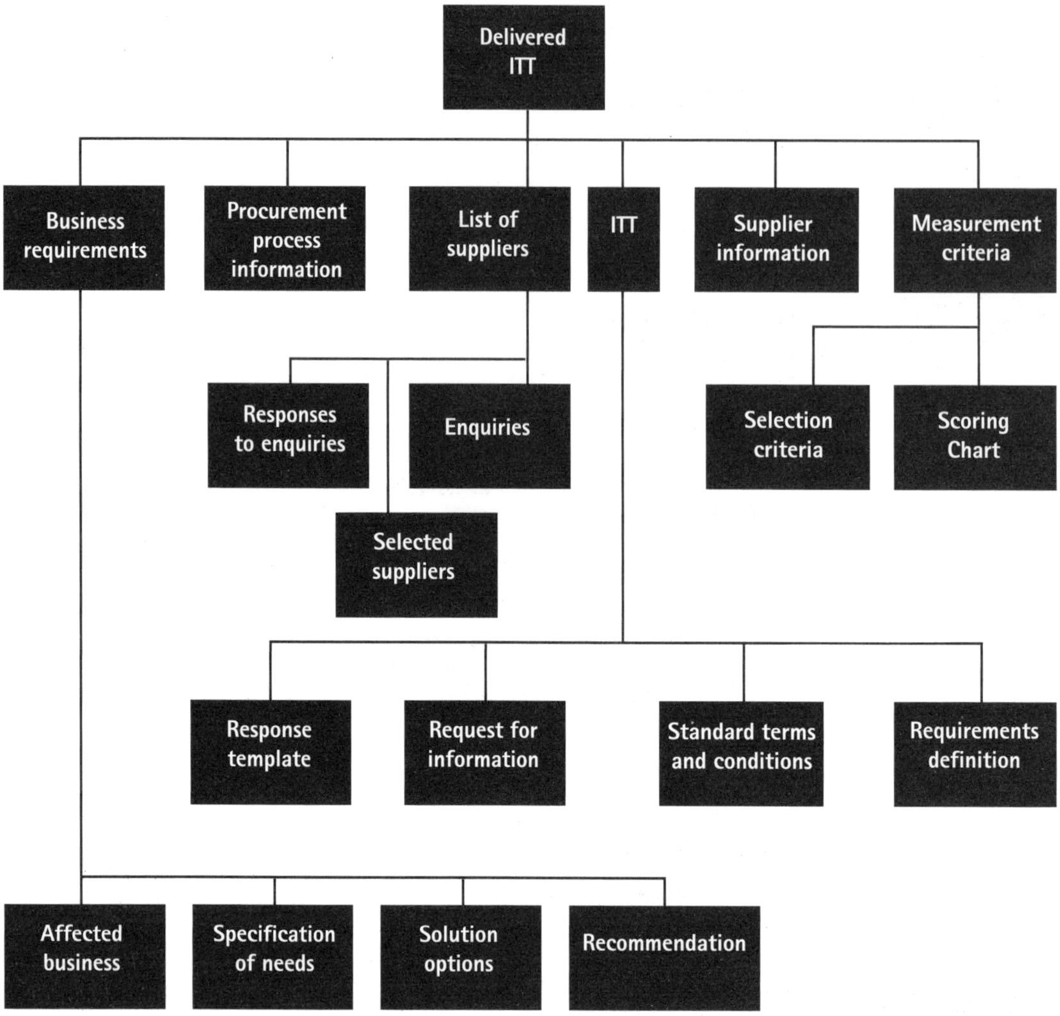

Figure 22.7 Stage Plan Product Breakdown Structure

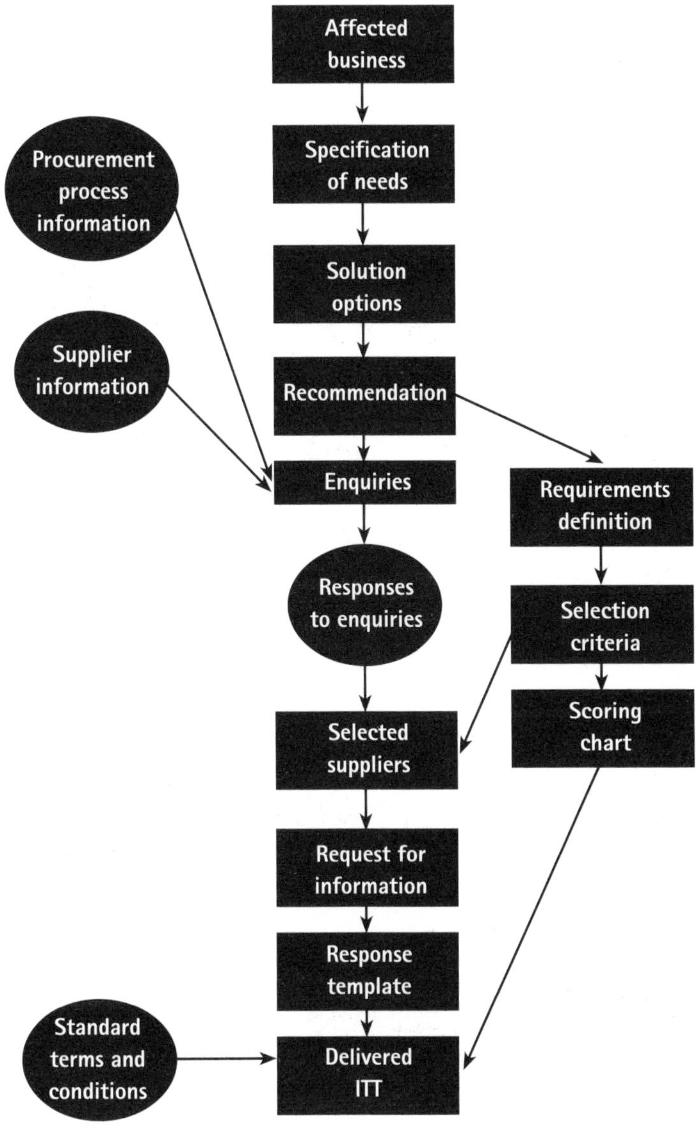

Figure 22.8 Stage Plan Product Flow Diagram

23 CHANGE CONTROL APPROACH

This chapter looks at the control of changes to specialist products, not management products. Two important points need to be made:

- If a product is to be changed, its Product Description should be checked for any necessary changes
- Once a product has been approved, the Project Manager should not authorise any work that would change it without the approval of the Project Board.

A programme or organisation may have its own change control procedure and forms. This is not a problem as long as its key points are compatible with the approach detailed in this chapter.

For those without a mandatory change control procedure, the following will ensure that changes are controlled during the project.

23.1 Change control steps

All changes are treated as types of Project Issue and are handled through the same approach. Chapter 20 (*Change Control*) should be read in conjunction with this.

Changes can be:

- A request to change what the project is set to deliver, for example, the specification of requirements (Request for Change)
- A suggestion to improve one or more of the project's products (Request for Change)
- A record of some current or forecast failure to meet a requirement (Off-Specification).

Figure 23.1 shows the steps involved in capturing issues and then managing those issues that are changes through to resolution.

23.1.1 Issue Log

Whatever its type, every issue raised is logged as a Project Issue in the Issue Log. Suggested content for this log is given in Appendix A, *Product Description outlines*. A unique number is allocated, plus the author, date and type of Project Issue.

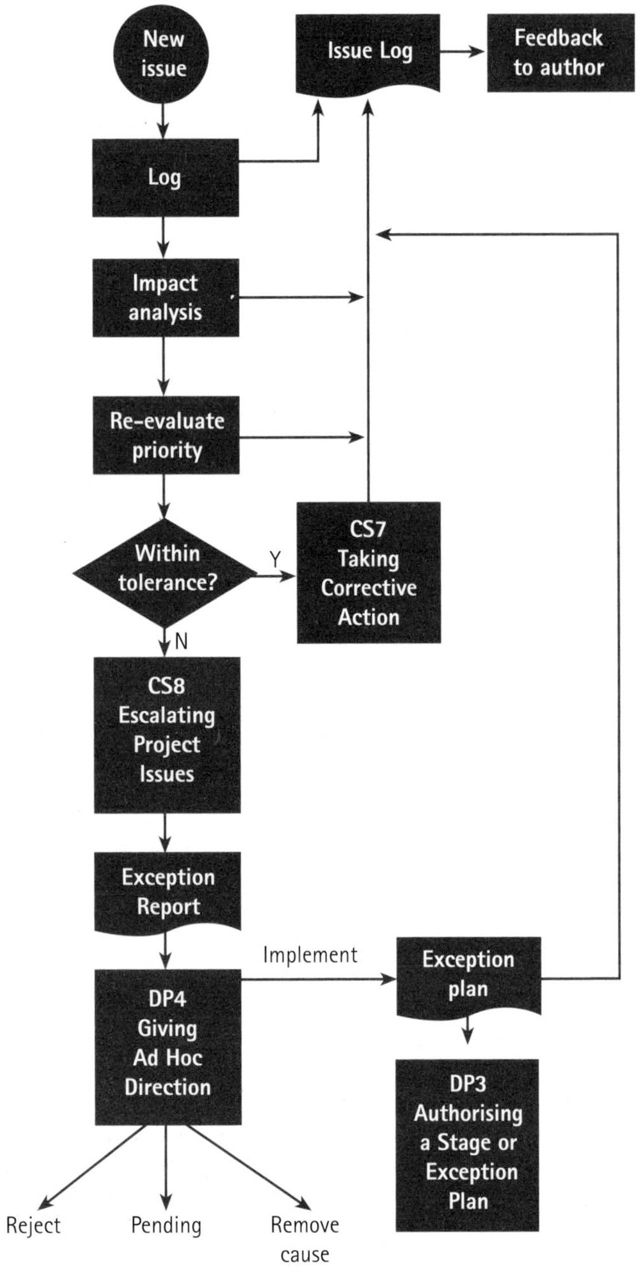

Figure 23.1 Change control steps

23.1.2 Prioritise

Each Project Issue should be assessed to indicate a priority. A suggested priority rating is:

1. A must; the final product will not work without this change
2. An important change; its absence would be very inconvenient, although a work-around is possible for a while
3. A nice-to-have but not vital
4. A cosmetic change; of no importance
5. This does not involve a change.

A copy of the Project Issue is returned to the author to acknowledge its receipt and entry in the project's Issue Log.

Any Project Issues that are questions or are based on misunderstandings should be answered directly. A reply is sent to the author, a copy filed and the Issue Log updated to reflect the action.

23.1.3 Impact analysis

An impact analysis is carried out on each remaining Project Issue to identify:

- What would have to change
- What effort the change would need
- What the impact on the team, Stage and Project Plans would be
- Whether the impact would cause deviation beyond team, stage or project tolerances
- What the impact on the Business Case would be
- What the impact on the risks would be.

The change may impact just the customer, just the supplier or both. The priority should be re-evaluated after the impact analysis. This can be done in a number of ways, depending on the project's circumstances. The Project Board may wish to do the re-evaluation. The Project Board may have decided to delegate such decisions on Project Issues to a change authority.

23.1.4 Authorisation

The use of a change authority is described in Chapter 20 (section 20.3).

For Off-Specifications, the Project Manager tries to solve the problem within the stage tolerance margins. This may mean changes to the plan(s) to include extra activities. Where correction of the Off-Specification is not possible within tolerance levels, the Project Manager follows the exception procedure, *Escalating Project Issues* (CS8), to bring the matter to the attention of the Project Board *Giving Ad Hoc Direction* (DP4). If the decision of the Project Board is to accept the Off-Specification without any corrective action, this is called a 'concession'.

The Project Manager decides which Requests for Change, if any, should be implemented within the current Stage Plan constraints. Even for those that the Project Manager is prepared to implement without extra funds or time, there should be discussion with the Senior User and Senior Supplier. This is particularly important in circumstances involving an external supplier.

Where the Project Manager does not wish to take the decision personally on whether or not to implement changes, the relevant Project Issues are passed to the Project Board/change authority. This authority can decide to reject Project Issues, put them in 'pending' status, remove the cause of the problem or ask for their implementation. The Project Issues are updated with any change in priority and the Project Board's directives.

The Project Issues are returned to the Project Manager, the Issue Log updated and an updated copy sent to the author.

Any Project Issues whose implementation would cause deviation beyond stage or project tolerances will form the basis of an Exception Report, created in *Escalating Project Issues* (CS8). According to the project environment, this may be formal or informal. The likely result will be a request for the Project Manager to produce an Exception Plan, which will include the extra work, to be submitted via *Producing an Exception Plan* (SB6).

NOTE: Where the Project Board has delegated decisions on the implementation of changes to some separate change authority, the name of this body should be substituted for that of the Project Board in this technique.

Hints and tips

Evaluating the impact of potential changes can be erroneously taken to mean only the impact on the customer. Impact analysis must cover the three areas of business, user and supplier. Before a change goes to the Senior User for consideration, the impact on the supplier must be known – for example, the cost and effort required and what products would have to be changed.

Where the project is partially or fully funded by the supplier, this may change the decision-making authority within the Project Board about changes. It may become more of a joint decision based on the contract terms or including contract modification. Any changes in responsibility and authority should be reflected in the job descriptions.

Where the project is part of a programme, is the project in a position to judge the impact on other projects? Does it have the authority to make decisions? There are two potential approaches:

- Screen all changes at programme level to determine where the decision should be made
- Ensure a programme representative is part of the project's change authorisation loop.

24
QUALITY REVIEW TECHNIQUE

24.1 What is a quality review?

A quality review is a structured procedure designed to assess whether a product is 'fit for purpose' or conforms to requirements. The procedure begins with the identification of individuals or groups who have a vested interest in the product under review. The product is presented for review and comments from reviewers are discussed during a structured meeting. Any required changes to the product are agreed and a complete list of required actions is taken. The procedure is completed when all the required changes have been made and the product is formally 'signed off', meaning that it meets the quality criteria that were set and the product is now approved.

24.2 Quality review benefits

The following benefits can be achieved from the effective use of quality reviews:

- A structured and organised approach to the examination of a product against predefined quality criteria
- Early identification of defects in products and, therefore, a platform for product improvement, with attendant reduction in the costs of the final product during development and in operation
- An objective measurement for management progress control is provided. It is one thing being told by the developer that a product is complete, but far more useful to know that a group of peers have examined the product and accepted it. This gives the Project Manager far more certainty about the status of the product
- It provides the opportunity for all vested interests to work together to improve product quality. This helps build the team approach to development
- Once a product has gone through a quality review, user(s), who are represented on the quality review team, are more willing to commit to that product.

24.3 Context

A quality review can be invoked at any point in the project, since any product could be subject to a quality review if there are subjective elements of quality to be monitored. It has close ties with the following processes:

- *Planning* (PL) for the pre-planning and resourcing of major quality reviews at the level of Stage or team plan

- *Managing Product Delivery* (MP), which is the process covering the production of the project's products and hence where the application of most of the quality reviews will take place
- *Authorising Work Package* (CS1), which addresses the hand-over of responsibility for product production and will include any requirement for quality reviews
- *Assessing Progress* (CS2), which deals with progress monitoring and reporting, and which will receive details of completed quality reviews.

24.4 Overview of the quality review technique

24.4.1 Objectives

The objectives of a quality review are to:

- Assess the conformity of a product against set criteria
- Provide a platform for product improvement
- Involve all those who have an interest in the product in checking its quality
- Spread ownership of the product
- Obtain commitment from all vested interests to the product
- Provide a mechanism for management monitoring and control.

24.4.2 Responsibilities

There are four specific roles involved in the quality review procedure.

Review Chairperson

This role runs the quality review. This is a different role from that of the Executive who chairs the Project Board.

The role has the following main responsibilities:

- Check that the product is ready for review
- Ensure that the quality review is properly organised (venue, date, time, attendees, duration)
- Gather in the question lists and set the review meeting agenda
- Chair the quality review meeting
- Ensure that the quality review does not stray from its main aim
- Ensure that actions and required results are agreed
- Together with the reviewers, determine the quality review result
- Keep the Project and/or Team Manager aware of the status of all quality reviews
- Provide final review sign-off

- Institute exception procedures via the Project and/or Team Manager where problems with the product cannot be resolved within a short timeframe.

Producer

This role represents the creator(s) of the product involved. Typically, the person who has produced the product or who has led the team responsible will fill it. The role has the following responsibilities:

- Provide all reviewers with the relevant review products
- Prepare for the review meeting
- Assess question lists prior to the review meeting and use them to assist the review chairperson to set the review meeting agenda
- Answer questions about the product during the review procedure, agree errors and explain any implications of these errors
- Agree action to resolve errors
- Ensure any agreed actions are carried out
- Obtain sign-off from reviewers for changes made to the product
- Obtain final sign-off from the review chairperson when the reviewers have approved all changes.

Reviewers

The reviewer role has the following responsibilities:

- Review the product
- Assess the product against the quality criteria specified in the Product Description
- Document their questions on the product against the pre-set quality criteria
- Ensure errors are fully understood by the producer and are subsequently resolved satisfactorily
- Sign off any follow-up action list items where they are identified as checkers.

Scribe

The major responsibilities of this role are:

- Assist the chairperson in the review administrative details, such as arrangement of venue
- Take notes of agreed actions during the review meeting
- Read back the agreed actions at the end of the meeting and note who is to take corrective action and who is to check the corrections.

In addition to the specific roles involved, there are responsibilities that need to be taken by other people. These are responsibilities that form parts of their standard job, but that are particularly relevant to quality reviews:

Project Manager

- Plan the quality reviews in outline
- Plan to overcome any identified exception conditions raised as a result of a quality review
- Act as reviewer where appropriate.

Team Manager

- Plan quality reviews in detail
- Identify any quality review resources required from the team (additional to any reviewers chosen by Project Assurance roles)
- Monitor quality review progress against plan
- Report progress to the Project Manager.

Note that often the Project Manager will be directly managing the work that is being quality reviewed. If this is the case, the responsibilities of Project Manager and Team Manager will be combined.

Project Assurance roles

- Advise on suitable reviewers for each quality review
- Check that everyone involved with the quality review process is aware of their role and responsibilities and that adequate training in the technique has been given
- Ensure that the quality review procedure is being properly followed
- Check that reviewers are being correctly selected and that they are being correctly briefed for the work
- Check that follow-up actions are being properly monitored
- Log and report on the use of corporate standards and advise on improvements and amendments
- Act as reviewers where appropriate.

Project Support roles

If Project Support is available to the Project Manager, it can be used to assist the review chairperson and producer to organise a review venue, prepare and distribute the review documentation, act as scribe and progress-chase the follow-up action list until all errors have been corrected and signed off. People in support roles can act as reviewers where appropriate.

24.4.3 Steps in a formal quality review procedure

A quality review has a number of activities, the central element being the review meeting, where all participants gather to identify and agree on any defects in the product.

There are three basic steps in a quality review:

- Preparation, consisting of:
  - confirmation that the product is ready for review
  - confirmation of the availability of the nominated reviewers and agreement on dates for the return of comments and the review itself
  - distribution of a copy of the product and its Product Description to reviewers where this is possible, for instance if it is a printed document. Alternatively, making the product available for inspection by the reviewers
  - assessment of the product against the quality criteria
  - entry of questions or suspected errors on a question list
  - annotation of minor errors (e.g. grammar and spelling) on the product
  - return of the annotated product and question list to the producer
  - a plan of the review meeting and agreement on the agenda
- Review meeting, consisting of:
  - discussion, clarification and agreement on each of the points raised by the reviewers
  - agreement of the follow-up actions appropriate to each agreed error
  - documentation of the follow-up responsibilities
  - summary of the actions at the end of the meeting
  - agreement on the quality review outcome, and sign-off of the product, if appropriate
- Follow-up, consisting of:
  - notification to the Project and/or Team Manager of the quality review result
  - a plan of any remedial work required
  - sign-off of the product following successful remedial work.

Tables 24.1, 24.2 and 24.3 show the detailed job contents for the quality review roles for each of the steps.

Preparation

Table 24.1 Preparation for quality review

Review Chairperson	Producer	Reviewer	Project Manager/ Team Manager
Check product ready	Confirm product available for review	Read Product Description of review product	Check quality review on schedule
Confirm reviewers available and still appropriate	Distribute the product and Product Description to reviewers	Schedule preparation and review time	Ensure quality review procedure is being followed

Quality review planning

It is important that quality reviews are properly planned, with input from the Project Assurance function. There is therefore an additional quality review planning step consisting of:

- Identifying the products that will be subject to quality review
- Planning the timescale for each quality review
- Identifying the reviewers and adding them to resource plans.

This is carried out as part of creating a Stage or team plan in the *Planning* (PL) process.

24.4.4 Quality review results

At the end of a quality review, the review chairperson should obtain a consensus agreement on the result of the review. If any of the reviewers is not prepared to sign off the product, then the product has not met its quality criteria and hence is not ready for use. If the reviewers' comments cannot be resolved for any reason – for example, contention between reviewers – a further discussion and agreement on the matter should be raised as an item on the follow-up action list. If the problem affects other products than the one reviewed, it should be raised via a Project Issue and this action recorded on the follow-up action list.

The result of a quality review will normally be one of three:

- The product is error free and can be approved immediately
- The product can be approved once the identified errors are corrected and signed off
- Correction of the errors found will radically alter the product and it should be reviewed again.

The review chairperson may also decide to postpone the review meeting if:

- Insufficient reviewers attend to cover the quality issues addressed by the product's quality criteria
- The reviewers who are attending are not qualified to comment on the issues being addressed
- It is clear that the reviewers have not studied the product during the preparation step
- It becomes obvious that the product is not fit to be reviewed.

24.4.5 Key criteria

- Have the product's quality criteria been specified?
- Has the Product Description been passed to the reviewers, together with the product?
- Have the reviewers fully checked the product prior to the review meeting?

- Have the question lists been sent to the producer or review chairperson prior to the review meeting?
- Has the review meeting concentrated on error detection, not error fixing or redesign?
- Have the follow-up actions been documented and allocated?
- Have reviewers been asked which changes they wish to sign off?
- Has agreement been reached on the result of the quality review?

Hints and tips

Quality review is there for error/opportunity identification NOT correction.

The temptation to agree solutions for the defects found in a product can be inviting. Should resolution become a feature of quality review, then the review procedure will lose much of its effectiveness because discussion of solutions takes time and effort away from the key objective of the quality review procedure, that is, the identification and agreement of defects in the product, to provide the platform for product improvement. Also, there may be more than one solution to a problem and the group of people assembled to review a product may not be the best qualified to select the best solution. Any solutions suggested during the review process should be noted for later consideration.

There is a need to address the producer/reviewer psychology. The aim of the quality review is to identify defects in the product not in the producer. Reviewers and producers should approach the review in a constructive 'team' attitude to achieving quality products. If the team approach is not adopted, conflict can arise and be destructive to the quality review procedure. It helps if reviewers can refer to **the** product, rather than **your** product.

Quality review is not an ad hoc gathering of individuals. It is not a first sight of the product for the purpose of problem identification. As in all good meetings, all the participants should attend having checked the product involved and should be prepared to contribute, knowing the agenda and objectives and the role they should perform at the meeting.

Quality review participants must prepare for the review by identifying major questions or suspected errors on a question list, annotating the product where possible with minor errors and informing the chairperson of their findings. Not to do so wastes the time of the other reviewers and devalues the eventual product sign-off since it is more likely that errors will be left undiscovered.

Care must be taken that managers do not attend a quality review in a people management role. They do not attend to assess the performance of their staff. This is particularly true of the producer's manager; it would devalue the meeting and would cause extra stress on the producer. However, managers may attend in the role of reviewers.

Checklists should be in existence.

A major means of assessing a product's quality is against the Product Description, which defines the composition, format and quality criteria of a product. Should this not be available, a checklist of the standard criteria for this type of product should be available. Without one or other of these, the reviewers will be left with no guidance as to what the acceptable quality is.

Ideally, the chairperson should not act as a reviewer. It is difficult to both chair the review meeting and review the product involved. The review chairperson should be there just to run the meeting.

Non-attendance of a reviewer:

- If a reviewer cannot attend the meeting, the review chairperson can decide either to accept a question list from that reviewer and arrange for its points to be discussed at the meeting or replace the reviewer. If the number of non-attendees is such as to undermine the effectiveness of the review, either because of the lack of people to form discussions or because of the lack of key skills, it may be necessary to postpone the review meeting. Where reviewers are not prepared for the review or have not submitted question lists, it may be appropriate to postpone the review if it is felt that the review might be ineffective
- A project may decide to ask for reviewers to submit question lists, then hold the review meeting with only the chairperson and producer in attendance, the chairperson acting on behalf of the reviewers. In such cases, the chairperson should have any actions signed off directly by the reviewer(s) who submitted the question.

For inter-project products, there should be cross-project representation at quality reviews.

The producer can take the suggested scribe role, especially in an informal quality review. It should not be done by the chairperson, as the distraction of note-taking may impair the control of the meeting.

Errors in other products:

- A quality review may turn up an error in a product other than the one being reviewed. This should be recorded as an action item, but closed on its transfer to an appropriate Project Issue. Quality reviews may reveal not only faults on the part of the creator(s), but also defects caused by deficiencies in the quality standards and development methods. Failure to use a standard may indicate that the standard is no longer practical or suitable. Such events should cause a review of the suspect standards area.

GLOSSARY

Acceptance Criteria

A prioritised list of criteria that the final product(s) must meet before the customer will accept them; a measurable definition of what must be done for the final product to be acceptable to the customer. They should be defined as part of the Project Brief and agreed between customer and supplier no later than the project initiation stage. They should be documented in the Project Initiation Document.

Activity network

A flow diagram showing the activities of a plan and their interdependencies. The network shows each activity's duration, earliest start and finish times, latest start and finish times and float. Also known as 'planning network'. See also Critical path.

Baseline

A snapshot; a position or situation that is recorded. Although the position may be updated later, the baseline remains unchanged and available as a reminder of the original state and as a comparison against the current position. Products that have passed their quality checks and are approved are baselined products. Anything 'baselined' should be under version control in configuration management and 'frozen', i.e. no changes to that version are allowed.

Benefits

The positive outcomes, quantified or unquantified, that a project is being undertaken to deliver, and that justify the investment.

Benefits realisation

The practice of ensuring that the outcome of a project produces the projected benefits claimed in the Business Case.

Business Case

Information that describes the justification for setting up and continuing a PRINCE2 project. It provides the reasons (and answers the question 'Why?') for the project. It is updated at key points throughout the project.

Change authority

A group to which the Project Board may delegate responsibility for the consideration of requests for change. The change authority is given a budget and can approve changes within that budget.

Change budget

The money allocated to the change authority to be spent on authorised requests for change.

Change control
The procedure to ensure that the processing of all Project Issues is controlled, including the submission, analysis and decision making.

Checkpoint
A team-level, time-driven review of progress, usually involving a meeting.

Checkpoint Report
A progress report of the information gathered at a checkpoint meeting, which is given by a team to the Project Manager and provides reporting data as defined in the Work Package.

Communication Plan
Part of the Project Initiation Document describing how the project's stakeholders and interested parties will be kept informed during the project.

Concession
An Off-Specification that is accepted by the Project Board without corrective action.

Configuration audit
A comparison of the latest version number and status of all products shown in the configuration library records against the information held by the product authors.

Configuration management
A discipline, normally supported by software tools, that gives management precise control over its assets (for example, the products of a project), covering planning, identification, control, status accounting and verification of the products.

Configuration status account
A report on the status of products. The required products can be specified by identifier or the part of the project in which they were developed.

Contingency budget
The amount of money required to implement a contingency plan. If the Project Board approves a contingency plan, it would normally set aside a contingency budget, which would only be called upon if the contingency plan had to be implemented.

Contingency plan
A plan that provides an outline of decisions and measures to be taken if defined circumstances, outside the control of a PRINCE2 project, should occur.

Critical path
This is the line connecting the start of a planning network with the final activity in that network through those activities with the smallest float. Often this is a line through the network connecting those activities with a zero float, i.e. those activities where any delay will delay the time of the entire network.

Customer
The person or group who commissioned the work and will benefit from the end results.

Deliverable
An item that the project has to create as part of the requirements. It may be part of the final outcome or an intermediate element on which one or more subsequent deliverables are dependent. According to the type of project, another name for a deliverable is 'product'.

End Project Report
A report given by the Project Manager to the Project Board, that confirms the hand-over of all products and provides an updated Business Case and an assessment of how well the project has done against its Project Initiation Document.

End stage assessment
The review by the Project Board and Project Manager of the End Stage Report to decide whether to approve the next Stage Plan (unless the last stage has now been completed). According to the size and criticality of the project, the review may be formal or informal. The approval to proceed should be documented as an important management product.

End Stage Report
A report given by the Project Manager to the Project Board at the end of each management stage of the project. This provides information about the project performance during the stage and the project status at stage end.

Exception
A situation where it can be forecast that there will be a deviation beyond the tolerance levels agreed between Project Manager and Project Board (or between Project Board and corporate or programme management, or between a Team Manager and the Project Manager).

Exception assessment
This is a meeting of the Project Board to approve (or reject) an Exception Plan.

Exception Plan
This is a plan that often follows an Exception Report. For a Stage Plan exception, it covers the period from the present to the end of the current stage. If the exception were at a project level, the Project Plan would be replaced.

Exception Report
A report that describes an exception, provides an analysis and options for the way forward and identifies a recommended option. The Project Manager presents it to the Project Board.

Executive
The single individual with overall responsibility for ensuring that a project or programme meets its objectives and delivers the projected benefits. This individual should ensure that the project or programme maintains its business focus, that it has clear authority and that the

work, including risks, is actively managed. The chairperson of the Project Board, representing the customer and owner of the Business Case.

Feasibility study
A feasibility study is an early study of a problem to assess if a solution is feasible. The study will normally scope the problem, identify and explore a number of solutions and make a recommendation on what action to take. Part of the work in developing options is to calculate an outline Business Case for each as one aspect of comparison.

Follow-on Action Recommendations
A report that can be used as input to the process of creating a Business Case/Project Mandate for any follow-on PRINCE2 project and for recording any follow-on instructions covering incomplete products or outstanding issues. It also sets out proposals for post-project review of the project's products.

Gantt chart
This is a diagram of a plan's activities against a time background, showing start and end times and resources required.

Gate review
A generic term, rather than a PRINCE2 term, meaning a point at the end of a stage or phase where a decision is made whether to continue with the project. In PRINCE2 this would equate to an end stage assessment.

Highlight Report
Report from the Project Manager to the Project Board on a time-driven frequency on stage progress.

Issue Log
A log of all Project Issues including requests for change raised during the project, showing details of each issue, its evaluation, what decisions about it have been made and its current status.

Lessons Learned Report
A report that describes the lessons learned in undertaking the project and that includes statistics from the quality control of the project's management products. It is approved by the Project Board and then held centrally for the benefit of future projects.

Off-Specification
Something that should be provided by the project, but currently is not (or is forecast not to be) provided. This might be a missing product or a product not meeting its specification.

Outcome
The term used to describe the totality of what the project is set up to deliver, consisting of all the specialist products. For example, this could be an installed computer system with trained staff to use it, backed up by new working practices and documentation, a refurbished and equipped building with all the staff moved in and working, or it could be a new product launched with a recruited and trained sales and support team in place.

Peer review

Peer reviews are specific reviews of a project or any of its products where personnel from within the organisation and/or from other organisations carry out an independent assessment of the project. Peer reviews can be done at any point within a project but are often used at stage-end points.

Phase

A part, section or segment of a project, similar in meaning to a PRINCE2 stage. The key meaning of stage in PRINCE2 terms is the use of management stages, i.e. sections of the project to which the Project Board only commits one at a time. A phase might be more connected to a time slice, change of skills required or change of emphasis.

Post-implementation review

See Post-project review.

Post-project review

One or more reviews held after project closure to determine if the expected benefits have been obtained. Also known as post-implementation review.

PRINCE2

A method that supports some selected aspects of project management. The acronym stands for **PR**ojects **IN** **C**ontrolled **E**nvironments.

PRINCE2 project

A project whose product(s) can be defined at its start sufficiently precisely so as to be measurable against predefined metrics and that is managed according to the PRINCE2 method.

Process

That which must be done to bring about a particular outcome, in terms of information to be gathered, decisions to be made and results that must be achieved.

Producer

This role represents the creator(s) of a product that is the subject of a quality review. Typically, it will be filled by the person who has produced the product or who has led the team responsible.

Product

Any input to or output from a project. PRINCE2 distinguishes between management products (which are produced as part of the management or quality processes of the project) and specialist products (which are those products that make up the final deliverable). A product may itself be a collection of other products.

Product-based planning

A three step diagrammatic technique leading to a comprehensive plan based on creation and delivery of required outputs. The technique considers prerequisite products, quality requirements and the dependencies between products.

Product Breakdown Structure
A hierarchy of all the products to be produced during a plan.

Product Checklist
A list of the major products of a plan, plus key dates in their delivery.

Product Description
A description of a product's purpose, composition, derivation and quality criteria. It is produced at planning time, as soon as the need for the product is identified.

Product Flow Diagram
A diagram showing the sequence of production and interdependencies of the products listed in a Product Breakdown Structure.

Programme
A portfolio of projects selected, planned and managed in a co-ordinated way.

Project
A temporary organisation that is created for the purpose of delivering one or more business products according to a specified Business Case.

Project Assurance
The Project Board's responsibilities to assure itself that the project is being conducted correctly.

Project Brief
A description of what the project is to do; a refined and extended version of the Project Mandate, which has been agreed by the Project Board and which is input to project initiation.

Project closure notification
Advice from the Project Board to inform the host location that the project resources can be disbanded and support services, such as space, equipment and access, demobilised.

Project closure recommendation
Notification prepared by the Project Manager for the Project Board to send (when the board is satisfied that the project can be closed) to any organisation that has supplied facilities to the project.

Project Initiation Document (PID)
A logical document which brings together the key information needed to start the project on a sound basis and to convey that information to all concerned with the project.

Project Issue
A term used to cover either a general issue, query, a Request for Change, suggestion or Off-Specification raised during a project. Project Issues can be about anything to do with the project.

Project management
The planning, monitoring and control of all aspects of the project and the motivation of all those involved in it to achieve the project objectives on time and to the specified cost, quality and performance.

Project management team
A term to represent the entire management structure of Project Board, Project Manager, plus any Team Manager, Project Assurance and Project Support roles.

Project Manager
The person given the authority and responsibility to manage the project on a day-to-day basis to deliver the required products within the constraints agreed with the Project Board.

Project Mandate
Information created externally to the project, which forms the terms of reference and is used to start up the PRINCE2 project.

Project Plan
A high-level plan showing the major products of the project, when they will be delivered and at what cost. An initial Project Plan is presented as part of the Project Initiation Document. This is revised as information on actual progress appears. It is a major control document for the Project Board to measure actual progress against expectations.

Project Quality Plan
A plan defining the key quality criteria, quality control and audit processes to be applied to project management and specialist work in the PRINCE2 project. It will be part of the text in the Project Initiation Document.

Project records
A collection of all approved management, specialist and quality products and other material, which is necessary to provide an auditable record of the project.

NB This does not include working files.

Project start-up notification
Advice to the host location that the project is about to start and requesting any required Project Support services.

Project Support Office
A group set up to provide certain administrative services to the Project Manager. Often the group provides its services to many projects in parallel.

Quality
The totality of features and characteristics of a product or service that bear on its ability to satisfy stated and implied needs. Also defined as 'fitness for purpose' or 'conforms to requirements'.

Quality Management System

The complete set of quality standards, procedures and responsibilities for a site or organisation.

Quality review

A quality review is a quality checking technique with a specific structure, defined roles and procedure designed to ensure a product's completeness and adherence to standards. The participants are drawn from those with an interest in the product and those with the necessary skills to review its correctness. An example of the checks made by a quality review is 'Does the document match the quality criteria in the Product Description?'

Quality system

See Quality Management System.

Request for Change

A means of proposing a modification to the current specification of a product. It is one type of Project Issue.

Reviewer

A person asked to review a product that is the subject of a quality review.

Risk Log

A document that provides identification, estimation, impact evaluation and countermeasures for all risks to the project. It should be created during the start-up of the project and developed during the life of the project. Also known as Risk Register.

Risk profile

A graphical representation of information normally found on the Risk Log.

Risk register

See Risk Log.

Senior Responsible Owner

This is not a PRINCE2 term, but is used in many organisations. Its equivalent in PRINCE2 terms would be the 'Executive' role.

Senior Supplier

The Project Board role that provides knowledge and experience of the main discipline(s) involved in the production of the project's deliverable(s). Represents the supplier(s) interests within the project and provides supplier resources.

Senior User

A member of the Project Board, accountable for ensuring that user needs are specified correctly and that the solution meets those needs.

Sponsor
Not a specific PRINCE2 role but often used to mean the major driving force of a project. May be the equivalent of Executive or corporate/programme management.

Stakeholders
Parties with an interest in the execution and outcome of a project. They would include business streams affected by or dependent on the outcome of a project.

Supplier
The group or groups responsible for the supply of the project's specialist products.

Team Manager
A role that may be employed by the Project Manager or a specifically appointed alternative person to manage the work of project team members.

Tolerance
The permissible deviation above and below a plan's estimate of time and cost without escalating the deviation to the next level of management. Separate tolerance figures should be given for time and cost. There may also be tolerance levels for quality, scope, benefit and risk. Tolerance is applied at project, stage and team levels.

User(s)
The person or group who will use the final deliverable(s) of the project.

Work Package
The set of information relevant to the creation of one or more products. It will contain the Product Description(s), details of any constraints on production such as time and cost, interfaces and confirmation of the agreement between the Project Manager and the person or Team Manager who is to implement the Work Package that the work can be done within the constraints.

APPENDIX A: PRODUCT DESCRIPTION OUTLINES

This Appendix contains Product Description outlines for the standard management products. These outlines do not include all of the standard headings and content of a Product Description, such as 'format' and 'quality method'. These may vary from project to project, so no attempt has been made to define what a specific project will need.

Those wishing to turn these outlines into full Product Descriptions will need to add the missing information. This is a good opportunity to compare the given material against the circumstances of a specific project and tailor the text to be a more precise fit. A full description of the contents of a Product Description is given in A.20.

A.1 Acceptance Criteria

A.1.1 Purpose

A definition in measurable terms of what must be done for the final product to be acceptable to the customer and staff who will be affected.

A.1.2 Composition

This will vary according to the type of final product. Suggestions are:

- Target dates
- Major functions
- Appearance
- Personnel level required to use/operate the product
- Performance levels
- Capacity
- Accuracy
- Availability
- Reliability (mean/maximum time to repair, mean time between failures)
- Development cost
- Running costs
- Security
- Ease of use
- Timings.

A.1.3 Derivation

Acceptance Criteria are derived from:

- The Senior User
- Customer's quality expectations.

The criteria are either provided by programme management or developed during *Starting up a Project* (SU).

A.1.4 Quality criteria

- All criteria are measurable
- Each criterion is individually realistic
- The criteria as a group are realistic, for example, high quality, early delivery and low cost may not go together
- Acceptance Criteria form a complete list of criteria to define what will constitute a product acceptable to the customer.

A.2 Business Case

A.2.1 Purpose

To document the justification for the undertaking of a project based on the estimated cost of development and implementation against the risks and the anticipated business benefits and savings to be gained. The total business change must be considered, which may be much wider than just the project development cost.

The Business Case is used to say why the forecast effort and time will be worth the expenditure. The Project Board will monitor the ongoing viability of the project against the Business Case.

A.2.2 Composition

- Reasons
- Options (brief description of the different options considered for the project)
- Benefits expected (expressed in measurable terms against today's situation)
- Risks (summary of the key risks of the project)
- Cost (extracted from the Project Plan)
- Timescales (summary of the Project Plan)
- Investment appraisal.

A.2.3 Derivation

Information for the Business Case is derived from:

- Project Mandate/Project Brief (reasons)
- Project Plan (costs and timescales)
- The customer.

The existence of a provisional Business Case is checked during *Starting up a Project* (SU). If the Project Mandate does not contain a Business Case, this would be created. The Business Case is baselined during *Initiating a Project* (IP).

A.2.4 Quality criteria

- Can the benefits be justified?
- Are the Project Plan and Business Case aligned?
- Are the reasons for the project consistent with corporate or programme strategy?

A.3 Checkpoint Report

A.3.1 Purpose

To report, at a frequency defined in the Stage Plan and/or Work Package, the status of work for each member of a team.

A.3.2 Composition

- Date held
- Period covered
- Follow-ups from previous reports
- Activities during the period
- Products completed during the period
- Quality work carried out during the period
- Actual or potential problems or deviations from plan
- Work planned for the next period
- Products to be completed during the next period.

A.3.3 Derivation

- Verbal reports from team members
- Stage or team plan
- Previous checkpoint (checkpoints are held as part of *Executing a Work Package* (MP2)).

A.3.4 Quality criteria

- Every item in the Stage or team plan for that period covered
- Every team member working to an agreed schedule
- Every team member's work covered
- An update on any unresolved problems from the previous report.

A.4 Communication Plan

A.4.1 Purpose

To define all parties with an interest in the project and the means and frequency of communication between them and the project.

A.4.2 Composition

- Interested parties (for example, stakeholders, accounts staff, user forum, internal audit, quality assurance)
- Information required
- Information provider
- Frequency of communication
- Method of communication.

A.4.3 Derivation

- The Project Board
- The Project Brief
- The Project Quality Plan
- The Project Approach.

A.4.4 Quality criteria

- Have all the listed derivation sources been checked?
- Have all stakeholders been identified and their communication requirements defined?
- Is there agreement from all interested parties about the content, frequency and method?
- Has a common standard been considered?
- Has time to carry out the identified communications been allowed for in Stage Plans?

A.5 Configuration Item Record

A.5.1 Purpose

A record of the information required about a product's status.

A.5.2 Composition

- The project identifier
- Type of product
- Product identifier
- Latest version number
- Product Description
- A description of the life cycle steps appropriate to the product
- 'Owner' of the product
- Person working on the product
- Date allocated
- Library or location where the product is kept
- Source – for example, in-house, or purchased from a third-party company
- Links to related products
- Status
- Copy holders and potential users
- Cross-reference to the Project Issue(s) that caused the change to this product
- Cross-references to relevant correspondence.

A.5.3 Derivation

- Product Breakdown Structure
- Stage and team plans
- Work Package
- Quality Log
- Change control.

A.5.4 Quality criteria

- Does it reflect the status of the product accurately?
- Are all Configuration Item Records kept together in a secure location?
- Does the version number match the actual product?

- Is the copyholder information correct?
- Do the copies held by the copyholders match the version number?

A.6 Configuration Management Plan

A.6.1 Purpose

To identify how and by whom the project's products will be controlled and protected.

A.6.2 Composition

This plan forms part of the Project Quality Plan. It consists of:

- An explanation of the purpose of configuration management
- A description of (or reference to) the configuration management method to be used. Any variance from corporate or programme standards should be highlighted together with a justification for the variance
- Reference to any other configuration management systems with which links will be necessary
- How and where the products will be stored (e.g. project filing structure)
- What filing and retrieval security there will be
- How the products and the various versions of these will be identified
- Where responsibility for configuration management lies.

A.6.3 Derivation

Details of the plan might come from:

- The customer's quality management system (QMS)
- The supplier's QMS
- Specific needs of the project's products and environment
- The project organisation structure
- Any configuration management software in use or mandated by the customer.

A.6.4 Quality criteria

- Responsibilities are clear and understood by both customer and supplier
- The key identifier for project products is defined
- The method and circumstances of version control are clear
- The plan provides the Project Manager with all the product information required.

A.7 Daily Log

A.7.1 Purpose

To record required actions or significant events not caught by other PRINCE2 documents. It acts as the Project Manager's project diary.

A.7.2 Composition

- Date of entry
- Action or comment
- Person responsible
- Target date
- Result.

A.7.3 Derivation

- Risk Log
- Stage Plan
- Checkpoint Reports
- Quality Log
- Conversations and observations.

A.7.4 Quality criteria

- Entries are understandable at a later date
- Anything of a permanent nature is transferred to the appropriate record, e.g. Project Issue
- Date, person responsible and target date are always filled in.

A.8 End Project Report

A.8.1 Purpose

This report is the Project Manager's report to the Project Board (who may pass it on to corporate or programme management) on how well the project has performed against its Project Initiation Document, including the original planned cost, schedule and tolerances, the revised Business Case and final version of the Project Plan.

A.8.2 Composition

- Achievement of the project's objectives
- Performance against the planned target time and cost
- The effect on the original Project Plan and Business Case of any changes that were approved
- Final statistics on change issues received during the project
- The total impact of approved changes
- Statistics for all quality work carried out
- Post-project review date and plan.

A.8.3 Derivation

The End Project Report is derived from:

- Updated Project Plan (including team, Stage and Exception Plans)
- Project Initiation Document
- Risk Log
- Quality Log
- Lessons Learnt Report(s)
- End Stage Report(s)
- Issue Log.

The End Project Report is produced during *Closing a Project* (CP).

A.8.4 Quality criteria

- Does the report describe the impact of the approved changes on the Project Initiation Document?
- Does the report cover all the benefits that can be assessed at this time?
- Does the quality work done during the project meet the quality expectations of the customer?

A.9 End Stage Report

A.9.1 Purpose

The purpose of the End Stage Report is to give a summary of progress to date, the overall project situation and sufficient information to ask for a Project Board decision on what to do next with the project.

The Project Board uses the information in the End Stage Report to decide what action to take with the project: approve the next stage, ask for a revised next Stage Plan, amend the project scope or stop the project.

A.9.2 Composition

- Current Stage Plan with all the actuals
- Project Plan outlook
- Business Case review
- Risk review
- Project Issue situation
- Quality statistics
- Project Manager's report on any events that affected stage performance.

A.9.3 Derivation

Information for the report is obtained from:

- Stage Plan and actuals
- Next Stage Plan (if appropriate)
- Updated Project Plan
- Risk Log
- Lessons Learned Log
- Quality Log
- Issues Log
- Exception Report/Plan
- Completed Work Package data.

The End Stage Report is an output from *Managing Stage Boundaries* (SB).

A.9.4 Quality criteria

- Does the report clearly show stage performance against the plan?
- Are any abnormal situations described, together with their impact?
- Do any appointed Project Assurance roles disagree with the report?

A.10 Exception Report

A.10.1 Purpose

An Exception Report is produced when an approved Stage Plan is forecast to exceed tolerance levels set. It is prepared by the Project Manager in order to inform the Project Board of the adverse situation.

An Exception Report will normally result in the Project Board asking the Project Manager to produce an Exception Plan.

A.10.2 Composition

- A description of the cause of a deviation from the Stage Plan
- Consequences of the deviation
- The available options
- The effect of each option on the Business Case, risks, project and stage tolerances
- The Project Manager's recommendations.

A.10.3 Derivation

The information for an Exception Report may come from:

- Current Stage Plan and actuals
- Issue Log
- Risk Log
- Project Plan
- Quality Log
- Highlight Reports
- Checkpoint Reports
- Project Board advice of an external event that affects the project.

An Exception Report is output from *Escalating Project Issues* (CS8).

A.10.4 Quality criteria

- The current Stage Plan must accurately show the status of budget and schedule
- The reason(s) for the deviation must be stated.

A.11 Follow-on Action Recommendations

A.11.1 Purpose

To pass details of unfinished work or potential product modifications to the group charged with future support of the final product in its operational life.

A.11.2 Composition

- Date of the recommendations
- Requests for Change that were considered to have merit but were not implemented during the project
- Off-Specifications recording missing products or products that do not meet the original requirements
- Risks identified during the project, which may affect the product in its operational life
- Any identified hand-over or training needs
- Any other activities needed to take the product to the next stage of its life.

A.11.3 Derivation

- Issue Log
- Lessons Learned Report
- Quality Log
- Risk Log.

A.11.4 Quality criteria

- There must be an entry for every open Project Issue
- The relevant Project Issues should have been closed with an entry to signify that they have been transferred to these recommendations
- Any available useful documentation or evidence should accompany the recommendations.

A.12 Highlight Report

A.12.1 Purpose

To provide the Project Board with a summary of the stage status at intervals defined by them.

The Project Board uses the report to monitor stage and project progress. The Project Manager also uses it to advise the Project Board of any potential problems or areas where the Project Board could help.

A.12.2 Composition

- Date
- Period covered
- Budget status
- Schedule status
- Products completed during the period
- Actual or potential problems and risk update
- Products to be completed during the next period
- Project Issue status
- Budget and schedule impact of any changes.

A.12.3 Derivation

Information for the Highlight Reports is derived from:

- Checkpoint Reports
- Issue Log
- Project Initiation Document.

Highlight Reports are output from *Reporting Highlights* (CS6).

A.12.4 Quality criteria

- Accurate reflection of checkpoint information
- Accurate summary of the Issue Log
- Accurate summary of plan status
- Highlights any potential problem areas.

A.16 Off-Specification

A.16.1 Purpose

To document any situation where a product is failing, or is forecast to fail, to meet its specification.

A.16.2 Composition

- Date
- Issue Log number
- Status
- Description of the fault
- Impact of the fault
- Priority assessment
- Decision
- Allocation details, if applicable
- Date allocated
- Date completed.

A.16.3 Derivation

An Off-Specification can be raised by anyone associated with the project at any time. It would be gathered in as part of *Capturing Project Issues* (CS3). The Project Manager may also decide that a Project Issue is an Off-Specification during *Examining Project Issues* (CS4).

A.16.4 Quality criteria

- Logged in the Issue Log
- Accurate description of the problem.

A.17 Post-Project Review Plan

A.17.1 Purpose

The purpose of the Post-Project Review Plan is to define for the Executive how and when a measurement of the achievement of the project benefits can be made. The plan is presented to the Executive at the end of the project.

The plan has to cover the effort to find out:

- Whether the expected benefits of the product(s) have been realised
- Whether the product(s) has caused any problems in use.

Each expected benefit has to be assessed for the level of its achievement so far or any additional time needed for the benefit to materialise. Use of the product may have brought unexpected side effects, either beneficial or adverse. Time and effort have to be allowed to document explanations of why these side effects were not foreseen. The plan must include time for recommendations on how to realise or improve benefits or counter problems.

A.17.2 Composition

- How to measure achievement of expected benefits
- When the various benefits can be measured
- What resources are needed to carry out the review work
- Other areas that may need consideration, such as user reaction.

A.17.3 Derivation

- Business Case
- Discussion with the users and product support people.

The post-project review is planned as part of *Identifying Follow-on Actions* (CP2), but the Executive is responsible for ensuring that the review happens after the project has finished.

A.17.4 Quality criteria

- Covers all benefits mentioned in the Business Case
- Describes a suitable timing for measurement of the benefits, together with reasons
- Identifies the skills or individuals who will be needed to carry out the measurements
- Is realistic in terms of effort when compared to the anticipated benefits.

A.18 Product Breakdown Structure

A.18.1 Purpose

To show all products to be developed and quality controlled. To understand the content and function of all products to be developed.

A.18.2 Composition

Top-to-bottom diagram showing breakdown of all products to be developed. External products must be clearly distinguished from the products developed by the project. The usual PRINCE2 convention is for project products to be shown as rectangles and external products as ellipses.

A.18.3 Derivation

- Project Brief
- Project Quality Plan.

A.18.4 Quality criteria

- Are all external products and project products clearly identified and distinguished?
- Is the PBS consistent with the Product Checklist?
- Are genuine super-products (i.e. non-bottom level but requiring a separate product description) distinguished from convenient product groupings (memory joggers)?
- Are management and specialist products identified and distinguished?
- Can Product Descriptions for the bottom-level products be written without further decomposition?
- Have enough bottom-level products been identified to meet management control requirements?
- Will all the products identified fulfil the business need?
- Have all quality products been identified that meet the needs of customer, audit and quality assurance as described in the Project Quality Plan?
- Is the numbering of each product unique and consistent with the level of the product in the hierarchy?
- Has responsibility for the monitoring of the quality of external products been clearly identified?

A.19 Product Checklist

A.19.1 Purpose

To list the products to be produced within a Stage Plan, together with key status dates.

Used by the Project Board to monitor progress.

A.19.2 Composition

- Plan identification
- Product names (and reference numbers if appropriate)
- Planned and actual dates for:
  - draft ready
  - quality check
  - approval.

A.19.3 Derivation

Extracted from the Product Breakdown Structure. Produced as an output from *Defining and Analysing Products* (PL2) and finalised in *Completing a Plan* (PL7).

A.19.4 Quality criteria

Do the details and dates match those in the Stage Plan?

A.20 Product Description

A.20.1 Purpose

- To understand the detailed nature, purpose and function of the product
- To identify the sources of information or supply for the product
- To describe the required appearance of the product
- To identify the level of quality required of the product
- To enable activities to develop and quality control the product to be identified
- To define the people or skills required to develop and check the product.

A.20.2 Composition

- *Identifier*: unique key, probably allocated by the configuration management method used
- *Title*: name by which the product is known
- *Purpose*: this defines the purpose that the product will fulfil. Is it a means to an end or an end in itself? It is helpful in understanding the product's functions, size, quality, complexity, robustness, etc.
- *Composition*: this is a list of the parts of the product. For example, if the product were a document, this would be a list of the expected chapters or sections
- *Derivation*: what are the source products from which this product is derived? Examples are:
  - a design is derived from a specification
  - a product is bought in from a supplier
  - a statement of the expected benefits are obtained from the user
  - a product is obtained from another department or team
- *Format and Presentation*: any standard appearance to which the product must conform
- *Allocated to*: the person, group or skill type needed to create this product
- *Quality criteria*: to what quality specification must the product be produced and what quality measurements will be applied by those inspecting the finished product? This might be a simple reference to one or more common standards that are documented elsewhere or it might be a full explanation of some yardstick to be applied
- *Quality method*: what kind of quality checking, e.g. test, inspection or review, is to be used to check the quality or functionality of the product?
- *Quality check skills required*: either identification of the people who are to check the quality, an indication of the skills required to do so or a pointer to which area(s) should supply the checking resources. Identification of the actual people may be left until planning the stage in which the quality check is to be done.

A.20.3 Derivation

- Product Breakdown Structure
- The end users of the product
- Existing customer or supplier quality management systems.

A.20.4 Quality criteria

- Is the purpose clear and consistent with other products?
- Is the product described to a level of detail sufficient to plan and manage its development?
- Is the composition of the product more like a requirements specification than a description of the contents/elements of a product?
- Is responsibility for the development of the product clearly identified?
- Is responsibility for the development of the product consistent with the roles and responsibilities described in the project management team organisation and the Project Quality Plan?
- Are the quality criteria consistent with the project quality standards, standard checklists and Acceptance Criteria?
- Can the quality criteria answer the question: 'How will I know when work on this product is finished as opposed to stopped?'
- Are the types of quality check required able to verify that the product meets its stated quality criteria or not?
- Have people with the right knowledge and skills written the Product Description?

A.21 Product Flow Diagram

A.21.1 Purpose

To show the required sequence of delivery of a plan's products and identify dependencies between those products, including any external products.

A.21.2 Composition

A diagram showing the product delivery sequence from top to bottom or left to right, plus the dependencies between those products. Arrows indicate dependencies between products. External products must be clearly distinguished from the products developed by the plan. The normal PRINCE2 convention is for project products to be shown as rectangles and external products as ellipses.

A.21.3 Derivation

- Product Descriptions (derivation field)
- Product Breakdown Structure (external products).

A.21.4 Quality criteria

- Are all external products identified and the dependencies understood?
- Are all bottom-level products on the Product Breakdown Structure (PBS) identified on the diagram?
- Are all 'super-products' identified on the PBS shown on the Product Flow Diagram (PFD)?
- Are all products identified in the PFD identified as products on the PBS?
- Are there any products without dependencies?
- Have dependencies been identified at a level suitable to that of the plan of which the PFD is a part?
- Are the dependencies consistent with the derivation fields (from Product Description) of all the products?

A.22 Project Approach

A.22.1 Purpose

To define the type of solution to be developed by the project and/or the method of delivering that solution. It should also identify any environment into which the solution must fit.

A.22.2 Composition

- Description of approach
- Type of solution, for example:
  - bespoke
  - contracted out
  - current product modified
  - design from scratch
  - use company staff
  - hire in contract staff
  - buy a ready-made solution
- Reasons for the approach (for example, part of programme approach).

A.22.3 Derivation

- Project Brief
- Design authority or equivalent
- Marketplace – that is, what is available.

A.22.4 Quality criteria

- It must conform to the strategy that relates to the product's operational environment
- It must be achievable within all known time and cost constraints for the project
- It must be achievable with known technology.

A.23 Project Brief

A.23.1 Purpose

To provide a full and firm foundation for the initiation of the project.

The contents are extended and refined into the Project Initiation Document, which is the working document for managing and directing the project.

The Project Brief is a key document in its own right. It is the basis of the Project Initiation Document, which gives the direction and scope of the project and forms the 'contract' between the project management team and corporate or programme management. Any significant change to the material contained in the Project Brief will thus need to be referred to corporate or programme management.

A.23.2 Composition

The following is a suggested list of contents, which should be tailored to the requirements and environment of each project:

- Background
- Project Definition, explaining what the project needs to achieve. It will contain:
  - project objectives
  - project scope
  - outline project deliverables and/or desired outcomes
  - any exclusions
  - constraints
  - interfaces
- Outline Business Case
  - a description of how this project supports business strategy, plans or programmes
  - the reasons why the project is needed
- Customer's quality expectations
- Acceptance criteria
- Any known risks.

If earlier work has been done, the Project Brief may refer to the document(s) containing useful information, such as Project Plan outline, rather than include copies of them.

A.23.3 Derivation

The Project Brief is developed from the Project Mandate supplied at the start of the project, produced by *Starting up a Project* (SU), and accepted via *Authorising Initiation* (DP1).

If the project is part of a programme, the programme should provide the Project Brief. In such circumstances it will not have to be derived from a Project Mandate.

If no Project Mandate is provided, the Project Manager has to generate the Project Brief from scratch in discussions with the customer and users.

A.23.4 Quality criteria

- Does the Project Brief accurately reflect the Project Mandate?
- Does it form a firm basis on which to initiate a project (*Initiating a Project* (IP))?
- Does it indicate how the customer will assess the acceptability of the finished product(s)?

A.24 Project Initiation Document

A.24.1 Purpose

To define the project, to form the basis for its management and the assessment of overall success.

There are two primary uses of the document:

- To ensure that the project has a sound basis before asking the Project Board to make any major commitment to the project
- To act as a base document against which the Project Board and Project Manager can assess progress, change management issues and ongoing viability questions.

A.24.2 Composition

The following are the base elements of information needed to direct and manage a project. They cover the following fundamental questions about the project:

- **What** a project is aiming to achieve
- **Why** it is important to achieve it
- **Who** is going to be involved in managing the process and what their responsibilities are
- **How** and **when** it is all going to happen.

The information will be held in various ways, and the following contents should be read not as a list of contents for one document but rather as the information needed in order to make the initiation decisions. The sections have been divided into 'Stable' and 'Dynamic' to indicate those sections that will need to have new versions created as the project progresses.

Stable

- Background, explaining the context of the project and how we have arrived at the current position of requiring a project
- Project definition, explaining what the project needs to achieve. Under this heading will be:
  - project objectives
  - defined method of approach
  - project scope
  - project deliverables and/or desired outcomes
  - exclusions
  - constraints
  - interfaces
  - assumptions

- Project organisation structure, explaining who will be on the project management team
  - Project management team structure
  - Job descriptions
- Communication Plan (see the separate Communication Plan Product outline)
- Project Quality Plan (see the separate Project Quality Plan Product outline)
- Project controls, laying down how control is to be exercised within the project and the reporting and monitoring mechanisms that will support this; it will include the exception process.

Dynamic

- Initial Business Case, explaining why the project is being undertaken
- Initial Project Plan, explaining how and when the activities of the project will occur (for details of the Project Plan content, see the separate *Product Description outline*)
- Initial Risk Log, documenting the results of the risk analysis and risk management activities.

A.24.3 Derivation

- Supplier's project management standards (if known)
- Customer's specified control requirements
- Much of the information should come from the Project Mandate, enhanced in the Project Brief. The Project Initiation Document will be completed during the initiation stage. Parts of it, such as the Risk Log, Project Plan and Business Case, may be updated and refined by each pass through *Managing Stage Boundaries* (SB) and will finally be archived as part of *Closing a Project* (CP).

A.24.4 Quality criteria

- Does the document correctly represent the project?
- Does it show a viable, achievable project that is in line with corporate strategy or overall programme needs?
- Is the project organisation structure complete, with names and titles?
- Have all the roles been considered?
- Does it clearly show a control, reporting and direction regime that is implementable and appropriate to the scale, business risk and business importance of the project?
- Is the project organisation structure backed up by agreed and signed job descriptions?
- Are the relationships and lines of authority clear?
- Does the project organisation structure need to say to whom the Project Board reports?

- Do the controls cover the needs of the Project Board, Project Manager and Team Managers?
- Do the controls satisfy any delegated assurance requirements?
- Is it clear who will administer each control?

A.25 Project Issue

A.25.1 Purpose

A generic term for any matter that has to be brought to the attention of the project and requires an answer. After receiving a unique reference number, Project Issues are evaluated in terms of impact on the product, effort and cost, risks, Project Plan and Business Case. The Project Manager may make a decision on what action to take or the Project Issue may be referred to the Project Board. A Project Issue may have a negative or positive impact on the project. Project issues include:

- Request for Change
- Off-Specification
- Question
- Statement of concern.

A.25.2 Composition

- Author
- Date
- Project Issue number
- Description of the Project Issue
- Priority
- Impact analysis
- Decision
- Signature of decision maker(s)
- Date of decision.

A.25.3 Derivation

Anyone may submit a Project Issue. Typical sources are users and specialists working on the project. *Capturing Project Issues* (CS3) deals with collating Project Issues. They are then examined during *Examining Project Issues* (CS4).

A.25.4 Quality criteria

- Is the problem/requirement/opportunity clear?
- Have all the implications been thought out?
- Has the Project Issue been correctly logged?

A.26 Project Mandate

A.26.1 Purpose

The information in the Mandate is used to trigger *Starting up a Project* (SU). It should contain sufficient information to identify at least the prospective Executive of the Project Board and indicate the subject matter of the project.

It will be used to create the Project Brief.

A.26.2 Composition

The actual composition of a Project Mandate will vary according to the type and size of project and also the environment in which the Mandate is generated. The project may be a completely new piece of work that has just arisen, it may be the outcome of an earlier investigation or it may be part of a larger programme.

The following list contains suggested contents, which should be tailored to suit the specific project:

- Authority responsible
- Background
- Project objectives
- Scope
- Constraints
- Interfaces
- Quality expectations
- Outline Business Case (reasons)
- Reference to any associated documents or products
- An indication of who are to be the project Executive and Project Manager
- The customer(s), user(s) and any other known interested parties.

If the Project Mandate is based on earlier work, there may be other useful information such as an estimate of the project size and duration and a view of the risks faced by the project.

A.26.3 Derivation

A Project Mandate may come from anywhere, but it should come from a level of management that can authorise the cost and resource usage. It is input to *Starting up a Project* (SU).

A.26.4 Quality criteria

- Is the level of authority commensurate with the anticipated size, risk and cost of the project?

- Is there sufficient detail to allow the appointment of an appropriate Executive and Project Manager?
- Are all the known interested parties identified?
- Does the Project Mandate describe what is required?

A.27 Project Plan

A.27.1 Purpose

The Project Plan is a mandatory plan that provides a statement of how and when a project's objectives are to be achieved, by showing the major products, activities and resources required on the project.

It provides the Business Case with planned project costs and it identifies the management stages and other major control points.

It is used by the Project Board as a baseline against which to monitor project progress and cost stage by stage.

A.27.2 Composition

This product forms part of the Project Initiation Document and will contain the following.

- Plan description, giving a brief description of what the plan covers
- Project prerequisites, containing any fundamental aspects that must be in place at the start of the project and that must remain in place for the project to succeed
- External dependencies
- Planning assumptions
- Project Plan, covering:
  - project-level Gantt or bar chart with identified management stages
  - project-level Product Breakdown Structure
  - project-level Product Flow Diagrams
  - project-level Product Descriptions
  - project-level activity network
  - project financial budget
  - project change budget
  - project-level table of resource requirements
  - requested/assigned specific resources
  - project-level tolerance (time and budget, for example)
  - Contingency plans, explaining how it is intended to deal with the consequences of any risks that materialise.

A.27.3 Derivation

- Project Brief.

Refined from the outline Project Plan in the Project Brief during *Planning a Project* (IP2). Modified during Updating a *Project Plan* (SB2).

A.27.4 Quality criteria

- Is the plan achievable?
- Does it support the rest of the Project Initiation Document?

A.28 Project Quality Plan

A.28.1 Purpose

The Project Quality Plan is part of the Project Initiation Document.

The purpose is to define the quality techniques and standards to be applied, and the various responsibilities for achieving the required quality levels, during the project.

A.28.2 Composition

- Customer's quality expectations (from the Project Brief)
- Acceptance criteria
- Quality responsibilities
- Reference to any standards that need to be met
- The quality control and audit processes to be applied to project management
- Quality control and audit process requirements for specialist work
- Change management procedures
- Configuration Management Plan (see *Configuration Management*, Chapter 19, for an explanation of the term)
- Any tools to be used to ensure quality.

A.28.3 Derivation

The Project Quality Plan is derived from:

- Organisational standards
- Customer's quality expectations
- Supplier and customer quality management systems (QMS)
- Configuration management requirements
- Change control requirements.

It is produced as an output from *Planning Quality* (IP1).

A.28.4 Quality criteria

- Does the plan clearly define ways in which the customer's quality expectations will be met?
- Are the defined ways sufficient to achieve the required quality?
- Are responsibilities for quality defined up to a level that is independent of the project and Project Manager?
- Does the plan conform to the corporate quality policy?

A.29 Quality Log

A.29.1 Purpose

- To issue a unique reference for each quality check planned
- To act as a pointer to the quality check documentation for a product
- To act as a summary of the number and type of quality checks held.

The log summarises all the quality checks that are planned/have taken place and provides information for the End Stage Reports and End Project Report as well as the Lessons Learned Report.

A.29.2 Composition

For each entry in the log, the following should be recorded:

- Reference number
- Product
- Method of quality checking
- Staff responsible, name, role
- Planned date
- Actual date
- Result
- Number of action items
- Target sign-off date
- Actual sign-off date.

A.29.3 Derivation

The first entries are made when a quality check or test is entered on a Stage Plan. The remaining information comes from the actual performance of the check. The sign-off date is when all corrective action items have been signed off.

An initial, blank Quality Log is created during *Planning Quality* (IP1).

A.29.4 Quality criteria

- Is there a procedure in place that will ensure that every quality check is entered on the log?
- Has responsibility for the log been allocated?

A.30 Request for Change

A.30.1 Purpose

To request a modification to a product or an acceptance criterion as currently specified.

A.30.2 Composition

- Date
- Issue Log number
- Class
- Status
- Description of the proposed change
- Impact of the change
- Priority assessment
- Decision
- Allocation details, if applicable
- Date allocated
- Date completed.

A.30.3 Derivation

A Request for Change can be submitted by anyone connected with the project. A Request for Change can be submitted as such and gathered in by *Capturing Project Issues* (CS3), or a Project Issue can be defined as a Request for Change by the Project Manager as part of *Examining Project Issues* (CS4).

A.30.4 Quality criteria

- Source clearly identified
- Logged in the Issue Log
- Accurate description of the requested change
- Benefit of making the change clearly expressed and, where possible, in measurable terms.

A.31 Risk Log

A.31.1 Purpose

The purpose of the Risk Log is to provide a repository of information about the risks, their analysis, countermeasures and status.

A.31.2 Composition

- Risk identifier: unique code to allow grouping of all information on this risk
- Description: brief description of the risk
- Risk category (e.g. commercial, legal, technical)
- Impact: effect on the project/programme/organisation if this risk were to occur
- Probability: estimate of the likelihood of the risk occurring
- Proximity: how close in time is the risk likely to occur
- Countermeasure(s): what actions have been taken/will be taken to counter this risk
- Owner: who has been appointed to keep an eye on this risk
- Author: who submitted the risk
- Date identified: when was the risk first identified
- Date of last update: when was the status of this risk last checked
- Current status: e.g. dead, reducing, increasing, no change.

A.31.3 Derivation

Some risks may have been identified in work that led up to the Project Mandate. Risks may have been identified in the Project Brief and should be considered during project initiation when the Project Plan is being created. There should be a check for any new risks every time the Risk Log is reviewed, minimally at each end stage assessment. The Project Board has the responsibility to continually check external events for external risks.

Risks to a Stage Plan should be examined as part of the production of that plan. They should be reviewed each time the Stage Plan is updated.

The Risk Log is created during *Preparing a Project Brief* (SU4).

A.31.4 Quality criteria

- Does the status indicate whether action has been taken or is in a contingency plan?
- Are the risks uniquely identified (including to which project they refer if it came from a programme)?
- Has the risk been allocated to an owner?
- Is access to the Risk Log controlled?

- Is the Risk Log kept in a safe place?
- Are activities to review the Risk Log in the Stage Plans?

A.32 Stage Plan (or Exception Plan)

A.32.1 Purpose

- Used as the basis for project management control throughout the stage
- Identifies all the products that the stage must produce
- Provides a statement of how and when a stage's objectives are to be achieved, by showing the deliverables, activities and resources required
- Identifies the stage's control and reporting points and frequencies
- Provides a baseline against which stage progress will be measured
- Records the stage tolerances
- Specifies the quality controls for the stage and identifies the resources needed for them.

A.32.2 Composition

This product will contain the following:

- Plan description, covering:
  - a brief description of what the plan covers
  - a brief description of the planned approach
- Quality plan
  - the quality control methods to be used for each major product
  - the resources to be used in each quality test or check
- Plan prerequisites:
  - containing any fundamental aspects which must be in place at the start of the stage and which must remain in place for the plan to succeed
- External dependencies
- Tolerances (time and budget, for example)
- How will the plan be monitored and controlled?
- Reporting
- Planning assumptions
- Graphical plan, covering:
  - diagram showing identified resources, activities, start and end dates (usually a Gantt or bar chart)
  - Product Breakdown Structure
  - Product Flow Diagram
  - activity network
  - financial budget

  - table of resource requirements
  - Risk assessment

- Product Descriptions for the major products.

An Exception Plan or any other detailed plan will have the same format as a Stage Plan.

A.32.3 Derivation

- Refined from the Project Plan during *Planning a Stage* (SB1)
- Based on resource availability.

Updated during *Assessing Progress* (CS2) and may be modified during *Reviewing Stage Status* (SB5) and *Taking Corrective Action* (CS7).

A.32.4 Quality criteria

- Is the plan achievable?
- Do all Team Managers involved in the plan's operation believe that their portion is achievable?
- Does the Stage Plan support the Project Plan?
- Does it take into account any constraints of time, resources and budget?
- Has it been taken down to the level of detail necessary to ensure that any deviations will be recognised in time to react appropriately – for example, within the stage tolerances and within the activity 'floats'?
- Has the Stage Plan been developed according to the planning standard?
- Does the Stage Plan contain activities and resource effort to review the Issue Log?

A.33 Work Package

A.33.1 Purpose

A Work Package is a set of information about one or more required products collated by the Project Manager to pass responsibility for work or delivery formally to a Team Manager or team member.

A.33.2 Composition

This product will vary in content – and, indeed, in degree of formality – depending on circumstances.

Where the work is being conducted by a team working directly under the Project Manager, the Work Package may be a verbal instruction, although there are good reasons for putting it in writing, such as avoidance of misunderstanding and providing a link to performance assessment. Where the work is being carried out by a supplier under a contract and the Project Manager is part of the customer organisation, there is a need for a formal written instruction in line with standards laid down in that contract.

Although the content may vary greatly according to the relationship between the Project Manager and the recipient of the Work Package, it should cover:

- Date
- Team or person authorised
- Work Package description
- Product Description(s)
- Techniques/processes/procedures to be used
- Interfaces to be satisfied by the work
- Interfaces to be maintained during the work
- Quality checking method to be used
- Configuration management requirements
- Stage Plan extract
- Joint agreement on effort, cost, start and end dates
- Sign-off requirements
- Work return arrangements
- How completion is to be advised
- Any constraints to be observed
- Independent quality-checking arrangements
- Reporting arrangements
- Problem handling and escalation.

There should be space on the Work Package to record its authorisation and acceptance of the return of the completed Work Package. This can be enhanced to include an assessment of the work and go towards performance appraisal.

A.33.3 Derivation

- Product Description(s)
- Stage Plans.

A.33.4 Quality criteria

- Is the required Work Package clearly defined and understood by the assigned resource?
- Is there a Product Description for the required product(s), with clearly identified and acceptable quality criteria?
- Does the Product Description match up with the other Work Package documentation?
- Are standards for the work agreed?
- Are the defined standards in line with those applied to similar products?
- Have all necessary interfaces been defined?
- Do the reporting arrangements include the provision for exception reporting?
- Is there agreement between the Project Manager and the recipient on exactly what is to be done?
- Is there agreement on the constraints, including effort, cost and targets?
- Are the dates and effort in line with those shown in the Stage Plan?
- Are reporting arrangements defined?
- Is any requirement for independent attendance at, and participation in, quality checking defined?

APPENDIX B: PROJECT MANAGEMENT TEAM ROLES

The following roles explain the normal responsibilities and tasks of each member of the project management team. They can be tailored to suit the needs of the roles for any project. Tailoring may include combining roles or dividing a role between two or more people. The important thing to remember is that all the responsibilities must be held by someone, whatever the size of the project. Responsibilities may be moved from one role to another, but should never be dropped. The *Organisation* chapter (Chapter 14) gives clear indication of which roles may or may not hold certain responsibilities, e.g. the Project Manager should not hold Project Assurance responsibilities.

B.1 Project Board

The Project Board is responsible to corporate or programme management for the overall direction and management of the project and has responsibility and authority for the project within the remit (the Project Mandate) set by corporate or programme management.

The Project Board is the project's 'voice' to the outside world and is responsible for any publicity or other dissemination of information about the project.

B.1.1 Specific responsibilities

The Project Board approves all major plans and authorises any major deviation from agreed Stage Plans. It is the authority that signs off the completion of each stage as well as authorises the start of the next stage. It ensures that required resources are committed and arbitrates on any conflicts within the project or negotiates a solution to any problems between the project and external bodies. In addition, it approves the appointment and responsibilities of the Project Manager and any delegation of its Project Assurance responsibilities.

The Project Board has the following responsibilities. It is a general list and will need tailoring for a specific project.

- At the beginning of the project:
  - approving the start of the project via acceptance of the Project Brief
  - agreement with the Project Manager on that person's responsibilities and objectives
  - confirmation with corporate or programme management of project tolerances
  - specification of external constraints on the project, such as quality assurance
  - approval of an accurate and satisfactory Project Initiation Document, including that it complies with relevant customer standards and policies, plus any associated contract with the supplier
  - delegation of any Project Assurance roles
  - commitment of project resources required by the next Stage Plan.

- As the project progresses:
  - provision of overall guidance and direction to the project, ensuring it remains within any specified constraints
  - review of each completed stage and approval of progress to the next
  - review and approval of Stage Plans and any Exception Plans
  - 'ownership' of one or more of the identified risks, as allocated at plan approval time – that is, the responsibility to monitor the risk and advise the Project Manager of any change in its status and to take action, if appropriate, to ameliorate the risk
  - approval of changes
  - compliance with corporate or programme management directives
- At the end of the project:
  - assurance that all products have been delivered satisfactorily
  - assurance that all Acceptance Criteria have been met
  - approval of the End Project Report
  - approval of the Lessons Learned Report and the passage of this to the appropriate standards group to ensure action
  - decisions on the recommendations for follow-on actions and the passage of these to the appropriate authorities
  - approval, where appropriate, of a Post-Project Review Plan
  - project closure notification to corporate or programme management.

The Project Board owns the process, *Directing a Project* (DP).

The Project Board is ultimately responsible for assurance that the project remains on course to deliver the desired outcome of the required quality to meet the Business Case defined in the Project Initiation Document. According to the size, complexity and risk of the project, the Project Board may decide to delegate some of this Project Assurance responsibility. See section 14.2.4 and B.7 for more detail.

One Project Board responsibility that should receive careful consideration is that of approving and funding changes. Chapter 20 on *Change Control* should be read before finalising this responsibility of approving and funding changes.

Responsibilities of specific members of the Project Board are described in the respective sections that follow.

B.2 Executive

The Executive is ultimately responsible for the project, supported by the Senior User and Senior Supplier. The Executive's role is to ensure that the project is focused throughout its life cycle on achieving its objectives and delivering a product that will achieve the projected benefits. The Executive has to ensure that the project gives value for money, ensuring a cost-conscious approach to the project, balancing the demands of business, user and supplier.

Throughout the project, the Executive 'owns' the Business Case.

B.2.1 Specific responsibilities

- Oversee the development of the Project Brief and Business Case
- Ensure that there is a coherent project organisation structure and logical set of plans
- Authorise customer expenditure and set stage tolerances
- Monitor and control the progress of the project at a strategic level, in particular reviewing the Business Case continually (e.g. at each end stage assessment)
- Ensure that any proposed changes of scope, cost or timescale are checked against their possible effects on the Business Case
- Ensure that risks are being tracked and mitigated as effectively as possible
- Brief corporate or programme management about project progress
- Organise and chair Project Board meetings
- Recommend future action on the project to corporate or programme management if the project tolerance is exceeded
- Approve the End Project Report and Lessons Learned Report and ensure that any outstanding issues are documented and passed on to the appropriate body
- Approve the sending of the project closure notification to corporate or programme management
- Ensure that the benefits have been realised by holding a post-project review and forward the results of the review to the appropriate stakeholders.

The Executive is responsible for overall business assurance of the project – that is, that it remains on target to deliver products that will achieve the expected business benefits, and that the project will be completed within its agreed tolerances for budget and schedule. Business assurance covers:

- Validation and monitoring of the Business Case against external events and against project progress
- Keeping the project in line with customer strategies
- Monitoring project finance on behalf of the customer
- Monitoring the business risks to ensure that these are kept under control

- Monitoring any supplier and contractor payments
- Monitoring changes to the Project Plan to see whether there is any impact on the needs of the business or the project Business Case
- Assessing the impact of potential changes on the Business Case and Project Plan
- Constraining user and supplier excesses
- Informing the project of any changes caused by a programme of which the project is part (this responsibility may be transferred if there is other programme representation on the project management team)
- Monitoring stage and project progress against the agreed tolerances.

If the project warrants it, the Executive may delegate some responsibility for the business assurance functions.

The Project Board is not a democracy controlled by votes. The Executive is the key decision maker with advice and commitments from others.

B.3 Senior User

The Senior User is responsible for the specification of the needs of all those who will use the final product(s), for user liaison with the project team and for monitoring that the solution will meet those needs within the constraints of the Business Case in terms of quality, functionality and ease of use.

The role represents the interests of all those who will use the final product(s) of the project, those for whom the product will achieve an objective or those who will use the product to deliver benefits. The Senior User role commits user resources and monitors products against requirements. This role may require more than one person to cover all the user interests. For the sake of effectiveness the role should not be split between too many people.

B.3.1 Specific responsibilities

- Ensure the desired outcome of the project is specified
- Make sure that progress towards the outcome required by the users remains consistent from the user perspective
- Promote and maintain focus on the desired project outcome
- Ensure that any user resources required for the project are made available
- Approve Product Descriptions for those products that act as inputs or outputs (interim or final) from the supplier function or will affect them directly
- Ensure that the products are signed off once completed
- Prioritise and contribute user opinions on Project Board decisions on whether to implement recommendations on proposed changes
- Resolve user requirements and priority conflicts
- Provide the user view on Follow-on Action Recommendations
- Brief and advise user management on all matters concerning the project.

The assurance responsibilities of the Senior User are that:

- Specification of the user's needs is accurate, complete and unambiguous
- Development of the solution at all stages is monitored to ensure that it will meet the user's needs and is progressing towards that target
- Impact of potential changes is evaluated from the user point of view
- Risks to the users are constantly monitored
- Quality checking of the product at all stages has the appropriate user representation
- Quality control procedures are used correctly to ensure products meet user requirements
- User liaison is functioning effectively.

Where the project's size, complexity or importance warrants it, the Senior User may delegate the responsibility and authority for some of the assurance responsibilities.

B.4 Senior Supplier

Represents the interests of those designing, developing, facilitating, procuring, implementing and possibly operating and maintaining the project products. The Senior Supplier is accountable for the quality of products delivered by the supplier(s). The Senior Supplier role must have the authority to commit or acquire supplier resources required.

It should be noted that in some environments the customer might share design authority or have a major say in it.

If necessary, more than one person may be required to represent the suppliers.

B.4.1 Specific responsibilities

- Agree objectives for supplier activities
- Make sure that progress towards the outcome remains consistent from the supplier perspective
- Promote and maintain focus on the desired project outcome from the point of view of supplier management
- Ensure that the supplier resources required for the project are made available
- Approve Product Descriptions for supplier products
- Contribute supplier opinions on Project Board decisions on whether to implement recommendations on proposed changes
- Resolve supplier requirements and priority conflicts
- Arbitrate on, and ensure resolution of, any supplier priority or resource conflicts
- Brief non-technical management on supplier aspects of the project.

The Senior Supplier is responsible for the specialist integrity of the project. The supplier assurance role responsibilities are to:

- Advise on the selection of development strategy, design and methods
- Ensure that any supplier and operating standards defined for the project are met and used to good effect
- Monitor potential changes and their impact on the correctness, completeness and integrity of products against their Product Description from a supplier perspective
- Monitor any risks in the production aspects of the project
- Ensure quality control procedures are used correctly, so that products adhere to requirements.

If warranted, some of this assurance responsibility may be delegated to separate supplier assurance personnel. Depending on the particular customer/supplier environment of a project, the customer may also wish to appoint people to carry out assurance on supplier products.

B.5 Project Manager

The Project Manager has the authority to run the project on a day-to-day basis on behalf of the Project Board within the constraints laid down by the board.

The Project Manager's prime responsibility is to ensure that the project produces the required products, to the required standard of quality and within the specified constraints of time and cost. The Project Manager is also responsible for the project producing a result that is capable of achieving the benefits defined in the Business Case.

B.5.1 Specific responsibilities

- Manage the production of the required products
- Direct and motivate the project team
- Plan and monitor the project
- Agree any delegation and use of Project Assurance roles required by the Project Board
- Produce the Project Initiation Document
- Prepare Project, Stage and, if necessary, Exception Plans in conjunction with Team Managers and appointed Project Assurance roles and agree them with the Project Board
- Manage the risks, including the development of contingency plans
- Liaise with programme management if the project is part of a programme
- Liaise with programme management or related projects to ensure that work is neither overlooked nor duplicated
- Take responsibility for overall progress and use of resources and initiate corrective action where necessary
- Be responsible for change control and any required configuration management
- Prepare and report to the Project Board through Highlight Reports and End Stage Reports
- Liaise with the Project Board or its appointed Project Assurance roles to assure the overall direction and integrity of the project
- Agree technical and quality strategy with appropriate members of the Project Board
- Prepare the Lessons Learned Report
- Prepare any Follow-on Action Recommendations required
- Prepare the End Project Report
- Identify and obtain any support and advice required for the management, planning and control of the project
- Be responsible for project administration

- Liaise with any suppliers or account managers
- May also perform Team Manager and Project Support roles.

B.6 Team Manager

The Team Manager's prime responsibility is to ensure production of those products defined by the Project Manager to an appropriate quality, in a timescale and at a cost acceptable to the Project Board. The Team Manager reports to and takes direction from the Project Manager.

B.6.1 Specific responsibilities

- Prepare plans for the team's work and agree these with the Project Manager
- Receive authorisation from the Project Manager to create products (via a Work Package)
- Manage the team
- Direct, motivate, plan and monitor the team's work
- Take responsibility for the progress of the team's work and use of team resources and initiate corrective action where necessary within the constraints laid down by the Project Manager
- Advise the Project Manager of any deviations from plan, recommend corrective action and help prepare any appropriate Exception Plans
- Pass back to the Project Manager products that have been completed and approved in line with the agreed Work Package requirements
- Ensure all Project Issues are properly reported to the person maintaining the Issue Log
- Ensure the evaluation of Project Issues that arise within the team's work and recommend action to the Project Manager
- Liaise with any Project Assurance roles
- Attend any stage assessments as directed by the Project Manager
- Arrange and lead team checkpoint meetings and produce Checkpoint Reports as agreed with the Project Manager
- Ensure that quality controls of the team's work are planned and performed correctly
- Ensure that the appropriate entries are made in the Quality Log
- Maintain, or ensure the maintenance of, team files
- Identify and advise the Project Manager of any risks associated with a Work Package
- Ensure that all identified risks are entered on the Risk Log
- Manage specific risks as directed by the Project Manager.

B.7 Project Assurance

Assurance covers all interests of a project, including business, user and supplier.

Project Assurance has to be independent of the Project Manager; therefore the Project Board cannot delegate any of its assurance responsibilities to the Project Manager.

B.7.1 Specific responsibilities

The implementation of the assurance responsibilities needs to answer the question 'What is to be assured?'. A list of possibilities would include:

- Maintenance of thorough liaison throughout the project between the supplier and the customer
- User needs and expectations are being met or managed
- Risks are being controlled
- Adherence to the Business Case
- Constant reassessment of the value-for-money solution
- Fit with the overall programme or company strategy
- The right people are being involved
- An acceptable solution is being developed
- The project remains viable
- The scope of the project is not 'creeping upwards' unnoticed
- Focus on the business need is maintained
- Internal and external communications are working
- Applicable standards are being used
- Any legislative constraints are being observed
- The needs of specialist interests (for example, security) are being observed
- Adherence to quality assurance standards.

It is not enough to believe that standards will be obeyed. It is not enough to ensure that a project is well set up and justified at the outset. All the aspects just listed need to be checked throughout the project as part of ensuring that it remains consistent with, and continues to meet, a business need and that no change to the external environment affects the validity of the project.

See each of the Project Board role descriptions, B.2 Executive, B.3 Senior User and B.4 Senior Supplier for details of Project Assurance tasks.

B.8 Project Support

The provision of any Project Support on a formal basis is optional. Tasks need to be done by the Project Manager or delegated to a separate body and this will be driven by the needs of the individual project and Project Manager. Project Support could be in the form of advice on project management tools, guidance, administrative services such as filing, and the collection of actuals, to one or more related projects. Where set up as an official body, Project Support can act as a repository for lessons learned and a central source of expertise in specialist support tools.

One support function that must be considered is that of configuration management. Depending on the project size and environment, there may be a need to formalise this and it quickly becomes a task with which the Project Manager cannot cope without support. See B.9 for details of the Configuration Librarian role.

B.8.1 Specific responsibilities

The following is a suggested list of tasks:

- Administer change control
- Set up and maintain project files
- Establish document control procedures
- Compile, copy and distribute all project management products
- Collect actuals data and forecasts
- Update plans
- Administer the quality review process
- Administer Project Board meetings
- Assist with the compilation of reports
- Specialist knowledge (for example, estimating, risk management)
- Specialist tool expertise (for example, planning and control tools, risk analysis)
- Specialist techniques
- Standards.

B.9 Configuration Librarian

The Configuration Librarian is the custodian and guardian of all master copies of the project's products. The role also maintains the Issue Log.

Major tasks are:

- To control the receipt, identification, storage and issue of all project products
- To provide information on the status of all products
- To number, record, store and distribute Project Issues.

B.9.1 Specific responsibilities

- Assist the Project Manager to prepare the Configuration Management Plan (during initiation)
- Create an identification scheme for all products
- Create libraries or other storage areas to hold products
- Assist in the identification of products
- Maintain current status information on all products
- Accept and record the receipt of new or revised products into the appropriate library
- Prevent changes to a product version once it has been declared ready for inspection
- Control the allocation of new version numbers to changed products
- Archive superseded product copies
- Ensure the security and preservation of the master copies of all project products
- When authorised to do so, issue copies of products for review or information
- When authorised to do so, issue a new version of a product for change or correction
- Maintain a record of all copies issued
- Notify holders of any changes to their copies
- Maintain the Issue Log
- Monitor all Project Issues and ensure they are resubmitted to the configuration library after any authorised change
- Collect and retain information that will assist in the assessment of what products are impacted by a change to a product
- Produce configuration status accounts
- Assist in conducting configuration audits
- Liaise with other Configuration Librarians where products required by the project are common to other systems

B.10 Project Support Office (PSO)

The concept of a Project Support Office is one of a central pool of skilled resources to provide the roles of Project Support, such as clerical support, Configuration Librarians and possibly PRINCE2 consultants to individual projects. The overall objectives of a Project Support Office are to:

- Support managers in project administration
- Ensure correct and efficient use of PRINCE2 standards across all projects.

A Project Support Office is not essential, but can be useful:

- Where resource shortages, either in numbers or skills, make it difficult to supply people to perform project administration for each current project
- Where there are a number of small projects of a diverse nature that individually require only limited support from Project Support
- Where there is a large programme, requiring co-ordination of individual projects.

A Project Support Office provides continuity of standards across all projects. The office can be the centre of expertise in the PRINCE2 method, any software packages used (such as planning and control software), configuration management and the quality review technique. Often, a member of the Project Support Office can handle aspects of the Project Support role for several projects. Typically, the Project Support Office role includes some or all of the following.

B.10.1 Special responsibilities

- Operating a central filing system for several projects
- Liaising with individual Project and Team Managers
- Being a centre of expertise for estimating techniques
- Providing expertise in the planning and control software used
- Advising on the preparation of plans
- Updating plans with actuals
- Producing management reports
- Producing multi-project reports
- Keeping a historical database of how long specific activities take
- Keeping track of the actual use of contingency
- Analysing productivity
- Providing PRINCE2 expertise and advice

- Advising on cost/benefit analysis
- Co-ordination of standards
- Acting as quality review scribe (and even chairperson)

APPENDIX C: RISK CATEGORIES

The following categories can be used as a starting point for identifying your organisation's main areas of risk in relation to projects or programmes.

Strategic/commercial risks

- Under-performance to specification
- Management will under-perform against expectations
- Collapse of contractors
- Insolvency of promoter
- Failure of suppliers to meet contractual commitments, this could be in terms of quality, quantity, timescales or their own exposure to risk
- Insufficient capital revenues
- Market fluctuations
- Fraud/theft
- Partnerships failing to deliver the desired outcome
- The situation being non-insurable (or cost of insurance outweighs the benefit)
- Lack of availability of capital investment.

Economic/financial/market

- Exchange rate fluctuation
- Interest rate instability
- Inflation
- Shortage of working capital
- Failure to meet projected revenue targets
- Market developments will adversely affect plans.

Legal and regulatory

- New or changed legislation may invalidate assumptions upon which the activity is based
- Failure to obtain appropriate approval, e.g. planning, consent
- Unforeseen inclusion of contingent liabilities

- Loss of intellectual property rights
- Failure to achieve satisfactory contractual arrangements
- Unexpected regulatory controls or licensing requirements
- Changes in tax or tariff structure.

Organisational/management/human factors

- Management incompetence
- Inadequate corporate policies
- Inadequate adoption of management practices
- Poor leadership
- Key personnel have inadequate authority to fulfil their roles
- Poor staff selection procedures
- Lack of clarity over roles and responsibilities
- Vested interests creating conflict and compromising the overall aims
- Individual or group interests given unwarranted priority
- Personality clashes
- Indecision or inappropriate decision making
- Lack of operational support
- Inadequate or inaccurate information
- Health and safety constraints.

Political

- Change of government policy (national or international), e.g. approach to nationalisation
- Change of government
- War and disorder
- Adverse public opinion/media intervention.

Environmental

- Natural disasters
- Storms, flooding, tempests
- Pollution incidents
- Transport problems, including aircraft/vehicle collisions.

Technical/operational/infrastructure

- Inadequate design
- Professional negligence
- Human error/incompetence
- Infrastructure failure
- Operation lifetime lower than expected
- Residual value of assets lower than expected
- Increased dismantling/decommissioning costs
- Safety being compromised
- Performance failure
- Residual maintenance problems
- Scope 'creep'
- Unclear expectations
- Breaches in security/information security
- Lack or inadequacy of business continuity.

APPENDIX D: PRINCE2 HEALTHCHECK

It can be very useful for an organisation to check on the correct use of PRINCE2 in its projects. The following set of questions forms a good basis for any such healthcheck. The questions can be the basis of a table or spreadsheet, with entries in extra columns to indicate whether and how well each element of the method is being used.

Start-up

- Was there a Project Mandate?
- Was the Project Board designed/appointed before initiation was authorised?
- Was a Project Brief produced?
- Is the Project Brief to PRINCE2 standards?
- Are quality expectations set?
- Has the Project Approach been defined?
- Was an initiation Stage Plan produced?
- Was the initiation Stage Plan approved?
- Was the Risk Log created?

Initiation

- Was the initiation stage formally authorised?
- Were the *Authorising Initiation* (DP1) agenda items covered?
- Is there a Project Initiation Document (PID)?
- Is the PID produced to PRINCE2 standards?
- Are the project objectives stated?
- Have project constraints been identified?
- Is project tolerance defined?
- Are any project interdependencies stated?
- Is the project scope stated?
- Are reporting procedures, contents and frequency defined?
- Is there a Communication Plan covering both inward and outward communication needs?
- Does the PID contain the Project Plan?

- Is there a Business Case in the PID?
- Are the reasons for the project given?
- Is there an investment appraisal or cost/benefit analysis?
- Was the PID quality reviewed?
- Did the Project Board formally approve the PID?
- Was the Project Board committed to the process?
- Was initiation done before work on specialist products began?
- Was there an initiation end stage assessment (*Authorising a Project* (DP2))?
- Was the next Stage Plan presented at the initiation end stage assessment?
- Were issues affecting the PID managed effectively?
- Was formal approval to proceed to the next stage given?

Organisation

- Is there a Project Board?
- Are any limits to the authority of the Project Board documented?
- Is it clear to whom the Project Board reports?
- Which member of the Project Board reports to senior management?
- Does the Senior User adequately represent all user areas?
- Are Project Board members contributing fully to all exception assessments and end stage assessments?
- Are Project Board members carrying out their other project duties?
- Is there a Project Manager?
- Have Project Assurance roles been agreed?
- Has any role for Project Support been clarified?
- Does each person have a job description?
- Has each person agreed/signed their job description?
- Was the organisation agreed by the end of *Starting up a Project* (SU)?
- Is the documented version of the organisation correct?
- Is the role of the supplier(s) clearly defined?
- Have any changes to the management team been recorded?
- Has the Project Board received training for its roles?
- Is the Team Manager role used effectively?
- Are job descriptions agreed with any late appointments?

Business Case

- Is there a Business Case?
- Are the reasons for the project clearly defined and valid?
- Is there an investment appraisal?
- Are figures based on defined items that can be measured?
- Is the Business Case passed down from pre-project work?
- If so, have the figures been checked out?
- Are costs based on the Project Plan or some other figures?
- Are benefits stated in terms that can be measured in the post-project review?
- Have 'before' measurements been taken in order to assist comparisons in the post-project review?
- Is the Business Case updated and reviewed for each end stage assessment?
- Who measures the impact of changes on the Business Case?
- Is the impact of changes on the Business Case assessed?
- If the project is part of a programme, is the programme's Business Case fully reflected in the project?

Risk

- Is there a Risk Log?
- Is it being kept up to date?
- Are risks to each plan identified, analysed and acted upon?
- Is a formal procedure for the management of risk in use?
- Is risk assessment part of each end stage assessment?
- Were the major risks entered in the Business Case?
- Have risk 'owners' been identified?
- Are risks monitored on a sufficiently regular basis?
- Is risk assessment part of each major change request assessment?
- Were risk probability and impact assessed?
- Have proactive risk actions been taken where necessary?
- Were any needed contingency plans prepared?
- Were all obvious risks covered?
- Were the risks and countermeasures discussed with the Project Board?
- Were appropriate countermeasures taken?
- Were risks reassessed when plans were changed?

Project Plan

- Is there a Project Plan?
- Does the Project Plan comply with PRINCE2 requirements?
- Are planning assumptions stated?
- Does the Project Plan show the stage divisions?
- Has each risk to the plan been added to the Risk Log?
- If an end date was imposed, is it realistic?
- Was the Project Plan quality reviewed?
- Were the assurance roles involved in the review?
- Was the product-based planning technique used?
- Is there a checklist of key products?
- Are there Product Descriptions for each major product?
- Are the Product Descriptions to the standard PRINCE2 format?
- Are Product Descriptions being reviewed before the start of building those products?

Stage Plan

- Is there a Stage Plan for each management stage?
- Do Stage Plans comply with the PRINCE2 standard?
- Is stage tolerance defined?
- Are stage controls identified and suitable?
- Are planning assumptions stated?
- Are Stage Plan risks identified and included in the Risk Log?
- Are Stage Plans consistent with the Project Plan?
- Is next stage planning carried out correctly in each stage?
- Is the quality of Stage Plans reviewed?
- Was the current Stage Plan approved?
- Is product-based planning used in stage planning?
- Is there a Product Checklist for each stage?
- Are there Product Descriptions for each product on the checklist?
- Are the Product Descriptions to standard?
- Are Product Descriptions reviewed prior to the start of the build process?
- Were Team Managers/team members involved in planning?
- Did the assurance roles review the draft Stage Plan?

- Did Project Assurance add quality checks to the draft Stage Plan?
- Did Project Assurance add names to these quality checks?
- Is time and effort allowed for project management activities?
- Is time allowed for the analysis of Project Issues?
- Has a reasonable rate of staff effectiveness been chosen?
- Is the method of quality checking identified for each product?

Control

- Are checkpoints held at the frequency stated in the plan?
- What actual progress information is captured?
- Are actuals used to update the Stage Plan regularly?
- Is the update frequency commensurate with the plan size?
- Is there a record of Work Package authorisation and return?
- Are estimates collected to complete any further information?
- Are Product Checklists kept up to date?
- Are Checkpoint Reports produced?
- Are Highlight Reports produced when stated in the plan?
- Are Highlight Reports produced to the agreed standard?
- Is the Stage Plan regularly checked against tolerances?
- Are Exception Reports used when tolerances are threatened?
- Were any required Exception Plans produced?
- Were exception assessments held to approve any Exception Plans?
- Can Stages be completed within the agreed tolerance levels?
- Are end stage assessments carried out at the end of each stage?
- Is there an End Stage Report for each stage?
- Is the End Stage Report to standard?
- Is end stage assessment documentation circulated prior to the meeting?
- Is the End Stage Report accepted at the end stage assessment?
- Are unfinished products included in the next Stage Plan?
- Does the Project Board sign off stages and give approval to proceed?
- Do relevant project members attend end stage assessments?
- Are end stage assessment actions recorded?

Quality

- Has the customer specified quality expectations?
- Is there a Project Quality Plan?
- Will the Project Quality Plan achieve the customer's expectations?
- Does the Project Quality Plan point at specific quality procedures?
- Are quality responsibilities defined in the Project Quality Plan?
- Are there stage quality plans?
- Are individuals and quality methods identified in the stage quality plans?
- Is there a Quality Log?
- Is the Quality Log up to date?
- Do the teams maintain one central Quality Log?
- Does the Project Manager get sufficient feedback to ensure quality is OK?
- Are Project Assurance roles sufficiently involved in quality checking?
- Do the quality file and Quality Log match?
- Is any external quality assurance function happy with its involvement?

Quality reviews

- Has training in quality reviews been given to attendees?
- Have the chairperson and reviewers been identified at stage or team planning time?
- Are products sent out before quality review meetings?
- Are Product Descriptions and blank question lists sent with the products?
- Are products reviewed against their Product Descriptions?
- Are products reviewed by the means stated in the Product Description?
- Is enough time planned for preparation, review and follow-up?
- Are question lists completed prior to quality reviews?
- Is there an agenda for each quality review meeting?
- Do reviewers unable to attend quality reviews send question lists?
- Do quality reviews generate follow-up action lists?
- Are corrections signed off by the reviewers?
- Are product authors always present?
- Are second reviews carried out if needed?
- Is there a review result for each review?

Change control

- Is there a documented procedure for change control?
- Is that procedure the same as stated in the Project Plan?
- Are Project Issues recorded?
- Is there an Issue Log?
- Are Project Issues assessed regularly?
- Is the impact of Project Issues on the Business Case assessed?
- Is the impact of Project Issues on the Risk Log assessed?
- Are all Project Issues actioned?
- Is the status of Project Issues monitored?
- If the impact of a Project Issue exceeds tolerance, is it escalated to the Project Board?
- Are plans updated to incorporate agreed changes?
- Is a distinction made between Off-Specification and Request for Change?

Configuration management

- Is there a formal configuration management method in use?
- Are products controlled once submitted to configuration management?
- Are products uniquely identified?
- Are relationships between products identified?
- Are products identified as complete?
- Do products have version identifiers?
- Are product records up to date?
- Is the accuracy of the product records checked regularly?
- Are all old versions preserved?
- Is it easy to retrieve old versions?
- Are the configuration management records in line with the support requirements?
- Is the Configuration Librarian role well defined, allocated and agreed?
- Are new records created during product-based planning?

Project filing

- Is there a recognisable filing system?
- Is its structure documented and available?

- Does it cover management and specialist products?
- Does it cater for multiple versions – for example, of plans?
- Does the filing system provide an audit trail?
- Is it easy to find things in the filing system?
- Is the filing kept up to date?
- Is filing responsibility clearly defined in a job description?

APPENDIX E: PROJECT DOCUMENT MANAGEMENT

PRINCE2 offers this suggested document management structure to be used by a project.

There are two major types of file in PRINCE2:

- Management file, which contains the planning, reporting, control and quality products identified in the Product Breakdown Structure (see Figure 22.1)
- Specialist file containing the products identified in the specialist section of the Product Breakdown Structure.

E.1 Management files

These comprise:

- A project file
- A stage file for each stage
- A quality file.

Project file

This has sections as shown in Table E.1.

Table E.1 Project file sections

Organisation	The project organisation chart and signed job descriptions
Plans	The Project Plans. These should include any versions developed, not only the one approved as part of the Project Initiation Document. The various components of each version should be kept (such as Product Breakdown Structures, Product Flow Diagrams) with clear identification of their date, version number and reasoning, such as change of assumptions, scope, stage results or resource availability. The Project Plan should be updated at least at the end of each stage
Business Case	Versions of the Business Case, updated at each stage end or when Exception Plans are created
Risk Log	Updated details of all identified risks, their status and countermeasures
Control	Copies of project initiation and closure.

Stage files

These have more sections than the project file. One of these would exist for each stage of the project (see Table E.2).

Table E.2 Stage file sections

Organisation	Stage organisation, details of team members. These should reflect all work assignments, achievements and the Project Manager's or Team Manager's assessment of work performance
Plans	Copies of Stage Plans, team plans and Exception Plans, updated as available
Control	Copies of Work Package authorisations, Checkpoint Reports, Highlight Reports, Exception Reports, end stage assessments plus any exception assessments held
Daily Log	The Project Manager's notebook of events, problems, questions, answers, informal discussions with Project Board members and actions for the stage
Correspondence	Copies of management correspondence or other papers associated with the stage

Quality file

The objective of a quality file is to permit an audit, at any time, of the quality work being done and to confirm adherence to quality standards. There is one quality file that runs through the whole project and is not divided into stages. It has four major divisions: Project Quality Plan, Configuration Item Records, quality inspection products and Project Issues.

- *Project Quality Plan*: the original and any subsequent versions of the Project Quality Plan should be filed here
- *Configuration records*: there should be minimally a Product Description for every product in the project. As more information is created, a full configuration record for each product can be produced
- *Quality inspection products*: it is useful to head this section with the Quality Log, giving a number to each check, the type of quality check or test (for example, quality review), the product and date. This is a quick reference to see or show how many checks have been held in a particular stage and a guide to where the appropriate documentation can be found
- The subdivision of the quality section will depend on the type(s) of check or test being made. There should be a separate file for the documents relating to each entry in the Quality Log. This file should keep details of the method used, the resources used, the sign-off document where appropriate, details of the tests made, expected and actual results. The filing for quality reviews should include:
  - invitations
  - action lists
  - result notifications

- *Project Issues*: this should have a log, the Issue Log, at the front to facilitate sequential numbering and to record the status and allocation. The Project Issue masters should be filed in sequence behind it. The subject of Project Issues is covered fully in Chapter 23, *Change Control Approach*.

E.2 Specialist file(s)

This contains all the versions of documentation about the specialist products of the project.

Specialist correspondence

There may also be a need to create this section of the specialist file, where correspondence or external documents cannot be specifically related to one product. The section should have its own log of entries, showing cross-references to the products concerned.

FURTHER INFORMATION

Best Practice guidance from OGC

OGC has developed a wide range of guidance covering strategy, programme management, service management, procurement and performance management.

Details of OGC guidance may be obtained from:

The OGC Service Desk
Rosebery Court
St Andrews Business Park
Norwich NR7 0HS

Telephone: (0845) 000 4999
Email: ServiceDesk@ogc.gov.uk
Website: http://www.ogc.gov.uk

PRINCE2 accreditation and qualifications

APM Group Ltd

7–8 Queen Square
High Wycombe
Buckinghamshire HP11 2BP

Telephone: (01494) 452450
Fax: (01494) 459559
Website: http://www.prince2.org.uk

User Group

The PRINCE User Group Ltd (PUG)

PRINCE User Group
c/o Intracite Ltd
Murrells House
6 Murrells Lane
Frimley Road
Camberley
Surrey GU15 2PY

Telephone: (0870) 901 5583
Fax: (0870) 901 6581
Website: http://www.pug.mcmail.com

Useful Information and Contacts

THE PRINCE USER GROUP

The PRINCE USER GROUP is an independent not-for-profit organisation whose aims are to encourage the use of the PRINCE2 methodology and to support users of the method and suppliers of PRINCE2-related products and services.

Membership is open to individuals and organisations in the UK and abroad and brings a range of benefits, including regular newsletters, subscription to Project Manager Today, the opportunity to attend two conferences each year and to take part in research and collaborative feedback activities relating to PRINCE2.

The PRINCE User Group is represented on the PRINCE2 Examinations Board and regularly hosts speakers from OGC at its conferences.

The PRINCE2 Prize is awarded each year at the Autumn Conference, in conjunction with APM Group and OGC.

Further details may be found on the PRINCE User Group web site at **www.pug.mcmail.com** or by contacting the Administrative Officer on 0870 901 5583, e-mail pug@mcmail.com.

PRINCE User Group Ltd

CERTIFICATION BODY

The APM Group Limited (APMG) is the certification body for PRINCE2 accredited by UKAS in accordance with EN45011 and EN45013.

They have been working as a strategic partner of OGC since 1996 on the development and promotion of professional standards associated with the use and implementation of PRINCE2.

Their activities extend beyond the UK and full information can be seen on their website at **www.prince2.org.uk**. Telephone +44(0) (1494) 459559

APM GROUP

INDEX

References in *italics* are to items contained in the Glossary; references in **bold** are Product Outline Descriptions (Appendix A) or Roles (Appendix B); Fig = Figure.

T

U

W

Dear customer. . .

We would like to hear from you with any comments or suggestions that you have on how we can improve our current products or develop new ones for the PRINCE2 method. Please complete this questionnaire and we will enter you in our monthly draw. The winner will receive a copy of Tailoring PRINCE2 worth £25!

1 Name ....

Organisation ....

Job Title ....

Department...

Address ....

....

Telephone Number
(Direct Dial if possible) ....

E Mail ....

2 Nature of organisation (tick one box only)

- ☐ Consultancy/Training
- ☐ Computing/IT/Software
- ☐ Industrial
- ☐ Central Government
- ☐ Local Government
- ☐ Academic/Further Education
- ☐ Private Health
- ☐ Public Health (NHS)
- ☐ Finance
- ☐ Construction
- ☐ Telecommunications
- ☐ Utilities
- ☐ Other

3 How did you hear about the **PRINCE2** Method?

- ☐ Work/Colleagues
- ☐ Internet/Web (please state)

....

- ☐ Marketing Literature
- ☐ Other (please state)

....

4 Where did you purchase this book?

- ☐ Web – clickTSO
- ☐ Web – Other (please specify)

....

- ☐ Bookshop (please specify)

....

- ☐ Training Course
- ☐ Other

5 How many people use **PRINCE2** in your company?

- ☐ 1–5
- ☐ 5–10
- ☐ 10–50
- ☐ 50–200
- ☐ 200+

6 How many people use your copy?

- ☐ 2–5
- ☐ 5–10
- ☐ 10+

7 Overall how do you rate Managing Successful Projects with **PRINCE2**?

- ☐ Excellent
- ☐ Very Good
- ☐ Good
- ☐ Fair
- ☐ Poor

[PTO]

8 What do you like most about the book?

(Tick all that apply)

- ☐ Ease of use
- ☐ Well structured
- ☐ Contents
- ☐ Index
- ☐ Hints and Tips

9 Do you have any suggestions for improvement?

....

....

....

....

10 How do you use this book?

- ☐ Problem solver
- ☐ Reference
- ☐ Tutorial
- ☐ Other (please specify)

....

11 What types of projects do you work on?

- ☐ IS/IT
- ☐ Procurement
- ☐ Other (please specify)

....

12 Do you use the **PRINCE2** CD?

- ☐ Yes
- ☐ No

13 What business change guidance/methods does your company use?

- ☐ ITIL (IT Infrastructure Library)
- ☐ Managing Successful Programmes
- ☐ Successful Delivery Toolkit
- ☐ Business Systems Development (BSD)
- ☐ Other (please specify)

....

14 Which three websites do you visit most?

1 ....

2 ....

3 ....

15 Which three professional magazines do you read most?

1 ....

2 ....

3 ....

Any further enquiries or questions about PRINCE2 or the Office of Government Commerce should be directed to the OGC Service Desk:

The OGC Service Desk
Rosebery Court
St Andrews Business Park
Norwich NR7 0HS

Email: ServiceDesk@ogc.gsi.gov.uk
Telephone: 0845 000 4999

☐ Data Protection: The Stationery Office and the Office of Government Commerce may wish to keep you informed about our products, services and special offers. Please tick the box if you do not wish to receive this information.

Please return this form to:

The Stationery Office
Scott Deakin
Freepost ANG4787
Norwich NR3 1YX